Empty Cradle, Broken Heart

Empty Cradle, Broken Heart

Surviving the Death of Your Baby

THIRD EDITION

Deborah L. Davis, Ph.D.

Parts of chapter 9 were adapted from the author's book *Loving and Letting Go: For Parents Who Decided to Turn Away from Aggressive Medical Intervention for Their Critically Ill Newborns.* Omaha, Neb.: Centering Corporation, 2002.

The information contained in this book, although based on sound medical judgment, is not intended as a substitute for medical advice or attention. Please consult your doctor or health care provider for individual professional care.

Please note that URLs are subject to change. If a URL is incorrect, please contact Fulcrum Publishing via fulcrumbooks.com.

Library of Congress Cataloging-in-Publication Data

Names: Davis, Deborah L., 1955- author.
Title: Empty cradle, broken heart : surviving the death of your baby / by
  Deborah L. Davis, Ph.D.
Description: Third edition. | Golden, CO : Fulcrum Publishing, [2016]
Identifiers: LCCN 2016023559 | ISBN 9781936218240 (paperback)
Subjects: LCSH: Perinatal death--Psychological aspects. |
  Bereavement--Psychological aspects. | Adjustment (Psychology) | Parent and
  child. | BISAC: SELF-HELP / Death, Grief, Bereavement. | FAMILY &
  RELATIONSHIPS / Death, Grief, Bereavement.
Classification: LCC RG631 .D38 2016 | DDC 618.3/92--dc23
LC record available at https://lccn.loc.gov/2016023559

Printed in the United States of America

0 9 8 7 6 5 4 3 2 1

Fulcrum Publishing
4690 Table Mountain Drive, Suite 100
Golden, CO 80403
(800) 992-2908 • (303) 277-1623
www.fulcrumbooks.com

CREDITS

Elizabeth (Heineman) is the author of *Ghostbelly* (Feminist Press, 2014). She is quoted in part from (1) her 2011 essay "My Stillborn Child's Life after Death" at http://www.salon.com/2011/10/07/my_stillborn_childs_life_after_death/; (2) her 2012 essay "Still Life with Baby" at http://newmillenniumwritings.com/showdb.8.php?w=88; and (3) an interview by Lisa Morguess at http://www.lisamorguess.com/2014/05/15/birth-death-interview-giveaway/.

Nicola (Daly) is quoted from her book *Sasha's Legacy: A Guide to Funerals for Babies* (Steele Roberts Publishers, 2005).

Mel (Scott) is quoted in part from her memoir, *After Finley*, which is available through her website, www.finleysfootprints.com.

Lori (Martini) is quoted in part from her personal account, which appears on her website, www.HealingFromTheStart.com.

Nathan (Oldfield) is quoted in part from *Stillbirth & Surfing: A Grief Journey*, a short taken from his feature-length surf film, *Seaworthy* (2012, https://vimeo.com/28056957).

Ben (Welnak) is quoted in part from a post on his blog *Mountain Bike Radio* at http://mountainbikeradio.com/life/life/.

DEDICATION

To all of your babies, loved and remembered always

A MOTHER'S LOVE SONG

Last night, I awakened to sounds of laughter outside my window
But the nearer noise of my fast-beating heart enveloped me
With memories of soft, sweet baby cries when you were born
Before the ones in white tore you from my arms
And bore you to your first and last crib, a small white casket.

An old, old wound, a long time closed, the pain now dull,
Unhealed and bled afresh and red from my mourning heart
Absorbed by earth, your eternal bed, my second born
In unfair death, in wretched, selfish death
That cheated me of a lifetime of loving you.

Part of me, deep and secret, lies with you in a maternal embrace
Wrapped in infant arms I never touched or kissed
Near a tiny face I saw but one too brief moment
Just long enough to engrave forever in my heart a question—
What would you have given this world if not your life?

—Carol J. Curtis
For Tom Eric Wilcox
Born 12/7/68, Died 12/7/68

CONTENTS

PREFACE

Since the second edition of this book was published twenty years ago, much has changed in the field of perinatal bereavement. First and foremost, there have been vast improvements in the quality of bereavement care following the death of a baby at any time during pregnancy, birth, or infancy. Quality care in most hospitals used to mean keeping parents away from their dead or dying babies, or perhaps offering them a mere glimpse or a scant hour, all in a misguided effort to spare them emotional pain. As it turns out, shielding parents can cause far more harm than good.

Change, to a large extent, has been and continues to be spurred by distressed parents speaking out about what they found or would've found helpful. Change is also due to the efforts of compassionate caregivers who have seen the need, become parent advocates, and pushed for policy changes from within their hospitals and clinics. This kind of inside-out change is powerful and enduring.

So nowadays, the gold standard of care is to approach parents with the knowledge that this baby is *theirs* and to support them in spending as many hours or days and nights as they want with their little one. Parents are also reclaiming important mourning traditions, such as taking the body home to provide after-death care until burial or cremation. Gentle, reassuring guidance is also offered, particularly for parents just meeting their babies, who have died *at any time* during pregnancy, labor, or shortly after birth. With compassionate support, the vast majority of parents are eager to welcome their infant, express their love and nurturing devotion, share their baby with family and friends, and engage in formal rituals as well as spontaneous, informal moments of profound sacredness.

Parents are also more comprehensively supported in collecting mementos. Instead of being left to wish for an image of their baby, or maybe cherishing the one blurry Polaroid photo taken by a caring nurse, parents nowadays often receive many high-quality digital images, some taken by professionals who volunteer their services or by caregivers who seek out training in the art of bereavement photography. These photographs are often their most treasured possessions.

Perhaps most remarkable is the enormous progress in medical ethics and end-of-life care. When the prognosis is uncertain, instead of being told what kind of medical care their critically ill baby will receive, parents are being included as collaborators and trusted decision makers. And when a baby is diagnosed in utero with a life-limiting condition, instead of being told that their only option is to terminate the pregnancy or submit their baby to a futile but required course of intensive care, more and more parents are offered the option of continuing their pregnancy and delivering their baby into hospice and palliative care. Known as "perinatal hospice," this movement has spread into pockets around the globe. Perhaps within the next decade, offering *and providing* this option to parents will become standard care.

Across the board, there is still room for improvement. Fortunately, there is a growing recognition of the importance of training caregivers in the specialty of bereavement care and the need for hospital administrations to support this kind of care—not as optional, but as *mandatory*, hospital-wide. The concepts of family-centered care, patient-centered care, developmentally supportive care, and relationship-centered care are also burrowing into medical culture and form the cornerstone of quality care. And finally, at long last, more research is being done on the effects of bereavement care as well as the causes and prevention of death, particularly during pregnancy.

National and international organizations involved in this groundswell, whose leaders I've had the honor of collaborating with, include the Pregnancy Loss and Infant Death Alliance (PLIDA), Share Pregnancy and Infant Loss Support, PernitalHospice.org, Sands New Zealand, STELLAR Research (Australia), Resolve Through Sharing (RTS) Bereavement Services, National Perinatal Association (NPA), International Stillbirth Alliance (ISA), March of Dimes, and Kaiser Permanente. Equally important are the efforts by individuals, hospitals, and nonprofits (which are often labors of love by bereaved parents) to meet the needs of grieving mothers and fathers in communities the world over. They *are* the change they want to see.

There has also been progress in the fields of grief counseling and psychology, notably Kenneth Doka and Terry Martin's conceptualization of grieving styles and the observation that activity-oriented grieving and emotion-oriented grieving are equally adaptive. Brain research has given us a window into how the brain is affected by grief and trauma, resulting in brain-based therapies that are often more effective and more efficient at treating trauma than medication, traditional talk therapy, or cognitive-behavioral approaches. Brain research also shows that mindfulness practices are effective at calming the brain and reducing unnecessary suffering. And there is mounting evidence that mindfulness-based coping strategies can be better than medication for treating anxiety and depression, as well as for reducing the stress of grief and mourning. It really is a new era.

As a result of this significant progress, I've observed a significant overall improvement in the well-being of bereaved parents. In the first two editions of this book, the parents I interviewed got what benefits they could from whatever meager bereavement care and decision-making support was offered (which was sometimes *none* in the 1980s and 1990s), but as a whole they suffered terribly, were likely to feel traumatized, and were filled with regrets and longing that seeped into their lives, including their subsequent pregnancies and parenting. But this time around, twenty and thirty years later in my interviews with parents whose babies died after the turn of this century, it is clear to me that at least anecdotally, this generation of parents is faring far better. Parents express deep gratitude for the compassion shown by medical practitioners, and for the validation of their grief and the affirmation of their babies. And unlike the parents from twenty-plus years ago, many have no regrets. Fortunately, my observations are backed by the past ten years of diligent, published research, which is what informs evidence-based care. And the news is spreading: Quality bereavement care really can make a difference to the quality of a parent's mourning, adjusting, and healing.

If you are in the trenches with grieving parents, know that your openness, respect, and empathy make an enormous impression. Parents are deeply touched. They continue to hold you in spirit as they mourn, and they continue to derive comfort from the warmth you showed them.

The Internet played a significant role in this edition, in that it brought parents to me from around the world. Five continents are represented, and even across cultures, it is noteworthy that parents share a shattering grief and acres upon acres of common ground. Some parents corresponded with me over the course of many months or even years, so as you read different quotes, you get a window into not just their deep distress, but also their transformation and healing. The parents who contributed to this third edition have my deepest gratitude—their modern voices add breadth and depth to the original voices that continue to grace these pages.

Bereaved parents are special. You are survivors, and I am always inspired by your demonstration of courage and strength, as you face your deepest pain and find healing after this most devastating death.

To all the parents who've contributed to my work: this book would be nothing without you. If you consider it part of your baby's legacy, I am honored.

PLEASE READ THIS FIRST

HOW TO USE THIS BOOK

Empty Cradle, Broken Heart is meant to accompany you along your journey. It doesn't try to tell you how you should feel or what you must do. Rather, it strives to show you the wide range of experiences that can follow the death of a baby, and it offers many different strategies for coping.

With factual information and the words and insights of other bereaved parents, you can establish realistic expectations for your grief and mourning. You can also gain reassurance that you are not going crazy. You are not the only one who has felt betrayed, powerless, or angry; you are not the only one to cradle pillows in your empty arms, or shed a river of tears, or hit the trail and hit it hard.

Along with helpful information, this book provides suggestions for managing your thoughts and feelings of grief. It offers ideas about mourning, getting support, and finding resources. It encourages you to do what *you* need to in order to survive your baby's death. Whether your baby died recently or long ago, this information can be useful to you.

It is not necessary to read this book from start to finish. Some sections may feel more appropriate than others at different times, depending on your unique situation, your personality, and where you are in your grieving. Some sections simply won't apply; others might seem like they were tailor-made for you.

At first, you may want to only focus on the quotes of the mothers and fathers featured in these pages. This approach is recommended, as reading a book about grief and mourning can seem daunting. As always, take in whatever seems helpful, and pass by whatever isn't. Come back to the passages that are particularly comforting, and try reading other parts later.

If reading this book moves you to cry, try to accept this reaction. These are healing tears—of grief and empathy, even joy. They are also tears of courage, health, and strength that merge with those of other grieving parents. You are not alone.

1

WHY IS THIS SO HARD?

THE "D" WORD

If only more people would say, "I acknowledge your pain and I am here with you." I wish I had had this. I look back now and fail to understand the words and actions of people around me, people who are meant to love and "know" me, at a time where I was at my weakest and most fragile. We know that our pain cannot be fixed, but worse than that pain is feeling isolated and alone in it.
— Emmerson

Society wants us to be invisible. No one wants to talk about dead babies or acknowledge the mum whose baby has died. Society just wants us to hide away like a dirty secret. You almost feel like a leper. We'd see people shy away, just so uncomfortable with our situation. If only we had that option, to shy away or choose to ignore it just because we are uncomfortable. But this is our reality. There is no "off switch" for us. We have to live with this for the rest of our lives. And as much as we would like to escape the unbearable pain, we can't.
— Melanie

As much support as there is today versus twenty years ago, there still needs to be more. If this happens to one in four pregnancies plus all the infant deaths, why is it still so "hidden" from the public? It's not the majority, but still a good number are forced into this "club."
— Anne

In many societies, unfortunately, death is not talked about freely. Rather than being seen as an inevitable and natural part of the cycle of life, death has become something we consider distasteful—even disgusting—and best avoided. We want to prevent it from happening to us or to our loved ones. Indeed, we've made great strides in this endeavor. With modern sanitation and advances in medicine, we've come to expect to broaden children to survive into adulthood, and most of us expect to live until we are very, very old. With new developments in medical science and technology, many previously fatal conditions or injuries are now curable, and it is possible to prolong life, although sometimes without regard to quality.

We also avoid contact with the dying and the dead. This wasn't always the case. Before the mid-1900s, most people died at home. Family members bathed and dressed the body, and friends and relations gathered to view the body and grieve together. Now, most people die in hospitals or other facilities, and the body is quickly dispatched to the morgue and then shipped off to be cremated or buried according to community health standards. Additionally, families and friends are more far-flung, so being present at the death of a loved one, or even attending the funeral, is less likely. Children are particularly sheltered, as we don't want to scare them or tarnish their innocence. Unfortunately, these modern trends separate death and dying from the continuity of life and the living, which makes death more foreign to us. Having so little experience with dying or death, no wonder many of us feel uncomfortable or afraid.

> *I'd carried his body inside me for nine months; I'd felt it kicking for the last five or six of them. That body had forced its way out of me early in the morning . . . and along the way it had turned from a living body to a dead body, but it was still Thor. Why should the body that was Thor transmogrify from a beloved member of the family, from a familiar part of my own body, into a repellent object just because it had died? This was my child.*
>
> *— Elizabeth*

We also avoid talking about death. We have all kinds of euphemisms for referring to death: the delicate "passed away," the vague "expired" or "is no more" or "has been taken," the spiritual "met her maker" or "transitioned" or "departed this life," the technical "demise" or "deceased," or the crude "croaked" or "kicked the bucket." Indeed, people may find it easier to use softer, more socially palatable terms like "baby loss." Unfortunately, such expressions make a baby's death sound inconsequential or akin to carelessness rather than the profound tragedy it is.

And finally, we avoid those who are mourning. This is understandable. Because of our discomfort and inexperience, we've lost some of our know-how and traditions for supporting the bereaved. After the funeral, it is considered almost impolite to talk about the death of a loved one or any struggles with grief. These attitudes leave mourners to grieve in isolation, which only adds to their suffering.

The death of a baby is even more hidden, more disturbing, and more taboo, as it's considered relatively uncommon and unexpected. But statistics tell a far different story. In the United States, the death rate for babies between twenty weeks gestation and one year of age is similar to that of people in their sixties, when death starts to be considered normal and sometimes expected. Furthermore, for every four confirmed pregnancies, one baby dies before birth at some point during the pregnancy. That's about twice the death rate of adults eighty-five and older. So where do we get the impression that babies never die?

Because nobody wants to talk about it. Unsure of what to say, friends, relatives, and coworkers often feel uncomfortable around bereaved parents. They aren't sure how to respond to emotional expression, often avoid asking parents about it, and may ultimately avoid the parents as well. Such attitudes merely compound the parents' grief and isolation. Suffering is further intensified by people not recognizing the parents' bond with this child, and therefore misunderstanding their grief and failing to notice their need for support.

> *A Maori friend told us that the way we were treated by our family was very "white," and over time we have come to realize that she is right. There is a very different attitude toward baby/infant loss in our culture that lends itself to the hierarchy of death, whereas in Maori custom, the closely bereaved are considered "tapu" or sacred, and the family comes in close to offer compassion and support no matter the age of the deceased.*
>
> *— Emmerson*

> *It doesn't have to be anything big. Just say, "I'm thinking about you and your baby."*
>
> *— Elizabeth*

A VIOLATION OF EXPECTATIONS

> *I was so excited. This was going to be the neatest thing in my whole life. I figured everything was going to go great because you always assume that with your first child. I had a beautiful pregnancy. You couldn't have asked for a nicer one. No morning sickness, I stayed active, it was great.*
>
> *— Lena*

> *My partner was beside herself with joy, as she has always wanted to have biological children of her own. I was also excited, as I do love children, but also, it was so good to see her in such a joyful space. She was blossoming. The pregnancy was uncomplicated. Everything was normal and looked perfect.*
>
> *— Lavender*

> *For Blake, we were so happy. Over-the-moon happy! We had wanted this so badly and we both felt that all the heartache, doctor appointments, and financial commitment had finally paid off. We were going to have our baby!*
>
> *— Sonya*

During the past century, at least in wealthier, privileged societies, people have come to expect babies to be born healthy and ultimately outlive their parents. Modern medicine and living standards have greatly improved the prospects of having a healthy pregnancy, a thriving infant, and children who pass all their milestones with flying colors.

As such, expectant parents are not likely to seriously consider the possibility that their baby might die, particularly after the first trimester of pregnancy. They naturally assume that a healthy baby will be born, and if sick, the baby will nevertheless survive. This assumption accompanies the belief that by "doing all the right things" during pregnancy, even before conception and certainly after delivery, a healthy baby is guaranteed.

> *With Emily, it was like my pregnancies with Matthew and Ryan. Just "commonplace," almost taking our pregnancies for granted to a certain level. You just expected to get pregnant, and have a healthy baby, full-term. I never thought that our baby could die while in my womb.*
> — *Anne*

Because parents assume they have control over what happens to them, they make plans and are increasingly likely to plot when and how many children to have. In addition to the assumption that they will have a healthy baby, they have an enormous emotional investment in conceiving within a few months, each pregnancy having a positive outcome, and each child surviving infancy.

> *We were excited to have a sibling for our older daughter, wondering if it would be a little sister or a little brother.*
> — *Shellie*

> *I went off the pill for a year and a half in anticipation because I knew that was something to think about. I did not drink any caffeine; I did not drink any alcohol; I did not smoke; I did not do anything. I led my life so perfectly as far as going by the rules. . . . I really wasn't aware that babies could die. I remember feeling so serene the week before the baby's birth. I didn't have any worries. I thought when you made it past a certain point . . .*
> — *Bryn*

> *This pregnancy was very much planned. It was our second pregnancy. It was going to be our last baby and we wanted a girl. I read many articles on the Internet on how to increase the chances of conceiving a girl. I liked to think that I could control the outcome of most things in life if I were well prepared and equipped myself with enough information. I wore the badge of a control freak proudly.*
> — *Destrida*

When a baby dies, the parents' expectations are cruelly violated, their dreams shattered, and emotional commitments dashed. Even when they "do all the right things," bad things can happen. This tragic turn of events upends their worldview, and nothing will ever be the same.

> *Things seemed to be right on schedule with the "plan," and like my first pregnancy, things were going very smoothly until the twenty-week ultrasound. Now I know how much the "plan" really means and that it doesn't always match the reality.*
> — *Shellie*

It's hard to fathom that we went from everything going along smoothly to Amy being induced into labor.

— Ben

Tanya was induced at the hospital the day after Oren died, and he was born a day later. I don't remember much of the labor and birth; I felt like I was in a tunnel the whole time. There was no joy, only a crushing grief in the room. There was calm and love and uncertainty and a feeling of just making it be over. Nothing like what I had anticipated when we planned a homebirth.

— Lavender

Everybody thinks of pregnancy as a positive outcome . . . and then to have two miscarriages on top of a stillbirth. After the second miscarriage, it was, like, this is just ridiculous, and what am I doing to deserve this? . . . I remember meeting the mother of a test-tube baby and thinking, "They can do this but they can't take my seven-and-a-half-pound healthy girl and get her out safely"—now come on! There's something not right here.

— Holly

Unfortunately, I was too trusting and put my faith in the hands of the professionals, so many professionals. I thought that is what you do.

— Victoria

Now, when I hear people talk about statistics with different situations I get a little upset because, you know, statistics are fine until you become one of them, and then they take on a different meaning!

— Sara

One is so unprepared for this. You are thrilled to be expecting a child, you are in a total honeymoon of your first pregnancy, and you never think that such things could happen to you.

— Annalaura

THE DEPTH OF YOUR GRIEF

Intuitively, I think that I recognized that something so grave and serious had happened in my life—I had lost a child—that I knew that it could break me.

— Nathan

Whenever and however it occurs, your baby's death is a profound sorrow because your emotional investment was already established. Even if the pregnancy is unplanned, a special bond materializes as you think about your baby and the reality of becoming a parent to this child. Throughout the pregnancy, you are primed to nurture and protect. You and your partner look after your baby's well-being and become deeply, intensely invested in this budding relationship. Other people may also count on the new baby joining your family.

It was so special. My partner was super-attentive and loving. Everything we did was for her from the moment we knew she existed. We played music for her, I read her stories in the evening, and Ben would talk to my tummy.

— *Emmerson*

My partner Lavender and her son Derek were both supportive and excited. My mother loves young children. She was ecstatic.

— *Tanya*

Throughout this bonding process, you fantasize about the future. You eagerly await the chance to experience your potential as a parent to this child, who may be your first or your fourth. You may wonder about your baby's familial characteristics and envision summertimes, wintertimes, holidays, birthdays, graduations, weddings, and even grandchildren. You look forward to the special "firsts" of childhood, such as baby's first smile, first wobbly steps, first words, first day of kindergarten, and first school dance. You imagine sharing all kinds of special experiences with your child. In such heartfelt and intimate ways, you forge a bond with your baby long before the birth.

When your baby dies, you never get the chance to know him or her in the way that we normally think of knowing someone, yet your hopes and dreams for this child have already become a part of your life. You have not only lost a child, you have lost the chance to see your baby grow, become a vital part of the family, and realize his or her potential. Your baby's death represents a deeply felt loss of a wished-for child and all your related fantasies, hopes, and dreams. Death thwarts your best intentions and breaks your heart.

Given that I was older, naturally I was afraid to share the news until after the three months, and even then, I waited an extra month "just to be safe." In retrospect, the pain you feel when losing a baby is the same whether you have told family and friends or not.

— *Helen*

The minute you get that positive pregnancy test, your life changes. Our hopes and dreams start then. So, when your baby dies, it's hard. So incredibly hard.

— *Anne*

If you've experienced the death of one or more babies from a multiple birth, the depth of your loss is compounded. Not only must you bear the death of a baby, you may be bearing the death of more than one, as well as the crushing loss of the special chance to raise two or more babies together. (See also "Multiple Birth and Multiple Realities" in chapter 2.)

A Traumatic Bereavement

The doctors were on it right away. They rushed us into a room, completed some tests, and before we knew it, the doctor was telling us our son, who we got to know through his heartbeats, movements, and daily size changes, was gone. In that moment, it was hard to tell if it was a dream or reality.

— Ben

I'll never forget my husband waiting outside for me to tell him our daughter's diagnosis. That moment changed the trajectory of our lives.

— Julie

Trauma happens when you experience an emotionally painful event over which you have no control, and it leaves a lasting imprint on your brain—and your life. Most bereaved parents, looking at their shock, grief, and mourning, can attest that the death of a baby is traumatic. A large part of what makes an experience traumatic is that everything is okay—and then suddenly, it's not.

Pearl's diagnosis day . . . before we even began the ultrasound, Josh said to the nurse, "Would you please tell Laura everything is going to be okay with the baby? She has been worried the whole time about something and just needs to hear everything is okay." Silence . . .

— Laura

We didn't seem to know what to think. All of the last five to six months had been positive and exciting and now a whirlwind two days crushed it all.

— Ben

You may have had a number of traumatic experiences during your pregnancy, your baby's birth, the postpartum period, and/or during your baby's infancy. And even after your baby's death, the trauma can continue to reverberate. As Ben says, "It was a surreal moment that will be with us forever."

Every day is a struggle at the moment. I feel exhausted and as desperate as I am to find "my" new balance, it eludes me. What comes with it is that sense of failure and disappointment that I know all too well. I feel sad and when I look in the mirror, I know I look sad. It is so painful living with empty arms.

— Emmerson

It is incomprehensible, the extremely personal aftermath of having my child die inside the only home he has ever known: me. And I can't just pick up the pieces. Some are too tiny to find; snippets of my innocence, and the little things I'm missing, like the heavy warmth of a sleeping baby in my arms.

— Tanya

*The events leading to and on that day will remain with me forever.
The shiny lights in the operating theater, the reflections, the panic,
the pandemonium, the empty sound, the crowds of people,
the absence of a perfectly formed human being—and these are
just hospital reminders. I have not only the mental scars, but also
the physical ones, which dominate my everyday life. Then there
are the everyday prompts such as my son, Tom, asking awkward
questions, the discussions I hear outside his day nursery, birth
stories, and idle chatter concerning "your next child." It is constant
and exhausting.*

— *Victoria*

When there is trauma, time is warped. It may seemingly stop, slow down, or cease to exist. Tanya remembers, "Time stopped. It seemed like the longest moment in history. Then the doctor said, 'I am sorry. I cannot find a heartbeat.'" Ben recalls, "After they induced Amy, I was the father and husband just standing there and basically doing whatever Amy told me, and time just seemed to creep." Sonya adds, "Time did not exist right after Blake passed away. I was in such denial, and I thought I was having a nightmare and would wake up and things would be okay."

This can be both a blessing and a curse. It can be a blessing when you're in shock and cannot tolerate anything that moves. The curse is that time often continues to creep along, especially during the early months after your baby's death. Nothing is familiar when your world has turned upside down. You don't know how to navigate the countless details of this new landscape, and you can't help but focus on each present moment of distress and longing. As a result, each day can seem endless, which makes grieving more grueling. When people suggest that "time heals all wounds," you can only note that you often feel suspended in time and stuck in brokenness.

*It's never-ending! I feel like we were just able to start making some
progress with our grief for Kate when we lost Zac. I think I will never
stop grieving. They say time is a great healer but at times it sure does
not feel like that. The actual physical response to grief (your heart
is so heavy it feels like it will actually break in two) lessens, but the
actual grief, it just never goes away.*

— *Melanie*

In addition to trauma, there are many layers of loss and special challenges that can affect the course of a parent's mourning, making a baby's death that much more difficult to endure. Your layers of loss, challenges, and trauma will be unique to you, but bereaved parents share many layers in common. It can help to identify them, so that you can make sense of why this journey is so complicated and difficult.

A Loss of Innocence and Faith

We had someone tell us that when you lose your baby, you lose your innocence. I can totally understand that now. I certainly feel like I have lost mine.
— Emmerson

To this day I struggle with the loss of that blissful notion of pregnancy.
— Abby

I also struggle with people saying "when the baby arrives . . ." I just want to shake them and say, "You have no guarantees. There is no guarantee that you will have a live baby at the end of a pregnancy." People are so blasé and if this had not happened to me, I know I would be too.
— Melanie

Many parents notice that this experience challenges the way they view life, nature, or the universe. They lose faith in their invincibility or the idea that they are somehow protected from bad things happening to them. All innocence is lost when they reach the frightening realization that they cannot keep death from invading their lives nor can they protect their babies from that fate. Their beliefs are shaken to the core, and they struggle with the senselessness of their baby's death. Moreover, many parents are faced with the difficulty of feeling intensely angry and having no one to hold accountable, except maybe God, which can trigger a crisis of religious faith. Or as Abby puts it, "How could God 'allow' this to happen?"

I questioned everything about everything at first. I had never gone through anything remotely painful or hard so in a sense I felt protected or maybe even favored by the God I had always believed in. I suddenly felt like He had turned His face from me and forgotten me or was punishing me for something.
— Embry

After Miriam I decided it was all crap. Nothing meant anything anymore. There was no big picture, no grand plan. I was just a pawn like everyone else in the world.
— Tanya

The Weight of Responsibility

When a baby dies, parents may feel especially responsible for what happened. These intense feelings arise from the natural and biological urge to protect your children. Because babies are so vulnerable and helpless, your guardian instincts can be at their peak. Even though your baby's death was beyond your control, feelings of responsibility can be magnified if you had to make decisions about continuing the pregnancy or enlisting aggressive medical intervention.

Mothers tend to feel principally responsible. You may wonder about things you did or did not do that might have contributed to your baby's plight. A father, too, can feel responsible. You may wonder if you failed to protect your baby and your partner from this tragedy. All of these normal feelings originate from the common belief that we have control over what happens to us.

> *Everything was "normal"—heart rate strong and steady. That night we did the kick count and everything was fine—well, truth be told, I was one kick short of eight and my husband and I didn't think twice about it. . . . Something that I looked back on and felt tremendous guilt over.*
> *—Helen*

> *At thirty-eight weeks we had a scare and went to the hospital because of concerns about my amniotic fluid level. At the hospital, we were assured everything was all right after they did all the measurements. She was small but not concerning. They didn't need to see me until my forty-week appointment. To this day that haunts me. I wish we would've gone in the next week or just induced labor so she'd be in our arms today.*
> *— Abby*

LOSS OF PURPOSE AND MASTERY

When your baby dies, you may be overcome with feelings of utter helplessness. Your baby's death undermines your sense of being masterful, in control, and able to solve any problem. Feelings of helplessness also go against the grain of an accomplishment-based life. In particular, many fathers feel this keenly. Like Ben, you may be rendered speechless and deflated, all the wind taken out of your sails. This was *not* on the agenda.

> *Once Bodhi was born, I felt pretty helpless. Now, with him in front of us, lifeless, I couldn't help, I couldn't fix the situation, and I didn't know what to say.*
> *— Ben*

Unable to control death, you must admit defeat, which may cut you to your core. And while some of your anguish may be focused on the loss of connection and opportunity to nurture your baby, a lot may be centered on performance failure. Later, feelings of helplessness may give way to anger as you become driven to recover from your loss of purpose and mastery. Charlie says simply, "It's just aggravating. Aggravating to think about and I don't like talking about it."

LOSS OF A PART OF YOURSELF

> *Bits of yourself just fall away. It is as if everything that coexisted to create "the self that is you" dies too.*
> *— Tanya*

Because wishes and dreams about your baby often reflect personal desires or attributes getting ready to bloom, a baby's death may magnify a sense that you have lost a part of yourself or potential. Likewise, if you and your baby shared similar qualities (or you hoped to), you may feel like a part of you is missing. Claudia had a strong kinship with her baby and feels this loss keenly. She says, "Jacob was such a strong, independent little guy. I felt like I could have really understood him because he would have been so much like me, like I would've been able to understand his rebelliousness, especially as a teenager." This loss of self is often particularly acute for a mother, as the life growing inside was physically and psychologically a part of her. You may also sense that you have changed as a result of your experience, which can make you feel adrift. As Emmerson says, "I feel like a different person, still trying to figure out who that is . . ."

> Before Camden was born, my pregnancy was full of hope and excitement. I was the happiest I had been in many years. All those fertility treatments had finally paid off. When we lost him, I lost myself too.
> — Fleur

Loss of Identity

When you found out you were pregnant, your identity as a parent to this child began to form. When this child dies, you have to figure out what it means to be a parent to a child who is no longer with you. Particularly if you don't have any other surviving children, you may question whether you're still a mother, or still a father.

> What ensued after all this was just terrible depression. One day, one is an expectant mom and another day, one is . . .? I don't know . . . a survivor?
> — Annalaura

Also, before your baby died, you may have seen yourself as emotionally sound, responsible, in charge, and invincible. Now you must develop a new identity as someone who is actually limited and vulnerable. You may also have to redefine what it means to be a woman or a man —or an adult.

> There have been a lot of dark, ugly, bitter, and incredibly painful sides of our grief. At times I felt like the worst version of myself that I could be. I remember asking someone (my doctor, I think), "How do I go through this with any form of dignity?"
> — Emmerson

Your role as a friend and family member may change too, as you may find it impossible to interact as one normally would when new parents rejoice in glad tidings. And if you quit your job in anticipation of staying home with the baby, you may feel adrift, uncertain of your financial role, your career, or what to do about it. As Tanya notes, "I left work to be a stay-at-home mother. Who on earth am I now?"

LOSS OF A PART OF YOUR FUTURE

When your baby dies you lose a part of your future. You grieve not only for your baby but also for your visions of parenthood. Times you had looked forward to—maternity leave, family gatherings, and holidays—can seem worthless or trivial without your baby. If you preferred to have all your children by, say, age thirty-five, or spaced a certain number of years apart, the death of your baby means that your family will not be what you imagined. If you were anticipating the birth of twins, you will grieve for the lost chance to raise babies together. Indirectly, any death represents a missing branch of the family tree as you consider the prospective generations that might have been. All of these deficits in your future make it particularly painful to get on with your life.

> *I didn't get to take him fishing, and he didn't get to take swimming lessons, he didn't get to throw rocks in the pond and make snowballs or have a frog collection. I would've let him have one too. I was made to be the mother of a little boy.*
>
> *— Lena*

Perhaps most painful of all, you lose some measure of hope for the future. Your baby's death makes you feel vulnerable to tragedy and reluctant to count on your plans coming to fruition. You may feel particularly hopeless if infertility, multiple deaths, or complications make you doubt that you will ever fulfill your dreams for parenthood.

> *My doctor said I was "technically pregnant" but most likely had a blighted ovum. I felt a little sting when those words came out of his mouth. There is no "technically" about being pregnant. I **was** pregnant. And it doesn't matter if it was an egg or an embryo or a full-term baby, I experienced pregnancy loss once again. And I lost a little hope that I hadn't realized I was hanging on to.*
>
> *— Jolie*

> *I was fourteen weeks pregnant. I had made it to the second trimester, and, I kid you not, I saw a giant rainbow in the sky. Surely this was a sign! Surely we would make it this time? But sometimes rainbows just mean it has been raining. Just two weeks later I would learn my daughter died. Now I found my anger. I felt betrayed. I felt that hope was stupid. What was the point in being hopeful in life when all my babies died and nothing ever works out?*
>
> *— Tanya*

Simply put, your baby's death puts you on a different path. Anne concurs, "I never realized that losing a baby while pregnant could be so life changing."

LACK OF MEMORIES AND RITUALS OF MOURNING

Coping with a baby's death is particularly difficult because the length of time spent with the infant is so brief. When you never or barely get to know your baby outside the womb, you may feel cheated of the chance to learn about this child's special qualities and how he or she would have graced your life. If you were blocked from spending sufficient time with your baby before death or before relinquishing the body, these are other losses to bear.

Your baby's brief life also means you're lacking memories, which are important for the bereaved. Dwelling on memories is a way to experience a more *gradual* goodbye. When the "hello-goodbye" is abrupt, mourning is more painful and complex. Many parents speak of experiencing a glowing pregnancy, an uncomplicated delivery, or even the return home of a healthy baby, and suddenly the baby is gone. And the brief time spent with their baby is not enough to fully express their devotion and gather precious memories. Especially if your baby dies before or shortly after birth, your keepsakes of your baby's life are few, and you have little tangible evidence that he or she really existed. It is unclear how this baby fits into your family.

*A friend of mine lost a baby when he was six months old, and she was saying, "You just don't know how lucky you are that your baby was taken at birth." I said, "At least you have some memories!" I really **wanted** to have some memories.*

— Bryn

Many parents are also not sufficiently encouraged to engage in rituals of mourning. Spending time with the body, arranging a funeral, attending the burial, making formal public announcements of the death, and recognizing a mourning period—all of these are rituals designed to support the bereaved. Lost rituals such as taking care of the body at home for many days, having a home funeral, and green burial are coming back, and these can be tremendously comforting for parents. Alas, mourning rituals take time and run deep, which is at odds with fast-paced, skate-on-the-surface, modern societies. As such, these rituals are often denied, overlooked, or minimized, especially when a baby dies. Rose remembers the limousine driver on the way to the gravesite making little jokes and chatting about local and national news events. To her, it summed up the feeling that her life had frozen and the whole world was going on without her, that her baby's death was but a droplet of mist that made no ripples when it hit the water.

LACK OF SOCIAL SUPPORT

Unfortunately, many friends and relatives do not recognize the depth of your pain. It is difficult for them to imagine your grief over a baby you never saw or perhaps held only briefly. Even if your baby died later in infancy, you may feel as though you are expected to grieve minimally and be "back to normal" after the first few weeks or months have passed. Add to this the fact that death is an uncomfortable topic to discuss, and you may begin to feel isolated, unwelcome to talk and share your feelings. Anne observes, "Others do not ask how I am doing or anything like that. It is over and done with to them. 'You're still thinking about your babies?!'" Emmerson recalls, "Ben's mum questioned to my face how I could love someone that I didn't know, how could I love someone who never lived. I try so hard to make sense of this." Bess notes, "It surprised me how few people will cry with you. I don't know where this idea of strength comes in, that you're strong if you don't cry."

> We had complete strangers signing Emily's online guestbook. One woman said that she appreciated us publicly acknowledging our loss. She had had three losses of her own. She wrote, "So many of us, grieve silently." That really struck me.
>
> — Anne

Because your grief is ignored or considered unnatural, you may wonder if your baby and the events surrounding his or her life and death are insignificant. Moreover, friends and relatives may have never seen your baby, so you have even fewer memories to share with others. These feelings of isolation, being the only one who knew your baby or the only one who cares, can make grieving very painful.

> If my mom died, or my sister, or anybody that had lived for years and years, I would talk about them every now and then. But because my baby wasn't born alive, people think I'm harping on it if I talk about it, which isn't true, not to me.
>
> — Cindy

> It's been four years and I haven't closed the book on it. She was still a part of my life. She was a daughter just like my other daughters are now. I don't think anybody would expect me to forget if Lori or Anna were to die now. I don't think they would force me to get over it, because they're not a newborn, like newborns are something less.
>
> — Rose

> I think it's hard because I think I'm the only one that's thinking about her, and maybe my husband and I wonder if anyone else is thinking about her.
>
> — Kitty

In the depths of mourning, it's normal to feel alone and untouchable. Even if you have a lot of support, mourning is still a lonesome journey.

You may lack the energy to deal with people. You may also feel set apart from everyone else, as your path is so different now. It is normal to withdraw and stand alone, although unfortunately this increases your isolation. Even if you prefer to grieve privately, you benefit from knowing others who have traveled this way.

> *I could see the path that everyone else was on, our paths so close they almost touch but never quite manage. They share the same environment and I can talk and interact with everyone on the other path, but I'm always separated.*
>
> — *Karen*

> *It was painful to be known as "the woman who lost three baby boys." Being in a small town, word got around and the pity people showed was the last thing I needed, let alone wanted. I would hide away from a lot of people. I'd take off, leaving shops or the supermarket if I saw someone I didn't want to talk to or face. I shut a lot of people out— worst of all, my husband. It took a huge toll on our marriage.*
>
> — *Fleur*

LACK OF PROFESSIONAL SUPPORT

For parents who have experienced the death of a baby, mourning is necessary and healthy. It has only been in the last few decades, however, that health care practitioners too have begun to recognize that these parents need to mourn. Before then, it was widely assumed that parents would not mourn this death because, after all, "They never really had a chance to know their baby." And when parents did grieve, they were admonished for feeling upset or sad, because these feelings were considered destructive and unhealthy, evidence that the parents were "dwelling on the baby" or "crying over spilt milk." Parents were pressured to forget about the baby and to think about having another one. They were dissuaded from cradling their dying baby for fear they might have to endure painful memories. After death, the baby was whisked away to spare the parents the sight of their dead child and the grief they might have experienced if they had been allowed to hold him or her. If parents were still grieving more than a year later, they were considered to be abnormal, maladjusted, or have a mental disorder.

As a result of these attitudes and the medical community's stance, most parents were deprived of expressing love to their baby in physical ways. Emotionally abandoned, they buried their feelings or felt alone and crazy for having them. When friends and family echoed these attitudes, bereaved parents were left with little or no support for grieving, coping with, or adjusting to their baby's death.

> *I was filled with extreme fear and feeling morbid to be spending time with my dead baby. I didn't know how to see the beauty in those*

final moments. Knowing what I know now, it did not have to be this way. If I'd had a compassionate nurse who was experienced and properly trained in perinatal bereavement care and who could have gently guided me, openly talked to me about fears, and how to spend quality time loving and parenting my baby, it could have been a special, cherished, and tender time of getting to know my child's body. And I possibly could have even experienced very meaningful and healing last moments with my son.

— Lori

I never saw him or held him. Before the delivery the nurse asked me if I wanted a service, but I was in a state of panic. I couldn't relate to such finality, so I said, "No." They never asked me again. Now I wish they had. I regret not seeing him.

— Karin

Remnants of these beliefs persist today, as many mothers and fathers or partners still aren't offered the compassion and guidance they need. For example, too many parents are pressured to hand over their baby when they are still overwhelmed and in shock, or before they've had time to settle into taking care of the body, sharing their little one with friends and relatives, or participating in meaningful rituals. This lack of support only adds to their grief, regret, disorientation, and the depth of their pain. But as research accumulates on the effects of a baby's death and what parents find supportive and beneficial, more and more health care practitioners are finally understanding what parents have known all along: The death of a baby is a profound and traumatic loss, and parents benefit from quality bereavement care that honors their parental bonds from the moment the terrible news is delivered, and all along the journey of mourning this child.

I still do not quite understand this, but when I found out that our baby had died, the two ultrasound technicians left me. I felt so alone as it was. I swung open the door, and called out after them (or anyone). I said, "You cannot leave me alone. I was just told that my baby died." I probably startled a few in that office that day, but I needed someone—anyone to just sit with me, until my mother or husband could arrive and be with me.

— Anne

I had good care in the hospital, but even so, I had to challenge the staff's claim to authority over Thor's body. I had to fight to have him with me for several hours rather than the thirty minutes they initially had told me I could have. Most of all, I was lucky to have the funeral director I had. He's the one who let me know I could take Thor home. It never would have occurred to me.

—Elizabeth

Health care practitioners and funeral directors are in fact in a position to provide a critical first line of support, and great strides have been made in the quality of bereavement care and providing the training necessary for delivering this highly skilled, sensitive care. Quality bereavement care reduces trauma and avoidable suffering, and has a significant impact on immediate and long-term psychological well-being, even reducing anxiety during subsequent pregnancies. Perhaps most telling, parents are filled with gratitude. As Fleur says, "I am most grateful for the comfort and support shown to us by hospital staff . . . and I got to hold my baby boys. The first two passed away in my arms."

We were blessed to have a nurse whose passion was working with bereaved families. Her calm presence and extraordinary skill in this stressful situation helped me to stay calm too.

— Lavender

They were wonderful about telling us to take our time. We never felt pressured to leave her. If anything, I was the one wondering when we needed to leave. They encouraged us to spend the night with her and from that moment on we just cherished every second.

— Abby

*When I go to leave, I am being wheeled out with Zac in my arms. As we go past the midwife station, they all come out to see us and say goodbye. I am so incredibly touched by this gesture, the acknowledgment of Zac and me. The midwives could have stayed in their station and I would have been wheeled straight past and been invisible to them. But they chose to come out and say goodbye to Zac and me. They **wanted** to. It made me feel validation of Zac's life even though he was gone.*

— Melanie

A New Era

Mourning a baby's death will always entail some degree of trauma, deeply felt losses, and emotional complexities. But quality bereavement care is becoming standard, and parents are reclaiming traditional rituals. Grieving is now considered normal and necessary. Grief counseling is more accessible, and brain-based techniques are being developed to effectively treat trauma. Greater awareness is also spreading across the lay public, as social media and the Internet provide forums for grieving parents to meet each other and shout from the rooftops. Overall, parents are receiving more of the respect, attention, and tenderness they deserve from their caregivers and their communities.

May you ride this wave of progress, and draw on the increasing quality and availability of compassionate support. You are not alone.

All the work to create this baby, summoning his soul from who knows where, all to end as ashes in a little box. I can't stand the endless goneness of him.

— Claudia Putnam

Points to Remember

- Many people find death difficult to talk about.
- People do not expect babies to die. For you, the death of your baby is a cruel violation of expectations.
- Your baby's death is untimely, unfair, senseless, and a devastating loss to bear.
- The death of a baby is considered a traumatic bereavement because it often involves a number of emotionally painful events, and mourning is complicated by many layers of deeply felt losses.
- Many people do not recognize the depth of your bond and your grief. In fact, you may be surprised by the intensity of your mourning.
- When your baby dies, you not only lose a child but also your dreams, your innocence, a part of yourself, a part of your future, and a sense of purpose and mastery.
- The brevity of your baby's life can make grieving complex and painful. You can't get fully acquainted with this special child, and the lack of memories makes it harder to experience a gradual goodbye.
- A lack of mourning rituals and a lack of support from friends, family, or health care professionals can make you feel desperately alone with your grief.
- In spite of all these barriers and difficulties, you *can* grieve and survive the death of your baby.
- You are not alone.

2

GRIEF AND MOURNING

---

*A week later, we gave our daughter's ashes to the sea. . . . It was
a beautiful day, but we were still numb with shock and sadness. In
some ways we naively thought the worst was over. Little did we know
that the grief journey had just begun, with all its despair, rawness,
sharpness, longing, and pain. It has been a long journey to travel and
I wouldn't wish it on anyone.*

—Nathan

For a bereaved parent, the journey of grief and mourning encompasses
a multitude of painful feelings, distressing thoughts, and uncomfortable
sensations. You may feel completely unprepared for the intensity of this
journey and how impossible it is to know or anticipate how you will feel
from day to day, or hour to hour. Your life seems hopelessly altered and
uncertain. You may wonder if you are going crazy.

Because mourning the death of a baby is a bewildering experience, it
can help to learn about what to expect and what other bereaved parents
have experienced. By knowing about the grieving process, you can be
reassured that your emotions are valid and normal. By knowing what's
involved in mourning and how others have mourned similarly, you may
feel less isolated and better able to cope with your grief.

*It would have helped if somebody had educated us and told us what
it was going to be like and said, "You're going to feel these things.
Don't think you're going crazy, because it's normal." I didn't know what
was going on. So I thought I was going crazy and I didn't want to tell
anybody about the feelings.*

— Desi

That there is no right or wrong way to grieve is perhaps one of the
most important points to remember. And there is no established length of
time for mourning. The bereaved parent who expects to feel a certain way
after a certain amount of time will only be distressed to discover that grief
is not so predictable.

Moreover, no two people grieve in the same way or with the same
intensity. Different feelings surface at different times for different people.
(See also chapter 10, "Especially for Fathers"; chapter 11, "You and Your
Partner.")

WHAT ARE GRIEF AND MOURNING?

- **Grief** is your *automatic internal reaction*—the thoughts, feelings, and bodily sensations you have in response to your baby's death, or diagnosis and death. Grief consists of emotions, which are like bits of energy that seek to flow along an avenue of expression.
- **Grieving** is the *process of giving grief expression*. Grieving means letting the thoughts, feelings, and sensations flow, whether they find expression through emotional avenues like crying or journaling, through mental avenues like planning a memorial, or through physical avenues like going for a run.
- **Mourning** is the *process of coming to terms with your baby's death*. Mourning includes grieving, as well as remembering, memorializing, adapting, adjusting, transforming, and healing.

Grief is *involuntary*—it is a biologically based emotional reaction that exists regardless of your intentions, and whether you are aware of it or not. Grief is also an instinct that drives mourning, which enables you to adapt and adjust to all the unexpected and unwanted changes created by your baby's death.

Mourning, on the other hand, is *voluntary*—and you can refuse to do it. Indeed, mourning your baby's death is a painful journey. However, it is also *the path of healing*.

THE GRIEF REACTION

Throughout our lives, we form durable emotional attachments to others. When a loved one dies, we feel deprived, reduced, and resistant to the changes and adjustments that must be made. Grief is the painful price we pay for our heartfelt connections with others. Grief involves many symptoms of distress.

Distress can be mental and emotional:
- numbness, detachment
- yearning, preoccupation, thinking about your baby or what happened
- confusion, disorientation, disorganized thought, difficulty concentrating
- anger, irritability, envy, guilt, regret
- fear, anxiety, worry, helplessness
- sadness, hopelessness, despair
- illusions of seeing, hearing, or feeling the presence of your baby

"No heartbeat." You'll never understand the emotions and thoughts that can possibly go through your head within a two-minute period.
— Ben

I was full of fear. I saw the top of his head—curly, dark, wet hair. It was unbelievable to see this perfect-looking being, but too still and too soft, unmoving, and nothing I could do.

— Lavender

I wanted to believe it was just a dream and I didn't have to plan a funeral or hold our dead son. It felt like a dream.

— Charlie

Guilt. I feel that I have failed as a mother to protect my daughter.

— Destrida

We were devastated. Instead of deciding whether to get blue or pink snuggies, we needed to plan the memorial service.

— Fred

Emptiness, sadness, continuous thinking about the baby, yearning, longing for him. Crying at the sight of other babies. Envy towards pregnant women.

— Annalaura

In the early weeks, a good day was one where I had eaten once and managed to dress.

— Mel

I thought I was not going to make it. It did not make sense for her heart to stop beating while mine kept going.

— Destrida

Distress can also be physical:
- shortness of breath
- tightness in the throat
- heavy or aching arms
- empty feeling in the abdomen
- fatigue
- sighing
- crying spells, tearfulness
- sleeplessness, restlessness
- change in appetite—eating too much or not enough
- heart palpitations and other manifestations of anxiety

Physically painful, and at times it felt never-ending. I felt like this big black ball had taken possession of my chest and was consuming me. I felt it when I breathed. I felt it when I wanted to sleep or rest. It just never went away.

—Lorna

My heart literally yearned and ached to hold my son. My chest hurt so badly that one night, I finally went to the Emergency Room. I thought there was something wrong with my heart. I went through every test and nothing was wrong. I was literally heartbroken.

—Jolie

The biggest thing I remember was empty arms. My arms just ached. I've read about this and it's hard to believe, but to me there was actually a physical emptiness. I could almost feel my arms cradling, but there wasn't anything there.

—*Meryl*

Distress can be social/emotional:
- experiencing loneliness, withdrawal
- feeling marginalized, isolated, avoided, misunderstood
- feeling hurt by others' clueless or insensitive remarks
- feeling put off by others who want to "fix it" for you
- resenting others who insist you should be "over it"
- wondering if you're the only one who has ever felt this way

It was so painful seeing pregnant women and hearing birth stories amongst "playground mums."

—*Victoria*

*After Kate died, people were very weird with us as she was just under the twenty-week threshold. They had real trouble acknowledging her as "a baby" and they were **so** uncomfortable.*

—*Melanie*

I feel like sometimes I am avoided because people do not want to "catch" what I have. It could all be in my head, but I feel it from time to time.

—*Anne*

*We found we sometimes had to make things "right" for people and pretend to be okay so **they** could cope with our situation.*

—*Emmerson*

The hardest emotion to deal with throughout this process is the feeling of betrayal from the people around me and distrust. The realization that I am essentially alone.

—*Karen*

Distress can be spiritual:
- Why did this happen? Why me? Why my baby?
- How could this happen when I did all the right things?
- Did I do something to deserve this?
- How could a loving God/Universe let this happen?
- Am I more vulnerable to tragedy than I thought?
- Can I trust, believe, or have faith in anything anymore?
- How can I go on when my trust in the future has been shattered?
- If I'm not in charge of my destiny, in control of my fate, why bother making plans?
- What's the point?
- What is the meaning of life?

- What's my purpose?
- Where do I go from here?

I'm still trying to process and make sense of Emily dying. The due date has passed, and I am just sad that she is never coming back. Death is so final.

—Anne

Profound fear and confusion; the self-imposed questions of Why me/us? What have I done to deserve this? What is the lesson to be learned?

—Emmerson

I think the prenatal diagnosis was God's way of preparing my heart for what was about to come—even though my heart was screaming every time the thought came to my mind that I was carrying a baby that was going to die.

—Laura

There may also be changes in personality or habits brought out by the distress of grief. A fastidious person may become careless; an outgoing person may become withdrawn; an active person may lose interest in working out; an even-tempered person may become quick to anger. Many bereaved parents also report illusions of seeing, hearing, or feeling the presence of the baby. Many behaviors and perceptions may seem peculiar, but they are normal aspects of grief.

Charlie is a weight-lifting fiend. Normally that is his outlet, but after Judah was born it took him a long, long time to get back to the gym.

—Jolie

After my first miscarriage, I remember feeling overwhelmed by the grief and thinking that I was "not handling it well." I talked to my midwife and she offered some good advice: "Grief is like labor. You don't do it, it does you." So I couldn't "do it wrong." That really helped.

—Tanya

UNDERSTANDING GRIEVING

Grieving is how your grief finds expression. For example, you may feel an ache in your empty arms, you are reminded of your little baby, and perhaps you feel sadness and longing at this thought, and you cry, or you get out your journal and write, or perhaps you turn to your partner and talk. Or maybe it's more your style to engage in a variety of meaningful activities and your grief finds expression as you build your baby's casket, plant a tree in your baby's honor, or make a charitable donation to an organization that supports grieving parents. Or maybe you feel restless and a need to get busy or get out and move your body. All of these activities, when they keep you connected to yourself and your body, are healthy ways of grieving. Your grieving tendencies are shaped by many factors, including

- your brain's arousal tendencies;
- your personality and temperament (e.g., sensitivity, intensity);
- cultural influences, including society, family, and religion;
- prior experience with loss and grief;
- your emotional and cognitive strengths;
- your adaptive strategies; and
- the support you receive.

There are four common misconceptions about the structure and nature of grieving, and it can be immensely helpful to steer clear of them. Instead, adopt these antidotes, which are examined on the following pages.

- Healthy grieving does NOT require expression of deep feelings— it requires that you grieve according to your nature.
- Grieving does NOT happen in stages—it is unpredictable.
- Grieving is NOT complicated just because it lingers—grieving takes all the time it needs.
- Grieving does NOT come to an end, with healing beginning directly thereafter—instead, grieving and healing coincide continuously. As grieving gradually winds down and recedes into the background, healing gradually winds up and proceeds into the foreground.

GRIEVING ACCORDING TO YOUR NATURE

I think the important thing to remember is that grief is a very personal journey, and each of us treads the path in different ways. I don't think that there is one particular "right way" to grieve.

—*Nathan*

Ken Doka and Terri Martin, in their book *Grieving Beyond Gender*, have created a useful framework for explaining how people internally experience grief and then outwardly express it. They identify two basic styles of grieving: *emotion-oriented* and *activity-oriented*. Practically everyone experiences a blend, landing somewhere on the continuum between the two extremes, although many people have strong tendencies toward one or the other. Reading the two lists below, you'll likely see yourself reflected in both—perhaps a balanced mix, or you may clearly favor one over the other.

Emotion-oriented grievers focus on *feeling and expressing*:

- Emotions of grief are intensely, deeply felt.
- Their narratives tend to be emotional accounts that reflect on *feelings about what happened.*
- Inwardly, they experience grief as an emotional challenge full of intense feelings.

- They direct their grief energy toward exploring emotions, and they find relief in expressing them.
- They connect to grief in the body through the feeling and expression of emotions.
- Outlets include crying, writing or talking about their experiences, attending support groups, sharing feelings with a friend or partner, spending contemplative time at the baby's grave or memorial spot, looking at photographs of the baby, handling keepsakes, and reviewing memories.
- They tend to immerse themselves in painful thoughts and feelings. They fulfill their most important tasks and responsibilities in manageable doses, so they can go with the flow of their grief emotions.
- It's as if grief and mourning flow emotionally.

Activity-oriented grievers focus on *assessing and doing:*
- Emotions of grief are not as intensely or deeply felt.
- Their narratives tend to be factual accounts that reflect on *what happened when.*
- Inwardly, they experience grief as an energizing physical restlessness.
- They direct their grief energy toward assessing and accomplishing what needs to be done.
- They connect to grief in the body through activity, including physical exertion.
- Outlets include gathering information; writing, thinking, or talking about what happened; identifying problems and solving them; keeping the household running; getting back to work; organizing rituals, events, or good works to commemorate the baby; creating or building memorials; advocating for the family or bereaved parents in general; and physical activities such as sports or working around the house.
- They tend immerse themselves in activity. They experience grief emotions in manageable doses, skirting emotional triggers so they can focus on finding solutions, setting goals, and completing tasks.
- It's as if grief and mourning flow mentally and physically.

All bereaved parents encounter much of the same mental, emotional, social, physical, and spiritual distress, but primarily emotion-oriented grievers experience distress more intensely. This does not mean they are better at grieving, more caring, or more loving; it means, simply, they are more inclined to *feel and express emotion in the face of adversity.* In turn, primarily activity-oriented grievers are more inclined to *assess and do* in the face of adversity. And while parents who tend toward "feeling" excel at tolerating a lot of pain, parents who tend toward "doing" excel at moderating the amount of pain they experience. And when it comes to mourning, any griever can be adept—whether it's finding emotional release or physical/mental release. (See also "Grieving Styles" in chapter 11.)

Remember, even though these lists clearly delineate the two styles of grieving, most people experience a blend of both, such that even if you are clearly inclined toward one (your primary style), you'll have moments or periods of being inclined toward the other (your secondary style). This means that a primarily activity-oriented griever can also experience moments of deep feeling and might benefit from a good cry. Likewise a primarily emotion-oriented griever can experience moments of assessing and doing, and can benefit from engaging in meaningful activity. As you may have noticed throughout this book, mothers and fathers alike talk about diving into emotion *and* jumping into action. (See also "Understanding Your Blend of Grieving" in chapter 10.)

Most importantly, whatever your blend of grieving, you can succeed at coming to terms with your baby's death and finding a sense of peace and healing. The first key is *staying connected to your body and its sensations*, as that is where the tension of your grief is held when it is seeking expression. The second key is *letting grief find expression in alignment with your internal experience of it*. If you're sensing a welling up of emotion, where you feel sensations in specific parts of your body, your grief is likely seeking emotional expression; if you're sensing a generalized physical or mental tension or restlessness, your grief is likely seeking physical/mental expression. If you're not sure what you're sensing or if you're sensing both, then your grief is likely demanding a mix of expression, such as crying during a hike.

Whether you're in feeling mode or doing mode, you are grieving. By being true to your inborn tendencies, you can tap into your strengths. You can find your natural flow and you can know which adaptive strategies fit and work best for you. You can even expand your repertoire. This profound experience may inspire a range of grief responses and adaptive strategies, all of which can enrich *and* ease your mourning journey.

GRIEVING IS UNPREDICTABLE

It has been like riding waves in the ocean. Just when you think the big wave has passed and you are okay, out of nowhere, another one hits.
—Anne

Unfortunately, grieving is not a linear, smooth, or timely progression. Your emotions don't adhere to a schedule, nor will you march through distinct stages. The process of grieving is far more complex, unpredictable, and bewildering. While there *is* a general progression toward feeling better over the long run, grieving is a fluid experience of many emotions, thoughts, and sensations. Many parents describe the experience in terms of a roller coaster, waves, or a host of painful feelings to let flow.

> It comes and goes in waves! Some days I am fine and "just get on with it!" Other days, in my head I go over and over what happened, and the aching pain that I have to have them here with us is overwhelming sometimes.
>
> —Kylie

> Grief is like a roller coaster. Good days and bad. You think things are good, then something small would pop up and rock your world, and the grief hits you all over again.
>
> —Fleur

> For sure, I remember my wife and I talking about grief coming in waves. Sometimes there would be a lull, and sometimes an onslaught. But there wasn't really a rhythm to it.
>
> —Nathan

At times, grieving may be gentle or intense, and it is quite typical for the thoughts, feelings, and sensations of grief to occur in waves. Each wave might last from several minutes to an hour or more—and especially in the early days or months, sometimes *way* more.

Over the course of grieving, you will also experience many ups and downs, as you would on a roller coaster. At first the "down" days will outnumber the "up" days. But as time goes on, the down days will become less frequent and the up days will occur more often, with progress consisting of one underlying theme: coming to terms with your baby's death.

Over the course of several years the downs can become less intense, but for many parents, the downs can remain as painful and powerful as ever. This can be discouraging, but eventually you *will* have more prolonged ups and you *will* survive the occasional downs. And after a time, the waves of grief and the ups and downs of grieving simply get woven into the bigger picture of your life.

> When you surf for a lifetime, you can understand the sea and different swells and the patterns of waves. Grief of course is much less easy to read.
>
> —Nathan

> After a year, a surge of grief can be as hard as ever, but it only lasts a couple hours instead of days on end. . . . It becomes slivers of pain. As time goes on it is still very painful but less consuming and less overwhelming, like you find a small place for it instead of it being your whole existence.
>
> —Claudia

During acute episodes, it can benefit you to give in to grieving. Whatever your style, grief is energy looking for an outlet, and in the long run, *it's far better for you to consistently engage in grieving rather than put it off.* By taking a time-out (even if just momentarily) and mindfully going with this flow, you're able to let that wave of grief pass, calm returns, and you take another healing step forward. After a time-out, you may resume responsibilities more safely and attentively than if you'd suppressed the wave.

> *My feeling is that it is important to make space for yourself to experience loss. Again, how that works is different for different people. For me, being naturally a person who enjoys his own company rather than being a people person, I gravitated towards solitude. I spent time alone in nature hiking and surfing. I spent time alone making things with my hands. I wrote poems and songs. I made photographs and films and surfboards.*
>
> —Nathan

What if you can't take a time-out in that moment? In those early months, when a wave might take longer than you can afford, you may be able to distract or soothe yourself when grief rears up, and then take your time-out later. Grief will always wait for you.

Many parents are proactive and pace themselves, making room for grieving outlets so the tension of holding their grief energy doesn't build up too high. You might set aside uninterrupted time to invite the waves to come—you could tend the grave, look at photos, or cuddle a weighted teddy bear and let the tears flow. Or perhaps you'll set aside an hour each evening for a workout, or a weekend afternoon for a project. You can determine proactive timing by checking in with your body and noticing how much tension you're carrying, or by being mindfully aware of a mounting desire to engage in behaviors that aren't good for you. By giving yourself regular and ample room to grieve, you free yourself to focus on your other responsibilities *and* you avert symptoms of suppressed grief. (See also "Claiming Your Grief" in chapter 10; and chapter 4, "Mindfulness-Based Coping Strategies."

> *Some days I knew I just needed to let it out—I felt on edge, like I was just full of emotion and I knew I just needed to cry.*
>
> —Jolie

Grieving Takes All the Time It Needs

You cannot hurry grieving, and there is no finish line anyway. Instead, grieving is open-ended with a progressive lessening. Over time, waves of grief generally wind down in terms of frequency and intensity. After many months or years, intense spikes of grief become rare occurrences, instead of a daily grind. But it never truly ends. As Ben says, "It's tough and still never easy to relive and think about. Basically it's a constant hole there." Melanie agrees: "I think I will never be 100 percent happy again. But that is okay and I can accept that." Many parents experience this "shadow grief," where sadness remains in the background and occasionally reappears. But over time, waves of grief become fleeting rather than dominating, and healing feels bittersweet.

> Grief is my companion. It will always be with me. Some days I am content with that, some days I am still angry about that, but it is what it is. Emma will always be in my life so of course grief will, too. I'm okay with that.
>
> —Abby

> I have to say that I agree completely with the words "some things in life cannot be fixed, they can only be carried." I carry Adisyn's short life and death every day.
>
> —Emmerson

> What a journey, and yet those "moments" still catch me every so often. Watching Tom play a part in the Nativity last week, I was drawn to the four-year-old angels thinking, "That would have been Alex," but then the moment passes.
>
> —Victoria

GRIEVING AND HEALING COINCIDE

Grieving has no definitive end, nor does it conclude or reach a resolution whereupon you grieve no more. Similarly, healing is not a destination, nor does it require grieving to stop. Instead, all along your journey, as you are grieving, you are also healing. Each moment you let the energy of grief flow, its corresponding moment of relief is a sign of your healing. As time passes and your grief becomes less energetic and softer, this marks the corresponding progression of healing.

> I don't really think that we grieve for a time, then we are eventually healed. That hasn't been my experience. For me, grief and healing coexist, side by side, and they both somehow minister to me.
>
> —Nathan

UNDERSTANDING MOURNING

As you mourn, you weave your way through grieving, adapting, and adjusting to your baby's death. With the support of companions, counseling, mindfulness, and other adaptive strategies, you come to terms with the changes that your baby's death has wrought, and seek respite from the ravages of grief when you can. Over time, you can reinvest your time and energy in regular activities and relationships. In this way you begin to re-organize your life and experience a sense of acceptance, peace, and healing.

As with grieving, mourning is rarely a predictable or smooth progression toward healing. You gradually adjust, adapt, and regain steady functioning, but over time, you may also identify more losses, delve deeper into your sorrows, find more problems to solve, and experience unexpected waves of grief. You may worry that you are regressing, but mourning is often two steps forward and one step back. Many parents point out that "healed" is an unrealistic goal, in that they are never completely "over it" or "back to normal." Instead, they move into a "new normal," as this experience has changed them forever.

TASKS OF MOURNING

As your varied thoughts and feelings of grief find expression according to your nature, mourning begins to unfold. But this journey needn't be passively endured. Passivity only compounds suffering. Instead, you can actively and mindfully *feel what you need to feel* and *do what you need to do* along this journey of mourning. For bereaved parents, this means engaging in the following, often concurrent, tasks of mourning over the course of many months and years.

- Affirm your baby's existence and importance.
- Acknowledge the reality of your baby's death.
- Identify your losses (of self, identity, dreams, faith, control, etc.)
- Reflect on your experiences and memories, and create a clear account of what happened.
- Be aware of your distress, staying connected to your body and going with the flow.
- Grieve in ways that are consistent with your inner experiences of grief.
- Implement adaptive strategies that ease your suffering and promote healing.
- Seek out and accept the compassion of others who can be supportive as you mourn.
- Honor and keep your bond to your baby, moving from a relationship of presence into a relationship of memory and/or spirit.
- Accept *what is*, letting go of *what might have been.*
- Adjust your beliefs, worldviews, roles, relationships, and ways of being,
- Search for meaning and explore spiritual/philosophical foundations (that are perhaps new) for living your life with a renewed sense of purpose, mastery, and gratitude.

This is basically a to-do list for engaging fully in your journey of healing. It may seem like a *very* tall order. But there are no time limits, and when and how you go about each one is up to you. For instance, you choose how to affirm your baby; you determine what your losses are; you discern when to go with the flow of your distress; you discover what a comfortable relationship with your baby looks like. Also, this list is meant to be a vague outline to loosely guide you as you feel your way along your journey. You can pace your mourning, or if you're feeling uncertain or adrift, pick a task that speaks to you in the moment. By doing what you need to do and doing it well, you can boost your feelings of competence, purpose, and hope. (For more detailed information on these tasks of mourning, boosting the quality of your mourning, and what healing looks like, turn to "How Do I Acquire a Sense of Healing?" in chapter 8.)

There are many resources to light your way (including this book). You can tap into your own experiences and self-knowledge to determine the what, how, and when. You can seek the advice of compassionate counselors, therapists, clergy, teachers, coaches, friends, and relatives who've also faced adversity—and talk to other bereaved parents. There are self-help books, self-improvement books, spiritual books, medical books, science books, philosophy books, and bereavement memoirs written by parents who've walked this path before you. There are websites run by parent support organizations, bereaved parents, and advocacy groups, and there are websites whose content is contributed by the general pubic. You can find wisdom in social media, journalism, and storytelling, including magazines, newspapers, radio, television, film, and TED Talks. You can deem what advice, perspectives, philosophies, tools, and skills work best for you. As your journey unfolds, you may discover a variety of ways to approach each of your tasks of mourning.

Reading about other bereaved parents' grief journeys, and also reading about how they went on to have inspiring, happy, fulfilling lives . . . gave me "some" hope for my own future happiness I guess. And reading about others' grief thoughts and feelings in these books helped me to feel normal, supported, and better understood.

—Lori

But where is the healing? As you navigate your way through these tasks of mourning, you can gradually accept *what is* and integrate your baby's life and death into the fabric of your life. This acceptance and integration is the hallmark of healing, and creates your "new normal."

By actively mourning, you are actively grieving, coping, adjusting, transforming, and healing. In fact, even when you cannot detect it, each and every moment of mourning brings you along your path of healing.

Why Is Mourning Required?

As was pointed out earlier, mourning is voluntary. But it is not really optional. This may seem counterintuitive, but *the path of healing requires you to mourn.*

When bereaved persons refuse to mourn, they may consciously or unconsciously believe they are successfully avoiding pain by controlling grief and its expression. They might think that after they have a few "good days" or get past a certain period of time, they should be "over it." Or perhaps they are desperately trying to maintain an image of strength and stoicism. Maybe they are listening to those people who urge them to "buck up" or "hold it together" or "quit complaining." They might have nobody to turn to. It *is* more painful to mourn without any affirmation.

Unfortunately, grief is like a wild horse, and your baby's death puts you into a tiny stall with it. You might plot your escape and reach for the door. But always, that wild horse gets there first because it wants out even more than you do. You might deny its presence, but it's always there. You can pretend it's nothing, but it keeps reminding you that it's quite something. You can hide it behind you, but it still exists. You can try to avoid it, but it's still in the way. You can try to force it to stay in one corner, but that only increases its fury. You can ply it with tranquilizers, but then its mass barricades the door so you're still trapped with it. So try as you might, your attempts to escape, deny, hide, avoid, control, or anesthetize never lead to freedom. Indeed, by trying to control or fight against the wild horse of grief, it actually ends up controlling and fighting you. You become a prisoner of grief, spending untold amounts of energy to suppress or avoid the involuntary waves that demand expression. (See also "What if I Try to Avoid Grieving?" in chapter 5.)

Mourning, on the other hand, is your ticket out. It does, however, require that you squarely and realistically face that wild horse of grief. It requires you to surrender at times to your distress. But in doing so, you also discover ways to accept and embrace the wild horse—ways that are inaccessible to you if you try to maintain control over it. You ultimately befriend the wild horse of grief, and it becomes an ally for living your life with integrity and authenticity. That's why, as scary and painful as mourning can seem, you'd be wise to do it. And because it's voluntary, you can choose to do it well. (See also "Welcoming Your Grief" in chapter 4.)

> I would describe my grief as "grief done well" because I had so many chances to create memories and to do what I needed to do, as I needed to do it. A bit of advice I was given was **do not let anybody tell you, "You are not grieving right." How would they know? Your grief is right for you.**
>
> —Sarah

A Long, Soulful Journey

While mourning includes the practical—expressing grief, implementing adaptive strategies, finding the support you need—it is also a soulful journey that invites you to search and question, adjust and change. You may adopt new skills that help you better acknowledge, express, and cope with your thoughts and feelings. You will likely ask big questions about medicine, relationships, life, death, destiny, meaning, God, spirituality, nature, and the Universe. You may reflect on what's really important to you and build a new foundation for living your life. You will likely experience personal growth as a result of surviving this adversity, and find strength and other talents you didn't know you had. All along the way, you'll be developing new facets to your identity. And like many parents, you will come through this journey utterly changed—for the better.

As every parent in this book can attest, mourning and surviving a baby's death demands change. Some of your old ways of being and doing are simply inadequate. It's as if you've been broken and forced to become wiser. Or as Lavender notes, "I have been going through enormous transformations, in all parts of my life." Transformation can be frightening, exhausting, and difficult, but ultimately you'll see that what you've experienced is a *healing transformation.*

> *Meeting Pearl was one of the holiest moments of my life, actually holding someone who wasn't meant to be part of this world. She was created to come for a moment and live the rest of her days in heaven.*
> —*Laura*

> *Alex's death has allowed me to bring purpose to everything and create a phoenix to rise from the ashes.*
> —*Victoria*

As you might imagine, mourning can take a long time. In fact, you *need* time. Because your bond to your baby is deep and enduring, you cannot immediately and fully confront the reality of your baby's death, nor fathom the extent of your losses. To do so would be emotionally overwhelming. Indeed, many feelings of grief, including numbness, denial, and anger, are forms of avoidance or protest, which permit a gradual adjustment to the death and its full impact on your life. You also need time to assess the damage and experience your grief. You need time to dwell on your baby and adjust your relationship. You need time to find support and practice new ways of coping. You need time to try to make sense of your baby's death. You need time to find meaning and rebuild your personal foundation.

Like most parents, you may be impatient to feel better sooner. But the passage of time, although it can be agonizingly slow, is your friend. Time makes it possible for your soul to wallow in the twists and turns of your life and your mourning. Time grants you room to breathe as you learn to cope, adapt, acquire insights, come to terms, and grow into your healing transformation. (See also "The Bittersweet Path of Healing" later in this chapter; and chapter 8, "The Journey of Healing.")

I view my grieving process as being fluid, it changes constantly. Grief is like an old blanket that I'm familiar and comfortable with, and I know that I will wear it less and less.

—Karen

MULTIPLE BIRTH AND MULTIPLE REALITIES

When they handed Caitlyn to me to hold, as I did with Sophie, I said, "It's okay darling. Mummy and Daddy are here." We had turns at holding her and taking photos with her while she was barely still alive. I remember Jaysen saying to one of NICU team that had been looking after her, "It's not any easier the second time around is it?!" and the NICU team member started to cry with us also. This was such a heartfelt moment.

—Kylie

If you have gone through a pregnancy with multiple babies, and one, some, or all of your babies died, you may face special challenges to your mourning. The tasks of mourning remain the same for you, but some might be more complicated. For example, you have many more losses to acknowledge. Not only must you grieve for the death of one or more babies, you must also mourn for the lost chance to raise twins, triplets, quads, quints, or more. If more than one baby died, you have more than one traumatic bereavement to bear. In addition, unless all your babies died similarly and simultaneously, multiple babies usually mean multiple realities. These might include stillbirth, illness, neonatal intensive care, emergency hospitalization, surgery, treatment decisions, death and—with survivors—homecoming. If you used selective reduction, you have not only the agony of that decision and the risks, but at best, you are excited and bereft at the same time.

You may also have more than one baby to affirm, more than one relationship to adjust, and more grief to express. If you are raising a surviving baby, you have a challenging balancing act, and your mourning may be prolonged. (See also "What if I Have a Surviving Baby?" and "Anniversaries and Other Reminders" in chapter 8. If you made agonizing decisions during the pregnancy, see chapter 9.) You may also mourn for a sole surviving child who will never know the unique kinship of a sibling who's the same age.

If you are dealing with multi-realities, you will react and respond to any one of them differently from a parent for whom a particular event is the only reality. You will benefit from finding people who can understand and listen to all of your experiences with each baby. This will help you celebrate each life and mourn each death. Remember that the realities you have endured would be considered overwhelming for any family to deal with over a number of pregnancies and several years. You've experienced them *simultaneously.*

As we cried tears for Brian, we got another phone call saying Marc was close to death. Again we went down that long hallway to NICU. We held Marc and watched as his heart rate and respiration slowed. Rick was crying and saying, "Come on, Marc, you're a fighter—you can make it!" It was breaking my heart. As I was holding Marc, his vital signs picked up—did he know I was his mother? Was he going to make it? . . . His heart rate began to drop and we watched our son die. . . . We felt the crushing weight of our children's deaths—not once, but twice within two hours. I can still feel my heart breaking, a piece of me lost with each of my boys.

—Sheila

This moment is the epitome of bittersweet. On one hand, we are celebrating the birth of our new son, Cody Alexander; however, we are also mourning the loss of son Robert Evan. Although I had three months to prepare for this moment, the tears were quick to flow from a well I thought I had buried deep inside.

—Ron

COMMON FEELINGS OF GRIEF

This is an overview of the most common and salient feelings of grief experienced by bereaved parents. While parents share much common ground, remember: everyone's grief is different. Not everyone will experience denial, guilt, failure, resentment, or deep depression. Furthermore, your grief may be intense or gentle, overwhelming or manageable, somewhere in between, or vacillating between extremes. This is simply a guide and an orientation to the general landscape of grief following the death of a baby.

SHOCK AND NUMBNESS

I came to, still on a wheelie bed . . . Mathew told me that the baby didn't make it and only lived a few hours. I was told that the baby was next to me in a bassinet. I looked. No wires, nothing, just a perfect baby. He looked so much like his older brother. And then I cried and closed my eyes. I was too exhausted to speak. I fell asleep.

—Victoria

Sometime after eight p.m. we handed Willow's body over to a very compassionate, weeping midwife. Leaving the hospital was very difficult, especially hearing the cries of healthy newborn babies. I wanted to get Eliza out of there as quickly as I could. We were both so numb.

—Nathan

There will be times, especially right after you receive the terrible news, when you may feel as though you are in shock. It's nearly impossible to absorb information, much less make important decisions. You may not even be able to recall certain information or events.

The NICU team was explaining to us what was happening, and what the equipment was for, and what it was doing for our little girls. I remember parts of this and other parts are a complete blur. As I look back now, I was in major shock!

—Kylie

Even the fact of your baby's diagnosis or death may not fully register for several days, almost as if your mind tries to protect you from the awful reality. For a while, you may appear to be unaffected by this tragedy or that you're taking it in stride—largely because it hasn't hit you yet. Throughout the months following your baby's death, you may still endure occasional periods when the entire experience seems unreal, but pervasive numbness due to shock normally occurs during the early days and weeks.

The day James died I was very numb. It was very undramatic. I didn't start really feeling anything for a long time, for a couple of weeks, before I started to really hurt. It was like I was watching somebody else go through the whole thing. My husband fell apart and I watched myself go over and comfort him and I watched myself go for the next two weeks, feeling guilty as hell that I wasn't hysterical or that I was actually laughing. I watched myself do these things, but I wasn't a part of what was happening.

—Sara

At first you're in shock and when you come out of it, then it hits you what happened and then you're back in shock again. I'd say the first two months were like that, and then it started easing up a little bit at a time.

—Martina

Early on, numbness is a natural result of shock. It is also healthy and adaptive, helping you gradually face reality without becoming too overwhelmed. But because feeling nothing at all can be far preferable to the intense pain of grief, numbness can become a recurring way to avoid distress. If this is the case, you may benefit from counseling. Because of the traumatic nature of this bereavement, many parents benefit from extra support as they gradually say goodbye to their dreams, let grieving flow, and adjust to their baby's death. (See also "Common Concerns about Emotional Recovery" in chapter 5; "Claiming Your Grief" in chapter 10; "Counseling" in chapter 13.)

DENIAL AND YEARNING

As the reality of your baby's death registers, shock and numbness subside. Periodically, however, you may find yourself believing that the baby is still alive. This is normal. For a while, you may wonder if this is all a bad dream and you'll wake up soon to find a healthy baby in your arms. You may wonder if the ultrasound simply failed to detect the baby's heartbeat. Before the birth, you may believe that you detect fetal movement and the baby is fine. You may feel a strong desire to retrieve your dead baby, wanting to resuscitate the lifeless body or wondering if the dead infant really belongs to someone else and that your baby is somewhere, alive and well.

> *I did a lot of denial. I kept trying to believe all this really didn't happen and I kept hoping that I'd wake up tomorrow morning and everything would be all right. I felt like I was living in a nightmare. That lasted quite awhile.*
>
> *—Lena*

> *Even after she was stillborn, it was kind of a relief to finally have her in my arms. But then again, I wanted her to be awake and I wanted her to cry and I wanted her to act like a normal . . . I wanted her to be alive. I really didn't realize she was dead until I held her. I mean, I kept thinking during labor, "maybe, maybe." Even after seeing that monitor and that line where her heartbeat should've been was just a solid line, I still didn't believe it. . . . But my subconscious or me not wanting to believe the truth kept saying, "Maybe she'll cry and everybody will be shocked." A few days later in the funeral home I kept thinking, "Why don't you just wake up. Just wake up and cry. CRY and then we'll be all right, and I'll take you home!"*
>
> *—Cindy*

> *I think everybody must have little fantasies that are a part of denial that help you. Sometimes I feel like he didn't die, that somehow someone else had become attached to him and they realized it was going to be hard to separate them. I know that this isn't true, but it's a little fantasy that keeps me going. So every once in a while I have that feeling that this is **so** unreal that that's what really happened—that someone else took him.*
>
> *—Liza*

In yearning for your baby, you may feel totally preoccupied with thoughts of him or her. You may be able to feel the sensation of your baby kicking inside you. At times you may believe you hear the baby crying. When you peek into the nursery you may, for a split second, believe you see the baby lying in the bassinet. You may dream vividly about your baby. These illusions and dreams occur as part of your denial and are a normal protest that also enable you to gradually face the fact that your baby is gone.

As reality sinks in, your yearning turns into a longing to be close to your baby. Without a baby in your arms, you turn to keepsakes and photographs, memories, and talking about your baby. (See also "Is It Normal to Find Comfort in Nurturing Behaviors?" in chapter 5 and "Memories" in chapter 6.)

BLAMING YOURSELF, RESENTING OTHERS

As you squarely face your baby's death, you may experience feelings of failure, anger, envy, and guilt. These emotions are part of protesting and confronting death.

Feelings of failure tug at you as you wonder if you are able to produce a healthy baby. Clinical terms such as *genetic mutation, irritable uterus, incompetent cervix,* and *blighted ovum* can add to your discouragement. A sense of inadequacy, particularly for mothers, may arise from the idea that your body betrayed you, or that you are less of a woman or less of a mother because your baby died. Like many mothers, Kelly recalls, "I didn't feel I was a good mother, a good person, because I couldn't do this one thing right."

Bereaved mothers often feel anger or envy toward pregnant women or mothers with infants. You may envy their ease of good fortune, even as you acknowledge you don't know their full stories. You may resent the ones who seem to effortlessly produce healthy babies despite abominable habits during pregnancy. You may bristle when you hear about unfit parents. You may also feel angry at fate, God, doctors, or your partner as you search for reasons to explain your baby's death.

> Others friends having babies is a double-edged sword. I'm happy for them but it also feels like I am being stabbed in the heart. It's such a hard one to explain/describe and with it comes guilt.
> —Emmerson

> All these women who don't even want their babies or the ones who don't take care of their bodies can pop them out with no problem and practically no medical care. How come I couldn't do it?
> —Desi

> I suppose I should say, "It's so unfair, but I don't wish other moms and babies harm." But oh, I do. I know it's not right and I don't want children to die, but I want those mothers to feel what I feel so I'm less isolated, so I'm not the only one. I am slightly disappointed when a healthy baby is born—they don't know how lucky they are.
> —Stephanie

> At some point, Emma's cord kinked. This fact brought me to my knees. The news felt so unfair. How are so many babies delivered with their umbilical cords intact, and our baby is gone?
> —Abby

Guilt reflects a valiant sense of responsibility and the belief that you should be able to protect your children, absolutely. It is most apparent when you wonder whether there was something you did or did not do that caused your baby's problems. Was it genetic or environmental? Did you or your body contribute to your baby's death? Could you have somehow prevented this? Did you do something to deserve this awful tragedy? Bess remarks, "I thought maybe I was getting paid back for something I did that was wrong."

> It was the guilt that I have a baby inside of me. I'm the only person that could hurt or help that baby. What I consume in my body is what goes to that kid, and I couldn't even know when something's

wrong and I couldn't even act and get her out and take care of her. I mean, this is the inside of my body. That was the guilt. I just felt like people thought, "Well, gosh, she was inside of you; didn't you know something was wrong? Couldn't you tell?"

—Cindy

*At first I thought, "You're not a woman anymore if you can't have a baby that lives. It's your fault." But it's not your fault. You go through guilt and then you realize finally that it **wasn't** you that did it. And then you try to blame it on everybody else. But I can remember blaming it on myself more than anything.*

—Martina

Failure, anger, and guilt are very common but difficult feelings to cope with. For more information and adaptive strategies for dealing with these painful emotions, see chapter 4, "Mindfulness-Based Coping Strategies"; chapter 7 "Painful Feelings"; and chapter 9, "Making Peace with Agonizing Decisions."

DEPRESSION, DISORGANIZATION, AND DESPAIR

When Adisyn died, a total blanket of darkness fell over me. I remember feeling completely helpless, the raw despair. I have wailed and ached for my baby. Night after night, shrouded by nightmares, waking from my sleep crying.

—Emmerson

Shortly after Oren's birth it rained, not just a light rain, but it poured. I thought perhaps the sky was crying with us. It rained and rained that day and shortly after that we entered into a long period of drought. I will always remember that strange paradox of crying thousands of tears while the clouds would not rain. Drought during our mourning.

—Tanya

After Kate died, I fell into a big, dark, deep hole that I never thought I was going to be able to climb out of. I could barely function. I could just get through the day and that was all. To be honest I barely remember that time. My husband would get home from work and I would just crawl into bed. I left him to sort the kids, do the housework. I was just totally overwhelmed and consumed by my grief.

—Melanie

The world can become a very dark place. It can seem like you are fighting just to stay alive, there can seem to be no point to the day.

—Mel

As you begin to grasp the fact that your baby is gone forever, you start adjusting to the changes in your life. Naturally, you may feel depressed, disorganized, or extremely sad. You may feel apathetic and unable to enjoy your friends, hobbies, or other pleasurable activities. You may feel pessimistic, hopeless, victimized, deprived, isolated, vulnerable, and/or powerless.

I got real depressed, which I'd never experienced. . . . You know, everybody has days when they're down in the dumps, but I was why-even-get-out-of-bed depressed, where all I wanted to do was sleep. . . . I just couldn't think of any reasons why I wanted to continue, that's how depressed I was.

—*Sara*

Just any routine thing was like a major ordeal. It just seemed like your whole world had been totally turned upside down, and then to just go back to the mundane stuff like going to the grocery store when your baby had died, it was, like, what difference does it make?

—*Hannah*

For many parents, part of their despair is spiritual distress. You may wonder how such adversity could happen to *you*, question your assumptions about a protective God, and realize you don't have as much control over your destiny as you thought you did.

We had three perfectly straightforward pregnancies, followed by losing Kate just before twenty weeks, a miscarriage, another miscarriage, and Zac at twenty-seven weeks. Was this the universe telling me I was only meant to have three kids? What more would we have to endure in the pursuit of our much-wanted fourth child?

—*Melanie*

Feelings of vulnerability to tragedy can also make you feel anxious about the safety of yourself and loved ones. Vulnerability can discourage you from making plans and make you want to retreat to a cave or your bed.

This withdrawal and turning inward is a natural response to the trauma of your baby's death, and for some, a necessary part of mourning. You can view it as a therapeutic and protective mechanism. Especially during the first weeks or months, by figuratively or literally retreating to a safe haven and curling up into a ball, you avoid further injury. It can also be a valuable way to collect and preserve your inner resources for the long and trying journey ahead. Particularly during the first year or so, you may occasionally retreat and curl up to regroup or rejuvenate.

If you feel like your everyday functioning is impaired—that you lack energy, don't care anymore, can't concentrate, or feel so disorganized that it is impossible to get much accomplished—realize that this is normal. Set aside time for yourself and focus on self-nurturing. Do what doesn't require much energy or concentration. Make lists to help your memory and organization. If you can't handle much responsibility, have someone else take up the slack for a while. You can also benefit from finding a companion to journey with you through this thickest part of your mourning.

*There are days where you wonder if you'll make it to the next day,
and days where you don't even care if you do.*
—Claudia

*I went through a stage where I just didn't care. When it was time to
pay a bill I thought, "Well, big deal, if it gets paid, fine, if it doesn't,
fine." I mean, I didn't care about anything. Now I'm back to caring
about certain things. But I went through that feeling that nothing is
important anymore; I've lost what's important to me, so why should
anything else be important?*
—Martina

If you become concerned about depression or prolonged withdrawal
and distress, you may require more help and support than you're getting,
particularly if you're suffering from trauma, as many parents do. (See also
"About Trauma and Suffering" in chapter 3; "Postpartum Depression" in
chapter 5; "Is It Okay for My Grieving to Feel Prolonged?" in chapter 8.)

THE BITTERSWEET PATH OF HEALING

*I once read somewhere, "You never get over it; you just get used to
it." So true.*
—Winnie

Many people mistakenly believe that healing means you stop grieving, forget
about the baby, and move on. To the contrary, you will never forget your
baby, you will always feel some sadness, and you will always prefer that
it would have turned out better. But with time, the longing, failure, guilt,
and anger fade; the sadness becomes manageable.

*There are those moments when things still come crashing down.
Being asked, "Is it just Tom? I thought you had another." At the
beach, seeing two boys play. Interestingly, these moments have
become livable, but boy, they can still pinch hard and probably will
always.*
—Victoria

*We lost our baby girl ten years ago. Of course, I have never been the
same since, and I will carry a sense of brokenness with me for all of
my days. The ache of loss and longing is still raw and real for me, but
thankfully it is much less frequent. I still remember my daughter each
day, but the knowing grows less sharp and more soft.*
—Nathan

Healing also doesn't mean that you meekly abandon your baby, or
surrender to death. Instead, you search for answers and vow to prevent
a recurrence, even as you accept your vulnerability to tragedy. You also
continue to feel a bond to your little one. What changes is how you relate
to your baby. Your love remains intact, but instead of hanging on to a

relationship with a presence, you forge a relationship with the memories, and depending on your beliefs, perhaps with your baby's spirit. Or as Emmerson says, "Our daughter is inside my heart and I literally carry her everywhere we go." In fact, there is mounting medical evidence that mothers can continue to carry their baby's cells in their blood and organs, including the brain, breasts, and heart, as early as the seventh week of pregnancy. You may find this a comforting thought that the mother literally continues to carry a tiny part of her baby in her body. (For more information, look up "fetal microchimerism.")

In other words, as you mourn, rather than moving away from your baby, you're moving away from the raw immediacy of your baby's death. You continue to hold on to your baby and bring your memories with you as you move along your path of healing. Plus, your bond transcends the pain of grief. Even when you're not actively grieving, and even when you're no longer plunging into despair, your bond to your baby remains strong.

As mentioned earlier, "back to normal" is unrealistic, but you can acquire "a new normal" and with it, a sense of healing as you adjust and adapt to your baby's death. You learn to accept it and integrate this experience into your life. Your memories of your baby can evoke pleasant emotions and even gratitude. As you remember your baby fondly, thoughts become bittersweet: sadness merges with your happier memories, and you acquire a sense of peace. And you feel good about being able to say, "I will always be my baby's mother" or "I will always be my baby's father."

Her life and death feel like a very integrated part of my life right now and not something that I could or would change, just something that happened and I'm going to cope with it. I don't feel as though it's limiting anymore, it's just part of my life.

—Jessie

When I think about it, it's always going to be sad. I can look back on the time we had with him, and although it was the only time we'll ever have with him, I can smile. I didn't think I'd ever smile. Every time I thought about that, it would make me cry. It doesn't make me cry anymore. Now it makes me real grateful that I had that time. I feel really, really grateful that I had him for three days. And I didn't think I'd ever feel that way.

—Sara

I feel grateful for our babies, Emily and Michael. It is bittersweet. Bitter, because we had two babies die in the second trimester, but sweet because they are still our babies.

—Anne

*For me, a healing realization on my journey was realizing that I can and will always love my baby **and** I will always be sad that my baby has died too. But I didn't have to always suffer, like in the beginning*

*months and years after my baby died. Sadness is bearable, but
suffering is not.*

—Lori

Adjusting and adapting takes time. Of the parents in this book, most
needed more than four years to feel a solid sense of peace and calm. Some
parents needed less time, some parents needed more, and even with healing,
some still continue to feel intense sadness at times, many years later.

*It's been now three years since that day and I can say that the
pain has now [been] assuaged, although tears flow to my eyes as I
remember, as I write this.*

—Annalaura

*How do I feel now, seven years later? That there is a missing part in
our life, that the family is incomplete. . . . I still miss him and I don't
know that that ever goes away. It's less now—it used to be every
minute of every day and then it was just a few days a week and then
a few weeks in the month. Sometimes I'll be like this only once in a
year. Sometimes it's worse and sometimes it's not. I just wish it had
never happened, never, ever, ever.*

—Bess

The peaceful feelings that come with healing are a blessed change from
the ravages of grief, and you too can find this sense of peace and healing.
Chapter 4, "Mindfulness-Based Coping Strategies," explores mindfulness
and the many strategies that can help you along this journey. Chapter 8,
"The Journey of Healing," explores the tasks of mourning in more detail
and describes what acceptance, healing, and integration look like. Reassuring
hindsight perspectives are in chapter 17, "Living in Remembrance."

SURVIVING GRIEF

At times, you may doubt that you can survive this grief. Many parents
express this concern. The secret is to trust the process and go with grief's
ebb and flow. By accepting your grief as it comes and goes, you'll experience
less suffering than if you resist your grief, suppress it, or hang on to it.

*When I initially experienced grief, I was in this survival mode of hunting
to find information or someone to relate to or something to console me
in some way, and then after a while I kind of just found my own way of
coping and I became a little more comfortable in my grief.*

—Jolie

*I knew grief long before Elizabetta passed and I knew that the
intense pain would ebb and I would get to a place where my life
would continue without grief having an everyday presence. Grief
is part of the process of living and I know I can live with grief, it
comes to visit when you least expect it, but I can usually get to a
point where the pain that comes makes me smile through the tears*

because it reminds me that someone I love lived and that they were precious to me. I'm also not afraid of grief, I'm not afraid to let it slide into the background and to live. It doesn't mean I've forgotten if I don't think of the person constantly, it means I'm choosing to carry them as part of who I've become, not as who they were or what could have been.

—Karen

In fact, researchers in bereavement agree that *the quality of your mourning can determine the quality of your life.* By letting your grief flow, you increase your chances of healing and finding peace and happiness again. In contrast, suppressing grief increases distress. (See also "What if I Try to Avoid Grieving" in chapter 5; "Invisible Grief" in chapter 10; "How Do I Acquire a Sense of Healing?" in chapter 8.)

I take each emotion or memory as it comes. Enjoy them. Cry with them. Laugh with them.

—Sarah

I was scared for a while of what would happen if I let go of my feelings. I now believe that our minds only allow us to express that with which we can cope, saving the rest for another day.

—Mel

I tell myself, "Take it one day at a time." This journey is long and I need to pace myself.

—Destrida

I have dealt with things in my own way, one day at a time. I sought help when I needed it.

—Fleur

Many parents benefit from attending bereaved parent support groups, as well as individual counseling. Both resources offer a place where you can talk about your baby and express your thoughts and feelings. If you feel stuck, overwhelmed, at the end of your rope, that your life and relationships are unraveling, or if you feel numb or in shock or have physical symptoms for longer than you think you should, you may benefit from talking to a counselor. Doing so may help you experience your grief, tackle the tasks of mourning, and eventually acquire a sense of peace and healing. Seeking help is a sign of strength and courage—and demonstrates a wish to avert unnecessary suffering. You deserve to feel better. (See also "Parent Support Groups" and "Counseling" in chapter 13; "Keys to Survival" in chapter 8, where more parents reflect in hindsight.)

My husband and I have been having regular counseling from a qualified counselor in this area of bereavement. That has been invaluable.

—Victoria

Hands down, counseling helped the most.

                                          —Melanie

I sought out counseling on day one, and that has helped tremendously. Also, attending support groups helps me not feel alone in my feelings.

                                          —Anne

*Grief is so complicated. Whenever I get put in contact with other bereaved mothers, I tell them that grief is complicated, exhausting, and never-ending. Since that seems ridiculously depressing, I follow it up with the three points I believe that grieving parents must constantly recite to themselves: (1) You are **not** alone, (2) You **are** still a mother/father, and (3) Give yourself grace. I truly believe, even though those ideas seem so simplistic, that those are the guidelines for navigating through your grief journey.*

                                          —Jolie

POINTS TO REMEMBER

- Grief is your *automatic internal reaction*—the thoughts, feelings, and bodily sensations you have in response to your baby's death.
- Although everyone's experience of grief is unique, there are many feelings that parents commonly share, including shock, denial, yearning, failure, anger, guilt, sadness, and despair.
- Grief is like a wild horse that cannot be averted, controlled, avoided, denied, or anesthetized. By surrendering control over grief, you can learn to accept and eventually befriend it.
- Grieving is the outward expression of grief.
- Bereaved parents share many of the same powerful feelings and experiences of grief, but all people grieve in their own personal ways, with their own intensity, on their own timetable.
- Mourning is the process of gradually coming to terms with your baby's death. It includes grieving, coping, adjusting, transforming, and healing.
- You have little to no control over grief. It is what it is. You do have some control over your grieving and mourning in that you can decide to do it, and do it well.
- Stay connected with your body so you can acknowledge grief as it comes up and give it the expression that fits the tension-seeking release.
- The tasks of mourning include affirming your baby's importance, identifying your losses, being aware of your distress, grieving in alignment with your inner experience of grief, leaning on others, keeping your bond and adjusting your relationship with your baby, and exploring answers to your spiritual questions.
- Mourning is a lengthy, unpredictable process of ups and downs. Each and every moment of mourning brings you along the path of healing.
- However painful and time-consuming grieving may be, in the long run, going with the flow is actually less painful and time-consuming than suppressing or avoiding grief.
- The quality of your mourning determines the quality of your life.
- Be kind to yourself.
- You will survive.

3

HOW YOUR BRAIN IS AFFECTED

In the early days, my brain was definitely struggling to make sense of everything and many things were overwhelming. I was dazed, confused, in shock, and was expected to find my footing. . . . I felt like I was in a dark jungle where I had to actively carve a new path and fight off wild animals.

—*Karen*

While you probably think of *you, yourself,* as being in the process of grieving and adjusting, as in, "I'm devastated" or "I'm feeling a little better," that's actually you feeling the effects of your brain doing all the heavy lifting.

Your brain prioritizes your grief and mourning, compelling you to set aside your normal routines and concerns. In fact, at first you may feel like your life has come to a complete halt, while the rest of the world has gone on without you. But if you follow the lead of your grief-stricken brain, you will be able to gradually let go of *what might have been* and adjust to *what is,* and, step by step, you'll rejoin the rest of the world. Your brain, the seat of your grief, your trauma, and your bond to your baby, is also the seat of your adjustment and healing.

This chapter offers insights into how your brain is vastly affected by the death of your baby. You can benefit enormously from this information. Understanding your symptoms, feelings, and reactions in terms of how the human brain is wired can actually demystify and normalize the more bewildering aspects of your grief and mourning. By understanding your brain, you'll also realize how much of your internal reactions are not your fault, nor signs of weakness or maladjustment—it's just how you're built to respond to all the unique challenges of this bereavement. These insights can boost your self-awareness and compassion for yourself, and enhance your ability to practice mindfulness, which is covered in chapter 4. You'll also realize how much grief is beyond your control, making you appreciate why "going with the flow" of your grief is often the best approach.

BRAIN ANATOMY

The brain is extremely complicated, but for the purposes of gaining insight into "the brain and bereavement," your brain basically consists of three distinct layers—two layers make up the core brain, and the third is the outer brain.

- Your core brain includes your brain stem, which automatically runs your physiology (breathing, heart rate, digestion, etc.). Usually it operates in a calm state of "rest and digest." But it also reacts instantly to danger—before your thinking brain is even aware of it—mobilizing you with the survival modes of fight, flight, or freeze. When the danger passes, your nervous system quickly recovers and returns you back to "calm." Your core brain also includes your limbic system, which is the source of your quick assessments and intuitive snap judgments, your emotional reactions, your ability to read emotion in others, and your motivation to connect with others, including mating, and bonding to your babies. These automatic/reactive parts and social/emotional parts of your core brain are respectively referred to as the "reptilian" and "mammalian" brains, often affectionately called "lizard brain" and "mouse brain."

- Your outer brain, or neocortex, is responsible for thinking, including analyzing, reasoning, explaining, problem solving, and language. It's also capable of concentrating, planning, and making careful judgments and decisions. As the source of self-awareness and self-control, your thinking brain also helps you stay calm and regulates your emotional reactions—unless the core brain triggers survival mode, which kicks your outer brain offline and creates a temporary disconnect.

YOUR BRAIN ON THIS JOURNEY

When you first start to hope or wonder if you're pregnant, you use your thinking outer brain to do the math and decide to take a pregnancy test. When you first see or hear the positive results, your core brain reacts, triggering a small shot of stress hormones into your bloodstream, which has the effect of making you alert and focused. Your breathing quickens, heart rate increases, and perhaps your digestion feels queasy; to what extent depends on whether you're shocked, pleasantly surprised, or confirming your suspicions. Your core brain also reacts with the attendant emotion—delight, relief, fear, or ambivalence—depending on how this pregnancy fits into your life and what it means to you.

> *I found out I was pregnant with Pearl on a cruise we took for our tenth anniversary. I had a feeling I might have been pregnant before we left. I was in the middle of the blue ocean with the test; it came back positive. I woke Josh up with a big smile and let him know number four was on the way!*
>
> —Laura

When you accept the pregnancy, your core brain conjures feelings of protectiveness and devotion to this baby, and your thinking brain starts planning and dreaming. Your whole brain is well connected and harmonious, which is reflected in your feelings of overall well-being.

> *This was the first grandchild on both sides of the family and grandparents could not have been happier! I had cut out caffeine, watched my diet, gained the "right" amount of weight. Everything was great.*
>
> *—Helen*

> *I was nineteen weeks pregnant and feeling amazing. I had not been sick in any way, shape, or form. No morning sickness, no tiredness. I was working as I always did.*
>
> *—Sarah*

> *When Oren was alive, our lives were filled with joy.*
>
> *—Lavender*

Then tragedy strikes. When you hear the terrible news, your core brain instantly registers this as a dangerous situation and a traumatic event. It reacts intensely, triggering a massive flood of stress hormones, which launches you into survival mode.

> *The nurse was getting a little flustered because she couldn't find the heartbeat as quickly as I'd become accustomed to. I quickly realized my first flash of parental instinct, and it wasn't good. Amy looked at me with an expression that assured me that she felt the same flash of instinct. We knew something was terribly wrong.*
>
> *—Ben*

SURVIVAL MODE

> *The nurse decided to alert the hospital just a few blocks down the street rather than continuing to check for a heartbeat. We rushed over there, not knowing what to think or do. I tried my best to stay calm.*
>
> *—Ben*

> *My whole world shattered into pieces from eight words. "I'm sorry but we can't find a heartbeat." Hearing those words being spoken about my baby boy put me into shock.*
>
> *—Courtney*

In the face of danger, threat, or trauma, your core brain is wired to react, and you'll behave viscerally *without* your thinking brain's knowledge or consent. Your core brain instantly assesses the situation, and
- you might flee by withdrawing, detaching, or leaving the room;
- you may fight by protesting, denying, or getting angry; or
- you might freeze, unable to respond, feeling apart from your body or in a daze.

> *After a few minutes they told us they couldn't find her heartbeat and that she had passed away. My husband immediately left the room.*
>
> *—Daniela*

Hearing the confirmation put me into a bizarre state. I was there, holding Amy's hand, but my head was gone. It was as if half of my body just decided to leave and half was there for Amy, and to just do what we needed to do at that point.

—Ben

It wasn't real, this wouldn't happen to us. It was going to be okay. My beautiful boy would be born with his eyes wide open and his loud cries telling the world, "I'm here, I'm here!"

—Courtney

When Dayani was born, suddenly there was frenzy in the room. She was immediately taken by the neonatologist to a warmer. I had reached out my hands thinking I was going to hold the baby and start breastfeeding. My husband stood in a daze as he thought he was going to cut the cord. The shock started to set in.

—Destrida

This automatic stress reaction explains the shock, numbness, denial, disorientation, and seemingly calm detachment that many parents experience. The cascade of stress hormones is also responsible for intense physical sensations, such as a heart that feels like it's breaking, or symptoms of abject terror.

I remember lying on the table watching the nurse's face as she kept going over the same area on the baby. Her head. I knew there was something terribly wrong with the baby's brain. There was a black hole where there should have been white. The tech told me she was going to go get the doctor to talk to me. I was shaking, jumped off the table, cried as I tried to get dressed and put my shoes on . . . all at the same time yelling at Josh that "nothing was okay, we are not going to be okay." He asked me what was going on and I said, "We aren't going to have a baby, we are going to have a funeral!" He fell into a heap in the chair.

—Laura

They hooked me up to the ultrasound and I could see nothing on the screen. My heart sank but denial was also present. Another nurse was called. Then the on-call OB was called. She placed the transducer on me and still nothing on the screen. She said, "I don't see anything," and my world just fell apart.

—Helen

I don't think I have ever been so scared in my life. My blood pressure started rising and my son's heart rate started to drop. I sat helplessly as nurses started getting out garb for my husband; they started dressing for surgery; frantic calls were being made to the doctor. They wheeled me in to an operating room and then I was put under. The last thing I remember was bright lights, stainless steel, and my husband holding my hand and saying that he loved me.

—Sonya

The silence was deafening. It was horrible to look down at my beautiful boy that I carried for thirty-six weeks in my body, to see him so lifeless, so perfect, and so still. My heart was aching for his eyes to open, his mouth to open and let out the loudest of cries. My world was truly broken.

—Courtney

I felt like I was going to die of heartache.

—Embry

Your fight, flight, or freeze reaction can be so intense that you can't do anything else. Even if you try to collect your senses, your thinking brain is offline, and simply cannot fully grasp the terrible news, give you social graces, or help you make sound decisions.

As I opened the door to leave the room, my doctor walked in and asked me to stay so he could talk to me. I was sobbing and couldn't breathe . . . Josh was speechless and watching me to see what was next.

—Laura

Their language became a bit blurry. I remember the doctors mentioning a series of observations. Then they asked me to go to the hospital. I was certain that when I got to the hospital they would find her heartbeat again so I didn't allow the reality of the situation to affect me. At the hospital and during labor I think I went into survival mode.

—Daniela

Thankfully, my husband saved me from a lifetime of pain and regret. When Judah was first born, I told the nurse that I wasn't sure if I wanted to see him. Can you imagine? I can't now.

—Jolie

Being mostly in reactive "survival mode" can last for several hours or days. As your reactivity lessens, you may experience on-and-off shock, numbness, denial, or avoidance lasting several weeks, and slowly fading over several months. During this time, repeated floods of stress hormones can make your core brain become habitually hyper-reactive, resulting in you feeling easily overwhelmed by life. You may continue to experience marked physical and mental symptoms of survival mode, such as numbness, confusion, tension, tearfulness, insomnia, fatigue, no appetite, emptiness, and aching heart. (See also "Shock and Numbness" and "Denial and Yearning" in chapter 2.)

There were missions out into enemy territory—the real world—where everything seemed too bright, too loud, too happy, and full of traps to catch you. Booby traps like shelves of nappies in unexpected places in shops, or the screaming baby around every corner.

—Mel

*The words **aching, longing,** and **heart-wrenching**—my heart hurt like that for a few months. It would wake me up at night. It would keep me from sleeping. My chest felt heavy and my heart literally ached to hold my son. It felt unbearable.*

—Jolie

EMOTIONAL MODE

When the nurse took me to see Dayani in the NICU, my heart broke in so many pieces. I stood by her side, tears flowing freely on my face.

—Destrida

*I remember seeing Sophie, **so** tiny in this incubator, all "wired" up, and looking rather bruised (from the labor) and so helpless! I broke down crying straightaway and sat and stared at her for what seemed like ages. All I wanted to do was pick her up and hold her.*

—Kylie

As your initial shock wears off, your numbness lifts somewhat and the emotional and bonding parts of your core brain can step in. Feelings of connection to your little baby come to the foreground, and you can experience the intensity of your love and nurturing urges. Those surges of devotion can first happen during pregnancy, and they intensify after your baby is born.

When it was time for Ashley to enter the world, she was breathing! I cuddled Ashley on my chest. Mike and I watched in wonder as she slowly took quiet breaths. We even heard a few soft cries; it made me believe she could feel the love from her parents surrounding her.

—Shellie

*Seeing Judah the first time was the most amazing moment I've experienced in my life thus far, and I think it always will be. The pride you feel as a mother, the love and awe you feel . . . it is just indescribable. It is literally impossible to describe. It is an emotion you can only experience yourself. I was so proud as a mother to see Judah. He was so beautiful and perfect and just the fact that **I made this little boy with my husband who I love with all of my heart and it is just absolutely amazing.** Just the thought of that moment makes me cry as I type this.*

—Jolie

We received a call around five a.m., telling us we should probably come immediately to the NICU. But the one thing I remember and cherish, is when I got down to the NICU, I once again started talking to him and stroking the back of his little hand with one finger, and then he grabbed it—he grabbed my finger and held on to it. I will always remember that feeling. Pure love for both of us.

—Sonya

*We had her tiny body in the baby's bassinet bed. I had my hand on
her bed, the whole night. I just wanted to have her next to me. To feel
connected with her physical being, as long as I could.*

—Anne

*We weren't sure what she'd look like, but we were both so amazed at
how beautiful she looked. . . . The scary part was holding her at first
because she was little and fragile. But then we couldn't let her go. We
bathed her, dressed her, hugged and cuddled her.*

—Abby

Your core brain is wired to bond, and you are instinctively awed and
enraptured by your babies. Fathers are particularly enthralled at the first
sight of their newborns, experiencing a surge of love and joy, even if the
baby is born still or doing very poorly. Both of you may feel determined
to keep a watchful eye on your newborn, and you are intuitively attuned
and responsive to your baby's needs. If your baby's life is threatened or has
ended, when the shock has sufficiently worn off, every ounce of your being
wants to protect and hold your baby close. You do not need your thinking
brain to come online for this experience, and in fact, you can benefit if it
stays out of the way.

*How did I know what I needed before I'd had a chance to think things
through? Maybe that was the key: I had no time to think, no time to
over-intellectualize or get tangled up in the pros and cons of various
options. Maybe **intuition** is exactly the right word. In any case, I was
incredibly lucky that my intellectualizing brain shut up and my intuitive
brain took over. I didn't do it on my own. If my funeral director hadn't
let me know that taking Thor home was an option, it wouldn't have
occurred to me to ask. But once he put that option on the table, I didn't
lose a second mulling over the question of whether I should do it or
not. I knew immediately that it was the right thing to do.*

—Elizabeth

Your instinct to hold your baby close is why separation is so heartbreaking, whether your baby goes to intensive care or is transferred to another
hospital—or if hospital staff or a funeral home takes your baby's body
away. Permanent separation is nonstop heartbreak, as your core brain is
still primed to nurture and protect. You're driven to yearn and search for
your little one, so you can provide caregiving.

*When they brought Dayani in to see me before she was transferred,
I felt a desperation I never felt before. Here was my daughter, a few
hours old being taken away from me. I did not know whether I would
see her again, whether she was going to pass away on the way to the
other hospital. My heart broke into billions of pieces that day and I
don't think it will ever be whole again.*

—Destrida

That longing to hold my son again—I think about it often. It is one of the most distinct emotions and memories that I've felt throughout my grief journey with Judah. Even now, I often think about how I wish so badly that I could hold Judah again—even just as he was. If I could hold him again in my belly, if I could hold his lifeless body in my arms again, I'd do it in a heartbeat, and until someone told me I had to give him back again.

—Jolie

When you're with your baby, your core brain reacts with love, sorrow, and longing for your little one. It also triggers bursts of stress hormones. If the burst is too much—perhaps because you're struggling to recover from birth, you're sleep deprived, you're not getting the support you need, or separation is imminent—you might feel numb, fearful, or in a daze. If the burst is just enough, you'll be alert and focused.

Once I gave birth, we decided to keep him with us until sunrise the next morning. It was just hours of going between uncontrollable crying and trying to stop long enough to just look at him and cuddle him. I wouldn't wish those moments on anyone, the hardest thing I've ever experienced.

—Embry

When I held my little girl for the first time an overwhelming feeling of love come over me, and that she was so little and innocent and she looked like me! Jaysen sat beside me and we both held her tiny little hands and patted her forehead, while watching her chest rise and fall. It will always be one of the most precious moments of being with our little girl. With streams of tears falling down my cheeks, I remember telling her, "It's okay darling, Mummy and Daddy are here with you."

—Kylie

You may also remember times when calm reigned, even during intense situations. This happens because your core brain strikes a balance between "full-blown alarm" and "rest and digest." Then you get to experience a sense of alert-calm, remaining attentive and in touch with reality. For instance, if you were able to spend sufficient time with your baby and not feel too rushed, you may have been able to move out of the alarmed survival mode and into an alert-calm bonding mode, where you could meet and care for your baby and express your love. This alert-calm state also helps you remember what happened and how it felt, providing precious memories that can comfort you as you grieve.

She spent her whole life in my arms—she peacefully stopped breathing and died in my arms shortly after her baptism. I remember being relieved that it was so peaceful and beautiful. It was sad, but it wasn't scary. We sent her off with the blessing of baptism and surrounded by a room of people that loved her very much. It felt a bit surreal, too.

—Shellie

There was calm that came over the space after Oren was born, but this calm was sad. For the most part, I couldn't believe what was happening. I was stunned by how beautiful he was. I wanted to be as far away as I could, but I wanted as much time to stare at him as I could too. It was all very shocking; his lifeless little body made the whole thing so much more real.

—Lavender

There was this moment where I took a breath and tried to prepare myself to look at my child. Lavender encouraged me to see the baby. "The baby is beautiful." He was. As we cried, held him, and gazed at his sweet little face I had a moment of utter peace. I think it must have been grace.

—Tanya

Unfortunately, if you don't have quality support from at least one person who can give you the kind of compassionate, helpful care that would soothe your reactive core brain, you may not be able to have best-quality time with your baby. Lori attests to the paralysis and fear she couldn't shake, and how it interfered with her ability to connect with her baby. Melanie describes why it's so important for the mother to spend time with her baby after her medical condition—and her stressed brain—stabilizes.

__Why spend time__ with a dead baby? Why do those memory-making things? Why take pictures? I was very scared and tense the whole time I was holding Bryce. At times it even felt morbid to be holding my dead baby. I held him awkwardly. I did not know what his body might do. Would it twitch or leak fluids? Would it make noises? Would it smell? The only thing I could bring myself to do with Bryce was to caress his knee, which was the only part of his body sticking out of his blanket.

—Lori

I was very unwell. I couldn't sit up or I felt like I was going to faint. I could barely hold him as I was so weak from blood loss and they were so busy trying to get the placenta out and the bleeding to stop. I had had a lot of pain medication, so that added to my spaced-out-ness. I remember holding him and looking at him and trying to concentrate really hard, __thinking you need to remember this moment__. But I can't. And I hate that. Later, we got to spend a couple of hours with him. Just holding him. I couldn't stop touching him. He was just so lovely.

—Melanie

Emotional mode also allows the reality to sink in, and you can start to experience thoughts and feelings of grief, like fear, anger, guilt, sorrow, helplessness, and disorientation.

I have never been so sad and so heartbroken and scared of what I was going to see. I totally blamed myself. Had I done something?

I was distraught and angry at having to go through labor, for there would be no happiness at the end.

—Melanie

I asked the neonatologist what my options were, like if I could have Dayani stay the night with me so we can be transferred together, or have my pediatrician take a look at her condition because to be honest, who the hell was he to tell me my daughter was going to die? I did not know him!

—Destrida

I think the sadness really began to set in when I held her. The reality that she was gone began to surface within me.

—Daniela

Thinking Mode

It is less acute than it used to be. I can think about it now. Before I would just react to things. It came from my gut. Now my heart may hurt, but I can also think. Much less primal.

—Lavender

Eventually, after the initial shock wears off and whenever your core brain isn't overwhelming you with emotional flooding, your outer, thinking brain can get involved too. In fact, during the ensuing months and years, your thinking brain is perfectly suited for some of the tasks of mourning, such as

- getting information about your baby's death and the aftermath, so you can process and understand what happened;
- identifying your losses so you can grieve them and gradually adapt to all that your baby's absence entails;
- finding the words to label your emotions so they can feel more manageable;
- addressing issues, identifying problems, and solving them;
- implementing coping strategies that work for you;
- gradually adjusting your dreams;
- creating a relationship to the memory and/or spirit of your little one;
- reflecting on your baby's life and death;
- making meaning out of facing adversity, such as what you've learned; and
- eventually noticing and appreciating your healing transformation.

Our little girl had lessons for us. She was a wee teacher. She was made from love and felt nothing but love. Her short life will have meaning and her legacy will be us helping others.

—Emmerson

The entire labor with Bodhi was really meaningful to me. I learned a lot that I was able to help with in the births of our other two children. He taught both of us how to deliver his brother and sister. That's really cool and I'm really thankful for that.

—Ben

The blessings are of course my daughter, her memory, the lessons she taught me. She had to come the way she was in order to bring in the wisdom and compassion that were bestowed upon me by family, friends, and strangers. And I have learned to accept things for what they are, not what they could have been or should have been.

—Destrida

She was a huge blessing in my life. She made me grow up.

—Julie

Your thinking brain can also help you manage your life. It can be aware of your emotions and regulate them so you can tackle what needs to get done. Karen demonstrates this when she reports, "I think my brain came back online fairly quickly just with a few hiccups. I ended up doing what I've always done, pulled up my socks and got on with things."

If you tend to be an activity-oriented griever, you'll often find emotional regulation to be doable, partly because you've acquired the skill, and partly because activity-oriented grief is not as intense as emotion-oriented grief. Instead, thinking and action are natural outlets for your grief. You might analyze the events that unfolded, trying to make sense of it. You may try to understand how your baby's death is affecting you, your partner, and your lives, and how to solve the problems that are arising. You scan your world for problems to avert and get going on all the tasks, projects, and activities that need to be done. Ben is very much "a doer." He says, "Immediately after returning home, we made arrangements to be away from work, get some house repairs done that we had planned on doing, and talking to family."

If you tend to be an emotion-oriented griever, emotional regulation is a skill that you implement when you must accomplish necessary tasks or take care of priorities. But because your grief can be very intense, you benefit from going with the flow and not getting so much done for a while— except for grieving, which is a huge and important chore. Still, sometimes your thinking brain will question some of your grief reactions for seeming irrational, unkind, or unnecessary. Abby admits, "The news of pregnancies and births were really hard for me. And although I never want anyone to go through what we did, it made me feel more lonely and more envious when healthy babies were born. I feel bad even writing that!"

Whatever your primary style of grieving, your thinking brain may doubt the necessity of some of your thoughts, feelings, and behaviors. But your core brain doesn't care. Your grief simply exists as it is. That's why instead of fighting, ignoring, or trying to talk yourself out of your painful thoughts and feelings, it's far more productive to mindfully observe them as they come up, and go with the flow.

> *I sang "Twinkle, Twinkle, Little Star." Somehow that song just popped in my head. Little did I know how many times I would sing that song over the next one week and how I can't hear or sing it without tears waiting at bay now.*
>
> —Destrida

> *I see little children and think that Blake or Rylee should be that age—or see a toy that I would have loved to buy. Underneath I still have faith and hope a child will be in our family soon, but the emotions can get very raw on the surface.*
>
> —Sonya

Sometimes, especially early on, it is normal for your core brain to occasionally overwhelm your thinking brain, and you'll fall into intense emotional moments or physical displays of healthy grief. But much of the time, with your thinking brain online, you can observe and modulate grief reactions and implement your adaptive coping strategies. (See also chapter 4, "Mindfulness-Based Coping Strategies.") For instance, when you feel a twinge of guilt, you can reassure yourself that you aren't responsible for your baby's death. When you find yourself perseverating on what's not fixable, you can focus yourself on fixing what *is* fixable. When you see a mother with newborn twins, you can calm yourself with "I don't know this mother's full story." When you feel frustrated with people, you can remember that you're angrier than usual because your baby died, and not take it out on them. And you can engage in the many brain-calming and grief-releasing activities that work for you, enabling you to become ever more adept at emotional regulation as you heal. Ideally, both parts of your brain—the *reactive, emotional, social* core and the *rational, thinking, observant* outer—work in tandem as you mourn.

Unfortunately, for some parents, the trauma of their baby's death puts their brain into a state of chronic disconnect, which can feel like perpetual survival mode.

TRAUMATIC BEREAVEMENT AND BRAIN DISCONNECT

When your brain is well connected, both your core brain and your outer brain contribute to your living a fulfilling life, wherein you get your needs met for safety, satisfaction, and companionship. As mentioned earlier, your core brain's default setting is the calm of "rest and digest." Your core brain will react to what it perceives as threats, but ideally this reaction is regulated by your outer brain stepping in and thinking, "I know that I have to walk past the baby supplies aisle, but I can stay calm and go straight for the freezer section."

Unfortunately, as often happens with traumatic bereavement, your outer brain may have a hard time stepping in to keep you calm and feeling like a civilized person. Many of the events surrounding your baby's diagnosis, dying, and/or death can trigger your core brain into survival mode, which kicks your outer brain offline. If survival mode is prolonged or repeatedly triggered, the core brain can become hyper-reactive, resulting in a degree of disconnect between the core brain's limbic system and the outer brain's prefrontal cortex, or PFC. Disconnection renders the PFC unable to do its normal job of emotional regulation, which makes you more sensitive and more easily triggered. So, for instance, you might find yourself bursting into tears as you pass the baby supplies aisle or snapping at a shopper who accidently bumps into you while you try to make your escape. This hyper-reactive core brain and underresponsive outer brain indicate that disconnect in the brain. The disconnect is an especially common and normal experience in the early weeks and months after a baby's death, and this effect can linger for many months. Symptoms typically include:

- mental confusion, disorientation, poor memory
- mentally struggling to concentrate, indecisiveness, poor problem-solving ability
- emotional numbness, detachment
- emotional sensitivity, being easily triggered by situations or events
- physical distress, including trouble with eating, sleeping, pain
- emotional distress, including depression, anxiety, irritability, despair

Every day, waking up and living was painful. I felt as if my brain could not take any more stress and pain. I seemed to have blocked out a lot of what happened after his death. I had my parents, my in-laws, and my best friend visit within the space of three months. To be honest, I do not remember much about any of their visits or what we did or said. That is really sad but I think I just existed for a while.

—Lorna

Overall, this disconnect in the brain can make you feel overwhelmed, isolated, and less able to function. If the disconnect is mild, temporary, or occasional, it can slowly recede over the course of several months. But some parents suffer more serious aftereffects of trauma, where the core brain becomes *chronically* hyper-reactive, rendering the outer brain chronically disconnected. Signs of a chronically hyper-reactive, disconnected, traumatized brain include:

- being habitually sensitive or reactive, too easily triggered
- ongoing mental distress, including numbness, detachment, inability to concentrate or make decisions
- ongoing emotional distress, including depression, anxiety, irritability, rage

- struggling with intrusive painful thoughts, flashbacks, or panic attacks
- disrupted sleeping or eating habits that are negatively affecting emotional or physical health
- depleted energy levels that are interfering with functioning
- self-neglect
- addiction or substance abuse
- troubled or broken relationships
- emotional outbursts or uncontrolled displays of emotion
- difficulty controlling behavior
- disrupted work, difficulty handling responsibilities
- feeling disturbed by or unable to handle the process of mourning
- wondering if your grief and distress will last forever
- thinking about dying or being uncertain you'll survive
- feeling consistently overwhelmed and traumatized
- you or others wondering if you need professional help

These pitfalls are common effects of trauma, and are *not* integral to healthy grief and mourning. Treat them as red flags that indicate you need additional strategies and/or more support than you're getting. Indeed, these problems can be insurmountable if you try to go it alone or don't add new strategies to your toolbox. Essentially, a chronically disconnected brain is the root of *unnecessary* suffering.

> Particularly in the early months, trauma and grief were so interconnected that I suffered with nightmares, flashbacks, hyperarousal, panic attacks, you name it.
>
> —Tanya

About Trauma and Suffering

When you grieve, a certain amount of pain is unavoidable. And contrary to the popular saying, "suffering is optional," some suffering is actually quite normal and can even be a necessary part of your journey. For example, necessary suffering can be part of the trial-and-error process of acquiring new skills and practicing new ways of being, such as

- practicing forgiveness of others for their lack of support,
- coming around to letting go of your regrets,
- figuring out how to reframe feelings of responsibility or failure, or
- settling on answers to the questions "why?" and "what if?"

While suffering can be a natural part of your journey, it is *overcoming adversity* that contributes to personal growth, not the suffering. Therefore, *excessive suffering is unnecessary.*

What's excessive? You can determine for yourself where and when to draw that line. And certainly, for the first few days and weeks after your baby dies, you can expect to suffer mightily. But if you continue to feel overwhelmed for months, or if your despair seems bottomless or unending with no improvement, these are signs of deep trauma, and you are suffering unnecessarily. If you're a mother with some of these symptoms, it is important to be evaluated for postpartum depression. (See also "Postpartum Depression" in chapter 5). For many parents, professional help is key.

Why professional help? Because a deeply traumatized brain tends to not get better with the passage of time. It's not that the brain is "broken"—the brain is actually excellent at repairing itself. But trauma casts memories into frozen knots, and the brain cannot process and integrate them. It tries *and tries,* but the result is repetitive flashbacks, obsessing, and intrusive thoughts. That's when the brain needs assistance in the form of professionally administered, brain-based therapy, such as EMDR (Eye Movement Desensitization and Reprocessing), which unfreezes and untangles the memories so that the brain can process and integrate them. These therapies work by physically restoring connection and calm in the traumatized brain. (See also "First, a Note about Trauma" in chapter 4; "Counseling" in chapter 13.)

> *I am just starting EMDR therapy. This is the trauma therapy used to reprogram the brain that has been successful with war veterans. I am nervous about it but I really need help with the PTSD.*
> —Tanya

Note that the devastating effects of trauma are not just happening in the mind. It's not a matter of choosing which thoughts to have or snapping out of it by sheer force of will. Trauma is a physical condition in the brain. No one would expect a person to "snap out of" the physical conditions that affect other organs, such as heart disease, lung disease, kidney disease, and so on. And no one would expect talk therapy or mindfulness alone to be the cure. Even medication falls short when it's not combined with treatments that address the underlying mechanisms—in this case, a chronically hyper-reactive brain stem and limbic system. That's why it's key for many traumatized parents to seek brain-based therapies that directly treat trauma. The alternative, if you have a chronic disconnection, is that your core brain's continued hyperreactivity will become entrenched, adding to your struggles, compounding your suffering, dampening your spirit, and holding you back from reengaging fully with life.

There are also many mindfulness-based coping strategies you can implement in order to prevent or shake unnecessary suffering. But if your trauma runs deep, it is only after getting treatment for your brain that you can benefit from mindfulness practices, such as meditation and yoga, which can also promote calm and connection in your brain.

> *My husband went out of town for a family wedding. When he returned, I had an anxiety attack. Never had one before. Very*

scary—I thought I was having a stroke. I'm doing meditation and exercise to help keep it in check before seeking medication. That seems to be working.

—Anne

As you grieve, you can benefit from any strategy that fosters calm and connection in your brain and helps you avoid unnecessary suffering. A first step (or a second step after you are successfully treated for deep trauma) is to become mindful of your triggers so that you can manage your exposure to distressful situations.

Becoming Mindful of Triggers

As you mourn, your core brain's stress reaction may be triggered many times. You'll review painful memories. You'll miss and yearn for your baby. And you'll encounter a series of unfortunate events and experiences, such as planning a funeral, anniversary dates, the sight of pregnant women, and people making clueless remarks, or worse, avoiding you. (Even reading this paragraph may trigger your stress reaction and feelings of grief. Mindfully tune into your body; note and observe the physical sensations; focus on your breath so you're not feeding your reaction with additional inflammatory thoughts; watch those sensations dissipate; have compassion for yourself.)

Repeated triggering of your core brain means that your level of stress hormones is running high and often. When possible, prevent exposing yourself to triggers, as your brain will benefit from as much calm as possible while it recovers from the shock and trauma of your baby's death. Your brain can attest that an ounce of prevention is worth a pound of cure. So, rather than subjecting yourself to upsetting situations—like baby showers, toy stores, abrasive relatives, clueless friends, and social events—come up with solutions to help you avoid, deescalate, or limit your exposure to them. Or, in the case of the unavoidable, like your baby's anniversary dates, you can soothe your brain by pairing painful situations with something pleasant, as this makes them more bearable. For instance, you could plan a special outing or set aside part of the day for exceptional self-care, doing what soothes and nurtures you. Or you can see how the day unfolds and follow your present-moment desires and inspirations for ritual. Even a simple ritual, such as lighting a candle, can be a soothing way to mark the day. (See also "Anniversaries and Other Reminders" in chapter 8; "Informal Rituals" in chapter 6.)

In fact, brain research reveals how and why many time-honored mourning traditions soothe the reactive core of the brain and increase activity in parts of the brain that are responsible for feelings of well-being. For example, the Jewish tradition of "sitting shivah" surrounds the bereaved family with relatives and friends who visit the house and provide food, compassionate care, empathy, and companionship. For a whole week, the bereaved are symbolically wrapped in a cocoon, where they have no responsibilities, no cares about appearances, and are expected to focus on the deceased loved one and their grief. This tradition has many characteristics that soothe the core brain, including feeling safe, full acceptance, acknowledgment of losses, affirmation of grief, comforting connections with others, warm touch, easily available nutritious food, and respite from work and daily chores during this most stressful time.

You can also soothe your brain and foster its calm and connectivity on a daily basis by establishing habits that reduce physiological stress and nourish your brain, such as sufficient sleep, good nutrition, and getting exercise. In fact, inadequate sleep, poor nutrition, and a lack of exercise are devastating for emotional health—and brain health.

The next chapter looks in-depth at a variety of practices and mindfulness-based coping strategies that you can employ to soothe your mourning brain.

POINTS TO REMEMBER

- Your brain is vastly affected by your baby's diagnosis and death, your grief, and the lengthy process of mourning.
- Knowing how your brain is wired can actually demystify and normalize the more bewildering aspects of your grief and mourning.
- When you receive the terrible news about your baby, your core brain triggers a cascade of stress hormones, which launches a fight, flight, or freeze reaction of survival mode and knocks your outer brain offline.
- Survival mode is accompanied by mental and physical symptoms of distress, such as numbness, shock, disorientation, confusion, disrupted sleeping and eating, and aching arms and heart.
- Whenever the shock and numbness of survival mode start to fade, you can begin to feel the yearning and nurturing urges that reflect your bond with your baby. You can also experience thoughts and feelings of grief, like guilt, anger, worry, helplessness, and sadness.
- When survival mode lifts, your outer brain can get involved too. It can gather information, make decisions and arrangements, and verbalize thoughts and feelings.
- As the months and years go by, your outer brain is key to many tasks of mourning, as well as implementing adaptive strategies that can help you cope with grief, calm your brain, and reduce unnecessary suffering.
- Because a baby's death is often a traumatic bereavement, parents commonly struggle with symptoms of trauma. Some parents struggle occasionally, mostly during the early months, but some struggle chronically over many more months.
- When a parent continues to feel numb, emotionally distressed, and overwhelmed, this can indicate a deeply traumatized brain— the root of unnecessary suffering. Deep trauma requires a brain-based therapy first, which then enables the parent to also benefit from adaptive strategies, including mindfulness practices.
- If you're the mother and have troublesome symptoms of distress, also be evaluated for postpartum depression.
- Be aware of situations that trigger grief. Avoiding them and engaging in mourning rituals can help soothe your brain and foster internal calm and connectivity.

4

MINDFULNESS–BASED COPING STRATEGIES

Today I have felt crippled by my emotions—so many, so loud, and all at once. So tonight when I go to bed, I am going to try to relax and "breathe." And tomorrow when I am hopefully feeling better and if there is a break in the weather, I will head outside to sit on Adisyn's memory seat and fill my lungs with fresh air, focusing on breathing deeply and slowly, while watching the clouds in the sky or the birds in the trees.

—Emmerson

After your baby dies, your yearning, despair, powerlessness, disorientation, and restlessness may feel endless. Many parents talk about feeling "broken." At times, you may feel completely overwhelmed or "out of it," and not yourself. Naturally, you may feel like your regular coping strategies are not up to the task of helping you deal with your grief and mourning.

This is where mindfulness practices come in. Mindfulness comes out of Buddhist spirituality, but trailblazers like Jon Kabat-Zinn have translated this approach into a secular practice that can be applied across all religions and cultures, and as a result, practice is becoming ever more widespread.

In recent years, brain research has confirmed the value of mindfulness practices. Long-standing traditions like meditation, yoga, and tai chi have proven to be effective treatments for anxiety, depression, trauma, stress, hostility, and attention deficits. These practices can even reduce blood pressure and boost immune system function. Successful therapies have risen out of this approach, including mindfulness-based stress reduction (MBSR) and mindfulness-based cognitive therapy (MBCT). (See also "Counseling" in chapter 13.)

Here are the main features and benefits of mindfulness:

- A primary component of mindfulness is bringing your awareness to the present moment. Emotionally, this is a powerful way to reduce your distress. When you are focused on the present moment, you are not regretting or wishing for the past, nor are you planning or concerned about the future. Even in the midst of a huge wave or an intense storm of grief, *mindfully attending to the present moment* can instill a sense of peace. You can rest on knowing that you are safe and sound, right here and now.
- Mindfulness is the practice of observing thoughts, emotions, sensations, and behaviors as they are, without judgment, in the

65

present moment. This practice cultivates acceptance and self-compassion, which soothes you and your brain.

- Mindfulness comes from purposefully paying attention to what your body feels and what you are sensing in and around you. It cultivates mind/body awareness, which offers clarity, perspective, and depth to your experiences.

- Mindfulness enables you to be a witness to your own experience, and instead of living on autopilot, you realize that you have a choice: Do you usually go with the flow and let painful thoughts, feelings, and sensations come and go, which enables you to recover quickly? Or do you usually fight the flow, either by resisting or hanging on, and then spiral ever deeper into misery?

- Mindfulness lets you separate your thoughts from your emotions. It allows you to identify what you are thinking and identify what you are feeling, see the link, and stop the downward spiral of progressively worse thoughts and feelings.

- Mindfulness improves your ability to regulate your thoughts, emotions, and behaviors, such as directing your attention, gaining perspective, keeping runaway negativity in check, being flexible, and responding appropriately so you feel more sane and civilized. Emotional regulation is key to resilience and an antidote to stress.

- Mindfulness practices calm your core brain's reactivity and recover your thinking brain's strengths, thus restoring their connection. Having a connected brain can soften the ravages of grief and ease your journey of mourning.

- Mindfulness, by keeping your brain connected and regulated, improves your ability to solve problems, create plans, implement coping strategies, and make sound decisions so you can function better.

- Mindfulness practices change your brain, strengthening structures and connections and increasing your stress reactivity threshold, so you're less easily thrust into survival mode. These changes boost your resilience and reduce the physical and emotional effects of stress and trauma.

Overall, mindfulness practices nurture your grieving brain, reduce unnecessary suffering, and enrich your healing transformation.

If you're already overstressed by grief and wondering whether you have the time or energy to learn and practice mindfulness, it might help you to know that mindfulness can reduce your stress so significantly that rather than becoming yet another task to accomplish, it becomes integral to your achieving more calm *and* more success throughout the day.

Even more importantly, mindfulness can encourage you to stay connected to your body and help you embrace your grief rather than avoid it. Because grieving can be so painful, it's instinctive and normal to not want to "go there," especially in the beginning. But with the support of mindfulness practices, you can go there more willingly because mindfulness connects you to your body in such a compassionate way.

Mindfulness also creates an awareness of having access to more time than you thought possible. And as you'll see in the next section, mindfulness can be as easy as giving your body the sleep it actually needs, scheduling slow time and quiet time into busy days, getting outdoors, and taking a few minutes to breathe deeply while remaining focused on your body rather than your busy brain.

SIMPLE MINDFULNESS PRACTICES

I've been thinking about mindfulness. I guess I do, in my own way. Those quiet moments in the middle of the night when I am "alone" and I can absorb the moonlight or when I'm writing or absorbed in making something.

—Karen

For me, mindfulness involves spending a lot of time in nature. There is something that I have always loved about the seasons. Here, there is a definite change of seasons. There is something beautiful and healing about the inevitability of change. Being out as the seasons changed in those early months showed me that all things come to an end.

—Mel

If you've already have taken up mindfulness practices before your baby died, you can call on those skills to offset the trauma of your baby's death. As Mel recalls, "I used meditation a great deal. I was already in the habit of meditating daily and listening to a pregnancy relaxation CD, so it was very natural to me."

If you are new to mindfulness, you may wonder, *How can it possibly be helpful to do simple practices, such as directing attention toward breathing?* Mindfulness practices are helpful because they nurture and call upon the part of your nervous system that calms your brain and body. Interestingly, a busy, stressed brain tends to cultivate stress and dwell on the negative. In contrast, a calm brain cultivates calm and dwells on the positive. With the help of mindfulness practices, being able to rely on a source of internal calm can be extremely therapeutic while you mourn.

As you wend your way along your journey, you can try the practices that resonate with you. At some point, you may even branch out and give some others a try. The more tools you have in your toolbox, the better. Here are some simple practices to get you started:

- meditative breathing
- soothing habits of daily living
- calming activities
- mindful journaling

While meditative breathing is considered a mindfulness practice, soothing habits and calming activities can also be mindfully carried out, in that you are purposefully attending to your brain's and body's needs for nurturing, in the present moment.

First, a Note about Trauma

It is important to note that certain mindfulness practices like meditation, which require you to attend to your internal bodily sensations, can be counterproductive if you are suffering from severe trauma. You'll know this is the case if you feel more upset or agitated during or after meditating. Here, Tanya explains why:

> I think both Lavender and my therapist recommended that I try mindfulness and meditation to try to both calm myself down, and to be more aware of myself in the present moment. The trouble was that, due to the trauma I had experienced, I was flooded with flashbacks and a terrible negative downward spiral . . . I couldn't be in the present moment because I was frozen in the past. I couldn't calm down because when I tried to quiet my mind, my thoughts became even louder than before. Yoga and tai chi helped some as I was moving while doing mindfulness activities, but I really noticed a difference after EMDR. It was like my brain literally said, "YES, your children died, but that is over now. It has already happened. They are not dying right now. Now you can relax. Now you can grieve. There is nothing to figure out here. You did the best job you could at the time." EMDR gave my brain permission to shut up.
>
> —Tanya

If this resonates for you, *seek treatment with a brain-based, neurobiological therapy,* many of which are listed in "Counseling" in chapter 13. (See also "About Trauma and Suffering" in chapter 3.) Many parents have been greatly helped by professionally administered therapies like EMDR (Eye Movement Desensitization and Reprocessing), which directly reduce the effects of trauma on the brain. Particularly if you're feeling unmotivated, incapable, or stuck in despair, or if ideas like "accepting what is" or "embracing positive experiences" feel impossible or insulting, you may need to pursue this kind of therapy first. Then your brain can reap the healing benefits of mindfulness coping strategies. *You deserve to be relieved of unnecessary suffering.*

Meditative Breathing

Meditative breathing works by connecting you with your body, quieting your mind, and putting you in the present moment. This practice is simple and doable, even when you feel like you have very little brain space to spare. Here are the ten easy steps:

1. Get into a comfortable position where you can relax fully supported and aligned, such as lying down or sitting up, with legs uncrossed.
2. Close your eyes, or turn your gaze to the floor in front of you or the ceiling above you.
3. Scan your body, noting its sensations of pressure and touch, wherever there is contact with the surface you're resting on.
4. Move your attention to your breathing.
5. Notice how each inhale invites air into your lungs and each exhale empties your lungs. Notice the moments between inhaling and exhaling, exhaling and inhaling.
6. Become aware of how your abdomen rises and falls, resting a hand there if it helps your attention.
7. Naturally, your mind will wander. That's what minds do.
8. Become aware of your mind wandering away into thought. Escort your attention back to your body and breath.
9. Each time you become aware that your mind has wandered away into thought, escort your attention back to your body and breath. Be kind and patient, viewing your mind wandering as an opportunity to practice awareness and redirecting your attention.
10. Notice the infusion of calm.

Set aside ten minutes (or more) for this exercise. If you practice meditative breathing at least once daily, you may notice a perpetual calm replacing your perpetual distress. You may find meditative breathing to be a good way to start the day, as a midday respite, or a way to ward off insomnia at bedtime. It can also be used as needed to calm yourself in moments when you are feeling prone to being triggered or are already overwhelmed.

> *I spoke to my counselor this week and she said these were all normal thoughts and that my mind was racing away. No time for stillness. So I'll endeavor to try and be "still."*
>
> —Victoria

If you'd like to do a guided meditation, there are many free audio resources online. Look up "mindfulness and grief" or "guided meditation." Find the meditations that work best for you.

SOOTHING HABITS OF DAILY LIVING

There are certain habits of daily living, listed below, that can counteract the stresses of grieving—and modern life for that matter. You may already be successful or adept at many of them, and now you can be more mindful of their value. With some of the others, you can strive to be more mindful about cultivating and integrating them into your life. Notice how they all encourage you to live in the present moment. And they all connect you to what your brain and body thrive on. As a result, they all contribute significantly to your physical and mental health, your contentment, and your success. Here are eleven key habits:

1. Start each day with a calm routine, such as meditative breathing and lingering over breakfast.
2. Eat when you're hungry, sleep when you're tired, and wake up when rested.
3. Reduce multitasking, which is generally inefficient anyway.
4. Slow down for a period each day—walk somewhere, stop to smell the roses, have a cup of tea, or enjoy the view.
5. Schedule respite in the middle of busy days.
6. Surround yourself with people who are compassionate and enjoy connection.
7. Strive for live communication rather than virtual, so you get the benefit of touch, hugs, and eye contact.
8. Get outside or find other ways to connect with nature.
9. Move and stretch your body every day—even five minutes at a time has benefits.
10. Reduce screen time; reduce or eliminate television viewing.
11. Get sufficient sleep, especially during your natural sleep cycle(s).

By being consistent with as many of these as you can, you can make a real difference in the quality of your life—and your mourning. Your grief can seem more manageable, and healing can become more of a reality. (See also "Support Networks" in chapter 13.)

CALMING ACTIVITIES

My partner and I are learning to quilt, to help us with our grief. Like the beading, where I string together little pieces of memory and hope, quilting is another lovely metaphor for the process of transformation. We take all these different fabrics and piece them together. Somehow we arrive at something beautiful, though it is hard to see how it will all come together until the end.

—Tanya

Besides soothing habits of daily living and meditative breathing, there are a number of common, ordinary activities that can qualify as adaptive strategies because they soothe your grieving brain. They are soothing because they do some or all of the following (specific examples included):
- allow expression of grief (releasing tears, journaling, listening to music, being physically active)
- are creative and meaningful (blogging, scrapbooking, memorializing your baby)
- restore purpose and mastery (fulfilling responsibilities, taking care of your family)

- are productive and positive (gainful employment, self-improvement, volunteering)
- provide social support and reassurance (reaching out to friends, relatives, or other bereaved parents; reading personal accounts; counseling)
- move your body (engaging in sports, walking, gardening, dancing)
- relax or regulate your body (yoga, tai chi, qigong, therapeutic massage, guided relaxation)
- connect you with nature (being outdoors, tending to plants or animals)

Whatever your preferred activities, strive to engage in activities that encourage calm behavior, which results in a calmer mind. In other words, if you choose activities that make you agitated, riled up, aggressive, sleep-deprived, or frightened, your brain is producing and releasing stress hormones, which only aggravate the stress of mourning. In contrast, what you really need is the infusion of feel-good hormones that come with engaging in productive or meaningful activities that nurture you, connect you, revitalize you, or make you smile. Such activities also help nourish your brain, making it less reactive and more connected.

Walking in nature has always been an integral healing ritual for me. It encourages me to breathe, releases healthy "feel good" endorphins, clears my mind, and enables me to let out some of my anxious energy; it also helps with my disrupted sleep patterns and forces restful sleep.

—Emmerson

I found much comfort and coped by doing things in honor of my son. Such as, reaching out to others who were experiencing grief, creating memorial jewelry, creating a memorial garden (I have never gardened before in my life . . . but, love seeing the end result of Bryce's special place in my yard now). I also created a memorial baby photo album of Bryce.

—Lori

Indeed, one of the easiest and most therapeutic calming activities is communing with nature, including plants and animals. Many parents can poignantly describe heartfelt animal connections and the valuable respite nature offers.

Today we took some time out and spent a day outdoors helping at our neighbor's farm. The sunshine and fresh air were good for the mind, body, and soul. There are nine orphaned lambs I have been feeding, my adorable woolly babies. They are one of the highlights of my day at the moment. They are truly precious to me.

—Emmerson

We became butterfly moms—figuratively and literally. Over the summer and into the fall we raised and released twenty-one black swallowtails. I couldn't help but grow fond of them as we watched them on every step of their metamorphosis. For me, deeply connecting to something in nature helps lessen the intensity of the grief by adding a bit of wonder.

—Tanya

I'm the most comfortable being me in the outdoors. The best way to describe it is this: When you sit down and quiet your mind, where does it go? My brain goes directly to a certain fishing spot, pieces of single track, a certain tree, an experience with a bird I saw for the first time, and doesn't stop.

—Ben

Whatever your grieving style or degree of trauma, you can reduce unnecessary pain and suffering by calming your stressed brain and body. As you can see, many parents have a variety of ordinary pursuits they find helpful.

Loneliness and envy—two emotions I wasn't used to feeling. I had to reach out to cope so I went to therapy weekly. I found a women's group that was extremely healing and was the one place I felt less alone. I talked a lot and wrote in my journal daily for a while.

—Abby

I coped by crying a lot, in private mostly. I talked to other bereaved parents. My work allowed me some distraction time from my grief, which was healthy to have at times, I do believe. I spent time in nature, which I always find comforting. I listened to music. I exercised to relieve some of my grief stress.

—Lori

There are many things that helped. Being so open and talking about it with other people was extremely helpful for me. I kept a journal of sorts using an online format called CaringBridge—it was a way to update family and friends (but also served as a way to express my emotions). Having supportive family, friends, and church family was important.

—Shellie

My faith. Prayer. Journaling. Music. Reading books and blogs. Talking with a counselor. Meeting other bereaved mothers and becoming friends. Knowing that we were not alone on this journey. Talking with others who have gone through this. Though different, we all share the pain of losing a child. Our babies.

—Anne

Mindful Journaling

It's funny—the journaling was completely unexpected. I've never been one to keep a journal. Then suddenly, the morning after I came back from the hospital, I started journaling compulsively. It clearly filled some kind of need—to process things, but also to continue to

have Thor in my life. I was supposed to be taking care of a newborn, but there was no baby. Writing made Thor a continuing presence for as long as I wished to keep at it.
—Elizabeth

Typically, journaling entails recording and reflecting on daily events and experiences. *Mindful* journaling is a tool for growth. Besides writing about your experiences surrounding your pregnancy, your baby, your grief, and your mourning, you can also write about formal and informal rituals, the support you've received, what helps you cope, making peace with regrets, new ways of being, and finding meaning, hope, and strength. For a fuller account, include thoughts and feelings and actions, as well as the sensory details of your memories like sights, sounds, smells, touch, and what sensations you experienced in your body. The benefits of journaling are many. Mindful journaling can have many benefits:

- Mindful journaling reduces stress by boosting self-awareness, encouraging expression of grief, and revealing insights.
- Since many memories, thoughts, feelings, and insights tend to be vague or fleeting, writing them down in detail can help you create a coherent narrative and make sense of your journey.
- Putting your thoughts and feelings into words lends clarity to your internal experience and strengthens the part of your brain that regulates emotion.
- Instead of your grief and mourning being a hidden, dark, and dense mass that affects you from behind the scenes, you can bring it out into the light and see the individual threads and view it as more manageable.
- Whenever you write about your baby, you get to re-experience your bond.

Journaling can also be a satisfying creative endeavor. You can write poems, positive affirmations, or letters—to your baby or anyone else, including yourself, God, or fate. Besides writing, you can include drawings and other visual material. Enclose photos, clippings, stickers, ribbons, fabric, pressed flowers or leaves. Create images of dreams or goals. Compose abstract pictures of your positive and negative feelings and wishes. Use pens, pencils, markers, charcoal, paint, crayons—whatever feels right.

Compared to using a computer, journaling on paper forces you to slow down, to be more deliberate, concise. Writing with pen on paper also engages more areas of the brain that are associated with processing, memory, and learning. As a result, the insights you acquire are more likely to sink in. Paper also lets you experience the tactile experience of both creating it and reading it. If you are drawn irresistibly to the computer, the advantages are being able to add music, create a film, and more easily add photographs. You can always do both to reap all the benefits. Here are some general tips:

- Aim for simplicity and imperfection.
- Consider keeping a journal that is absolutely confidential. Otherwise, you start writing for others or for show. It is far more therapeutic to write for *you*.
- Do not censor yourself. Write in your journal without passing judgment on whether thoughts or feelings are acceptable or worthy.
- Consider keeping two journals, or dividing your journal into two parts: one for ranting or venting negativity, and the other for writing down memories, experiences, affirmations, insights, reflections, reframing, gratitude, and positivity.
- Date your entries. Time frames are important and revealing, particularly with regard to anniversaries.

Separating negativity and positivity can encourage mindfulness about how you perceive and interact with the world. More importantly, it can remind you to also journal about the positive, as journaling exclusively about the negative tends to breed more negativity. Plus, whereas you can find it calming and reassuring to read and reread the positive entries later, you'll likely find it distressing to read and feel transported back into the negative. Separating the two can help you avoid unnecessary suffering.

Indeed, journaling tracks your journey, which makes it such a great tool for self-reflection. Reading it is a way to affirm your baby, ponder what you've been through, and feel reassured of your healing. You can use it to question your thoughts and reframe your perspectives in line with the reframing strategies covered later in this chapter. You can also practice self-compassion by exploring thoughts and feelings without being a harsh critic or judging yourself for having them. Try writing kind, gentle, encouraging side notes to yourself.

Your journal can also become a treasured keepsake—a testament to your anguish, growth, and love for your child—and for yourself. Writing is a therapeutic outlet for many parents.

Writing helps. It helps my mind to unravel the chaos that occurred on that day of his birth, because that is what it was, pure and utter chaos.
—*Victoria*

I'm so glad I started writing so soon and that I kept it up, especially in that following year so I can look back on all that I went through and all that I've learned because of my sweet son.
—*Embry*

I like to keep a journal, so I voice my regrets there and work on them.
—*Fleur*

I made a few short movies about Oren and started to write about my experience after many months away from my journal. These helped open me up when I felt stuck.
—*Tanya*

Thor's death cracked something in my brain, and out of the crack came a creative energy I didn't even know I had.

——Elizabeth

If you'd like to follow the footsteps of published writers and go public with your story, consider mindful journaling first and let that inspire—and deepen—your memoir.

A SAMPLING OF MINDFULNESS STRATEGIES

The rest of this chapter looks at specific strategies you can use to manage your emotional distress and reduce unnecessary suffering. All of these strategies have components of mindfulness, including:

- seeing the present moment as a refuge from ruminating on the distress from the past or worrying about the future
- staying connected to your body, whose sensations hold your direct experience of reality
- seeing thoughts as how your mind interprets and thinks about your experiences, but not necessarily as an absolutely accurate reflection of reality
- seeing emotions as resulting from your thoughts, and not as proof that your thoughts are true
- being a nonjudgmental observer of your sensations, thoughts, and emotions; accepting them as temporary and releasing them as they flow through you
- accepting grief and necessary suffering
- reducing unnecessary suffering
- considering yourself worthy of self-compassion
- seeking out, creating, and embracing positive experiences

As you explore this world of mindfulness practices, be aware that there are many resources you can tap into. Keep watch for opportunities to expand and improve your own practice. Indeed, mindfulness practices can improve your quality of life during *and* beyond your journey of mourning.

PRACTICING SELF-COMPASSION

*I guess a lot of coping tools are about **being kind to yourself**. Many parents don't have a reason for why their baby died and are looking to blame something or someone. And when there is nothing or nobody to blame, you blame yourself, which is what I did. So those tools of relaxation, exercising, doing something for yourself, are all about taking care of yourself.*

—Melanie

Self-compassion means extending kindness, caring, and concern toward yourself, such as becoming a nonjudgmental witness to your thoughts and feelings. It means being clear about your boundaries—what is okay with you and what is not okay—not just in your interactions with others, but also how you want to be treated by you yourself. And self-compassion also means nurturing yourself and taking care of your needs, and can include any of the "Soothing Habits of Daily Living" and "Calming Activities" listed earlier in this chapter. Seeking support, getting professional counseling, and movement therapies (such as yoga, tai chi, and qigong) are all ways of nurturing yourself, taking care of your body, and calming your grieving brain.

Practicing self-compassion can significantly reduce your suffering. As Emmerson correctly observes, "Self-care is not about self-indulgence. It's about self-preservation. It is not selfish *or* optional."

> *The gift that I have gotten from bodywork and movement is being met at exactly where I am. The first day of meeting with my movement therapist she asked me to check in with my body and tell her where I was at in that moment. I told her I wanted to curl up in a ball. She told me that was what I needed to feel safe, so we built a "nest" with cushions and soft things in the corner of the room and after that I was able to slowly move out more freely. I needed someone to say it was okay for me to be exactly where I was and to start from there. With yoga it was the same . . . yoga after pregnancy loss. The class is part yoga, part therapy, and part support group. We cry and laugh. It is a safe space to build strength, breathe, and do as little or as much as your body tells you to. The teacher meets us where we are at, and that is the key to letting each of us open to healing.*
>
> *—Tanya*

> *Yoga sounds like a great idea. Also another way of meeting people and gaining some time to focus on me.*
>
> *—Karen*

Self-forgiveness is another critical piece of self-compassion. If you're holding yourself or your body responsible for your baby's death, there is much healing that can come from forgiving yourself for not being the "perfect mother" or the "perfect father," whatever that means to you. Another way to think about it—what if another bereaved parent came to you and said she was disappointed in her body, her reactions, or her decisions during this most traumatic time of her life? What would you say to her? Would you hold her at fault? Self-compassion is extending yourself the same empathy and forgiveness. Also, know that you can be a good parent and still have regrets. Welcome to parenthood, really.

> *I want to forgive myself for not being able to make Adisyn better like a mother should, forgive my body for not being able to carry her to term, forgive myself for caring so much about what people think and say and letting it hurt me. I am learning to let it go, let it wash over me. It's not always easy but I try really hard.*
>
> *—Emmerson*

If I had another mother tell me of her regrets, I would never hold her at fault. After Judah was born, someone who I probably only knew for about two weeks messaged me and told me that about five years ago she had a stillbirth. She had a little girl. She had never really talked to anyone about it until me, and she didn't have any pictures of her little girl. My heart broke for her. I told her that she did the best she could at the time. And she did—just as I did.

—Jolie

Still, many parents admit that self-care and in particular, self-forgiveness can be challenging. Tanya says, "It seems like it is a long journey from 'how to survive after loss' to 'how to love yourself after loss.'" And if you have other children, like Karen and Melanie, that presents a challenge too. But then, self-compassion is called "a practice" for a reason.

I really do need to make more of an effort to set aside some self-care time. I have a habit of hitting the ground running and not stopping because sometimes it's easier to be busy fixing everyone else and ignoring myself. Self-care just seems too hard.

—Karen

My counselor encouraged me to take time for myself and to not feel bad for it. We talked a lot about the pressure of trying to be the perfect mum while grieving, and that it is okay for things to not be perfect. It is okay to feed the kids something out of a can at night and not meat and vegetables. So to start, it was just taking a long bath and not feeling bad about that. Then, to make time to exercise, or to go out and do something that I enjoy—something that made me happy, which was really hard at the time as I was not happy with anything. But now I can see the benefits of doing this. And I am more aware of it now—I think it is really important to have time for myself and for the girls to see me having time to myself, and that it's okay.

—Melanie

I have never been that good at self-care. I tend to put others naturally before myself and I was happy doing so. But now I am trying to make myself and my healing a priority.

—Emmerson

I had a panic attack last spring. So now I know, when I start to worry in my brain and physical symptoms come on, I need to take care of myself. And make time to meditate and exercise. It is not just, "I would like to feel better by doing this." It is, "I have to do this, or else I could have another panic attack."

—Anne

The mindfulness-based coping strategies in this chapter all have self-compassionate aspects to them. Adopting the ones that fit for you is another way to practice self-compassion.

*I try to think of **what do I need right now?** And also see what **can** I control. Losing a baby, and then two, you can feel so out of control. So, it helps to look at what you can do to help you feel better and grieve honestly.*

—*Anne*

WELCOMING YOUR GRIEF

Welcoming your grief is a mindfulness practice, in that it involves focusing on your body in the present moment. Whenever a wave of grief washes over you, you can mindfully observe your physical experience of it in the present moment. Whenever there is calm, you can also observe and welcome the respite. By going with this ebb and flow, you avert the unnecessary suffering that comes with judging it, ignoring it, wishing it away, clinging to it, worrying about the future, or regretting the past.

Welcoming grief can be challenging at first. After your baby dies, you may soon realize that grief has become a constant companion. It may consume your every waking moment, as if it's sitting on your nose. As the days and weeks and months wear on, it may still accompany you almost everywhere, but it spends less and less time on your nose, and more time perhaps sitting on your shoulder. As the months and years pass, grief might start to fall in step behind you. It can still pop up regularly, whenever you invite it to and sometimes when you least expect it. Eventually, grief can wander off, and only visit on occasion. And as always, you can benefit from mindfully welcoming it.

My grief has absolutely eased. That doesn't mean that I don't have days where I'm brought to tears because I cannot believe my daughter isn't here to be raised and loved by us. But it just changes. Grief has become my companion, always with me, like Emma. Whereas once grief was an awful beast in my life!

—*Abby*

If you treat grief like an unwelcome intruder, you will fight it and resent it. You may hide from it, going to great lengths or expense to avoid it. And when you give in to it, you may feel depressed or worry about yourself. But grief doesn't intend to worry you, and it won't go anywhere just because you resist it. Grief will patiently wait for you wherever it's sitting—on your nose, your shoulder, your back. (See also "Why Is Mourning Required?" in chapter 2.)

But what would your journey look like if you welcomed grief? What if you didn't worry or feel depressed about its existence? What if you accepted grief as a worthy companion? What if you treated it as evidence of your parental bond to your baby? What if you considered it a natural part of being human? What if you took it as an opportunity for growth? What if you saw it as necessary for adjusting and healing?

Even when your grief is running hard and deep, you can let it flow through you. And rather than being overwhelmed by it, you can practice taking it in stride. As it flows through you, notice that you too keep moving, finding your way through each moment rather than feeling unable to go on. In this way, grief can be a dynamic journey, where grief ebbs and flows freely through you while you make progress freely along your way. Note that the alternative to freedom of flow and movement is to dam up the flow and halt all progress. Or back to the wild horse of grief from "Why Is Mourning Required?" in chapter 2—you are confined to a tiny stall with it, and by habitually avoiding, ignoring, repressing, or detaching from it, you become its prisoner. You can also become its prisoner by climbing into its belly and dwelling there. Either way, you remain stuck. You don't adjust and you don't heal. This is no way to live.

As scary, inconvenient, and draining as the grief journey can be, it *is* normal to feel stuck at times or fall into a seemingly bottomless pit. But the ebb and flow of grief, and your ability to mindfully ebb and flow with it and progress along your path, is always within reach. If you do feel stuck, whenever you're ready—and often with the assistance of a counselor, a brain-based treatment for trauma, and compassionate support from others or even yourself—you can pick up where you left off. (See also "About Trauma and Suffering" in chapter 3.)

MINDFULLY RESTORING CALM TO YOUR TRIGGERED BRAIN

When your core brain is triggered by a grief reaction, whether you're feeling a little bothered or quite distressed, here are some mindfulness-based stress reduction tips for restoring calm to your brain and body. As with other mindfulness techniques, you actually change your brain such that with consistent practice over time, your brain becomes able to return to calm more easily and automatically.

- With your outer, thinking brain, become a witness to your distress. Observe that your core brain has been triggered. (This first step can take time and practice to master.)
- See your grief reaction as normal. Remain nonjudgmental, compassionate, and in the present moment. Accept grief's presence. Embrace it.
- Observe the sensations in your body and note where you feel tightness, contraction, or discomfort.
- As you tune into your body, identify the sensations and their associated feelings. For example, a lump in the throat or heaviness in the chest typically indicates sadness. Tension in the jaw, neck, shoulders, arms, hands, or lower back can indicate anger. Twinges or flutters in the abdomen or weakness in the legs can indicate fear.
- Observe the sensations/feelings as they rise and let them flow through you. Don't resist. Don't cling. Just go with the flow.

Take your time. Stay connected to your body. Become aware
of your breath, breathe deeply, and let the bodily sensations
dissipate as your physiology calms. Any associated thoughts and
feelings will dissipate too.

- If you want to stay with a feeling, you can sink into it. Really feel it
  in your body and *physically* experience it. If you have any painful
  thoughts that trigger painful emotions, you can accept them mindfully
  without judgment or attachment to them, and just let them float by.
  Return your attention to your body, let the physical experience run its
  course, and notice the release of tension in your body.
- Take some long, slow, deep breaths. Breathe in your suffering and
  breathe out compassion for yourself. Breathing out reinforces
  your core brain's relaxation response and return to calm.
- Remain in the present moment. When you feel calm restored in
  your body, continue to breathe deeply and soothe yourself with the
  observation that right now, in the present moment, you are safe.

*I had a good understanding that feelings, although intense, cannot
actually hurt you, and that avoiding them actually makes it worse. I
have learned how to sit with painful feelings and know that they are
just that. They are a memory or a reaction to a memory, and the event
is not happening now. I talk a lot about "being in the here and now."
I often found that if I looked at the feeling, and allowed it instead of
suppressing it, it went very quickly.*

—Mel

At any time, when you want to move out of misery or avoid spiraling
down into negative emotion, you can move your attention away from
thought and into your body. Shifting your attention allows your physiology
to simply metabolize the stress hormones in the minute or two it takes.
Stay focused on your body and deepen your breath, mindfully witnessing
your abdomen or airway as it inhales, pauses, exhales, pauses. Notice the
air flowing naturally in and out of your lungs, like water on the seashore.

FEELING CONNECTED TO YOUR BABY'S ESSENCE

Spiritual philosophies like *we are all one* can help you feel a peaceful sense
of flow with life, the Universe, Mother Nature, or God. Many parents
also talk about continuing to hold their babies close, not just in terms of
honoring their babies' memories, but in terms of tapping into their babies'
spirit or essence. Whether you believe you will be reunited after this life,
or you wonder about the idea of an enduring soul or nonphysical essence
that never goes away and is everywhere around you, you can call upon
this connection to soothe you and calm your brain.

The idea behind tapping into this connection is that whatever connection
you felt with your baby, that connection still exists. When you want to feel
this continuing bond, dwell on your felt sense of your baby whether you

rely on cherished memories of being with your baby, or imagine communing with your baby's spirit. Get into a quiet state of openness and receptivity, and listen. Dwelling on this felt sense of your baby can take you deeper into the experience of your bond, which you can trace back to the sense of oneness or the source of all. You may also conjure up a sense of your baby's well-being, and with that, a sense of your own well-being—and peace.

One powerful way to feel connected to your baby is to write a letter. This can be particularly therapeutic if you harbor any regrets. If you are struggling with feelings of failure, anger, or guilt, writing your baby a letter, and then writing your baby's response as you imagine it, can be a way to release those feelings and find inner peace.

> *Our counselor once suggested that we write a letter to Judah, telling our baby everything we wish we could have said to him and done with him. I'm not sure if I ever ended up doing it. Charlie started to do it, and it revealed a lot of his inner emotions that it seems like he has a hard time expressing when asked directly. I guess the counselor knew the potential power of that assignment.*
>
> *—Jolie*

Some people believe that by focusing on your continuing bond, dwelling on your felt sense of your baby, or feeling connected to your baby's essence, you can touch a spiritual realm where grief and negativity don't exist. Also, it can be powerfully healing to feel deeply connected to an essence that exists in another realm.

Many people are skeptical about this kind of thinking. *Is it real?* One response to that question is, *It doesn't matter.* The whole point of mindfulness is to be in the present moment and a nonjudgmental witness to your internal experience. Your mind is powerful, and when you sit in the driver's seat with mindfulness, you can use that power to improve your well-being, even if that means "tapping into another realm."

When you can feel connected to your baby, it can inspire gratitude for your baby's life. By sinking deep into a meditative, present-moment, felt-sense experience of your baby's essence, you can tap into a sense of calm whenever you want. (See also "Is It Normal to Feel My Baby's Presence?" in chapter 5; "Spirituality and Religion" in chapter 8.)

Accepting *What Is*

Another calm-inducing mindfulness practice is accepting *what is.* Acceptance averts the needless suffering caused by wishing for something other than what has happened, what is happening, or what will happen. When we regret what happened in the past, we are wishing to change what cannot possibly be changed. When we resist what is happening now, we are in denial or frustration. When we are sure we can control what will happen, we are buying into an illusion. When we are attached to a certain outcome, we resist adjusting to the actual outcome. We may even worry about undesired outcomes that haven't even happened, and perhaps never will.

When you aren't accepting *what is,* you are essentially fighting with reality. Some would say you are fighting against "God's will" or trying to go against the flow of the Universe. There is nothing wrong with reaching for the stars, but wisdom is knowing when to set your sights on a different path.

Early on, you may not be able to fathom accepting that your baby has died. You may even be angry at the very idea. This is perfectly normal. But as you adjust and heal, you can warm up to the idea of rolling with the twists and turns of fate.

Coming around to accepting *what is* can also help you avoid ruminating on painful events and regrets. Such ruminating is a natural part of processing your experience, putting it into perspective, and learning lessons. But too much rumination only adds unnecessarily to your suffering. How much ruminating is too much? That is for you to determine. Jolie talks about where she drew the line. For her, recalling the joy of meeting her baby, born still, and essentially accepting *what is,* help her avoid ruminating on painful ideas about *what should have been.*

> I hold on to that amazing moment of first seeing Judah, and I avoid rehashing the regrets. I have questioned if whether me choosing not to relive or reevaluate the regrets—the moment I found out Judah was no longer alive, or why I didn't take pictures with my son, or why I was afraid to see him—means that I am delaying healing. I have come to the conclusion that it is not. Those moments will always cause me pain and those will always be my regrets. But there is simply nothing I can do about any of them, and there is no closure that I or anyone else can offer me. I know that I showed Judah what love is for forty-one weeks. He felt love and he felt safety and comfort. That didn't all go down the drain the moment I said I was unsure if I wanted to see him, or the moment I declined to take a picture with him. I was a good mom. I AM a good mom. I did what I could in that moment. But even those truths don't bring me any consolation, and I think that the only thing that will ease the pain of these regrets is just time—and not revisiting them.
>
> —Jolie

> Honestly, hindsight is twenty-twenty. I can start many sentences with "I wish . . ." but that was before I lived in a world where babies die. I didn't know any better and my doctor had no reason to be alarmed because I'd had such a normal, healthy pregnancy. So making peace with these feelings really means not going there anymore.
>
> —Abby

> Why didn't I lay complaint about that stupid guy who did my twenty-week scan with Camden and failed to pick up I was fully dilated, membranes bulging? Would things have been any different if that had been picked up? No point dwelling on the **what-ifs**.
>
> —Fleur

Philosophically, accepting *what is* involves adopting a sense of wonder about what the future holds. You make plans but you remain open to *what will be*. This, in contrast to pinning your hopes on specific outcomes and harboring feelings of vulnerability, fear, and desperation about the future. Thinking *I wonder what lies in store for me?* is a far calmer approach to life and its unpredictability. (See also "Doing 'The Work'" later on in this chapter; "Vulnerability" in chapter 7; "Making Sense of Tragedy" in chapter 8.)

BEING AWARE OF THINKING TRAPS

The whole experience of losing Oren was such a tremendous mental quagmire. It was easy to get wrapped around and around in this terrible downward spiral of thoughts . . .

—Tanya

The stress of your baby's death can bring all kinds of painful thoughts to mind. Unfortunately, when your thinking mind gets carried away with painful thoughts, these thoughts can give rise to runaway painful feelings.

Mindfulness entails seeing thoughts as stories your mind creates in an effort to make sense of the world. Sometimes our stories are warranted, such as, "My baby died and I am sad." But sometimes our stories are unwarranted, such as, "My baby died and I am a failure." And yet we believe them, and unwarranted painful emotions follow. Furthermore, it's tempting to think, "I feel terrible about this, so it must be true." The end result is a vicious cycle of unnecessary suffering.

All of us have fallen into the trap of clinging to an unwarranted, distorted story that makes us (and our lives) miserable. It is part of the human condition. But with mindfulness, we can strive to avoid or climb out of thinking traps—and be especially alert for the ones we tend to favor. In fact, we all have go-to habits of thought and feeling. Here are examples of seven common default settings and their associated emotions:

1. Others don't give me a fair shake (anger).
2. The sky is sure to fall (fear, anxiety).
3. There are no good options (frustration).
4. Things are not what I'd hoped (sadness, failure).
5. Other people think less of me (embarrassment).
6. It's my fault (guilt).
7. I should/should not have done that (shame).

You may regularly fall into one or more of these thinking traps, which act as default settings that get in the way of your ability to see what's really going on in front of you. Thinking traps can ultimately get in the way of your healing as well. But you can overcome traps by your willingness to consider alternative perceptions and conclusions. By considering alternatives, you unravel the vicious cycle of being triggered by painful, distorted thoughts. Positive alternatives engender positive emotions like compassion, forgiveness, and acceptance. Entertaining alternatives is key to the next two strategies. See which one fits you best, or combine the features you find most helpful.

MINDFULLY REFRAMING YOUR THOUGHTS

> *There are honestly still days where I would like nothing more than to hide under my duvet. When I am having a particularly "down" day, I use self-talk to lift myself up and out. I guess it is like redirecting my thinking. I also reassure myself that as bad as I am feeling in that moment, it will pass . . . and so I let the thoughts and feelings come and I try to let them go.*
>
> *—Emmerson*

> *I found it most useful to be able to recognize my thoughts and to know the effect of my thoughts upon my feelings. It really helped to have that witness-like detachment from the processes going on in my body.*
>
> *—Mel*

When you find yourself in a negative spiral, the first step of reframing is to stop and mindfully observe your thoughts and the resulting emotions, without judgment. Preface your awareness of each thought with *"I am thinking,"* as this powerfully underscores that it's just a thought—not a feeling, not necessarily true, and *not a part of you.* Mindfully approach your thoughts with self-compassion and curiosity. Here, some common distorted thoughts are posed as mindful observations:

- Hmmm, *I am thinking* I'm a failure because my baby died.
- Hmmm, *I am thinking* I did something to cause my baby's death.
- Hmmm, *I am thinking* my baby feels poorly or all alone.
- Hmmm, *I am thinking* no one else cares about my baby.
- Hmmm, *I am thinking* there is no way for me to feel better.
- Hmmm, *I am thinking* this grief will last forever and do me in.
- Hmmm, *I am thinking* I don't want to go on living.

Simply let those thoughts pass through your consciousness as you observe them, in the moment. Ignore the power they would hold if you chose to believe them. Don't buy into any emotions that are stirred. If you're already agitated and distressed, go into your body and identify the sensations you're experiencing, such as a tight jaw, lump in the throat, or queasy stomach. Continue this mindful observation for a minute or two, or until your ramped-up physiology calms down. (See the section "Mindfully Restoring Calm to Your Triggered Brain" earlier in this chapter.)

Then recall that you don't have to believe everything that goes through your head. Question your perceptions by exploring alternatives. Do some reality checking; for instance, make a list of all the evidence pointing away from your being at fault. Or ask your partner, a friend, or a relative if they ever think about your baby. Recall that there is no crystal ball proving you are doomed. Counseling can be an invaluable forum for exploring alternative ways of looking at your assessments of reality. Talk to someone who is a compassionate, insightful practitioner of mindfulness. Explore different spiritual or philosophical ideas.

> *One of the absolute hardest things for me was reconciling the fact that Oren lived and died **inside my body**. On the one hand, I was sacred space. I had been the whole world to a little boy. This made me gorgeous. How could I ever feel bad about myself when I was blessed to be his home? But on the other hand, at the same time I had been his coffin too. I felt indescribably contaminated, desecrated. How could I come to terms with this? This was the big gift from the Pilates teacher, not the bodywork itself, though I am sure it was good for me. What she said was something like this: "I have never had kids myself, but I know that if I was dying, the place where I would feel the safest, the most held, would be with my mother." This was so powerful to me. It was exactly what I needed to hear. My son died in the place that was the safest to him—the only place he had ever known.*
>
> *—Tanya*

> *Finley was born in the summer so I spent a lot of time in the peacefulness of the graveyard in the early weeks. Then autumn came and I found myself struggling about the fact that he was in the ground alone. So I would find myself thinking of him having a quilt of autumn leaves, or playing in them. Then, the first winter was hard, coping with the fact that my baby boy was frozen in the ground, and that's what really started my exploration of what my beliefs were about death. Some of the thoughts I had at the time were awful, things like wanting to dig him up and bring him home. I took control by writing about my thoughts, then finding a way to change them. For me this was changing my belief about where the part of Finley that made Finley **Finley** was now. It helps to say that I didn't bury my son; I buried his shell and my son is free.*
>
> *—Mel*

By noting the alternatives to your distorted thoughts, you can soothe yourself by choosing to believe kinder, gentler, *more accurate* perspectives, and reaping the benefits of the attendant positive effects. Mel gives an example of how she reduced her distress by reframing her interpretation of her crying: "I think of tears as being diamonds that fall from my eyes, another gift from Finley." Corresponding to the earlier list of distorted thoughts, here are examples of how those negative distortions might be reframed into positive assessments:

- Sometimes babies die, and it is not a reflection of a parent's worth. (I am worthy.)
- I did nothing to intentionally harm my baby. (I'm not guilty; I am loving.)
- My baby is not suffering. (I am at peace.)

- Others are silent as they don't know what to say, or they don't want to trigger my grief. (I am grateful for their efforts at caring.)
- I have many options and resources at my disposal, should I choose to follow through. (I feel satisfied.)
- Intense grief doesn't last forever. (I am hopeful.)
- I can ultimately grow from this tragedy and find peace. (I am resilient. I have faith.)
- As I mourn, I am healing and slowly reinvesting in the future. (I have confidence.)

Ironically, another common distortion that leads to unnecessary suffering is this thought: *I'm having a pretty good day and actually smiled. If I really loved my baby, I would remain grief-stricken at all times. I must do something to renew my misery.* In reality, grief naturally consists of unpredictable ups and downs, and you deserve—and benefit from—any respite you can find. (See also "Understanding Mourning" in chapter 2; "Mindfully Embracing Positive Experiences" later in this chapter.)

It sounds very strange but I worried what would happen to me if I had no sadness or pain. I thought I would just be empty, I thought that if I didn't feel sad then I didn't love Finley. Part of the reframing that I did for myself is to understand that I can be happy and still grieve. I can be happy and still miss Finley.

—Mel

Doing "The Work"

"The Work" is a powerful form of mindful reframing and transformative inquiry developed by Byron Katie, author of many books, including the seminal *Loving What Is*. The Work can help you truly and deeply understand that when you believe painful, unwarranted thoughts, the result is painful, unwarranted emotion—and unnecessary suffering. When done mindfully, The Work is a very effective method of writing, questioning, and releasing unwarranted thoughts. It also grants lasting insights that help you accept *what is*—and reduce suffering.

To do The Work, pick a thought that is associated with emotional pain and distress for you. Write it down. (As with journaling, writing down your thoughts helps you pin them down and face them.) Get into a quiet, open, meditative frame of mind, and ask yourself four questions, followed by a turnaround:

- First: Is it true? (Yes, or no—your response doesn't matter; simply contemplate that painful thought, reflect on that question "Is it true?" and then answer simply "yes" or "no.")
- Second: Can you absolutely know that it is true? (Contemplate how the answer could actually be a resounding *no*.)

- Third: How do you react, or what happens when you think that thought? (Describe, in writing, and reflect on your answer.)
- Fourth: Who would you be, or what would happen if you didn't believe that thought? (Describe, in writing, and reflect on your answer.)
- How can you turn it around? (Write down the opposite and try that on for size. Or change the pronouns, particularly if you are working on a thought you have about someone else, and maybe the way they treat you. Or switch subject and object. Who is this really about?)
- Is the turnaround true, or truer? (Write down three pieces of evidence that show the turnaround might be true.)

The Work demonstrates how *the truth will set you free*. When you get good at it, you can even jump straight to the turnarounds and the evidence that supports them, and watch your distress lift. For example, you can go from, "I am crying too much" to "I am *not* crying too much; this is what my grief is asking for, and if I go into my body in the present moment, I can see that it releases grief and its tension."

In general, when you question painful thoughts and discover that they are unwarranted, you avoid spiraling deeper into unnecessary suffering. Doing this kind of inquiry wakes you up so you can experience a shift in how you view the world and the stories you tell yourself. The powerful inquiry of The Work can put you back into your "true self," and you can see what you couldn't see before.

These are very big, game-changing ideas, and it's okay if you're having trouble wrapping your mind around them. If you are curious and want to learn more, go to Byron Katie's website. There you can see videos of people doing The Work—questioning their thoughts, vaporizing their distress, and gaining profound insights about themselves. You can also witness how powerful thoughts are when we mindlessly believe them—and how *powerless* they are when we *don't*.

I went through a phase of hating Lilly's father, but it just made me sad. Once I chose to not hate him anymore, the clouds started lifting and I was able to see rainbows again.

—Sarah

MINDFULLY EMBRACING POSITIVE EXPERIENCES

Finding reasons to smile has been a lot easier than I thought it would be. I put that down to listening to myself. Yes, I am always one step away from tears but I am also only one step away from laughter. The ball swings both ways. I've accepted that.

—Sarah

*I think just being a generally positive person really helped, too. The
experience wasn't only a tragedy—it was also a time of beauty and hope.*
—Shellie

Even in the depths of mourning, you won't mourn 100 percent of the time.
Your brain and body simply require breaks. In fact, they will demand
breaks, just as your mind wanders after a period of steady concentration
or your body stops, sits, rests, or sleeps after a period of steady exertion.
Just as you do not expect your brain to continuously study, create, analyze, or learn, nor do you expect your body to continuously exercise,
move, or do physical work, you cannot expect your brain and body to
continuously mourn. You need respite.

But after exertion, your brain and body don't thrive on just any
respite. They require *repair* in the form of positive, nurturing experiences. Positive experiences nourish your brain and body, boosting your
physical strengths as well as your emotional strengths, which you can
draw on to survive times of suffering and eventually, to heal. Seeking out
and embracing positive experiences might seem impossible at first and
disloyal to the memory of your precious baby, but it is actually a task
of mourning and important to do it well. (See also "Is It Normal to Feel
Happy Sometimes?" in chapter 5; "How Do I Acquire a Sense of Healing"
in chapter 8.)

The mindfulness piece is important because the brain is most efficient at
highlighting unpleasant experiences and emotions—often because alarms are
triggered—resulting in efficiently built and reinforced neural pathways that
focus on the negative. This tendency may have promoted human survival
over the eons, but unfortunately, it coincides with the brain's tendency to
ignore, gloss over, or dismiss pleasurable experiences and emotions—usually
experienced as more mild and no big deal—resulting in a relative lack of
positive neural pathways. To see this bias in action, you might recall that
if someone criticizes you, you probably take it to heart and it might bother
you for days. But if someone praises you, you'll likely shrug it off, or even
decline it outright, rather than feeling appreciated, being grateful, or even
graciously saying, "Thank you." Instead, "Oh, no, not me. You're too kind."
That's your brain easily absorbing the negative and rejecting the positive.
Unfortunately, this bias can lead to chronic stress, depression, anxiety, anger,
pessimism, and bitterness. Naturally after your baby dies, you are more even
prone to these kinds of misery.

Misery is part of mourning, for sure, but you needn't suffer prolonged
or unnecessary misery. Chronic misery is not a task of mourning. And to
ward it off, it's important to nourish your mourning brain by seeking and
embracing positive experiences. To do this effectively, you'll likely need
to offset your brain's bias toward the negative and actively focus on the
positive. Do this whenever you encounter a positive experience, by (1)
mindfully noticing it, (2) staying with it, and (3) absorbing it.

1. Mindfully notice, in the moment, when you've had a positive experience. This can take practice, especially if you're an expert at glossing over the positive. Be on the lookout for even fleeting moments where you experience laughter, wonder, awe, love, affection, peaceful contentment, being praised, being appreciated, being cared for, or anything else enjoyable.

2. After you note having a positive experience, stay with it. Don't brush it off or hurry away from it. Accept it, reflect on it, lean into it. Sense how it feels in your body, and sit up or stand a little straighter in the face of it. Commit to momentarily dwelling on it, knowing it will help your brain build positive neural pathways. By actively staying with it you enrich the experience, giving your brain something more impressive to hold on to.

3. Absorb the positive experience. Be a sponge. Imagine it making a real impression on your brain. Visualize folding the positive experience into your body. Lean into it *and let it land*. Rejoice in it. Feel gratitude for it.

Even ten to fifteen seconds of noticing, reflecting, and absorbing each positive experience can make it easier for your brain to build and strengthen positively inclined neural pathways. Over time, it'll become even easier. And having more positive neural pathways reinforces your positive traits and emotions, which contributes to your resilience and healing. By essentially "rewiring" your brain in a positive direction, you reap the benefit of having a more positive life.

Many people find focusing on the positive to be a challenging habit to adopt, just in the course of living a typical busy life. Needless to say, it can be very challenging while mourning. Here are several simple ideas to get you started:

- Give yourself credit for your triumphs, accomplishments, and responsibilities fulfilled, large and small.
- Accept compliments as gifts. Saying "thank you" shows your gratitude and fosters a sense of mutual connection, which benefits both you and the giver.
- Read, write, and say positive affirmations, which when done habitually, reinforces positivity in your brain and discourages negative self-talk.
- Seek out positive experiences that let you enjoy the present moment. Linger over your morning coffee or tea. Watch birds flit about. Lie in the sun. Explore a beautiful place. Engage in your favorite athletic or creative hobby—Mel says, "Photography helped me see the beauty in the world again." Jolie and Charlie took dance lessons. Set aside "positive time" to get your daily dose.

I feel like I'm always aware of and receptive to the moment when I'm shooting [with a camera], because I am doing my best to capture and compose the exquisite dignity and uniqueness of the moment as it unfolds.

—Nathan

Having something else for my mind to focus on was a blessed relief. I might not have gotten very good at quilting, or retained much of the Spanish that I learned, but at least I didn't spend those hours drowning in "whys."

—Tanya

When you're ready for more, here are three mindfulness practices that can help you create more positive experiences.

CULTIVATING POSITIVITY IN YOUR BODY

When Lavender would come home from work, she would find me sitting and crying, day after day. Then one day she found me laughing. I had been watching cute guinea pig videos online. A few weeks later she took me and Derek to the pet store and we came home with two little guinea pigs. They did not take away my grief. I had wanted a baby, not guinea pigs. But they did help as they came to love and trust us and let us snuggle with them when we were sad.

—Tanya

There is research pointing to the value of smiling and good posture—even when you think you have nothing to smile about or when you feel bent over by grief. Holding a full facial smile that includes the muscles around the eyes actually changes brain activity to create a happier mood. Holding upright posture, which includes engaging your core, straightening your spine, and putting shoulders back, chest up, and head high, engenders positive feelings of strength and enthusiasm. In contrast, a frown creates a sour mood and a slump engenders anxiety, sadness, and passivity. You could take a moment right now to compare and contrast, and see what you experience in your body and brain.

It's not as if habits of smiling and good posture will erase your grief, but they can soften the edges and reinforce your efforts to heal. Seek out experiences that make you smile and laugh, such as watching comedies, and look for opportunities to practice good posture, such as when walking, dancing, doing yoga, and waiting in line.

PRACTICING RANDOM ACTS OF KINDNESS

Practicing random acts of kindness nurtures you, even as it nurtures others. Because grieving often entails focusing inward, it can be immensely helpful to sometimes focus outward and feel connected to people, specifically by being compassionate, generous, and kind. By volunteering for a worthy cause, making charitable donations, and, especially powerful, practicing random acts of kindness, you can feel nurtured by knowing you can spread good in the world.

Today I smiled at and made eye contact with strangers. I told shop assistants to enjoy the rest of their day (and I sincerely meant it) when I left their stores with my shopping. I let traffic in to my lane and an elderly couple into the car park even though I had the right-of-way. I did our laundry at the Laundromat and left three dollars (the cost of a wash) by a machine with a "Random Act of Kindness" card with Adisyn's name on it. There is no better service than to pay it forward and the mantra I try to live by, which is to treat others as you would like to be treated. It does help to heal my world and it costs nothing to be kind. It is in giving you receive and receiving you give.

—Emmerson

PRACTICING GRATITUDE

Another powerful outward practice is the practice of gratitude. Gratitude induces the relaxation response in your nervous system. Even during your darkest days, you can find something to be grateful for by focusing on the present moment. It can be as simple as, "I am grateful for this sunny day." Or "I am grateful for my pillow." Reviewing the day and focusing on what you are grateful for can even reduce the amount of time it takes to fall asleep and can improve sleep quality. Gratitude also honors your baby's life.

I've made an intention for this year to explore lots of things that make me feel good and build in strategies to my daily life to heal. I am very much enjoying my new daily habit of writing a note each day to put into a blessings jar, which I will read on New Year's Eve.

—Mel

I wish they had never died, but I don't for a second, wish they had never lived. I am grateful and blessed to be their mother.

—Tanya

You can practice gratitude at a regular time as part of your daily routine, or peppered randomly throughout the day. The traditions of saying grace before a meal and evening prayers are gratitude practices that have been handed down through generations. (See also "Acceptance, Peace, and Gratitude" in chapter 17.)

ADVICE BEREAVED PARENTS WOULD HAVE GIVEN TO THEMSELVES

The parents quoted below answered this question: *If you could reach back in time and say something to yourself when your baby died, what would you say?* When you read their responses, notice the self-compassion and positive affirmations. These are the kinds of thoughts that reduce suffering. To tap into these bits of wisdom, pick and choose the ones that feel good to you, and treat them like anchors. Or you may have your own favorite mantras. Mindfully hold on to them, especially during the darkest, stormiest times.

It's hard when there are no answers and no explanations for what has happened. But be patient, embrace the love and support of others, and take time for yourself.

—Daniela

You are not a failure. You did nothing to cause this. You did everything you could for this baby to come into the world safely.

—Melanie

You will not only survive this, but so will your husband, so will your son, and, if you let it, it will make you better. Remember to breathe. Give grace to others—they don't know.

—Embry

Trust in yourself, in your strength and your love.

—Karen

You are not alone and you are going to get through this.

—Abby

It may not feel like it now, but you will survive.

—Emmerson

This is so hard. I am with you.

—Julie

Just to allow yourself to feel whatever it is.

—Anne

Be patient. Things are not always the way you plan or want, so just remain patient.

—Ben

You will be okay and you will be happy again. Ronin died in a safe place inside his mummy, knowing he was loved and wanted so much.

—Lorna

You are deserving of the same gentleness and compassion that you would show to another who was struggling with pain, fear, and grief.

—Tanya

***You are not alone.** This was not your fault. You are still a mother and a **good** mother. Judah knew nothing but love all the days of his life with you. It won't always hurt as bad as it does right now, and* *you and your husband will be okay—and you'll be okay **together**. Your husband will grieve differently than you, but he **is** grieving. Be patient and gentle with yourselves and each other, and give yourself grace.*

—Jolie

Remember you have to grieve, too. Being strong isn't holding it back. Cry, support your wife, and grieve together. It's okay to cry, it's okay to be upset. You're not weird, you're not odd. Don't be afraid to take time off work. Don't feel ashamed to talk about it. Go to a counselor. Talk to your wife about it. Talk to other people who have been through it. Remember that you'll live another day and you have to live for your wife and your children. Remember that you'll see him again, and he'll be alive and well.

—Charlie

*This is such a difficult and sad time. It's hard to imagine life going back to "normal." But you will find a **new** normal—and you **will** get through this. Over time, you will find many gifts that came out of such great loss. You will have the opportunity to help others in a similar situation. You will live with the hope that someday you will be reunited with your daughter. Ashley will always be part of your family and lives on in your heart.*

—Shellie

Grief does not own you forever. One day you will rediscover joy.

—Nathan

Points to Remember

- Mindfulness includes bringing your attention to the present moment, being a nonjudgmental witness to your thoughts and feelings, gently questioning the thoughts that result in painful emotions, and having compassion for self and others.
- Mindfulness practices reduce unnecessary suffering by soothing the core brain and enabling the outer brain to stay connected and regulate emotions.
- If you are suffering from deep trauma, you'll benefit from first seeking brain-based treatments, like EMDR, which will enable you to benefit from mindfulness practices.
- Mindfulness practices include meditation and yoga, and form the basis of therapies such as mindfulness-based stress reduction (MBSR) and mindfulness-based cognitive therapy (MBCT).
- Simple mindfulness practices include meditative breathing, soothing habits, calming activities, and mindful journaling.
- Mindfulness strategies include practicing self-compassion, welcoming grief, accepting *what is*, feeling connected to your baby's essence, mindfully restoring calm after being triggered, being aware of thinking traps, mindfully reframing distorted thoughts, and embracing positive experiences.
- You can reduce and avert unnecessary suffering by questioning thoughts that result in painful emotions and deriving kinder alternatives.
- By embracing positive experiences, you foster positive neural pathways, which in turn foster positive strengths, all of which contribute to your resilience and healing.

5

THE EARLY DAYS AND MONTHS

The early days and months after your baby dies can be especially grueling. You may be awestruck by the power of your thoughts and feelings. Your parental instincts and urges seem to come out of nowhere. You may be engaging in behaviors that previously you would have considered inappropriate or outrageous. And yet, the depth of your experience is somehow proof that you are encountering the biological essence of what it is to be human.

Parental bereavement is a social, emotional, intellectual, and spiritual experience, to be sure. But it is also a biological experience. Human babies need devoted and protective parents who are willing and able to supervise them for many years. Their very survival requires a strong, resilient bond felt by the parent toward the baby. This bond can begin forming before conception and becomes very powerful even before the baby's birth.

When this bond collides with death, parents still harbor irresistible biological urges to nurture their baby. If you are a mother, the biochemical changes that occur as a result of pregnancy and birth put you into parental overdrive. If you are a father, when you first lay eyes on your little one, your devotion blooms fully. As a result, you may feel like you should be able to revive this baby, if only you could figure out how. You may be obsessed with your baby's body, and want to be with it, know where it is, or make the perfect plans for burial or cremation. Your preoccupation can lead to hallucinations and nurturing behaviors that make you question your sanity. But you are not insane. You are bereft of the very one who would give these natural thoughts, feelings, visions, and behaviors meaning: your baby.

> I would go into Judah's room. With his hospital blanket, I'd wrap up the weighted bear someone gave me as a gift and put Judah's hat on the bear. I would rock him and hold him close to me and close my eyes and pretend it was my son. It made me sob, but it eased the heartache. It makes me cry now just imagining those feelings. Losing your child—it is heartbreaking. It is **heart-wrenching**. There is no better word for it than that. There is no better word to describe that awful, unbearable emotion that is so strong that it physically causes your heart to ache, to long, for your child.
>
> —Jolie

As time goes on, these emotions and urges will fade. Without a baby to reinforce this devotion, your instincts will move on. In the meantime, accept yourself for where you are. The resilience of your parenting urges is evidence of your biological inheritance as well as the depth of your parental love. (See also "Is It Normal to Find Comfort in Nurturing Behaviors?" later in this chapter; "Emotional Mode" in chapter 3.)

This chapter looks at the common concerns many parents share regarding (1) postpartum recovery and (2) emotional recovery, particularly in the early days and months of this journey when nurturing instincts can remain in high gear and grief can feel so endless and profound.

Concerns about Postpartum Recovery

I felt a real physical loss because she was attached to me for her whole life—then she was gone. And then I had all this milk and there was no baby. I felt as though a part of me had just been cut out, a real overwhelming, intense sadness.

—Jessie

Physically I am recovering like any mom would after giving birth. Emotionally . . . it comes and goes.

—Helen

When your baby dies, not only do you feel emotionally devastated, you may also feel physically devastated. Besides physical symptoms of grief, including fatigue, insomnia, and empty, aching arms, many mothers also experience a physical ordeal around the birth of their babies. And if your baby died in the womb or shortly after birth, you have all the physical signs of pregnancy and giving birth, but no baby. Your emotional load can be further increased by postpartum "baby blues," caused by the natural readjustment of your hormones to nonpregnant levels. This period may last several weeks and accounts for some of your mood swings and mothering urges. If these symptoms last longer or are more severe, you may be diagnosed and treated for postpartum depression. Finally, if your baby died while you were still breastfeeding (or getting ready to breastfeed), you must also cope with your breasts as they continue to produce milk.

These cruel twists of nature can make your physical recovery very painful, and add to your emotional distress. It can be hard to find the energy to take care of yourself. You may feel angry at your body or depressed about the signs of pregnancy, childbirth, or breastfeeding that remain, or impatient for them to disappear. For some women, the return of menses is another blow. It seems so unfair.

My body producing milk seemed cruel after the fact. It was a painful physical reminder of what was supposed to be, but wasn't. I had similar feelings when getting my period for the first time after losing Judah. The fact that I was getting my period because I was no longer pregnant was like pouring salt onto an open wound. Yes, thank you, body, for reminding me. Sometimes I would mentally feel like I was doing "okay," but then a physical reminder would occur (like breast milk leaking or getting my period), and I would have somewhat of a relapse when otherwise I was doing alright that day.

—Jolie

With time and by taking care of your body, you will soon recover physically. Good nutrition, rest, and emotional support can lessen the fatigue, anxiety, and depression normally associated with postpartum recovery. Bodywork, such as therapeutic massage and yoga, can also be a source of great healing. Attending to overall health is also good for emotional recovery and brain health, which is taxed by the journey of grief and mourning. After you feel better physically, you may find that you are better able to cope with your grief and focus on your emotional recovery. (See also "Practicing Self-Compassion" in chapter 4.)

BREAST CARE

For most mothers, giving birth stimulates hormones that make the breasts produce milk. In addition to physical discomfort, engorged breasts can make you feel emotionally distressed. If you planned on breastfeeding your baby, your sadness or anger is only heightened—here you are, beautifully equipped by nature to feed and nurture your baby, but there is no baby. Many mothers report that this is a very difficult part of postpartum physical recovery. If you have been breastfeeding, you may deeply miss this nurturing, loving act with your baby.

Milk usually comes in two to five days after a baby is born, and the mother's breasts may feel engorged and perhaps leak milk. The breasts will also feel full and uncomfortable when breastfeeding or pumping stops. This engorgement period lasts up to forty-eight hours.

If you experience painful pressure, swelling, or lumpiness, you can relieve it by expressing a little milk every few hours by hand or using a manual breast pump. Electric pumps are too powerful for this delicate operation—you need to leave in as much milk as is comfortable because a chemical present in the retained milk signals the milk glands to depress production. Over time your supply will naturally fade away.

Other measures that relieve discomfort include cold compresses and ibuprofen or acetaminophen. A warm shower or kneeling in a hot bath with breasts suspended might induce milk leakage and reduce painful pressure. While a well-fitting bra can help too, binding breasts is ineffective and might intensify your pain and increase the risk of infection.

It was the third day after my baby was stillborn. My milk had just come in and I had forgotten that was going to happen, and I thought, "Oh, is this another torture thing here?" My sister had a baby and she couldn't breastfeed, and here I was with all this milk.

—Elaine

I've never been so empty in my life. I pictured breastfeeding him, I pictured him just lying in bed with us. I woke up in the middle of the night, wanting to get up to nurse him.

—Meryl

There is another option that some bereaved mothers find therapeutic: expressing and donating their milk to a human milk bank. These banks make breast milk available to sick and premature infants whose mothers cannot provide this vital nourishment. Donating is a generous and compassionate act. For a bereaved mother, donation can feel like a meaningful way to turn a negative experience into a positive one. You can donate expressed milk in honor of your baby.

If you'd like to explore this option, a midwife, nurse, or lactation consultant can show you how to pump efficiently, and the human milk bank nearest you will provide instructions on collection, storage, and donation and if necessary can arrange for free overnight transportation. For locations, visit the nonprofit Human Milk Banking Association of North America at www.hmbana.org.

As long as you keep pumping, your body can continue to make breast milk. You can express and donate for however long you wish, even if it's just for a day or two. When you are getting ready to stop, pump at increasingly longer intervals and don't empty your breasts so the retained milk can signal your body to reduce your supply. Depending on how much milk you are producing, it may be helpful to discuss strategies with a lactation consultant, doctor, or midwife.

I donated his milk to a local milk bank for three months and got to know the twins who were the primary recipients. My milk even went to help the newest baby of the woman who had started the milk bank years ago when her son was stillborn! Talk about full circle.

—Tanya

Regardless of when and how you do it, reducing your milk supply can be an emotional process, so take your time, seek extra support, and be gentle with yourself. Call your doctor or midwife if regular measures don't address the pain of engorgement, or if you notice any signs of breast infection:

- any red, warm, hard, or tender areas in your breasts
- fever above 100 degrees
- general ill feeling
- tender lymph glands in the underarm area

Postpartum Depression

Most new mothers experience "baby blues," which consists of symptoms of mild depression, including mood swings, crying spells, anxiety, and insomnia. Symptoms typically start two or three days after the mother gives birth (but can start sooner) and can last up to two weeks. But some mothers experience more severe symptoms, known as postpartum depression (PPD).

Postpartum depression is rooted in physiology. Fluctuating postpartum hormones can affect the parts of your brain that are involved in memory, emotions, sleep, empathy, and bonding, and survival reactions like anxiety, aggression, and fear—hence the wide array of distressing symptoms.

> *I was placed on antidepressants and had to see a psychologist as I was a mess. I was given tablets to help my anxiety and to sleep. Without them I would not sleep.*
>
> —*Lorna*

As a bereaved mother, you may be more prone to PPD, and prompt treatment can relieve the unnecessary suffering it can cause you. But how can you tell whether you're distressed because of grief or because of PPD? In general, grief moves, with ups and downs; PPD feels like you're stuck in the down position. Ask your doctor or midwife for an evaluation if

- you have a history of depression;
- your symptoms last longer than two weeks;
- your symptoms become severe at any point within six months after the birth;
- you are unable to function (get dressed, eat properly, tend to personal hygiene, etc.);
- you feel unable to concentrate, think clearly, or make plans or decisions;
- you are preoccupied with feelings of guilt, shame, or worthlessness;
- you think about harming yourself or committing suicide;
- you have severe anxiety or panic attacks;
- your appetite is decreased or increased;
- you are unable to sleep or are sleeping too much;
- you experience overwhelming fatigue or lack of energy;
- you feel intense irritability or anger;
- you are uninterested in people or pleasurable activities;
- your thoughts, speech, or movements are slowed down;
- you have any symptoms of psychosis, such as agitation, incoherent speech, hallucinations, or delusions; or
- you are wondering if you have PPD.

PPD actually changes your brain's activity, and its effects can be clearly seen and measured with brain imaging. PPD is not a sign of weakness, failure, maladjustment, mental disease, an emotional issue, or something you just need to snap out of it. Nor is it your fault. PPD is a biochemical imbalance that affects many women after childbirth, and it is a medical problem that can be easily and successfully treated. There is no sense in adding unnecessarily to your suffering, as you have enough on your plate—particularly grief and mourning—following the death of your baby.

SEX AND CONTRACEPTION

Parents vary on their interest in sex after their baby dies. For some parents, sex provides the intimacy they want; for other parents, it seems like a worthless or painful activity, especially when associated with conception. When you are intensely grieving or if your relationship is stressed, you may feel too emotionally drained. It is also common for each parent to be at opposite ends of the spectrum.

As the mother who's just given birth, fatigue, soreness, and hormonal changes may also affect your interest in sex. And, you may be struggling with feelings of failure, feeling like your body betrayed you, and feeling like you are no longer even a sexual being. Winnie recalls, "I was *so* uninterested in being sexual. I felt incapable of it. It was like someone flipped a switch in my brain."

> *Sex, body image, and self-esteem are such enormous issues. I have been struggling, struggling with these. A friend of mine whose daughter was stillborn says that it took her a whole year to be able to look at herself in the mirror again. I think these are extra hard for me because this was my firstborn so I had never experienced the normal postpartum changes, let alone those with grief in the mix. The body stuff has been hard.*
>
> *—Tanya*

For a woman, interest in and eagerness for sex is made possible by living a low-stress life, having a calm brain, inhabiting her familiar body, and having an affectionate and engaged partner. For any postpartum woman, the playing field has been completely altered. She is more stressed, more reactive, and inhabiting an unfamiliar body, which makes her less available and less eager for her partner's advances. When the postpartum woman is also grieving, she is likely to have little, if any, interest in sex until the playing field can be repaired. Her partner's patience, nurturing, accommodation, and collaboration during this trying time can go a long way toward assisting her with her restoration and healing.

There are also medical issues. The mother may be advised to avoid any vaginal penetration until healing is checked at the six-week postpartum exam. Physically, you are able to tolerate penetration when your bleeding stops and when it feels comfortable to you. It is important to be gentle the first few times. Let pain be your guide. A water-soluble lubricant (such as K-Y Jelly or Blossom Organics) may be helpful in reducing discomfort. Try different positions to minimize discomfort caused by pressure on your episiotomy or other tender areas. You can also try other ways to express sexual intimacy and physical affection. (See also "Sex and Intimacy" in chapter 11.)

Many mothers long to be pregnant again immediately, but if you are still recovering from pregnancy, you need time to heal physically. If you are in a heterosexual relationship, to avoid conception, you need to use birth control as soon as you resume intercourse. Pregnancy can occur before your menstrual period reappears, as the first ovulation can happen anytime. Discuss birth control with your doctor or midwife to find the method that is right for you.

> *At first, birth control was just out of the question. I just couldn't use anything, I just couldn't! Then, after a couple months, I decided I was feeling a little bit better, and I wasn't going to risk any more pain. But at about the time we decided we weren't going to have any more children, I discovered I was pregnant.*
>
> —*Sara*

Trying for another pregnancy is a complicated decision for most couples. Whether you are still recovering from pregnancy or not, you need time to think about this important issue. Temporary contraceptives, rather than long-lasting ones, will keep your options open. (See also "When Should We Try Again" in chapter 14.)

COMMON CONCERNS ABOUT EMOTIONAL RECOVERY

Grief and mourning arouse many concerns, especially in the beginning.
- Will I survive this tragedy?
- How do I get through this?
- What will I feel tomorrow, next week, next month, next year?
- Are my feelings, thoughts, and behaviors normal?
- Will I feel better, ever?

In time, you will find some answers to these questions. For instance, yes, you will survive this, and in doing so, you will know you can survive *anything* life presents. But early on, like many parents, you may have doubts about this when you notice your distress actually intensifies after several months, with variable intensity continuing for many months thereafter.

> *I would describe my grief as nonlinear. Some days are better than others. I felt my strongest the first couple of months, until the shock wore off and I had to face reality. Now six months later, not a day goes by that I do not think about Dayani.*
>
> —*Destrida*

So what will you feel tomorrow, next week, next month, next year? Grieving is unpredictable. You will know what it's like when you get there. And since no two people grieve exactly alike, you will find your own path through mourning. One thing is certain: you can try to avoid grieving, but you will not benefit.

What if I Try to Avoid Grieving?

Over the long run, grieving cannot be avoided, only disguised. As the months and years go by, if you habitually suppress grief's expression and hinder mourning—that is, you deny your grief its natural expression, discount your experiences, and ignore your losses—it results in an overarching sense of numbness about your baby's death—and life in general. Whether you're a mother or a father, an emotion-oriented or activity-oriented griever, if you try to keep a lid on grief, you must keep a lid on your body and all your feelings, until you can honestly say you feel nothing at all—about anything. Over time, this pervasive numbness can result in living a diminished existence, including depression, anxiety, depleted energy, uncontrolled emotional outbursts, maladaptive behaviors, or even having the urge to create chaos so you can feel *something*. Keeping a lid on grief compromises your health and happiness, and puts you at risk for many physical and emotional ailments. (See also "Numbing" in chapter 10.)

More specifically, when you suppress grieving, grief can find expression in any of the following ways:

- physical illness due to poor immune system functioning, such as recurring viral or bacterial infections, fatigue, digestive distress, skin eruptions, allergies and sensitivities, aching muscles or joints
- hyperactivity, such as working overtime, being overextended, filling up the calendar with commitments, feeling restless or at a loss when not super busy
- anxiety, including specific fears or a vague, uncomfortable feeling of fear or dread, which may be accompanied by rapid breathing and heartbeat, nausea, diarrhea, headaches, sweating, irritability, insomnia, trembling, nightmares
- depression, including vague feelings of dissatisfaction, unhappiness, or boredom; loss of interest in life; excessive sleeping or insomnia; difficulty concentrating, making decisions, or keeping up with responsibilities; intense guilt; irritability; crying spells; being uninterested in health or self-care
- disrupted relationships, such as a troubled marriage, broken friendships, conflict in family relationships, isolation, difficulties with people at work, thinking others are "out to get you"
- substance abuse, including alcohol, food, cigarettes, tranquilizers, other drugs
- other compulsive or addictive behaviors, such as engaging excessively in exercise, religion, shopping, gambling, cleaning, television watching, gaming, sexual activity, romantic infidelities
- anger, bitterness, and violence, such as getting into verbal or physical fights with anyone—including family members—destruction of property, motor vehicle accidents

- self-destructive behaviors, such as impulsiveness, lack of good judgment, accidents that might have been avoided with normal caution or alertness, feeling suicidal

As you can see, if you habitually suppress grieving, you exchange the necessary pain of dealing with reality for the *un*necessary pain of dealing with self-made troubles. You reject a path of healing for a path of continued misery. So while you may think that you are successfully distracting yourself from grief and mourning, you are actually a prisoner of it. To free yourself, you can't go over it, you can't go under it, you can't go around it. *You just have to go through it.*

> It's a process. I don't think we ever get to the end of it, we just continue to process it in different ways and seasons. The first year felt unmanageable so many times, but we continued to face it head-on and make time for ourselves to process what we were going through. And that's what got us through that unbelievably hard first year.
>
> —Embry

Grief and mourning can be painful, but you will gradually feel better as the months and years go by if you can consistently let your grief's expression flow as it comes up. By letting it flow, you will move through your mourning more easily than if you try to forget about it or deny its role in your healing. Remember that grief and mourning are not signs of weakness; rather, it takes strength and courage to acknowledge your losses, give your grief its appropriate expression, let go of *what might have been*, and adjust to *what is*. This is a time to mindfully surrender to mourning, to look after yourself, to get the support you need, to engage in the nurturing behaviors and/or activities that offer release and purpose—and to stretch and grow. (See also "Why Is Mourning Required?" in chapter 2; "Welcoming Your Grief" in chapter 4; "Is It Okay for My Grieving to Feel Prolonged?" in chapter 8; "Invisible Grief" in chapter 10.)

Is It Normal to Feel Crazy?

When you are told your baby is in danger, dying, or dead, your core brain goes berserk. Literally. The most primal emotions of love, fear, anger, and sadness are triggered to the max. Your core brain is wired this way because these are the emotions that have ensured human survival throughout the ages. Love keeps you connected to others, which boosts survival. Sadness is what you feel when you lose an important connection, keeping you motivated to stay in contact, which boosts survival. Fear and anger are tied to the "fight, flight, or freeze" reaction, which boosts survival. And so when your baby's life is threatened and then gone, your brain goes crazy—crazy with fear, anger, sadness, love, and longing. (See also chapter 3, "How Your Brain Is Affected.")

Because mourning a baby's death can be such a powerful experience, full of bewildering thoughts and feelings, many parents wonder if they are going crazy. Some of the more worrisome disturbances include insomnia, fatigue, aching arms, lack of concentration, disorientation, forgetfulness, confusion, irritability, guilt, anxiety, despair, hopelessness, illusions of hearing or seeing the baby, and wishing for death. You may feel crazy for how deeply you long for your baby. You may feel crazy for having powerful urges to engage in nurturing behaviors. However, since most parents have these bewildering, intense, unpredictable, and overwhelming experiences, this "crazy journey" is quite common, and therefore *normal* and to be expected.

While these "crazy" reactions are normal, some of them do range from benign to serious. So if you have nagging concerns about your thoughts, feelings, or behaviors, or if you are feeling overwhelmed or "stuck," it may be helpful for you to talk to a professional counselor who understands bereavement and perhaps how to treat trauma. Therapy tailored to your needs can help you integrate traumatic memories, accept your powerful emotions and let them flow, and help you find ways to improve your functioning. (See also "Counseling" in chapter 13.)

It was hard going on with the daily living, all the little stuff. There wasn't a lot of sense to it for a while. I remember distinctly feeling like I was losing my mind.

—*Bess*

I tried to leave the hospital by way of jumping out the window. I can remember doing things like that, just trying to get away from it, thinking, "Now if I leave the hospital, everything will be okay." It just seems like your mind . . . you can really be a sane person, but when something like that happens, you just lose it.

—*Martina*

I knew that it wasn't crazy to feel crazy, but even though I had that understanding, it was helpful to have people around me who would say, "That's normal, it's okay to feel that way, let yourself feel that way."

—*Sophie*

Is It Normal to Find Comfort in Nurturing Behaviors?

The neighbor behind our house had a newborn, a couple of months older than Judah. I had contemplated many, many days asking her if I could come over to hold her baby. I just wanted to rock her and cuddle with her and attempt to fill that void and in hopes of that longing feeling subsiding for a while.

—*Jolie*

Powerful bonding instincts have promoted human survival through the ages. But for you, the bereaved parent, this instinct to long for and nurture your baby can feel like a cruel joke that serves no purpose but to deepen your agony. You may feel like every cell in your body is yearning, and you cannot help but dwell on your baby and your heartache. The alternative is to forget and move on, which of course is unthinkable as well as impossible, as you're wired to remain devoted.

> *The urn sits on a pink polka dot wrap that we had with her when we brought her home; I wrap her urn in this when we leave the house and carry her in my handbag. I used to take her everywhere—if I didn't I suffered from separation anxiety. If we travel, she still gets wrapped and comes with us, as I can't imagine going anywhere overnight and not taking her with us. At night I sleep with the wrap. I used to hold it, now it drapes over my pillow. It brings me some comfort and helps me feel close to her.*
>
> —Emmerson

> *There was a time where I realized with horror that I'd erased Thor's **smell** by tossing every piece of fabric that had ever touched him into the laundry. When I came home from the hospital, it felt very important to create sanity in whatever ways we could, and cleaning was part of that. Later, I desperately wanted to bury my nose in something that smelled like him.*
>
> —Elizabeth

Some parents become concerned when they find themselves or their partner cradling a pillow as if it were a baby or cuddling their baby's clothes. While these behaviors may seem strange to outsiders, you may find great comfort in these nurturing gestures. Particularly if your grieving style is "feeling/expressing," you may want to consider keeping your baby's nursery intact so you can spend time holding and caressing your baby's things. You may be comforted by

- smelling your baby's clothing,
- putting your baby's photograph under your pillow,
- sleeping with your baby's pajamas or a teddy bear meant for the baby,
- dressing a doll in infant's clothing,
- sitting in a rocking chair, cuddling a baby-sized stuffed animal,
- cradling your baby's ashes,
- writing your baby a loving note in your journal before starting the day or going to sleep at night, or
- talking to your baby.

Even though your baby is dead, your nurturing instincts may remain very strong. It is normal to find comfort in anything that helps you feel close to your baby or satisfies your nurturing urges. Engaging in these behaviors affirms your parental identity and enables you to gradually adjust to your baby's absence. These behaviors also fulfill many of the "tasks of mourning" (covered in chapters 2 and 8), including affirming your baby, dwelling on memories, acknowledging your losses, expressing thoughts and feelings, surrendering to grief, and honoring your bond. So do all the nurturing your mourning calls you to do.

> *The first time we went away for a weekend, I felt like I was abandoning Jamie. So I held the urn that holds her ashes and I wrote a little note to her, telling her how much I loved her and that we'd be back, and I put it on the dresser with her urn.*
> —Stephanie

> *I got out my favorite baby doll from my childhood and dressed her in a newborn sleeper. I slept with that doll for a couple of months around the due date. I just **needed** to have a "baby" nearby.*
> —Winnie

Is It Normal to Be Triggered by Pregnant Women and Babies?

In a word, yes, or as Julie puts it, "The year after, seeing pregnant people was a killer."

> *I struggled enormously with seeing pregnant women. It seemed like they were everywhere, taunting me. Seeing newborns felt like a dagger to the heart.*
> —Melanie

Particularly if you're a mother, pregnant women are emotional triggers because they serve as reminders of your many losses. They are reminiscent of promises broken and a blissful ignorance never to be recaptured. The same is true for newborns, who can evoke memories of your baby, remind you that your arms are empty, and renew a deep yearning for your little one. You may feel especially emotional when you see babies that trigger memories of yours—such as having any physical resemblance, being the same age as yours would have been now, or seeing a set of twins or triplets.

Being around pregnant women or babies can also arouse resentment and envy—even fury. It's so unfair! You may dread baby showers, baptisms, social gatherings, or even places where you know pregnant women or babies will be present. When your grief is most raw, it is perfectly acceptable to avoid these occasions and places in order to protect your heart.

> *It is most difficult seeing my friends and family having their children and not me! I often think how old the girls would be now and them being able to play together with our friends' and families' children and watching their milestones and knowing that I will never be able to have that with our girls!*
> —Kylie

> *We have close friends who discovered they were expecting around the same time, in fact only days separated our due dates. They had a*

*bouncy baby boy and I watch his milestones thinking of our baby girl.
He will be a constant reminder of where Adisyn would be.*
—Emmerson

Rest assured that over time, as your grief becomes softer, your emotional reactivity will subside and you can feel neutral or merely wistful. You might even have an experience where you're obligated to hold a baby, and come to realize that it's actually not as terrible or difficult as you had imagined. In fact, some mothers find it a healing step to take.

*My neighbor was pregnant the same time I was and she came over
with her baby. At first I thought, "This is really cruel." But I held her
baby and I realized, "This isn't my baby. Nobody's baby is going to
take the place of my baby. This isn't who I'm aching for. I'm aching for
that specific baby, MY baby." I was really relieved that she brought
him over and I didn't covet her baby.*
—Bryn

*My sister-in-law just had a baby girl. I was a weeny bit apprehensive
to be **so** close to a baby, but in fact it was okay. I have to say, when I
heard that she had a girl, there was a slight relief, and it just seemed
easier. Then when I saw her this afternoon, she was just that, a baby
girl and not Alex. I don't think it would have mattered even if it were a
boy; it was just a different baby. I kissed her and was kind of tempted
to pick her up, but never got round to it. I suppose there was that bit
of me that held back. However, another big hurdle, hey!*
—Victoria

IS IT NORMAL TO GRIEVE PAST LOSSES TOO?

Besides all the losses associated with the death of your baby, you may be reminded of other losses you've experienced. If other loved ones have died, you may revisit mourning for them too. If you've lost other children, you may feel that the death of this baby pushes you to the limits of your endurance.

If you find yourself dealing with old emotions or unfinished business, it helps to pinpoint those other losses—and not just those involving death. Human experience contains many different kinds of loss, all warranting some degree of grief. We all lose relationships through incompatibility, misunderstandings, shifting interests, moving to distant towns, divorce, graduations, changing jobs. These life changes can also involve loss of trust, status, opportunities, goals, familiar places, or favorite activities.

Symbolic losses deserve recognition too. For instance, if you lose your great-grandmother's jewelry in a fire, in a burglary, or by accident, you may feel as though you've also lost a part of your heritage or the last tangible part of her. Even losses and traumas you experienced long ago can be dredged up, such as giving up a pet; moving a lot as a kid; feeling neglected; being bullied, shunned, or teased; or experiencing a serious accident or illness.

When an overwhelming trauma and loss occurs, such as the death of a baby, it is normal for earlier traumas and losses to rear up and cause despair. Rather than trying to focus solely on your grief over your baby, give yourself permission to acknowledge your feelings about other losses as well. By also mourning lingering bereavements, you enhance your ability to mourn your baby's death.

Is It Normal to Feel Some Relief upon My Baby's Death?

Sometimes parents know ahead of time that death is possible or inevitable. Needless to say, anticipating death can be stressful due to the uncertainties, suspense, decision making, and worries about their baby's suffering. So when their baby dies, they may feel a sense of relief mixed with despair. Even if death is sudden and unexpected, you may feel relief that your baby does not have to suffer or okay that your baby has been released from this world or this life into the next.

> It wasn't until after she was stillborn that the doctors discovered she had a fatal heart defect. Although I'm really angry that something was wrong with her heart, and that they couldn't know it or do anything about it, I'm so thankful that she didn't have to suffer.
> —Stephanie

> I was devastated and brokenhearted for us, but relieved and happy that Dayani could now go on with her limitless and unbridled journey.
> —Destrida

You may also experience feelings of relief if the pregnancy was unplanned, or if your baby had disabilities and you weren't sure how you were going to manage long term. Margaret felt guilty about this until she realized, "I wasn't relieved that my baby died, but I was relieved that I didn't have the financial and logistical worries this child would bring."

Is It Normal to Feel So Irritable or Frustrated?

> A messy house doesn't usually bother me, but now the mess is annoying me. I think it's symptomatic of trying to control my environment and my diminished tolerance of things invading my personal space.
> —Karen

> I've set all these goals for myself that I wanted to accomplish by her birthday, and not being able to accomplish it all in time is also adding to the sadness. I want it to be special and I realize I am putting too much pressure on myself.
> —Daniela

Irritability arises because you are under a tremendous amount of stress. It isn't easy to cope with the minor inconveniences, delays, and annoyances that occur every day. You may notice that you have less patience for things that never bothered you before. Careless drivers or delays in the grocery store checkout line may bring you to the brink of violence. Your partner or other children may drive you to distraction. Frustration arises when something unplanned happens and it's hard to manage, or if you cannot find something you need, or if you simply aren't as accomplished as you're used to being. When you're mourning, it isn't so easy to shrug off these common aggravations.

> *My reactions were so strong that it was the closest thing to being insane. I'm a pretty emotional person anyway, but I don't think I've ever felt that intensely.*
>
> —Liza

> *About four months after Casey died I found myself turning around once—and I don't even know what it was, or why—and slapping my youngest child. Then I just fell to pieces, and I thought, "Oh my gosh, you can't even control yourself."*
>
> —Meryl

As discussed in chapter 3, your intense reactions are coming from your core brain being easily triggered, which is a result of being kicked up to "high alert" due to the trauma of your baby's death as well as the stress of grieving. And you'll tend to react with anger when that's the grief emotion seething under your skin. As time goes on and your grief softens, you will feel less stressed and less angry, and your patience will return. In the meantime, calm your brain by reducing stress wherever you can. Cut back on and say *no* to all but the *most* necessary commitments. For now, grief and mourning are your priorities. Even more key is to calm your brain by mindfully doing what relaxes you—draw a bubble bath, listen to music, take a brisk walk, talk to a friend, watch comedy clips, see a film. Yoga, meditation, getting adequate sleep, and being outside in nature are even more highly effective at soothing the brain. And when anger is triggered, become a mindful observer, go into your body, note the sensations, let them flow through you, and watch them dissipate as you calm. (See also "Mindfully Restoring Calm to Your Triggered Brain" in chapter 4; "Anger" in chapter 7.) It may help to remind yourself (and others!) that you are having a hard time because your baby died. Sometimes, just knowing strong reactions are a side effect of mourning can help you move more gracefully through moments of irritability and frustration.

Is It Normal to Feel Happy Sometimes?

At first many bereaved parents feel awkward if they laugh at something funny or enjoy a pleasurable activity. After all, their baby is dead. How can anything seem funny or enjoyable in the midst of such tragedy? If you aren't sad all the time, you may feel disloyal to your baby, as though you are desecrating his or her life and death.

To the contrary, it is normal—even healthy—to experience positive as well as negative emotions while you are in mourning. You deserve to have respite from the pain and still enjoy the positive experiences life has to offer.

One time I found myself whistling at work and I couldn't believe it, you know, that I'd forget for just a little while and I'd be happy. And then I'd feel guilty that I actually forgot about the baby.

—Kent

I remember the first time I laughed at something. It really hit me that I shouldn't be happy about anything, that it was wrong or disrespectful or something. But then again it was such a relief to know that I wasn't going to be this totally somber person for the rest of my life.

—Kim

In fact, it's good medicine to laugh, connect with others, and appreciate pleasures. Contentment can calm your stressed brain and body, sustaining you as you mourn. And you can actively strengthen your resilience and healing by noticing and embracing positive experiences. (See also "Mindfully Embracing Positive Experiences" in chapter 4.)

IS IT NORMAL TO GO BACK TO WORK RIGHT AWAY?

If you were employed outside the home before your baby died, you may feel pressure to give up your maternity or paternity leave and return to work. But if you'd prefer to take a leave of absence—as much as you can afford—you are completely justified in doing so for emotional and physical recovery, whether you're the mother or the father or coparent. In fact, you are justified in worrying about being able to concentrate on your work or having the energy to put in the necessary effort. You may prefer to be alone with your thoughts and your grief. The thought of having responsibility may feel overwhelming. In hindsight, Charlie wishes he'd taken off a lot more time. (See also "Advice Bereaved Parents Would Have Given to Themselves" in chapter 4.)

Depending on your duties, you might try to swing it anyway. For some parents, returning to work gives them a sense of worth, something to do, a way to be with people, or a helpful distraction from grieving.

I generally "take it easy" since returning to work. My employer is lucky enough that I can manage to convince myself to even come to work every day. And if I wear real pants (not leggings) on top of that, it's just a bonus.

—Jolie

Work has been my lifeline and the thing that gave me a sense of normality when I felt the rest of my life was falling apart. I am lucky that I love my job and it has kept my mind busy. In some ways it was nice to have one place that I could just forget my grief and act as if it had not happened for a few hours before the grief consumed me again.

—*Lorna*

Your decision may depend on finances, medical complications, whether your job is normally a stressful one, or whether returning to work requires job hunting due to quitting your job to be a stay-at-home parent. Remember, adjusting to the death of your baby has already put you under a tremendous amount of stress. To make a decision about returning to work, consider your financial, physical, and emotional needs and how you can best balance them.

Is It Normal to Feel So Alone?

Many people are unacquainted with the death of a baby until it happens to them. It is easy to feel alone and isolated when you are unaware of how many other families are struck by childbearing losses. Unfortunately, this isolation can add to feelings of self-blame and doubt.

When you feel that you're the only one, your mind can really convince you that it is directly related to your behavior, and you become paranoid. It took me so long to drop the intense guilt and questioning— "What did I do? Was I so sinful? Was this a punishment?"—on and on. When you see that it does happen to all kinds of people—through reading, seeing it on TV, joining a support group—it lessens the questioning and paranoia and helps you do the job of grieving for your child.

—*Rose*

After the first weeks or months following your baby's death, you may feel especially isolated from friends and family. You may notice that the initial rush of support from others subsides. People seem to expect you to be back to normal and may even say things like, "Aren't you over this yet?" or "Hang in there." Or "Is that still bothering you?" Because you are still mourning so intensely, these remarks can make you wonder if your feelings are silly or unjustified.

Unfortunately, as time passes and your initial numbness wears off, that's when you really start grappling with your varied losses and painful feelings. For many parents the third to sixth months can be most difficult, partly due to being discouraged by feeling worse instead of better, and partly due to feeling so alone when people aren't as supportive as they were in the beginning. For many parents, this time frame also includes the baby's original due date. You may feel distressed about grieving solo if you're worried that no one else thinks about your baby, or no one cares but you.

Today, I would have been thirty-five weeks pregnant with an adorable big baby bump. Instead I am twelve weeks without our precious baby girl, feeling lost and empty. At a time when I would have been finishing work in preparation for her arrival, setting up her nursery, nesting, and celebrating with loved ones at a shower, instead I am mourning her death, yearning for her presence, and taking each day as it comes. The sympathy cards have stopped, the flowers have died, and to a lot of people, Adisyn-Hope is but a distant memory or perhaps even considered something that never really happened at all. But for us, one of the hardest months is about to begin.

—Emmerson

Unfortunately, it is normal to find yourself in situations where people just don't understand what you are going through. And even if you want to keep it to yourself, this can feel intolerably lonely.

I went right back to work and got involved in that. I thought I had to put on this big front that everything was fine. So I was functioning and everybody expected things of me, and people were real sweet, but they didn't know that inside I was going crazy. I just remember not caring and being frustrated and just feeling like I was one big act and that inside I was dying. During the holidays, Thanksgiving was unbearable, Christmas was unbearable, everything was unbearable.

—Holly

It was hard because after a month, it seemed like everyone had "moved on," and I felt this sort of pressure to do the same. But my life had changed forever.

—Anne

Many parents turn to bereaved parent support groups, which can be a good place to meet people who will walk with you through your mourning, as you in turn walk with them. Befriending other mourning parents can reduce your feelings of isolation immeasurably. (See also "Support Groups" in chapter 13.)

IS IT NORMAL TO FEEL SO IMPATIENT ABOUT MOURNING?

Exhausting, isolating, and overwhelming. I wish grieving was a short process with a definite end date, but it doesn't work that way.

—Tanya

Mourning can be a long, often discouraging process. During the first several months you may feel that your baby's death will always be the center of your attention, that nothing positive will ever be realized, that you will never accept it or integrate it into your life, that you will never adjust or adapt. Other bereaved parents will try to reassure you that in time you will feel better, but when you are in such agony, that's hard to believe. Especially after a few months, when the shock has worn off and you are facing the stark, painful reality of your baby's death, you may feel more despondent than ever.

Even as you start feeling better, you may experience times when you feel worse. These setbacks are a normal part of the roller coaster of grief, but you may feel very frustrated and discouraged that you can still feel so terrible. Kim observes, "Time seems to be dragging, taking forever! The bad days are as bad as ever, less frequent but just as bad—like it happened yesterday, so fresh! I just try to get through one day at a time, although some days I feel like I'm just trying to get through one minute at a time."

As time goes on, these setbacks happen less frequently and, eventually, are less overwhelming. In hindsight, many parents can see that the passage of time brings healing.

I remember feeling impatient because I wanted my emotions and my heart to heal as quickly as my abdomen. I knew that wasn't going to happen, but the feeling was, "I want to be done crying, I want to be done being sad, I want to be done being angry, I just want to wrap this up and get on with my life."

—Sophie

It's a very sad thing, but you don't feel like such a victim after you get to a certain point. You just go on, and time will finally just do something that does kind of help.

—Bryn

*Time is a very good healer. I think for everything that happens to me, if I can just take a breath and think, **someday I'm going to see this from a different perspective**, I think it helps me get through.*

—Jane

Is It Normal to Feel Suicidal?

At some point, many parents feel it would be easier to die than to cope with their baby's death and the turmoil of grief. Some thoughts of suicide are harmless, while others can be quite serious, leading to an actual suicide attempt.

Basically, there are two kinds of suicidal feelings: passive and active. Passive feelings occur when you think about suicide as an option but don't make plans to actually do it. These passive thoughts of suicide are like fantasies—you comfort yourself by imagining death as an escape from despair, as a natural consequence of your devastation, or as a way to be reunited with your baby.

There were days I didn't want to keep living. I did not want to kill myself—there is a difference—I just didn't want to go on. Every day was exhausting. Why was I still here when Sam and Oren were gone? I would have died to protect them, but they were taken from me.

—Tanya

I remember that first week, waking up one night shaking and losing control. I told my husband, "I want to die, I just want to die, and I want to be with my baby and if that's what it takes, then I want to die, God just take me, please!" I couldn't take my own life, but if it happened, it would have been welcomed because I would have been with Nicole. I kept thinking, "Why didn't I die too, why didn't we both die together? And then we'd be together." At that time, Nicole was the only important thing in my life. I couldn't see ahead, I couldn't think ahead. All I thought was, "I want my baby and if that's what it takes, let it be."

—Cindy

There have been times when I have questioned whether I would survive or not.

—Emmerson

Active feelings are evident when you make concrete plans or have *even a moment of impulsive intention* for committing suicide. You may buy an overdose of sleeping pills or devise plans to drive over a cliff. Mira remembers, "I had a really bad night and I thought about overdosing on Valium, but then I thought about my husband and my two-year-old, and I couldn't do that to them."

That was the only thing that stopped me from taking my life—the knowledge of how much pain I was in and I could not do that to anyone else, even though I wanted to end the all-consuming pain.

—Lorna

I knew exactly where the gun was and I was wondering how I could do it where I would be sure that I would die and not be a vegetable. Then I would think, "No, I can't do that. I would really hurt a lot of people." And then I'd think, "No, I wouldn't, they would just go on with their lives just like after Jessica died."

—Rose

Whether thoughts of suicide are active or passive, without help, it can be a struggle to keep a clear perspective. If you have *any* concerns about your suicidal thoughts or feelings, talk to a loved one or one of the following resources:
- your doctor or midwife
- your counselor
- your faith community's clergyperson
- a suicide hotline
- a community mental health agency with a twenty-four hour or "crisis" number

For the mother, it is important to be evaluated for postpartum depression (PPD). Getting treated for PPD can alleviate many difficult symptoms, including feeling suicidal.

Even if your suicidal thoughts are merely passing fantasies, if they are more persistent than "rare and fleeting," or if you experience even one moment of serious intention, this is a sign of deep distress. Your body is telling you "I don't think I can stand it." *You don't have to struggle like this or go it alone.* In fact, there are noninvasive, brain-based therapies such as EMDR (Eye Movement Desensitization and Reprocessing) that can quickly and directly address the effects of trauma and restore wholeness and well-being far more effectively than if you try to "gut it out." Ask someone to help you reach out to one or more of the resources above. The sooner the better, as it's best for you and your brain to get this help early, rather than waiting until trauma, depression, or anxiety become entrenched. (See also "Postpartum Depression" earlier in this chapter; "Counseling" in chapter 13.)

Is It Normal to Think about My Baby So Much?

There may be times when your baby consumes your thoughts: you hear music you associate with your pregnancy, you see reminders of your little one, or you vividly dream about your baby. You may have trouble concentrating or remembering details because you are so preoccupied.

These illusions and thoughts are not abnormal or morbid. As mentioned earlier, much of the reason you dwell on your baby is that your nurturing urges are in overdrive. But also, going over your memories, hopes, and dreams is a central part of mourning. Ruminating is your mind's way of engaging in tasks of mourning, including processing experiences, integrating memories, acknowledging losses, surrendering to distress, and gradually adjusting your relationship with your baby and your future plans. For instance, you can benefit from telling your story over and over to friends and acquaintances. You also need to review, mourn, and adjust your plans, as you may have envisioned taking your baby to the beach during the summer or visiting your parents on vacation, baby in tow. Or perhaps you resent going back to work sooner than you had originally planned because you thought you would be staying home with the baby. As you dwell on your baby, you acknowledge these losses, surrender to your feelings, adjust your dreams, and make different plans. Repeatedly thinking about your baby and all the changes is the way you come to terms and gradually adjust.

Parents vary in how often they think about their baby. At first you may feel preoccupied with the circumstances surrounding your baby's life and death. As time passes and you adjust, you will gradually feel less preoccupied with your baby and you'll regain interest in other activities. Even years later, however, some parents report thinking about their babies every day or several times a week.

More important than how often you think about your baby is whether doing so prevents you from getting things accomplished. At first, this will be the case, but eventually you'll discover that you can think about your baby without dissolving into tears. If you stumble into the baby food aisle in the grocery store, you may think wistfully about what might have been, but you can still finish the shopping. If a colleague brings baby pictures to work, you can be reminded of your own baby and still finish the task at hand.

As the years pass, parents who think daily about their baby point out that it can become a ritual rather than an obsession. Some parents include their baby in nightly prayers or have a picture or other memento displayed in a special place.

It's kind of hard to describe, but I just thought about Laura all the time, just constantly. In the first few weeks I could probably think of maybe half an hour where I didn't think of her, when I was distracted. But it was just a real constant dwelling on her and talking about her and what had happened. Then it lessened and I was aware of thinking about her several times a day. But I thought about her an awful lot for an awfully long time—for at least a year, intensely for at least six months.

—Hannah

Is It Normal to Feel My Baby's Presence?

Particularly early on, you may experience mild hallucinations in which you hear, feel, or see your baby. You may feel movement in your recently pregnant abdomen. You may hear newborn nuzzling noises or a baby's cry. You may perceive motion in your peripheral vision. While you know these sensations are mirages, for a moment, they can be very convincing. As you are still struggling with shock and denial, and while your yearning is at its peak, the realness of these sensations may be quite disturbing.

At night, when I try to sleep, I hear Allex cry. His was the only baby's voice I heard. For a couple of weeks after the triplets were born, I could still feel them kicking inside me. A couple of weeks before that, it was comfort; now it's a nightmare because I know the kicks aren't real.

—Georgia

Many parents report feeling the presence of their baby's spirit. You may hold religious or spiritual beliefs that your baby exists in heaven or on another plane and that perhaps you will be reunited upon your own death. Or you may have acquired special associations that make you feel close to your baby. Many parents find symbolism in the natural world. These beliefs, symbols, and feelings of closeness can give you great comfort. Sometimes coincidences bring your baby to mind, and make you wonder.

The butterflies have been showing up at our house consistently since Oren died. Now I gather their eggs and rear the caterpillars, even being blessed with the opportunity to watch them emerge from their chrysalises.

—Lavender

When Caeden passed away, a monarch butterfly sat outside our [hospital] window till we left and it was the wrong season for them. Often when I think about the boys, a monarch butterfly will flutter by to say, "Hi, Mum." Also, every now and again I will be shedding a tear for my boys and a small white feather would appear out of nowhere as if to say, "Mum, I'm okay. I'm here with you."

—Fleur

As my grief unfolded I realized the color yellow reminded me of her. It was her visiting us. One day in the fall, our front tree at our new home turned yellow overnight. I woke up with the most peaceful feeling knowing it was her saying hello.

—Abby

Kate is buried in a native bush area and there are often tui birds in the trees, and every time I hear them up there I feel like it's Kate telling me she is okay. I find comfort in their sound. The cemetery where Zac is buried is on the flat, but from time to time I would hear a tui. I would often sit until I could hear one of them and then feel it was okay to go.

—Melanie

One evening I heard three slow knocks on the front door. I had a feeling no one would be there, but I opened the door anyway and I felt a rush of warm air. Was that Matthew?

—Kea

Do these stories show how close we are to our babies? Certainly when your baby is on your mind and always in your heart, you will be more open and sensitive to coincidences. Or are they synchronicities? Perhaps the veil between life and death is very thin, and your baby is often nearby—a thought many parents find comforting. There's so much to wonder about.

Whilst camping near Winnie the Pooh's Bridge in Sussex a few weeks back, we went into a shop and directly in front of us, we saw a solitary key ring hanging up on a display unit with the name "Alex" on it. Crazy. I bought it and it's now beside Alex's photo in my bedroom. These things continually happen to me.

—Victoria

(See also "Feeling Connected to Your Baby's Essence" in chapter 4.)

IS IT NORMAL TO FEEL LIKE A CHANGED PERSON?

I don't particularly think everything's going to go uphill all the time anymore. I don't count on things. I can't be quite as trusting as I maybe was before.

—Hannah

Not everything is as it appears. I no longer see the world through rose-tinted glasses, less naive, more discerning.

—Emmerson

I'm a new person. I don't recognize who I was before the baby died.
—Julie

I am grateful that the experience has changed me as a person . . . for the better. I cannot remember who I was before this time.
—Victoria

It has grounded me for life, and to love more deeply.
—Anne

Bereaved parents often remark that they feel changed. At first, while you grieve intensely, you may feel more temperamental, more pessimistic, and more sensitive than usual. But as you move through mourning, you will notice that it is more your perspective than your personality that changes. It's as if you are waking up, shedding your tunnel vision, and seeing a deeper level of existence. You may feel older, wiser, more vulnerable to tragedy, but also able to find comfort in being closer to what really matters. Like many parents, Anya observes, "I've learned more about myself, that I'm stronger than I thought I was." You may feel that certain things such as work, money, status, and expensive possessions have lost some of their value. Your interests may shift toward what your new priorities are. You may find a heightened appreciation for other things, including children, fertility, health, life, supportive relationships, and yourself. (See also "Recognizing the Positive" in chapter 8.)

When Jessica died, everything lost meaning. I just don't care about anything except spiritual things, eternal things, things that last. Relationships are much more important to me, deep relationships. My only long-term goal is raising my kids. Since Jessica died, being a mother means everything.
—Rose

In general, surviving great adversity often includes attaining deeper understandings, new perspectives, emotional growth, and spiritual development. For many bereaved parents, personal transformation is integral to their healing. (Read more about healing transformation in chapters 8 and 17; see also "Spirituality and Religion" in chapter 8.)

SHOULDN'T I FEEL BETTER AFTER A CERTAIN PERIOD OF TIME?

Throw deadlines out the window. Don't place expectations on yourself to feel consistently better after a certain amount of time. Give yourself permission to think your thoughts and feel your feelings, to feel bad when you feel bad and to feel better whenever that occurs. Remember that grief has its ups and downs, and you may feel discouraged when you think you're having setbacks. As long as you feel like you are generally making progress on your journey of mourning, setbacks are simply par for the course. And if you are feeling stuck, you can seek out the help and support you require.

Do what is best for you, what you need to do to grieve, manage, and adjust to your baby's death. You deserve all the time you need for mourning. (See also "How Long Will It Take?" in chapter 8.)

It's been nearly two years since Kevin died, and I'm having a hard time these days. I think I should be feeling better than this! Kevin would have been two years old this month. My baby daughter is now the age Kevin was when he died. It's the holiday season, and I should have three children, not just two. After my new baby was born, I grieved very hard. But after a few weeks I thought, "That's enough, I'm done," and I put Kevin's photo album away. But I guess I need to give myself permission to grieve some more.

—*Cathryn*

Points to Remember

- Taking care of your postpartum body can help you cope with grief and mourning.
- Lactation is a physically and emotionally painful issue for most mothers.
- As a bereaved mother, you may be more prone to postpartum depression (PPD). While grief consists of ups and downs, PPD makes you feel stuck in the downs. Prompt evaluation and treatment can relieve the unnecessary suffering this can cause.
- For the postpartum mother, fatigue, soreness, hormonal changes, and feelings of failure can affect her interest in sexual intimacy. Her partner's patience and nurturing can go a long way toward assisting her with her restoration and healing.
- It is normal to worry about your reaction to your baby's death and your ability to survive.
- It is normal to find comfort in nurturing behaviors; do what lets you remember and feel close to your baby.
- If you avoid grief, you spurn necessary suffering and get *un*necessary suffering in return.
- It is normal to feel crazy; mourning is a bewildering experience.
- After your baby dies, it is normal to feel relief that his or her suffering is over.
- It is normal to mourn previous losses; acknowledging these bereavements can enhance your ability to mourn your baby's death.
- It is normal to be irritable; reduce your stress by finding constructive outlets for your anger as well as engaging in relaxing activities.

- It is normal to be happy sometimes; accept any respite from your grief.
- It is normal to feel isolated; surround yourself with people who understand and care.
- It is normal to feel impatient with grief; let yourself have bad days whenever they appear.
- Get a medical evaluation if you are at all concerned about thoughts of suicide, or if your distress is making you think about dying.
- It is normal to think about your baby often; going over memories of your baby and what might have been can help you gradually adjust to your losses.
- It is normal to feel your baby's presence or find comfort in the belief that your baby continues to exist in a different form or on another plane.
- It is normal to feel like a changed person; many parents grow as a result of surviving this experience, and personal transformation can be integral to healing.
- It is normal to expect to feel better after a certain deadline, but allow yourself the time to mourn without regard to how many months or years have passed.

6
Affirming Your Baby

I was only pregnant for three months. So I felt no movement; I wasn't showing; I hadn't bought any maternity clothes; we told only a handful of people. But it was such a memorable time, being my first. And fortunately, a good friend bought me a pair of newborn socks, like, right away. She said, "It's never too early to collect baby things." Being older moms, we knew the risks of miscarriage, and her gesture was much appreciated at the time, as so many people wait, but then if something goes wrong, you have nothing. I am so grateful to have something that was given while the baby was alive. It truly affirms this little life.

—Winnie

Memories

I cherish my pregnancy with him, as that is the only time I knew him while he was alive. It was the only time I could feel his sweet little body moving around and guess what kind of personality and character he would have. He was very mobile which made it fun and especially neat that his daddy and brother could feel him so much too. I loved when I would be lying down reading my son a book and Jed would be moving like crazy. Those were such sweet times between the three of us.

—Embry

As soon as the sun started to reflect off the mountains, early in the morning, Pearl began to move for one last time in my womb. It was as if she knew a new day was dawning . . . the world was waking up and she was ready to go home! I was so thankful she came in the light . . . not at a secret, dark time . . . but a day all her own, when people were refreshed and ready to meet her. The day was hers!

—Laura

When Laure was born the room filled with joy. She looked so perfect. My doctor cried. My husband held her first and then my mother-in-law and my sister while the nurses tended to me. My mother-in-law sang to her and my sister held and kissed her. Everyone was saying their hellos and their quiet goodbyes.

—Daniela

After the nurse cleaned her up, she brought her over to us. I had already decided, immediately after we found out that she did not have a heartbeat, that I wanted to hold her. Holding her in my arms was an intense emotional experience—looking at the beautiful girl in front of me, noticing her father in her, weighed by the reality of our situation . . . the tears seemed to flow down my face for an eternity. My husband held her. We touched her face, her eyes, her lips. I asked if I could see her body. We took pictures with her—mom and daughter, dad and daughter, all of us together. I so desperately wanted to hear her cry. Every moment of silence was a cruel reminder of what was happening. I was filled with love and sorrow; overwhelmed with what was happening.

—Helen

I stared at her with all my power to never forget what she looked like. I touched every part of her fragile body and truly forgot about everything happening around me. For the twenty-eight hours we were with her, although she never took a breath or blinked her eyes, I know she was with us every moment. Emma's soul filled every inch of that room letting us know it was okay. She was okay.

—Abby

I started talking to him and stroking his hand, and I knew that he knew his mommy was with him. Though the meeting in the NICU was only about five minutes long, that was my special time with him. It was not so much about what I saw in him, but what I felt in my heart.

—Sonya

Our little girls were fighting for their lives. I remember looking at them both and thinking "these little bundles were inside me; we did this, we made these beautiful little girls" . . .

—Kylie

It was indescribable. Truly. But I will try—heartbreakingly sad and yet profound, awe-inspiring, transformative, and beautiful. This was my son. My firstborn child. I grew this. I birthed him. How could he be so beautiful, so perfect, so dead? I remember wanting to memorize every detail all the while fighting a deluge of grief and exhaustion and the knowledge that I am not a visual person and I would never be able to remember or know all the details of my son's body. I remember his big feet the most. Lavender said he had my nose. His eyes were closed and I wished he would open his eyes.

—Tanya

It was an experience so profound that we will likely never have such an amazing opportunity again in this lifetime. It was so peaceful to see her and watch her quietly pass away; it was nothing like the scary scenarios I played out in my head before her birth.

—Shellie

Memories are key to the process of mourning. Although often painful, recalling memories is a way for you to gradually adjust to your baby's absence. Memories allow you to reminisce about your pregnancy or the baby's special qualities and happier times. Memories enable you to create a coherent narrative that you can weave into the tapestry that contains all your life's stories. Memories make it possible for you to adjust your relationship to your baby at a gradual pace. If friends and relatives also had a chance to know this baby, their memories enable them to recognize the significance of your losses and to share your grief more easily.

I spent the days playing with her, talking to her, singing to her. Some days our son would join us at the hospital and he would talk and touch his sister. He was even jealous of her as he sensed the baby was getting more attention than he was. It was very heartwarming to watch. I will always cherish the moments that we shared with Dayani. The seven days we spent together are my most cherished memories and prized possessions. I would not trade it for the world.

—Destrida

I remember spending the most precious moments with them both— their last breaths, holding them in our arms, having photos taken with them, and being able to have them both at home. The photos are so, so precious to us now.

—Kylie

We did have a trip to Ireland planned about three weeks after her prenatal diagnosis. We debated about even going, but in the end decided to go. Ireland was the place to go with our sad and weary hearts. It was cold and gray but the fields were glowing green. We took her to a huge castle, lit a candle for her in an old cathedral, walked though one of the oldest cemeteries in the area, and cried a lot. I am so thankful for the memories of the time with her in that place.

—Laura

As discussed in chapter 1, a baby's death is more challenging to mourn because of the relative lack of time and memories to recall or share with others. This lack makes grieving difficult, whether you are able to recall a little person you got to know or simply a person who might have been. Your baby is gone, leaving little tangible evidence of his or her existence. Most notably, grieving can be painfully difficult because the lack of memories makes your adjustment seem overwhelming and goodbyes too abrupt.

In the past, parents were encouraged to forget their babies. It was assumed that a bond had not yet formed, and the less there was to remember, the easier it would be to forget and move on. However, it is not so easy. The parental bond can run deep even before conception. The mother in particular is physiologically invested in nurturing and raising *this* baby, and to forget is to abandon a part of herself. In fact, having less to remember can make grieving more complicated.

Indeed, remembering and affirming your baby facilitates your ability to grieve and adjust to a different future. You benefit from getting to know your baby and gathering as many memories as possible. Like most parents, you may ache for more.

A lot of people say, "It would've been worse if she had lived." But I think if I had even one hour with my child alive, thank God for that hour. I feel cheated. . . . I didn't have any time with her outside of my body. I thought, "If you just give me fifteen minutes, just a little bit of time—just to tell her that I love her and to know that she heard me and to know that she knew, that she was alive and breathing when I told her that." So I don't like people to tell me that it would've been worse.

—Cindy

I was holding Blake as he took his last breath. This is a part of my life that I will never be able to let go. It is a memory that I hold on to with every ounce of myself.

—Sonya

EVERY BABY IS IMPORTANT

Once upon a time, stillborn babies were whisked away and the mothers didn't see them. But now hospitals let parents hold their stillborn babies, so they can say goodbye. No one seems to understand that first they have to say hello. . . . Not for half an hour like the hospital staff wanted. Not for the six hours I negotiated when they couldn't give me a reason for the half-hour limit. . . . I said hello to my stillborn son in the days that followed, in visits to the funeral parlor, in his visits to our home, which should have been his. So began my life with Thor.

—Elizabeth

When your baby dies, you need to affirm your baby's life however possible—by gathering mementos such as ultrasound pictures or photographs taken during that time, sorting through your baby's things, or having opportunities to see or spend quality time with your baby. If you're lucky, you got the guidance you needed.

My sister's best friend's sister had a stillborn baby boy two years prior and her advice was so invaluable. She gently shared with us things she wished she'd done or what she did do. She was a familiar voice for us in a world we had no clue about.

—Abby

After your baby dies, you also need to affirm your baby's importance and the significance of your losses. To do this you may want to arrange rituals and create memorials that acknowledge your baby's life. By having a funeral or memorial service or by sending out announcements, you are inviting family and friends to recognize your grief, giving them a chance to realize your baby's importance and to grieve along with you. These rituals also provide you with more memories of your baby. Creating memorials can help you honor your baby's place in your life. Visiting the gravesite or the place where you keep the ashes also commemorates your baby's existence.

There is a park that has always been special to us so we dropped off Jedidiah's ashes near there and we visited the park every fourteenth day of the month for the first year. Now we go every year on his birthday, as well as whatever holidays or days we feel like going. We usually do a balloon release but not always. Initially it was an easy way to let big brother remember him and go through his own grief, but it has been so helpful for all three of us and at a place so beautiful that we have always loved.

—Embry

Sadly, some opportunities for making memories, collecting mementos, and engaging in certain rituals may have already passed. It may be too late to take photographs, clip a wisp of hair, or dress the baby. In retrospect you may wish you had decided on burial instead of hospital cremation. After a multiple birth, you may wish you could know whether your babies were identical or fraternal. But without guidance, how could you have known what would be comforting to do? These circumstances must be grieved also. Expressing anger, disappointment, and sorrow at these losses can help you mourn them.

*At this hospital they didn't take pictures, they didn't save anything, they didn't do anything. I didn't realize at the time that you need all these things. I didn't know that the mementos would be important, that the picture would be all-important, and that holding the baby is real important for the grieving process. . . . That's probably, above all, the thing that makes me the angriest or the saddest. It's like, if she **had** to die, they could've at **least** handled it right!*

—Holly

Kevin was our second child, and you know how it is with the second one. In the three months he was with us, I only took enough pictures to fill three pages in the photo album. I never clipped a wisp of his hair. I feel so bad about that. I wish I had more things to remember him by.

—Cathryn

If one or more babies died from a multiple pregnancy, you will especially benefit from the acknowledgment that "every baby is important." Even if you're not encouraged to do so, you can acknowledge all your babies as valued individuals, no matter how many have died and how many have lived, or the timing of death, even if months before. It can be particularly helpful for you to assign names, collect mementos for each baby, and label your keepsakes. If you wish, you can ask people to refer to the babies separately by name, instead of lumping them all together as "the twins," "triplets," "quads," or more. You may also find it meaningful to collect or notice artwork and other objects that contain two, three, or four of anything. Whether you are raising survivors or all the babies died, this can help you to recognize each baby as a separate identity, and at the same time the specialness of their twin, triplet, quad, and so forth, connection.

Even though you may have some regrets about decisions made or circumstances that may have been out of your control, there are still some things you can do. It's never too late to remember and memorialize your baby(s) in special ways.

> *I continue to honor Bryce's life, by keeping my promise that I made to him in my hospital room that very sad day, when we had our one-on-one time alone. I promised him that he would always be loved and always be included in our family forevermore. So, we keep the promise by including him in our daily lives. By keeping his picture in a frame for all to see, everyone knows that we are parents to **four** boys, not three!*
>
> —Lori

REMEMBERING YOUR BABY

> *I found that I was able to move forward in my life by realizing that I did **not** have to say goodbye to my son who died. Yes, I had to say goodbye to his body, but I did not have to say goodbye to his memory or to his very special and meaningful place in our family. Choosing to remember and include him was very healing and freeing for me.*
>
> —Lori

MEMORIES OF YOUR PREGNANCY

> *I loved the way Oren danced inside of me. How he would kick the floor of the yoga studio as I contorted myself into the pigeon pose on Monday nights. I loved how he would get really still after my partner would zerbert [raspberry] my belly. I am sure he was wondering, "What the heck was that?"*
>
> —Tanya

Your pregnancy holds a major chunk of memories of this baby. These memories can be especially important if your baby died early in the pregnancy, if you received a prenatal diagnosis, or if you were not able to spend adequate quality time with your little baby after the birth. You may recollect the day you discovered you were pregnant, the excitement of hearing the heartbeat, or the first time you saw your baby's image on an ultrasound screen. If you carried your baby well into the second trimester, you may be able to remember the first time you felt your baby move inside you. Was this a quiet or a rambunctious baby? Did he get the hiccups often? Did she like to stretch out? You may want to set aside a few maternity outfits that you especially associate with this time, instead of giving them away. Your "positive" pregnancy test slip or any ultrasound pictures may also be cherished as mementos.

You may even have photos taken during the pregnancy—of you or of places you went, carrying your baby along in your belly. Embry feels especially fortunate, noting, "We decided to have pictures done. So I happen to have maternity photos that I cherish so much!" Rituals and celebrations also provide memories. Tanya had a Blessingway (rooted in Navajo tradition) during her pregnancy with Oren. She says, "I am so grateful for my family and friends who celebrated my pregnancy with me and who had hopes and dreams for this baby." Whatever memories and mementos you have, they can be of benefit—and treasured.

> *I remember the few fluttery kicks that I felt a few days before she passed. I feel grateful that Elizabetta* **was**.
>
> —Karen

Still, it's common to wish you hadn't taken your pregnancy so much for granted, now that you realize the treasure trove of memories that time could hold. If your baby died before birth, you may wish you could go back in time and do more nurturing of your baby during the pregnancy. As meaningful as nurturing after death is, you want to know that during your baby's life, she or he actually be experienced your love.

> *I grew a perfect bump—all baby, many people would say—and my bump became "our basketball." The kicks I would get were so strong and definitely made my tummy wobble. . . . Oh, how I wish I could go back in time and cherish those moments. When you squirmed, moved around, and kicked inside of me you showed me a glimpse of your personality. I knew that you were going to be such a monkey just like your sister.*
>
> —Courtney

> *I wish I would have known that Oren was dying or was going to die. I would have wanted to spend more time intentionally connecting to him. If I had known he was dying I think I would have wanted to sing or play my cello for him as he died. No regrets, only oceans of sorrow.*
>
> —Tanya

If your baby was born at a hospital or clinic, you may find it helpful to go over the events of labor and birth with your doctor, midwife, and nurses, especially if you were medicated. If you have unanswered questions about your baby, even if it is years later, you can request medical records from your doctor, your midwife, or the hospital. The more you know, the more complex and detailed your narrative becomes, and the more meaningfully and fully you can integrate it into the story of your life. You may even discover something you didn't know about yourself or your baby, which can help restore wholeness.

> *I went back later to the hospital and met my primary nurse because I wanted to know everything that had happened. She answered all my questions and told me everything my mind couldn't fill in. She told me what the baby looked like, which was really sweet because that's really all I have, is what she told me.*
>
> —Holly

When my second baby died at eighteen weeks, they didn't let me see it. They wouldn't even tell me if it was a boy or a girl. The doctor just said, "You don't need to know that." So now, seven years later, after my baby girl Susan was stillborn, it brought back a lot of questions about my other baby. With the encouragement of my support group, I went back to that hospital and requested the medical records to get some answers. The baby was a little boy—I named him David—and now I feel like I have a better idea about what I lost, who I grieve for.

—Janet

MEMORIES OF BEING WITH YOUR BABY

*When our son was born I did not want to look at him. I had just felt the heavy silent baby slip out of me onto the bed. I was trying to catch my breath after labor and steel myself for the moment when I would have to look at the face of my dead child. Lavender, in a moment of profound wisdom said, "Look down, the baby is beautiful." This gave me the strength to look at our son and to hold him close on my chest. It was a boy and he **was** beautiful. What I found out later was that Lavender said this before looking at the baby herself. She knew what I needed to hear to be able to open my eyes, and if I could look at him then she could look at him too.*

—Tanya

I was not sure if I wanted to see Ronin, as I had never seen a dead body … but he was perfect and just looked like a sleeping baby. I held him, took pictures, changed his clothing, and just looked after him. I remember looking at his body and just looking at his hands and feet and his hair. Just marveling at something so perfect. The only thing missing was a heartbeat and those cute baby noises they make when they are just born.

—Lorna

This was my initial impulse: to get to know my baby. We didn't even know his biological sex till he was born. So we discovered he was a boy. We discovered that he had thin dark hair, and that he was big. We discovered that he was dead. We were discovering all those things at the same time, and we wanted to get to know him, with whatever characteristics he had.

—Elizabeth

We spent seven hours with Willow. We were given the choice but decided not to bathe her. We just wanted to savor her smell and her olive skin and her dark hair and her perfect toes and fingers.

—Nathan

As you grieve, you can reflect on memories of being with your baby. During your pregnancy, your baby was cradled inside you. If you were able to see and hold your baby, you can try to remember how he or she looked and felt. If your baby lived many days or months after birth, you had more opportunities to get to know your baby. Although it may never seem like enough, these memories can be cherished.

> *I remember when they brought David in. My husband was standing there at the bed and I was lying in the bed and the nurse walked in the door with the baby all wrapped up as a newborn, and I remember thinking in that short distance from the door to me, "What was she going to do? Was she going to put him in my arms? Was she going to lay him on the bed? What was she going to do?" And very naturally she walked in, didn't say a word, and handed me the baby and left. We immediately started to cry very, very hard, and I took his little hand and held it around my finger the way you do any baby and I just held him like that and kept looking at him . . . and then my husband leaned down and kissed him on the forehead.*
>
> —Bess

> *After what seemed like eternity, the neonatologist was able to stabilize the baby and he brought Dayani to my arms. I held her for the first time. My heart broke into a million pieces seeing all the wires and tubes going in her body. But suddenly her eyelids opened and she looked straight at me and her father. It felt like we made a connection. Like it was a purposeful look, not one of those newborn reflexes. It was beautiful moment. She never opened her eyes like that again after that . . .*
>
> —Destrida

> *Right before they took Stephanie off the machines, we each had hold of one of her hands. . . . Then she opened her eyes and she was gripping each of our hands, which was amazing because she was so sick. It was like she was acknowledging we were there. It was as though she were saying, "It's okay, I love you and I know you love me and I'm leaving." It was amazing we both had that same sense, that message from her.*
>
> —Sophie

Memories of being with your baby, before and after death, are important because they confirm the fact that a baby really existed. If you were able to see your baby, this experience helps you view him or her as an individual and gives you someone tangible to mourn. Seeing your baby satisfies curiosity about your baby's appearance and lets you admire family resemblances. Taking care of your baby affirms your role as parent. Shellie says, "I treasure the memory of treating her like any other baby—holding her, bathing her, taking photos, reading stories to her, and snuggling with her in my hospital bed. Abby agrees: "The bathing, dressing, holding of her are *such* cherished and memorable moments for me." Holding and touching your baby also gave you an opportunity to express your love in a physical way. Being with your baby gave you an opportunity to say hello *and* goodbye.

*He was **so little**. . . I knew there was no way he could live, he was just too little. As they were wheeling him by they let me hug him, and I told him his name and I told him how much I loved him . . . because I knew I wouldn't have much chance to do that.*

—Lena

I unraveled the blanket she was wrapped in and looked at her body. She was beautiful. The doctors allowed me to spend as much time as I needed with her, and my husband and I spent the night with her sleeping between us.

—Daniela

*We took our Emily home with us, until her funeral. I just wanted her with us. **Home** with us. For as long as possible.*

—Anne

I was only twelve weeks along, and being able to see the tiny baby helped. She fit right in the palm of my hand. . . . I wasn't sure what to wrap her in for the trip to the hospital, and then I thought of my grandmother's lace handkerchiefs. So I picked one out and wrapped her up very carefully.

—Clara

The midwife wrapped her up in a little blanket and handed her to me. I just marveled in her beauty. She was an identical image of her brothers, a perfect merge of the two of them together.

—Sarah

*I am grateful that I had time with both my children. I had the opportunity to hold them, kiss them, and cherish their little features. I even saw the start of my husband's nose in **my son** Blake.*

—Sonya

I think when I was going through nursing school, the attitude was more, "Just don't let the mother see the baby." And that's the opposite of what you really need. Holding her was good because we knew her from during the pregnancy, and now here she was and she was a real baby and a real person. That helped, rather than just, "She's gone, there's nothing to it, just like it didn't happen, you didn't have that baby inside you for nine months and just forget about it . . ." There really was a baby there.

—Hannah

Parents also find it immensely comforting and validating when relatives or close friends are able to meet their baby. Mel remembers, "Watching my friends meet my little boy seemed to validate his life. To prove that he was real and that he did exist." You may feel especially heartened when others hold and kiss your baby. Lori recalls, "I was so touched that my mom voiced the desire—and need—to spend time with her grandson. That means the world to me!" It may also have been important to you that your older children got to meet their sibling.

They all got to meet her, some with hesitation and some with absolute love. I'll never forget a friend asking if they could kiss her. Still brings tears to my eyes.

—Abby

We were debating showing our boys, Matthew (three) and Ryan (one), their sister, before we left for the funeral that Friday morning. Emily's body was already changing in the hospital, and what would she look like, almost a week later? It did not matter to me, what she looked like. She was beautiful when born, and remained beautiful. Some family members thought that it was too much doing that, but I do not regret it.

—Anne

Derek, who was twelve, arrived at the hospital unexpectedly with his grandmother, after the birth of his brother. He had been afraid to go but his grandmother had convinced him to come and meet his baby brother and to say "goodbye." This was a profoundly important moment for Derek and for our entire family. I think it gave Derek the chance to bond with his brother and to start his own healing and grieving. He has gone on to make several art projects in honor of his brother and to talk to other kids about loss.

—Tanya

Seeing the baby after birth also alleviates fears about the baby being horribly deformed. Fantasies are usually much worse than reality, and parents are often relieved at how normal and beautiful their baby looks. Even if the baby is malformed, parents focus on and find comfort in positive body features, as they are looking through eyes of love. If you were discouraged from seeing every part of your baby's body, you may regret missing out on this. As Emmerson says, "We weren't able to see her adorable face and I felt robbed of that because all I wanted to do was kiss her button nose."

If your baby died before or shortly after birth, some people will wonder if holding your baby makes grief more painful because you risk becoming too attached. You can remind them that you've already held your baby in your womb and felt a deep bond long before the birth. Abby sums it up when she says, "I'm grateful for the amazing time we had with her, and that both our families were there to meet her and love her." Plus, as the mothers below explain, seeing the baby after death can be therapeutic, helping the mind register and verify that the baby is dead.

*I thought the doctor was awful when he asked me if I wanted to hold Caleb after he died. I thought about it though, and agreed to. . . .
When I first saw him, he was gray and pale and I just screamed with devastation. It hurt so badly . . . but I did hold my son for the first and last time with no tubes or hoses in the way. It was the most fulfilling thing I could have done outside of taking him home with me. I now have a wonderful memory to carry me through the hard times.*

—Ginger

I was glad I held the baby. It helped a lot to be able to see him and hold him and know that they didn't take our baby and give it to someone else and give us a dead baby. It helped to know that he was ours.

—Martina

We did see her body changing, right before our eyes. It was hard. But it was then that I truly realized, she was gone. Her body was turning back to dust. Her soul was with God. And this was my daughter. My baby. It was life changing.

—Anne

If I hadn't seen her, definitely her—with the hospital band that said Jessica—dead, I don't think I could've settled it in my mind that she was really dead.

—Rose

After he was born they brought him up to the bed, and my husband and I sat and looked at him and touched him. I was glad. That was really the best thing that could've happened. I think I thought he was probably a monster, that he was deformed, that there was something wrong with him. He was a beautiful baby. I think it also helped to ease the sorrow and filled in all those empty areas where I could have wondered what he looked like. Just seeing him gave him a personality, a real concrete substance.

—Meryl

*Two nurses took time to go down and get my babies because I could not stop crying. How I **needed** to see them again—to undress them and look at them and create the only memories we will have. . . . They put Kayla and Regina on the overbed table and watched as I unwrapped them. One nurse silently cried while the other one stood by me telling me how beautiful they were. That made me feel so good—knowing they understood. Then they left us alone and closed the door so Rob and I could be alone with our babies. For an hour and a half, we were a family.*

—Deidre

If you were not encouraged or allowed to see your baby, you may feel angry or cheated or desperately curious about your baby's appearance. You may feel an added sense of loss that not only is your baby dead, but you were denied the only chance you had to hold him or her. If you had a miscarriage, you may not have known what to look for, or your doctor may not have allowed you to see the baby or the remains. Being able to see whatever there was might have been helpful.

If you had some babies survive from a multiple birth, you may not have been encouraged to see the baby(s) who died. This misguided effort to have you focus on the living robs you of memories and mementos. This also discounts the individuality and specialness of each baby you carried in your womb. Even if you were encouraged to see all your babies, you might not have had the opportunity to hold or see them all together, to validate the experience of "my twins," "my triplets," or "my quads." If you missed this chance, you may feel preoccupied with somehow getting them all together or being recognized as a parent of multiples. An artist's rendering of all your babies together can be quite healing.

Although researchers have found that most parents are very grateful for the time spent with their babies, there are some parents who fear that seeing the baby, having photographs, or taking the baby home would be too upsetting. Even with encouragement, many parents are in shock, reeling from the trauma of their baby's death. They cannot truly comprehend their options and find it very difficult to make decisions, figure out what they need, or attend to details. Some don't receive adequate support from the people around them. When parents are simply asked once, "Do you want to see your baby?" (or "have photographs" or "take your baby home"), many of those parents who reflexively or hastily say, "No," later regret missing out. If you said "No," you may not even remember doing so, and perhaps what you were really saying was, "No, I am too stunned, nor do I want to face this reality." (See also "Survival Mode" in chapter 3.) As a result, it's unfortunately all too common for these parents to have regrets.

> *Lavender says that when Oren was born they offered to let me take him home. Honestly, I don't really remember this, but much of that day was a blur. She says that I said "No," and I am sure that this was because of Derek. I did not want to bring the baby home because I thought that that would bring a sad memory of death into our house and I wanted our home to feel like a safe place for our twelve-year-old. Of course, now I wonder what it would have been like to have had Oren at home.*
>
> —*Tanya*

Fortunately, hospital policies are changing and more health care practitioners are getting the training they need to slowly and supportively walk parents through making informed decisions that are right for them. Perhaps you benefited greatly from receiving individually tailored reassurance and guidance. You might also have benefited from another bereaved parent offering you advice.

> *Another bereaved momma gently shared with us things she did or wished she'd done. She also told us to take lots of pictures and look at every part of her little body. And the nurses and doctors were amazing. They gave us all the time we wanted. And they held her with such love.*
>
> —*Abby*

And even if you didn't hold or see your baby, you can find comfort and meaning in the other ways you spent time with your baby, such as during the pregnancy, knowing your partner was with your baby, or hearing that your baby was tenderly cared for.

Alex was very active inside. I felt as though I knew him inside and not on the outside, and to this day, I'm comfortable with not holding him. I am grateful for seeing him. Specialists asked whether I wanted to hold him and within a nanosecond, my mum said in a softly spoken voice, but deliberate, "Don't do it, Victoria." My husband was right next to me and briefly explained that he had held him throughout intensive care and was very much part of his very short life, and that the hospital minister had come to baptize him. It is comforting and meaningful that my husband cherished, cuddled, and kissed Alex during the seven hours of his life.

—Victoria

With babies who die in the first or second trimesters of pregnancy, changes are coming about more slowly. If you wish you could have seen and held your baby, inform your doctor or midwife. You can also express other hindsight wishes, such as increased support during miscarriage or the option of labor induction rather than resorting to a more invasive surgical intervention. These options and opportunities may then be offered to others.

The doctor wouldn't tell me anything about Matthew. He just said, "The baby was normal. That's all you need to know." But I've had nightmares about him, what he is like in the grave, digging him up, things like that. I still wonder what he looked like. Every once in a while I think about what's happening in the grave, and I don't know why I do that. I guess I just wonder what it would be like to look at him now. I think I'm just obsessed. I needed to see him.

—Desi

Never Enough Time

I remember feeling conflicted. I wanted to hold my son and memorize his appearance and the way he felt in my arms, but I could see that, as time went on and he was handled more and more, his skin became damaged and his color grew mottled. I wanted him to go to the funeral home so that he could look as good as possible for the funeral. Now I wish I could have had time alone with him—time to rock him, sing to him, and to apologize to him for not being able to fight back death.

—Tanya

Parents who are able to see their baby are generally glad to have that experience. However, they also report regrets, such as wanting more time with their baby or wishing they'd done more nurturing things such as cuddling, examining their baby's entire body, bathing and dressing their baby, or taking their baby home to provide hospice or after-death care. You may also have specific regrets around what was made impossible by your baby's condition. Stephanie wishes she could have seen the color of her stillborn daughter's eyes or felt the grip of her tiny hand. These are common regrets of parents whose babies are born still, very sick, or premature.

With Emily, I regretted not seeing her back. I do not know why I did not turn her over to see her back. And I did not lay her on me to do kangaroo bonding.

—Anne

I have all the memories of him kicking, his somersaults inside of me, but I never got to see his beautiful eyes open or the way his tiny fingers would curl around my fingers.

—Courtney

I wish I had opened Oren's eyes. I don't know what color they were.

—Lavender

I wish I could've seen him move. I wish I could've held a warm baby, not a cold one.

—Charlie

Although it can be painful, it is necessary to grieve for these missed opportunities. You can cope more easily if you pinpoint these moments and talk or write about your thoughts and feelings instead of burying them and letting them fester. (See also "Mindful Journaling" in chapter 4.) It can also be comforting to know that you are not alone in feeling this way.

I remember her being brought to us and having the priest bless her. I was too unwell and asked for her to be put nearby as I worried I would drop her from the bed. A couple of hours later I got to spend some time with her, just talking to her but mostly I dozed with my hand on top of the box she was in. I regret that we didn't get to hold her, that no one suggested or facilitated getting more photos. I regret not being physically capable of being more "present."

—Karen

If your baby was placed in the NICU or transported to another hospital for treatment, you may regret that you were unable to spend more time with your baby before death. Rose's baby was transported to a children's hospital after delivery, but they didn't run any tests for two days. She says, "I'm really angry about that. . . . If she was just lying there, she could've been lying there with me. I just remember there was no concern about me being with the baby. Of course, at the time I thought I'd have a lifetime with her so I wasn't that concerned."

When Matthew was born they handed him to me and said, "Oh, this looks like a healthy little baby boy." He was beautiful. But the nurse picked him up right away because he was having trouble. So that was the only time that I got to hold him while he was alive and it just seemed like it was only a second. Looking back on it now, I wish I could've held him a little longer, but I just didn't see the tragedy that was going to occur. When he was in intensive care, we kept vigil as much as we could. I was right on top of him, as close as I could be to him. Then, after he died, I demanded that we see him. It was like, "You're not *taking my baby. I want to see him RIGHT NOW." Nowadays, I wish I could have held him much, much more before **and** after he died.*

—*Kara*

Whatever the circumstance, it is common for parents to wish that the doctors and nurses had been more adamant about connecting them with their little babies—before *and* after death.

I did not explore Bryce's body. I never even thought to do it. No one was there to talk to me about it. I so wish that I had a caregiver who could have explained why to do these things and helped me to see the preciousness of these final, once-in-a-lifetime parenting moments with my son.

—*Lori*

I remember after she was born and was taken away, waiting and waiting and watching the door. The midwife checked and rechecked whether we wanted to see her and then had to tell us that she was concerned, as the hydrops had affected her face. I remember crying and saying, "Have I not been punished enough, you took her from us and then we weren't even able to see her?" In the end they wrapped her so we could see and hold her perfect little hands and feet and we nursed her in the Moses basket. It was surreal. I think I may have been in shock. I recall Ben cradling the basket, looking lovingly at her and saying over and over, "You poor wee girl."

—*Emmerson*

Parents also benefit from having more time to recover from shock or from anesthesia so they can spend more meaningful time with their baby. Kelly points out, "I really resent not being awake for Scott's delivery. I can accept his death a lot better than I can accept not being with him for the few hours he was alive." Seeing their baby over a long period of time also helps parents remember more.

I still feel kind of cheated because I was in such a state of shock. I remember looking at the baby, but I cannot remember what he looked like. I remember asking the doctor to go ahead and take him away because I was afraid I was going to get crazy and say, "No, you can't have my baby." I don't think I would have, but you just don't know what you're doing. I wish they had offered him to us again later.

—*Bryn*

After I came out of the anesthesia I was really out of it, but the doctor brought her into the recovery room. . . . I held her and touched her but I couldn't really move or anything because I was in such pain. One of the things that's real frustrating to me is I can't remember her because I was so out of it.

—*Holly*

When parents don't have enough time with their little one, it may not occur to them to unwrap their baby and caress the little body or dress the baby in special clothing. As Erin says, "It would've helped me to be able to dress her, so she could've felt my touch somehow." Some parents wish they'd had more privacy so that they could have felt free to explore their baby's body or express emotions without feeling self-conscious. Kara recalls, "There were people there and it was great having their support, but I just kept feeling interrupted."

Some parents regret giving in to pressure from a partner or other relatives to not see the baby or to cut the visit short. Lena, Rose, and Kara had husbands or other relatives who were trying to protect them from their sadness instead of letting them face it.

Life support was taken off him, and we let him go for it. Looking back on it, I wish I had held him as he died. But at the time, I think my husband was trying to protect me because he knew how much I wanted that baby. So when he approached me about it, he said, "You don't want to hold him now do you?" and I went, "No. . . " I deferred to his judgment. I was a little mouse. Looking back on it, I wish that I had cuddled Stephen close. If I had to do it over again, I would pick him up and hold him, hug him, rock him, talk to him, and sing to him. Hugging him in his incubator isn't quite the same.

—Lena

*My husband felt like I needed to rest, so I remember he took me home. I was fighting and screaming all the way. I didn't want to go. I just wanted to spend the time with the baby. This was the first day I'd had with her and he was just **so** insistent and at the time I just wasn't as confident. I wasn't the kind of person who would say, "I'm staying. You can go home if you want to." I wasn't that person then. I was a lot younger, dumber, and less confident. So now I have all these things I should have done, to spend any second that I had with her.*

—Rose

*My mother-in-law was saying, "Well, you know, you need to let go. The longer you hold on to him, the harder it is to give him up." And I was kind of, "Well, maybe she's right." But I could've held on to him longer. I **wanted** to hold on to him longer.*

—Kara

Many parents give up their baby before they are ready, as they feel unsupported, confused, rushed, or morbid. Looking back, many parents wish that the nurses had offered the baby again, more than once or twice, or simply left the baby in the room until discharge. Some wish that the nurses had explained how to take care of the body and what other parents have found helpful to do and why. In hindsight, you too may wonder why you didn't demand more time with the baby or do more things like kissing and cuddling. But you did the best you could at the time with the support you were given.

The only regrets I have are not spending as much time holding and cuddling my daughter. I knew I could pick her up and cuddle her as often as I liked, but I wish the midwives had encouraged me to do it more. It is extremely difficult to bring yourself to pick up your dead baby. You really want to but it is the hardest thing to actually do.

—Sarah

*After I announced that we were ready to say goodbye, I was asked if I wanted to spend more time with Bryce, but it was not explained to me what I could have done with that extra time. With no in-depth explanation, I chose to say goodbye after only three hours. I just didn't see the point of prolonging things, I guess. But I would have spent more time with Bryce **if** it had been explained to me that a common regret that they hear from bereaved parents is **not spending more time** with their babies. Just knowing that other bereaved parents did such things somehow gives you permission to do it as well, or something similar.*

—Lori

I wish we had gone to see him at the funeral home. I wish I had gone and taken him for a walk, just me and him.

—Lavender

Parents may also regret that the option of taking the baby home was not offered, or that they decided not to do it because of inadequate support. But some parents are satisfied with not taking their baby home. Destrida notes, "I am not sure I would want to take her home. Once she died, I saw it was her physical being that we held, not our daughter anymore." Accommodating personal preferences is key and merely underscores how important it is for you to be guided in determining for yourself what would be meaningful. If you didn't receive enough guidance, this is another loss to grieve.

*The "natural funeral" movement, which can include caring for the body of your loved one at home, is simply unfamiliar to most people in our culture. For some people, the initial reaction is one of revulsion. But then, as soon as they stop to think about it, they often realize: yes, they **have** seen those old movies where the body lies in state in the family's living room and people visit to pay their respects, touching the hand or cheek of the deceased and whispering a few words. This can be a very loving and intimate way to say goodbye.*

—Elizabeth

There's simply no way around it: relinquishment is always hard. Lavender remembers a woman from the funeral home coming to collect their baby. She says, "When we actually put Oren into that stranger's arms, my heart broke a little more." Abby agrees: "I have no regrets, besides wishing we wouldn't have left her. That was the hardest thing I've ever done." Even parents who feel like they spent plenty of time with the baby will always wish they could have had more time, a lifetime with the baby. Jolie observes, "As bereaved parents, we will never be satisfied. We will always be left wanting more until we get our healthy, live baby back."

Part of me was not, and will never be ready to say goodbye. Part of me will always be there in the hospital room trying to memorize my son's features, wanting to hold him as closely as possible to my heart. Telling him that I love him in a thousand different ways and without using words at all. For a brief shining moment our souls danced together in one body and the deep violation of losing him produced an emptiness that I will never be able to fully heal.

—Tanya

The last couple of hours were just Eliza and I and our Willow. Despite holding her all day, her body inevitably cooled and stiffened and became less alive looking. We hung on to those last anguished moments with Willow. We held her tightly together and our souls wept and screamed as we said our final goodbye. And as we sat there, a summer storm whipped up outside the window of the birthing room, the blinds shook as thick, angry, heavy rain lashed against the windows and lightning and thunder filled the sky. Somehow the storm was comforting, as if God was raging beside us.

—Nathan

PHOTOGRAPHS

The pictures I have of Judah are the most precious, priceless things I own. I couldn't imagine not being able to picture my son. Even just having the physical pictures of him serves as evidence that yes, I had a son. He existed. He mattered. He is real.

—Jolie

I recently finally put a picture of Jed's sweet face out in our living room next to pictures of his brothers. I love the statement it makes, that he is just as much a part of our family as any one of us.

—Embry

Dayani's pictures are all over the house and on the fridge mixed up with other family pictures. Everyone who comes to the house can see that she is still very much in our lives and will continue to be in our lives.

—Destrida

Photographs can be some of your most treasured mementos. Particularly if you experienced an early miscarriage, any pictures of you during that pregnancy can be special, or you might have a photo from an ultrasound scan. As Tanya says, "The ultrasound photos . . . they still make me cry. There is a little fuzzy baby there who was my daughter." Courtney realizes she might actually prefer her ultrasound pictures as they were taken when her baby was still alive, whereas, "The only photos of Beau are when he is dead. My heart is breaking again at this thought . . . time to look for the scan photos."

If your baby never left the hospital, a health care practitioner may have taken photographs, or you may have been offered the services of a volunteer professional photographer. Perhaps you used your own camera. If your baby was at home, you may have many photographs to keep. Having at least one good quality photograph can help you remember your baby. Along with other mementos, a photo helps affirm your baby's existence and your bond, and can strengthen memories of that time.

I'm really glad we have pictures. I look at them a lot. Some people think that they're kind of gruesome, but they're real important to me.

—Jessie

I'm glad we've got a picture because you never forget the baby, but you can forget how they look, and later on if you want to look at it, you can.

—Martina

I have photographs of every inch of her body. From the tip of her nose right down to the curl of her toes. There is not a single millimeter of her body I do not have a picture of.

—Sarah

When they asked if we wanted them to take some pictures of him, at the time I thought, "You've got to be kidding me. That's disgusting!" And a week or so later someone from the hospital called and said, "I've got these photographs of Matthew and I'd really like to send them to you." I said, "Send them! I want them!" Now we treasure them. The pictures are something that really helps me go through the grieving process.

—Kara

You can tell which photos my best friend took because, as she tells it, she was looking at Oren with the eyes of love. In her photos you don't just see a dead baby, you see all the love in the world.

—Tanya

For many parents, photographs can be a mixed blessing. Photographs can trigger feelings of grief, and yet this expression can be healing. Photographs can stir memories of a sad time, but they can also let you see your precious baby again. You may only have photographs of your baby after death, but they prove there was life. Photographs might be lacking, and yet they are treasured record of reality. Photographs can also help you integrate your baby into your family.

Now I Lay Me Down To Sleep sent a photographer, and although it felt unsettling (like everything else about that day), those pictures mean the world to me! When they arrived in the mail it was like we lost him all over again, but I was also instantly overjoyed that at least I had those memories of him.

—Embry

Initially I was upset that I didn't have a "nice" photo of Zac and me at the hospital. I am so puffy and I couldn't brush my hair because of all the lines in my arms. But I can look at them now and see just how unwell I was. And that is okay. I look at those photos and all I see is love for our precious wee boy.

—Melanie

Having photographs of Ronin means that I get to show my children that they had a brother who was here before them, and so that I can keep his memory alive within our family, and that he can be talked about openly. Also my children can see who he is as they have physical proof of his existence, which for young children, they need.
—Lorna

If you don't have a picture of your baby, you may feel bereft over this lack of tangible evidence that your baby existed. Bryn wishes she had a picture to refresh her memory because she can't remember her baby's face. This is difficult for her "because he was a part of me." For others, like Dara, a photograph would have been their only chance to see what the baby looked like. Dara remembers that the pathology department at her hospital took photographs for research purposes, but they've never been able to get copies. She says, "That's something I go through in phases every once in a while, wanting to try again and get them." Desi was never able to see her baby, nor were photographs taken, but she believes her curiosity could be somewhat satisfied by seeing someone else's picture: "I want mothers in my support group to bring a picture of their dead baby so I can see what they look like. But I never have the nerve to ask anybody."

Parents who do have photographs may be dissatisfied with the quality or regret that they don't have close-up photographs of the face, the undressed body, or them holding their baby. After a multiple birth, many parents want a photograph of all the babies together. Anya has most of these regrets, but it still helps her to have photographs of twin daughter Rachel. She notes, "The pictures are blurry and fuzzy and don't look like much, but I know they're there. It's real important. It's something tangible."

My biggest regret is that I didn't have the photographer take pictures of us with Judah. When she mentioned taking photos with him, I pictured us holding him and smiling. I was thinking, "Yes, I want a picture with Judah. But is that weird? How is she going to take them? It seems really morbid and awkward to take a 'happy,' smiling family photo with my dead baby." It seemed really insensitive and disturbing to me. I think Charlie was thinking the same thing.

The thing was, I wanted to so badly, and I wish a million times over that I would have spoken up. But I felt so odd. I felt odd asking for pictures with my dead baby.

That moment right there has caused me so much pain and guilt. I look at my other bereaved mother friends who have pictures with their babies and I think, Why couldn't I? It was just as hard for them . . . but they did it and I didn't. Why couldn't I handle it? Why didn't I speak up? I feel like an awful mom. That is a moment, like so many others, that I can never get back.
—Jolie

I wish we did take photos of them together while both in NICU, especially when Caitlyn was still alive. And although Sophie had passed away, if we would have put her in the incubator with Caitlyn, she would have maybe "sensed" that Sophie was "with her."

—Kylie

If you don't have a photograph or if your photographs are disappointing, it can help to realize that *this is not your fault.* As a shocked and newly bereaved parent, you cannot know what you want and why, nor can you be expected to find the strength to overcome inhibitions, doubts, hospital policies, staffing, or the photographer's lack of knowledge about bereavement care. You did the best that you could, given your condition and the support at hand. (See also "Practicing Self-Compassion" in chapter 4.)

What would have benefited me is reassurance that "Yes, other mothers took pictures with their babies. It isn't weird. They cherish those photos." I needed someone to assure me that taking pictures is "normal" in this very abnormal situation, and that many mothers are glad they did—or regret that they didn't.

—Jolie

Any regrets are another loss that must be grieved. Some parents fulfill their need by having a portrait drawn or painted of their baby that suits their desires. One mother took her single blurry photograph to a portrait artist who did a wonderful job of capturing what her baby looked like. Another mother, whose baby died thirteen weeks into the pregnancy, took a collection of family baby pictures to an artist who drew a portrait of what the baby might have looked like as an infant. An artist could even render a touching portrait of the parents embracing their baby, or of babies from a multiple birth all together. You can also acquire art that shows the parental bond.

If you were offered Polaroid photos by the hospital, note that they fade over time—but you can take them to a custom film-developing lab and ask for a copy negative, which will last, or you can digitally scan them. Some custom photo labs, restoration artists, and digital computer programs can also sharpen edges in fuzzy or blurred photographs, or render them in black and white for an image that neutralizes skin discoloration.

Photographs and portraits are one way of preserving a memory, but not the only way. If you don't have a portrait of your baby, you can still imagine what he or she looked like and hold that picture in your mind's eye.

KEEPSAKES

Sometimes it feels like all we have been through is a dream—well, a nightmare. But having these photos and mementos, it affirms they were real and they are part of our lives and they are not forgotten.

—Melanie

They are so, so hard to look at, but at the same time I am glad I have these things. It's all I have of them. I do not have all these memories of them to rely on for life.

—Anne

Treasured mementos of your baby may include footprints, record of the baby's length and weight, locks of hair, hospital ID bracelets, the autopsy report, sympathy cards and flowers, any clothing or toys or stuffed animals you acquired, and baptismal, birth, and death certificates. You may collect recordings of special songs you associate with your baby or your pregnancy. Even if you were pregnant for a short time, you can save anything you associate with this time period. And it's never too late to make a baby blanket, buy a teddy bear, light a candle, do some writing, or display an ornament for your baby.

*I cherish them **all** very, very deeply. His lock of hair helps me to remember his true hair color. And his clay mold footprints, which again, are not the best quality—but knowing his feet touched that clay, and has left somewhat of an impression in the clay, makes me cherish them so much.*

—Lori

The keepsakes mean the world to me. The photographs, blankets, pink bows, hospital bracelets, the rattle toys I used to play with her while in the hospital, the dress she wore for the photo session at the hospital, the eighty-inch pearl necklace I got for her thinking she'd wear it for the rest of her long life—these are some of my treasured possessions. It's all I'll ever have as a physical proof of her existence to go along with my memories. That she was here, that it's not all a dream . . .

—Destrida

The nurse gave us a memory box with a picture of Melina, her hand- and footprints both in ink, and a plaster casting, and a lock of her hair. That box is the most valuable object in our home to me and my husband. Of half a lifetime of collectibles and memories, nothing comes close.

—Helen

We had a "treasure box" made that contains the hand and feet castings, along with a scan photo, their little bonnets, a little clock with the time they were born, and a wee angel for each. This has pride of place in our hallway and is a very treasured keepsake of ours. I think it will be even more valued when we have other little ones running around. It will help us tell them the story about their sisters. That is what means the most to me, that they will never be forgotten

—Kylie

We created a "memory shelf" where I keep things from her nursery, photos of her, our maternity photos, cards from her baby shower, pressed flowers from the hospital, her blessing certificate, her urn,

and anything that presently reminds me of her. They bring me
comfort. I feel as though she's in the room with us.

—Daniela

Some parents keep their mementos in a special box, baby book, or envelope and look through them as a way to spend time with and affirm their baby. Following traditional folk art, you can create an altar, totem, or shrine that honors your baby and your bond, using keepsakes you collected during your pregnancy and afterward. Even if your keepsakes are tucked away in a drawer, it helps to know you have them. However you arrange them, your mementos are a comforting affirmation of your baby's existence, importance, and connection to you.

I love my mementos. It's good for me, another thing that makes it real.
I have a picture of my baby; I have her hair. She was alive at one time
and she was my daughter, and you just can't pretend she isn't real.
So it does, it makes it real.

—Cindy

Doing things that commemorate her life helps me a lot, such a putting
pictures up on her memory shelf and creating projects with other
mothers who have been through this experience. I sleep with her
picture at my bedside table and I carry a lock of her hair in my purse.

—Daniela

I kept a pregnancy journal and wrote like mad. So that's an
important keepsake. And I have those socks—they were such
*a comfort. It was something that had **belonged** to this baby,*
something I could hold on to.

—Winnie

If your baby died before birth, you will likely not receive an official birth certificate. This can feel disappointing because it somehow denies the fact that your baby was alive inside you! Maybe to you it implies that your baby wasn't real, wasn't important, wasn't *human*. Much progress has been made for officially acknowledging the lives and deaths of stillborn babies, and many governments and hospitals now provide a certificate, which lists the baby's name, date of birth, and other life-affirming information. But acknowledging babies who died earlier in pregnancy is lagging. As Sarah points out, "If Lilly Marie had been born thirty-two hours later or weighing forty grams [1.41 ounces] more, she would have been classified as 'a stillborn,' not 'a late miscarriage.' She would have been issued a birth/death certificate. It does make a difference." For whatever reason, if you didn't receive a certificate but want one, you can find one online, design your own, or find a print shop to make one for you.

Baby gifts are another source of confusion. Many people assume that baby gifts would be meaningless or painful to the parents. To the contrary, these gifts can be viewed as acknowledgments of your baby and can serve as treasured mementos. If someone mentions it or if you know a gift was being made or planned for your baby, don't hesitate to express how meaningful it would be. You can also continue to create or acquire meaningful objects. As Emmerson says, "Anything that reminds me of her, I must have!"

> *When Judah was first born and I went to the store, I would still want to buy him things. So I did buy him some things—including a couple of English-Spanish baby books (Charlie is Puerto Rican).*
>
> *—Jolie*

Even if you feel pressured to pack up the nursery—or put away anything that reminds you of your time or plans with your baby—wait until you are ready, which may well be after you are done having babies. Putting away baby things is a big step in letting go of your dreams, and you certainly deserve to take all the time you need. Meanwhile, spending time in your baby's room or among your baby's things is a good way to feel connected to your baby. Eventually you will find special places in your home to permanently display or store treasured items. (See also "Feeling Connected to Your Baby's Essence" in chapter 4.)

> *I still have not been able to wash my bath towel, which I used before I delivered Emily. I am not ready to do that.*
>
> *—Anne*

> *I remember I would take Matthew's little cap he wore in the incubator and smell it after he died because I can remember that it smelled like him. . . . I saved everything I could. He was real important to us.*
>
> *—Kara*

RITUALS

Ritual is a ceremonial moment that becomes memorable because of the profound meaning and symbolism it carries and the way it touches you on a deeper level. Words like *sacred, soulful,* and *heartfelt* describe such moments. Rituals for your baby might include naming, religious or spiritual blessing, burial, scattering ashes, funeral or memorial service, as well as any informal ritual done in the moment, on occasion, or ongoing—whether simple or elaborate, formal or informal, structured or spontaneous. Ritual can be therapeutic in many ways, such as

- affirming your baby's life and importance;
- acknowledging the depth of your bond, your sense of loss, and your grief;
- heightening others' abilities to recognize your baby's life and death as significant;
- granting you a time and place to mourn and an outlet for emotion-oriented grieving;

- providing the opportunity to create, plan, organize, and carry out tasks, restoring a sense of control, being an outlet for activity-oriented grieving;
- generating social support if others participate or bear witness, or if you talk about it;
- offering opportunities to create meaningful moments that honor your baby and your bond; and
- applying a spiritual, comforting, or meaningful framework to your baby's life and death.

Whether ritual includes other people or not, it has a way of making you feel cloaked in support, which offers comfort and boosts your ability to cope.

A Name for Your Baby

My family decided that we weren't going to name him, and I can remember coming up out of that hospital bed and saying, "OH YES WE ARE!"
—*Desi*

Naming your baby is another way to acknowledge your baby's existence and individuality. A name is personal and lasting, and can integrate your baby into your family and its traditions or heritage. It is also a way to capture an essence or confer meaning onto your little one's life.

It was just the three of us in the hospital room. We love the name Grace but it didn't seem fitting, and then my husband came up with Emma and it fit her sweet button nose and rosy lips perfectly. So she became Emma Grace.
—*Abby*

Dayani means "compassion" in Sanskrit. Her middle name is Kirana, which means "a "beautiful ray of light" in Indonesian, like the rays of light you see coming out of the sun during an eclipse. Dayani's name is also two-thirds of my middle name, which is Handayani.
—*Destrida*

My paternal grandmother was Jewish and while I am not, Judaism still plays a small part in my life. I looked at one of those baby name websites and found the name Oren. This was perfect as it was Hebrew for "pine." I also liked how the name was a tree as both Lavender and I enjoy connecting to nature.
—*Tanya*

We saw the name "Bodhi" somewhere and it just stuck. It wasn't until after some time that a friend of ours who studies Buddhism told us what it means. This still really affects me now—Bodhi means understanding the true nature of things, traditionally translated into English as "enlightenment" or more literally "awakening." He was a turning point in our lives, and led to a new life and new normal.
—*Ben*

If your baby died early in the pregnancy or even at term but before birth, you may wonder if a name is appropriate. Do whatever feels right to you. Some parents may want to save a favorite name for a future baby. Others feel that the name originally chosen rightfully belongs to this baby. You may even discover your baby's name to be particularly fitting or comforting.

Jedidiah was already named before we lost him. We actually chose his middle name when his great-grandfather passed away during my pregnancy. When we lost Jed, it was comforting to know they were together now and shared a name.

—Embry

We were having a girl! I did a lot of research on baby names and we settled on Melina. We both loved the name and we even shortened it to Meli, which literally means "honey" in Greek (my cultural background), representing sweetness.

—Helen

I just always loved the name Emily for a girl. And my name is Anne, so it was a way of incorporating my name with her. Emily Anne. And Michael, I believe that his name was sent to me by God. I had a dream at three weeks pregnant, and I was naming my children. I said, "Matthew, Ryan, Emily, and Michael." I found out that we were pregnant shortly after that dream. Michael means "he who is closest to God."

—Anne

We named our daughter Willow Blue Lotus Ariel Oldfield several months before she was born. My wife Eliza and I kept it as a little secret between us. We decided she would have four given names. Even though we knew that some people would think that was over the top, we didn't care. We knew an over-the-top kind of love for her.

—Nathan

Giving the baby a nickname or other term of endearment may be most meaningful to you. Some parents use the Native American custom of choosing a name associated with nature, Mother Earth, or celestial bodies to encompass their intuitions about the baby's spiritual essence. Many parents have remarked how naming their baby, even years later, assigns a specific identity to the baby and gives them someone tangible to mourn. As Janet said earlier, "I named him David—and now I feel like I have a better idea about what I lost, who I grieve for."

Naming your baby also makes it easier for people to refer to your baby, and can instill a sense of formality that encourages people to remember him or her as a real member of your family. Even if relatives or friends resist using it at first, if you use it early and often, it may become familiar over time. Jolie noticed people started using her son's name more freely after her daughter was born.

Since Aviana has been born, so many people have mentioned her looking like Judah, and because of that I have heard so many more people say his name than they ever had after he was born. I found myself wondering if maybe it's because they feel more comfortable mentioning him now that I have a live baby? It's almost like Aviana softens the blow of his name, like it's okay to mention Judah because it is followed by "looks like Aviana . . . your baby that is alive and well and that you got to take home."

—Jolie

We all talked so much about her and we called her by name—Melanie. I was happy that people could say her name so easily.

—Kitty

Caring for Your Baby's Body

I was looking forward to bathing her. Because we didn't have a baby bath the nurses allowed me to undress her and pretend I was bathing her. My husband took video footage of her "bath." This was the most meaningful and special moment for me.

—Daniela

We don't have a single regret. We loved and honored our daughter. We took her home, we wrote her letters, we slept with her between us, and we farewelled her in a private ceremony followed by a cremation where we handed her over. I am grateful that we planned her farewell, that we did our best to be prepared, that we spent every waking moment we could with her. She was never alone.

—Emmerson

With Michael, I really do not have any regrets. I put him inside a container filled with saline solution. Another bereaved mother did this with her son, who died in the earlier part of her pregnancy, and she was able to see her baby so much better. It is like they are back in the womb. That was pretty incredible to see. I wish that I had done this with Emily too.

—Anne

Many parents find meaning in rituals that take care of the baby's body after death. Bathing, dressing, preserving, and carefully examining your baby's little body lets you do the nurturing your heart longs for. You're able to see and know your baby a little better, create treasured memories and mementos, and express your love in a physical way. You can also acquire a deep sense of your bond with and connection to your little one, and seal your identity as your baby's parent. If you also take your baby home, you get to experience having your baby be an integral part of the family and welcoming visitors to your home to meet your baby.

In retrospect, the many things we did allowed us to become first-time parents. The fact that we were able to have him in our home, surround him with his gifts, read to him, sing to him, hold him whenever we wanted, allowed us to get to know his body, to see who he looked like. . . . It gave us a chance to parent our child, and to begin our roles as parents. It gave us the chance to create myriad memories, which form a very warm and real connection with him outside of my womb.

—Nicola

It was comforting taking our babies home to show them their room and home, and spend time with them at home, in our arms. People who wanted to visit could and not have to worry about hospital visiting times.

—Fleur

Bringing your baby home deeply affirms your parental identity. You can experience the soothing balm of seeing and holding your baby whenever you want, folding your baby into your daily routine, or taking your baby outside and immersing yourselves in nature, where the sunshine can kiss soft cheeks and breezes can ruffle downy hair. Everything you do becomes a healing ritual.

Sasha Felix spent the next five days at home with us, tucked up in his drawer, surrounded by soft toys and blankets and many colorful bunches of flowers. He was read to and sung to and held by all his close family. We took hand- and footprints and more pictures. We showed him the night sky full of stars and even took him down to the beach in the early morning to dab salty water on his forehead. Sasha's father wrote his name in the sand, a kind of naming ceremony for him. Each night we took his drawer up beside our bed with us, and each night we lit candles all around the house for him. And then on the sixth day we took him up to Hamilton to bury him.

—Nicola

I just had a very hard time giving my babies up to the funeral home. I wanted them "home" with us. I asked the funeral director what they would do with our baby, if we handed our baby over to them. He said, "We would put your baby in our refrigerator. That is what we do with the bodies to preserve them." I said, "We have a refrigerator. We can put our baby in there. So, our baby can be home with us." I remember putting Emily in there, and saying, "I am so sorry that I have to put you in here. But, this is where it is best for your body." I would kiss her container every night, and say, "Good night. I love you."

—Anne

Having prolonged contact with your baby's body also gives you the opportunity to gradually and truly experience it as a lifeless shell, which can help you part with it at burial or cremation. Some parents feel like they get to witness the soul's leave-taking. As Nicola writes, "This also allowed us to adjust to the fact that he was dead; he really was dead."

Being able to take your baby home and provide after-death care until burial or cremation is a longtime tradition that is making a comeback in some parts of the world, and never left other parts. Taking the baby home circumvents the heart-wrenching separation of sending the baby to the morgue or the funeral home. Parents can benefit from the normalcy and closure of having easy access to their baby's body, and experiencing a very gradual goodbye. Taking the baby home is a welcome and therapeutic part of bereavement care for many parents.

We brought our baby home, in a container full of a preserving solution and with instructions to keep it refrigerated until we decided what to do with the body. I kept it for about five months, until the due date. Even other bereaved parents were uncomfortable with me doing that, but I got the whole nine months I felt entitled to! Until then, I just wasn't ready to let go.

—Winnie

It is natural for you to have protective urges toward your baby, even after death. If you weren't able to take your baby home, the thought of the baby being cold and alone somewhere in the hospital or funeral home may seem unbearable. When your baby's body is treated with warmth and respect, this confirms your baby's importance and worth. For your sake, your baby should be kept comfortable.

BAPTISM AND BLESSING

For some parents, a baptism or blessing is a meaningful way to have the baby recognized as a valued and real person. This ritual can hold special memories, and a baptismal certificate is another treasured memento. Meryl asked her priest to come to the hospital and bless her baby because she wanted acknowledgment that this baby was a person; that he had lived. She remembers, "Even though he wasn't born alive, he needed that blessing—*I* needed the blessing." Shellie remembers, "It meant a lot to us to plan a Christian baptism for Ashley. Our pastor was kind enough to baptize our daughter regardless of whether or not she was still living. To her, Ashley's exact status wasn't important when it came to baptism." You too may have been touched by a clergyperson's willingness to be compassionately flexible.

*We had her baptized two days before, when she was in my tummy. And then we had our priest come to the hospital to do it again. We just wanted to be sure that we did "everything" for her. Baptism is for the **living**, but I still wanted it.*

—Anne

Our tears came down to welcome this sweet little girl. I couldn't believe she stayed around to meet everyone and to be baptized. Toward the

*end of her baptism, she simply stopped taking her quiet breaths. It
was so unbelievably peaceful.*

—Shellie

INFORMAL RITUALS

*We burn a candle every night. We were told it helps her spirit find
her way home to us.*

—Emmerson

*I used to say goodnight to the girls every night in the early months as
I found it comforting to do so.*

—Kylie

*We used our blanket to wrap Emma in and I slept with that blanket
every night until our son was brought home in it from the hospital. I
plan to have that blanket for every one of our babies.*

—Abby

Rituals needn't be formal, nor sanctified by religion, culture, or authority.
In fact, informal rituals can be the most comforting because they are *personal*.
Some informal rituals are adapted or created by parents, planned in
advance, and carefully executed. Others happen in the moment, unplanned
or invented on the spot. Perhaps you've experienced a spontaneous ritual—a
moment in which you knew something special and sacred had just happened,
and it is burned into your memory. An informal ritual can be any moment
or activity that is meaningful, memorable, and deeply heartfelt.

*It was suggested to us by a NICU team member that we should put
my ring around Caitlyn's wrist and take a photo of this moment. It
became one of our favorite photos of Caitlyn, and I wished this had
been suggested with Sophie also. I am able to still wear this ring and
think that my little girl wore this on her wrist for a short time! I guess it
kind of gives me a sense of having a continuing bond with her, hence
why I wish we had also been told of this with Sophie too.*

—Kylie

*We wrote letters to Adisyn after we brought her home. It was truly
painful yet cathartic and healing at the same time. They were written
with such honesty, they were heartfelt. A story of our journey through
pregnancy, our Hopes and Dreams for our precious daughter,
written to help us grieve all the things that we would not be able to
experience as a family. We both read them to her before we took her
to her service and put them in her Moses basket with her.*

—Emmerson

*Since we brought the body home with us, I was able to take
photographs over the course of many days. I created backdrops
with flowers, my mother's vintage handkerchiefs, which I'd had
since childhood, and the baby held in my hand. It doesn't look*

much like a baby—the doctor estimated that I didn't go into labor for three weeks after the baby had died, so lots of details had "melted." But I knew that was my baby's body and I wanted to honor it and **remember**. *Looking back on those photo sessions, I guess they had elements of ritual.*

—Winnie

When I was pregnant with Oren, we had an enormous potluck picnic/ baby shower and all the kids decorated little shirts and onesies with fabric markers. Later when Oren was buried, we put all the little shirts under him in the basket he was buried in, so he was held by his community.

—Tanya

I find that every time we go to beach I write Elizabetta's name in the sand.

—Karen

What's nice about informal rituals is that you create them, for yourself, in a personal, sometimes evolving and often instinctive manner. Informal rituals can also arise mindfully and spontaneously, in the present moment. There is no time frame for creating personal rituals, and no standards you must uphold. It's just whatever you find meaningful, wherever you are on your journey. Or as Abby says, "I felt a lot of pressure, put on by myself, to have all of this figured out because you want to honor your baby in the best way. It took me a bit of time to realize it would all unfold in a beautiful way." Many parents create ritual in the care of their baby's ashes.

We have a sacred space for Adisyn in the living room and also in our bedroom. We used to carry her tiny urn between the two rooms each day so she is in our room with us at night. Now, she stays in our bedroom on my bedside table.

—Emmerson

We arranged for him to be cremated and carry him now, in his urn. He sits on our dresser and [comes with us on] any trip we take. Amy brings him along. And when I go to sleep at night, I just fall asleep knowing our family is together. Including Bodhi, for sure.

—Ben

Another informal ritual is having, noticing, or collecting memorial symbols. Many parents align their baby with elements of nature, including birds, insects, animals, plants, gemstones, a periodic element, a celestial being, and even weather. Anne notes, "There was this beautiful snow on the day that we had Emily's ceremony. That soft, falling snowfall makes me think of her. And it is wonderful."

Other symbols might be associated with a holiday that coincides with an anniversary date, the initials of the baby's name, a special color, or a certain object. If you're so inclined, a symbol can be whatever holds special meaning or associations for you. Symbols can be sweet reminders of your baby or expressions of your continuing bond. Symbols can be an easy way for other people to acknowledge your baby too.

I went through months of collecting things that remind me of her. I was taken with little birds the whole way through my pregnancy so they feature a lot!

—Emmerson

My symbol for Ashley is a butterfly, because they change form. Even though her physical body is no longer with us, we think of Ashley as being in a different form, still with us in some ways.

—Shellie

We use butterflies as a symbol for the girls and have them in the garden, along with two kowhai trees planted in their memory.

—Kylie

Someone in the hospital brought us each a penny and told us they were dropped by angels from heaven; now any time we find a penny, it's from Emma. We collect them in a jar that also holds her candle.

—Abby

Shortly after Emily was buried in the cold months of February, I was visiting her at the cemetery, crying and praying to her. Pretty soon one of those dandelion "wishies" went by at eye level. It caught my eye, and brought a smile to my face. It was a pretty good-sized one. Two weeks before her due date, there were thousands of them around here. For about two weeks straight. I am not kidding. A lot of the times, when I am thinking deeply about Emily and Michael, a "wishie" appears. It brings me such comfort. I believe they send them to me.

—Anne

BURIAL OR CREMATION

If you buried your baby, the gravesite can be a place where you go to be with the baby and express your sadness. If you cremated your baby's body, you may decide to scatter the ashes in a special place that you can visit. Or you may decide to keep the ashes. Many parents find comfort in knowing where the baby's body or ashes lie. If you decide you don't want to keep the ashes forever, it still may take you a long time to feel ready to scatter them or place them in a cemetery. No matter when you are ready, it may help you feel a sense of closure.

We got to bring her home, and buried her on Saturday. It was so, so hard knowing I would never physically get to see her again. But we found a beautiful spot in the hills above our house to lay her to rest.

—Melanie

Oren is buried in a little grove of trees at a nature preserve. It is about as lovely as lovely can be. Someday I hope I can be laid to rest nearby.

—Tanya

I think it helps us to know we have a place to visit and we can see where it says "David, Son of . . . ," and I think that's real helpful somehow.

—Bess

In hindsight you may wonder if you should have done some things differently. Holly wishes they had scattered her baby's ashes in a more accessible spot. Deidre wishes her triplets could've been buried together. Erin wishes she hadn't let the hospital handle her daughter's cremation and burial. She says, "I think if I could do it over again, I would take Barbie's little remains and say something, rites over her, and place her remains in a little tiny coffin box. I just think it would have helped me know that she's okay, she's all in one piece, she's all together. Sometimes I just wonder why we didn't do that. When we drive by the cemetery I always think of her. I think she's in there somewhere. I hope she's there."

Indeed, the decisions and rituals associated with your baby's cremation, burial, or spreading of the ashes can be deeply meaningful gestures. Ritual can give you a way to express your most profound feelings of love, honor, and grief. It can also offer you an intense and detailed memory that you'll always hold dear.

We chose a green burial for our son in a nature preserve nearby that had a cemetery. I wanted him to rest somewhere beautiful where we could see the trees and the animals when we went to visit him. His grave was dug by hand, by one man, in one day. He was buried in a beautiful handmade basket (made by a dad who lost his own son) wearing a sweater that my mother had made for me when I was a baby.

—Tanya

We had researched it ahead of time and decided to bury her in a Jewish cemetery. We had spoken with the head of the cemetery and he was so kind and helpful. We buried her next to other children. Her grave is not marked but we know where it is and we visit her whenever we attend a funeral at the cemetery.

—Julie

When we had Judah cremated, he wouldn't fit into just one little urn, so we actually have a sealed gold heart urn at home for him plus an extra urn with his ashes, which we decided to spread in meaningful places. Charlie and I spread some of Judah's ashes on Lookout Mountain, on the exact spot where Charlie and I first said, "I love you." We plan on making a trip to the Channel Islands where we met on the beach and spreading some there as well.

—Jolie

I chose to have Lilly Marie cremated; her ashes sit at home in the lounge where I see her every day. When it is my turn to die, Lilly Marie's ashes will go with me in my coffin and will be cremated again with me. She is my daughter and it is my responsibility to always look after her. That's what parents do, even when your child dies, you still have to parent them. It is just in a different way.

—Sarah

Exactly one year after Bryce was born, we had a private family memorial send-off for his ashes. It was only my husband, myself, and both of my parents. At sunrise we walked his ashes (which were in a biodegradable urn) down to a special place by the water. At that point we gently tossed his urn into the water, which made a very touching ripple effect that symbolized to me that his life would carry on and touch many people's lives forevermore. And this was definitely not the end of our bond of love. I did not want to view this as an ending. I saw it more as a freeing of his earthly remains.

—Lori

Dayani was cremated. We let her ashes go into the ocean several days later on a cold morning, four days after my birthday. My husband placed the urn containing her ashes on his head and submerged himself with it. I stood next to my husband while he submerged himself, but I did not go in. I had planned to initially but my husband was worried that I might catch a cold so he asked me not to. Some of her ashes did come out as the urn went underwater; we spread the remaining ashes with our hands. I stood alongside my husband and floated a paper boat in which I had written my hopes and dreams of Dayani the night before. No matter what happens in the future, those hopes and dreams will always belong to her and no one else. Once we scattered her ashes, there was a sense of peace that came over me, and my husband said he felt the same thing.

—Destrida

Particularly if you were not encouraged or given the option to take your baby's remains, you may wonder what the hospital or clinic did with them. Many places handle babies' remains sensitively, cremating and either scattering or burying the ashes with other babies in a meaningful place. Because of the tiny mass and lack of hard bones, if your baby died early in the pregnancy, cremation leaves no remains. The body simply evaporates and goes into the air.

If you want to know what happened to your baby's remains, call your clinic's or hospital's pathology department. You won't be the first or last parent to call for such information. If you wish you had been given the choice to take your baby's remains with you, tell or write to your caregivers and this choice may then be offered to others. If you are upset with the way your baby's remains were handled, you can register your complaint and suggestions with your caregivers, chief of pathology, and laboratory supervisors.

If you have regrets, express your anger and sorrow about them and then figure out ways to memorialize your baby—ways that hold meaning for you now. Even if you don't know where your baby's remains are, you can have a headstone or plaque made for your baby and put it in a special place. You can put flowers in a peaceful part of a cemetery. Any of these gestures can confirm your love and help you grieve.

> *I think my only regret with burying Kate and Zac is that we have now moved . . . and I don't have them here with me. I hate that they are there and I am not. I have some amazing friends who visit them for me, which gives me comfort. But at the time that was the right decision for us.*
>
> *—Melanie*

> *I somewhat wish I had kept a tiny portion of his ashes and put them in a memorial necklace to keep forever. I did not choose this option at the time because it felt like I was separating his body somehow. But, now I feel a little differently for some reason, so if I could do it again, I would have saved a tiny portion of his ashes.*
>
> *—Lori*

> *I felt a little hesitant to spread them at first—I kept on thinking that these ashes were all I really have of my son, so naturally I hesitated to let them go. I thought it was a beautiful little ritual though. We told him that we loved him and missed him, and the story behind where we were at.*
>
> *—Jolie*

FUNERAL OR MEMORIAL SERVICE

> *I wish we'd had a special memorial service for Bryce and invited all of our family and friends to come support us and see his picture displayed. I think a memorial service could have also allowed family and friends to truly see this was **our child who died**, and not just some tragic event that happened to us at a hospital.*
>
> *—Lori*

> *Because Kate was under twenty weeks we were able to bury her effectively wherever we wanted. We chose a spot in a native bush reserve above our house. It was a special place where we spent time with our girls so we thought that was pertinent. My father-in-law and brother-in-law dug the hole for us. I remember carrying Kate up the track just wanting the ground to open up and swallow me. I just couldn't believe what we were doing. The ceremony we had was beautiful. My husband lit our wedding candle, and my husband and I both spoke and some family members read poems. It was lovely.*
>
> *—Melanie*

At the time I did not see the significance in having it and my husband just thought it was a waste, as he felt he had said goodbye. But now we feel as if it gave us closure. And for me, it gave me a way to say goodbye to Ronin's physical presence on this earth. He may no longer be here with us in body but his spirit lives on inside us as we remember him.

—Lorna

Although it can seem sorrowful, a funeral or memorial service for your baby can be helpful in a number of ways. A service creates an opportunity to say a special goodbye. It acknowledges your baby's life and death and your need for comfort and support. Friends and family can share your sorrow and, in turn, lessen the isolation you may feel.

Organizing the service itself can be therapeutic, giving parents a purpose and a way to "parent" their baby in a meaningful way. Mel remembers, "In the war zone that had become my life, I discovered the battle of organizing the funeral and volunteered for this. I spent hours each day researching music, readings, flowers. We had tasks to do, even if they were incredibly hard."

We displayed the little gown that Adam wore, a couple pictures, a twelve-inch tape measure, a certificate of birth with tiny little footprints . . . and the hospital wristbands that were never used. There it was, life to death in three twenty-by-thirty-inch frames.

—Fred

My husband's dad and my brother built Zac's coffin. It was white and it had these beautiful teddy bear knobs for the handles. The day before the funeral all the family gathered around the coffin and my daughters and their cousins stuck stickers on the outside. Thinking about this makes me smile. It was a really special moment at such an awful time.

—Melanie

For me, it was very important to plan a more public funeral. My husband wasn't sure about this at first but he eventually agreed. I know he doesn't regret our decision, in hindsight.

—Shellie

Because most parents have not had experience arranging a burial, cremation, or memorial service, the process itself may seemingly pose too many obstacles. Bess wishes they could have done more than just arrange a private graveside service. Dara feels that it wasn't enough to just dedicate a mass to their baby. Rose had feared that no one cared, but after so many people attended the graveside service, she wished they had arranged a "full-blown funeral in a church." Holly also remembers thinking no one would come and now wonders if it is too late to have some kind of memorial service, just to "add to making it a more real thing, that she had been a *child*."

Services don't have to be stuffy, formal, or religious affairs. It is only important to do what is meaningful and manageable to you.

We had been in hospital for five days and when we were allowed to go home, we had a memorial/funeral service for the girls at home. That felt right for us, to have our family and close friends around home. We had the girls in their room and those who wanted to see them could do so, and I think pretty much everyone did! It was relaxed and a time to remember the girls and grieve with loved ones.

—Kylie

The beach was deserted and the sky was overcast on the day we scattered Dayani's ashes, and I let go of all my dreams for her. It was a good reflection of my feelings at that time . . .

—Destrida

It is important to remember that memorial services are appropriate any time you feel ready or decide it's something that you want to do. Any rituals that allow you to say goodbye can help. You can arrange a formal memorial service and invite a lot of people, or you can keep it small and private by inviting only a few people or even just your clergyperson. You can read something that has a special meaning as you spread the ashes. Any memorializing gesture like this can be a release—a way of letting go. What's important is that you make arrangements that suit your special needs.

To do nothing would be to act like she'd never existed. I had a need to acknowledge that she was here . . . to make a statement about her being here and what she meant to us. What we didn't anticipate was the response that we got from other people. As a result of both the announcement and the service, people were a terrific support for us. Also, I didn't account for the fact that a lot of those people and some of our close friends had a need to grieve. The service helped them do that as well. It was a good decision.

—Sophie

In ways I think it would've been good to have a service in order to have closure. But I got that closure when I went up to visit his grave. I realize talking to a stone on the ground is kind of absurd, but I managed to get out a lot of the things I would've said to him if he had lived and I'd had the time to say them. To me that was important.

—Lena

A week later, we gave our daughter's ashes to the sea at a little cove in the national park. It is a place that I have hiked to and surfed since I was a child. A sacred place, surrounded by towering sandstone cliffs and huge ancient trees with secret Aboriginal carvings hidden in caves in the thick forest of the quiet valley. It was a perfect early summer's day, not a hint of swell or a breath of wind or a single cloud in the sky. After Eliza, Noa, and I walked out along the finger of rock shelf and freed the ashes, family and friends placed Singapore orchids in the water to be carried away by the tide.

—Nathan

Memorializing Your Baby

All three of us have done countless art projects. Derek made projects in woodworking and with stained glass. Outside our house, Lavender put in a rock wall and a rock garden by our "little free library" with a sign: "This library is in honor of our boys: Derek, who loves to read and Oren, who would have." I made a prayer flag which I sent to Australia, which, along with hundreds more, was displayed at Infant Loss Awareness Day.

—Tanya

My husband and I made a little mini garden-like section in our backyard, and that made my spirit feel a little renewed and at peace. It looks nice and I feel like it's kind of a little spot that I can look at and think of Judah.

—Jolie

Most parents find it helpful to have the baby memorialized in a tangible way. There are many ways to publicly acknowledge your baby's existence. You can have your baby's name engraved in stone or brass and mounted somewhere meaningful. You can donate a tree to a botanic garden or park. You can write a poem or a story about your baby and publish it in a bereaved parents newsletter or website. You can post a video online. You can invite people to do good deeds in your baby's memory.

One of my dearest friends and her family had a star named after Adisyn; it is one that can be seen all year round.

—Emmerson

I maintain a memorial garden. The year after Oren died, I had a garden party and asked friends to bring plants for his garden. It was a sweet and sad occasion.

—Lavender

Every December since his death we have hung up a stocking for Oren and asked people we know to consider doing a small act of kindness or service in Oren's name, which means so much to me. They write it down on a slip of paper, which we put in his stocking. The results have been inspiring.

—Tanya

You may find it particularly comforting to memorialize your baby during holidays or anniversaries that are special to you. Doing so affirms your baby's importance and enduring place in the family. Commemorations can be public or private.

On Emma's birthday we honor her with a day of service in our community. It has been a wonderful tradition. For Christmas I pick out a book for her and write her a letter. I look forward to the day my other children pick out Emma's Christmas book.

—Abby

The fact that I am missing a child always feels a bit more obvious at Christmas. Only four stockings, no presents with her name on them . . . but we continue to have hope and remember her in sweet ways at Christmas. Her ornament, the string of pearls the kids decorate the tree with, and the gifts we buy for a little girl who doesn't have anything. Pearl made us better . . . hearts that are able to love big without regret.

—Laura

On Blake's birthday, my husband and I each wrote a note to Blake and attached them to a balloon. We watched them until they disappeared. In our hearts, this was a symbolic way for our son to know that we were thinking of him on that day. I know we will continue this tradition for both Blake and Rylee on their birthdates.

—Sonya

There are many private ways to memorialize your baby. You may find it comforting to plant a tree or a flowering shrub in your garden or keep a houseplant as a living memorial to your baby. You could display your baby's portrait in a special frame somewhere in your house, hang ornaments, or burn a candle. You could buy a piece of jewelry or another object of some value that symbolizes your baby; for instance, Kim wears a necklace with a gold, heart-shaped locket containing a wisp of her baby's hair. For many parents, writing about their baby, their experiences, and their mourning is a powerful way to affirm and commemorate that precious life.

*Writing about Thor kept me close to him. In a way, writing about him **created** Thor. One of the things that's so existentially horrifying about stillbirth is that stillborn children exist in this liminal state between having-been and not-yet-having-been. Even women who experience their babies as "real" prior to their births get to know them in a whole new way after they're born—when they get to see them, hear their cries, rock them, nurse them. Never mind what happens in the next few weeks, as, say, the baby turns out to have a good appetite but be a restless sleeper—as the baby really turns into an **individual**. Stillbirth banishes the possibility of even that most basic establishment of a child's presence. So at some level I was worried that if my partner and I just buried Thor, if we just "remembered him in our hearts," then it would be as if he'd never existed. I needed to make sure he existed.*

—Elizabeth

Getting a tattoo is another private and personal way to memorialize your baby. Creating or choosing a design, deciding where to put it, and then having it applied also has elements of ritual and the symbolism of an image that has meaning and association with your baby. On his forearm, Nathan has a tattoo that matches the design he put on the surfboard he made in memory of baby daughter Willow. Having this mark honors his baby and demonstrates his continuing bond.

For a long time after his death, I had wanted do something for me that would mean something. I looked into different things such as jewelry, but nothing seemed right. Then one day it popped into my head: a tattoo with his name on it. I have it on my right wrist. When I see it, I remember my son and know that he is also in my heart, but also, for all the times that I will never get to write his name or see his name written, I get to see it every day.

—Lorna

You may tap into your own creativity and talent to make your own memorials—like Nathan did with his surfboard and tattoo. The options are endless: patchwork, quilting, needlework, knitting, sewing, doll making, drawing, painting, writing, engraving, calligraphy, sculpting, making pottery, silk screening, woodworking, gardening, flower arranging, stained-glass working, or making music. Build a piece of furniture, display mementos, or frame anything that reminds you of your baby. Janet made her own memento by designing a card with her baby's name and date of birth and death. She included a poem and Susan's footprints and had it professionally printed and framed. John made a pine chest to hold mementos of Jacob.

We have done so much in memory of our precious baby girl. I just can't help myself. It's a balm for my broken heart and provides some comfort for my aching soul.

—Emmerson

Many parents find that the creativity involved in these projects gives them a sense of accomplishment and worth—that they are still capable of making beauty after their baby's death. And if you're tending a garden, a tree, butterflies, or houseplants, you get the soothing satisfaction of sustaining life. Eva received a potted plant upon William's death, giving her "something meaningful to nurture."

Some friends gave us a houseplant and I thought, "Oh, no, something else that will surely die." I put it in the extra bedroom and whenever I thought about it, which wasn't often, I'd toss some water on it. Then, by some miracle, a couple months later the flowers started to bloom. It was so meaningful. I felt like Micah's life was acknowledged by that plant.

—Ami

POINTS TO REMEMBER

- Memories and mementos help you mourn. They affirm your baby's existence and importance; they help you feel close to your baby as you grieve; they let you experience a gradual adjustment to your baby's physical absence.

- The time you spent in your baby's presence, whether during pregnancy or after birth, can provide cherished memories.

- Photographs and keepsakes make your baby's existence more tangible, honor your bond, and help you feel close to your baby.

- Rituals and memorials honor your baby's importance to you and signify his or her ongoing presence in your life.

- Rituals can be informal, spontaneous, ongoing ceremonial moments that touch you on a deep level and honor the bond you keep with your baby.

- If you have regrets, identify them and acknowledge your feelings—perhaps anger, disappointment, or sorrow. Remember, you could not have known at the time that certain activities or objects would be a comfort to you later. Show yourself the compassion you would extend to another grieving parent in the same boat.

- It is never too late to engage in ritual or memorialize your baby in meaningful, comforting ways.

7

PAINFUL FEELINGS

You always have regrets when you lose a child, because you believe (whether it is right or wrong to), "If I only did this or didn't do this or made this decision, he would be okay and he would be with me now."
—*Sonya*

Grief encompasses many painful thoughts and feelings, and some are especially difficult to deal with and release. For bereaved parents, thoughts and feelings of failure, anger, guilt, and vulnerability are among the most difficult.

If you are prone to these thoughts and feelings in other areas of your life, they may arise more intensely when your baby dies.

These thoughts and feelings can also be intensified by factors associated with fertility, pregnancy, birth, cause of death, and supportive relationships. If it took a long time to get pregnant or if this baby was your only living child, you may think you are doomed and feel an added sense of failure and vulnerability. If you have been told that future pregnancy is unlikely or a recurrence of genetic defects is probable, you may feel especially angry and ask, *"Why me?"* If, on the other hand, the pregnancy was unplanned or if you had a particularly difficult day before tragedy struck, you may feel intensely guilty when you think any negative thoughts or feelings somehow caused the baby to die. The particular circumstances surrounding your baby's death may point to someone or something to blame—or perhaps you blame yourself. If you had to make agonizing life-and-death decisions, you may harbor an additional sense of responsibility that can heighten self-blame. (See also "The Guilt and Anger" and "The Responsibility" in chapter 9.)

Anger, guilt, and failure all arise from the belief that you are in charge of your destiny. Until tragedy strikes, you may have thought you had control over what happens to you. You make plans; you follow them. You have goals; you attain them. You place a lot of faith in medical practitioners who have always come through in the past. You may have put your faith in God, fate, Mother Nature, or universal justice. Many people do this with their health, their finances, their careers, their relationships, and, of course, their children.

Guilt—why couldn't I save her? Questioning—what I could have done differently? Anger—I'm not an angry person but I have certainly experienced "the angry mummy bear protecting her young."
—*Emmerson*

The anger has been the hardest to deal with and I'd say it still creeps up at times. I was immediately angry at the God I had believed was protecting me from loss like that; I was angry at myself for letting something bad happen to my child.

—Embry

This upended sense of control is a source of many of your painful thoughts and feelings. You may be angry that your baby died in spite of happier plans; you may feel guilty you could not prevent it; you may wonder if there must be something wrong with you that such a terrible thing could happen. You want answers to ensure more control in the future. This crisis can be uniquely unsettling for fathers, whose key adaptive strategies are to regain mastery and control. Your baby's death shatters the illusion that you can fully accomplish either, and may leave you with a dreaded feeling of helplessness.

I've dealt with death throughout my life, and I've gained the perspective that it's part of life. It's tough knowing that most times there isn't anything you can do.

—Ben

Yeah, you feel powerless, but no one wants to say that—even to themselves.

—Charlie

When you start to realize that you don't always have the power to prevent bad things from happening, a sense of vulnerability is triggered. It is sobering to *know* that misfortune can strike, even when you least expect it. This vulnerability to tragedy can be a terrifying thought or feeling to face. To avoid the fear and helplessness that come with vulnerability, you may prefer to hold on to anger, guilt, or failure for a while. These emotions guard that comfortable illusion of being in total control.

You may also hold on to these thoughts and feelings as a way to avoid sadness and despair. If grieving is like a roller coaster, profound sadness and despair are at the bottom of the deepest dips. These emotions are so painful that you may try to build bridges so you don't have to plummet so far down. The thoughts that feed feelings like anger, failure, and guilt can serve as bridges, and you may be intent on using them. A sense of numbness can even result, which is a sign that you are suppressing important aspects of your grief.

I am not good with sad. I learned to be very stoic when I was a kid. I have held a lot of the sad tightly inside.

—Lavender

Guilt has been one of my most painful emotions as I kept thinking, "If only I had got to the hospital sooner—they may have been able to stop me going into labor and the outcome may have been different." This was hard for me. And that feeling that my body had failed me: "I'm a woman, I'm supposed to be able to carry children until full-term and have a healthy baby at the end of it." I would often cry myself to

sleep over this and as time has passed (though it is still early on) I
found myself just feeling a little numb.

—Kylie

You may wonder, "Why shouldn't I use these bridges to avoid feeling the depths of despair?" Unfortunately, holding on to these feelings forever can be incapacitating. An unforgiving stance of guilt or failure creates a harsh inner critic that can eat away at your feelings of self-worth. Anger begets a bitterness that can interfere with your enjoyment of life. You are entitled to say, "How can I ever feel good about myself and enjoy life? MY BABY IS DEAD!" But as time goes on, you may become weary of being angry or guilty or feeling inadequate or numb and want to move on. Dropping these defenses can be a sign that you are ready to embrace your sadness and despair over your baby's death.

I recall a time where I relented. I had nothing left. I was emotionally,
psychologically, and physically exhausted. I wanted to give my life
for hers. I couldn't sleep or stop crying.

—Emmerson

Sadness and despair can be excruciatingly painful. These feelings can make you feel broken, discouraged, and overwhelmed. You may be afraid that if you start crying, you may never stop. But, sadness and despair are also involved in many of the critical tasks of mourning, and in fact, you may notice that whenever intense sadness wells up, if you simply surrender to the pain and let it flow through you, you can then also feel relief from holding back these powerful emotions.

Parents have found many ways to release deep feelings of sorrow. For several months after her daughter died, Stephanie made sure that every morning before doing anything else, she would look at Jamie's pictures, talk to her, cry, and write about her feelings in a journal. She discovered that by doing this she felt better and was able to get through the day more easily. Likewise, Kitty knew that when she was feeling stress, she needed to take the time to go through her "memory box" where she kept pictures and mementos of her baby. Tearfully she would examine the keepsakes. Afterward she would feel better, relieved of the tension. Nathan spent hours in his man cave, building a surfboard and shedding his tears. Ben headed for the hills on his mountain bike. Depending on your blend of emotion-oriented and activity-oriented grief, you can discover your own rituals to help you release your deepest held grief energy.

There were times when I made it hurt. I'd look at the pictures; I'd
go to her grave and I'd cry. I'd want to hurt and I couldn't figure
out why, but I guess I knew I needed to grieve. I'd feel the pain
like it had just happened. And now I can't feel that pain anymore.
I can look at the pictures, I can do everything I would have done a
year ago, and it doesn't hurt like it did. It's just, I've dealt with it. If I
hadn't done that, the pain would still be in there and I wouldn't even

be able to talk about it. And then it would be harder to deal with. I believe that as the years go on, if you don't let it out, it's going to be harder.

—Cindy

*I made myself do what I had to do to get through it. I think the reason I feel as good as I do now is because I **made** myself grieve for my son, by forcing myself to confront how I was feeling. As your grieving goes on, when you first cry, you cry all the time. After a while you can stop your tears and put them away, but I **always** took them back out again and I made myself look at my picture of Jamie and I made myself read all the literature and I made myself grieve for him. Grieving is not fun. It's very easy to go on, go to the movies, or change the subject. It's something that you have to force yourself to do, and I think because I did, that is the reason I feel so much better now.*

—Sara

Parents who give themselves time and permission to grieve are more likely to feel they are on the road to recovery. Those who hold back may eventually recognize that their lives are still compromised by the grief they have tried to avoid. And if trauma is what's holding them back, getting brain-based treatment can put them back on a healing path. (See also "Why Is Mourning Required?" in chapter 2; "About Trauma and Suffering" in chapter 3; "What if I Try to Avoid Grieving?" in chapter 5; "Invisible Grief" and "Claiming Your Grief" in chapter 10; chapter 8, "The Journey of Healing"; "Counseling" in chapter 13.)

Holly, Lena, and Anya provide testimony to the fact that grief is painful and easy to avoid, but letting it flow makes the journey easier in the long run.

I think I've been in a fog for two entire years. I have functioned beautifully to the outside world and pulled an incredible workload and accomplished an incredible amount of things, but personally I've just been in a fog. It's amazing to me that I've pulled it off, but I think by avoiding grief, I've caused myself more agony.

—Holly

I immediately immersed myself in volunteer work as an escape mechanism. I kept myself so busy that I didn't have time to think. At the time I think that's what was needed. I didn't want to wallow in self-pity. I did bury a lot of my feelings and I'm sure there are some feelings I haven't even come to grips with. I still feel a little pit in my stomach when I think about it, so I know there still must be something there. I probably should go back to counseling . . .

—Lena

I've learned it's okay to let yourself hurt. You may feel that you're falling apart and going crazy, but it's okay. You'll come back together again.

—Anya

As you adjust to your baby's death, you can gradually accept that you are not in charge of everything that happens in your life. And eventually, you may discover that life can be even more positive, fulfilling, and *liberating* when you embrace vulnerability and release trying to exert total control.

You just realize that's the way life is. There's a lot of things we don't like and a lot of things that aren't fair. You can't change it, so you just deal with it so you can move on. What else can you do? If you don't, then you lose yourself.

—*Cindy*

FAILURE

*I guess I had been "hoping" that the autopsy would have been able to tell me that Bryce died due to something being wrong with **him**. It really, really upset me to know that he was healthy, full-term, normally developed, and just days away from being born . . . but then he died anyway because **my body** somehow failed him. That was very hard to get over.*

—*Lori*

I wasn't there to hold him when he died—I failed him. I had all these hormones that were trying to be mothering and here was my big opportunity and I blew it. And everybody said, "Well, he didn't know if you were there or not." But who knows? I felt like I really failed him.

—*Sara*

Thoughts and feelings of failure arise when you believe there was something you could have done better or more competently. The mother may especially struggle with a sense of failure, because she carries the pregnancy, births the baby, and is often the primary caregiver of the infant. As the mother, if you have trouble conceiving or if there were problems with your uterus, cervix, hormone levels, or placenta, or if things went wrong during labor or delivery, you may feel like your body failed you. If your baby was born with genetic anomalies, you and your partner may feel a great sense of failure that your genes are somehow defective. You may even feel ashamed or embarrassed, and question your ability to bear a healthy child or worry that you don't deserve to be parents. You may wonder if you are a failure as a woman or a man.

I felt really betrayed by my body. I felt like there was something wrong with me physically that I could not complete a pregnancy, and that got to be a goal almost as much as having a baby—to complete a pregnancy successfully. I just really hated my body for a while. I felt like it just wasn't working right.

—*Jessie*

I don't like the term "incompetent cervix." It sounds like I got an F in the class. Incompetent. I've never been incompetent at anything in my life!

—*Lena*

Some parents feel an intensified sense of failure because they have experienced the death of more than one baby, or the death of a baby or babies from a multiple gestation. Or perhaps they are raising a child with birth defects or problems associated with pregnancy complications, prematurity, or other unfortunate circumstances. These difficulties invite a whole new level of questions and regrets stemming from feelings of failure.

> *Everybody was so excited because we were having twins. So when Jeffrey died, I felt so sorry because I was disappointing everyone. Like I was letting people down . . . I was worried what people would think, like, "You fool, you can't do anything right."*
>
> —Shannon

> *All my premature births were upsetting and ended badly. I felt like I was liar, as one day I was pregnant and the next day I wasn't. And I didn't have a baby to show for my pregnancy.*
>
> —Fleur

> *Sometimes I've really felt a lot of failure because both my other kids have problems. . . . So you know, you just feel like you haven't done anything right. I've felt like I couldn't make a baby right!*
>
> —Rayleen

> *Horrible feelings of failure—that I couldn't carry a pregnancy to term, that I couldn't keep two babies alive, that my body had bailed out on me. I had tried to do all the things you're supposed to do and it hadn't worked. My next pregnancy went fine, but it wasn't twins. It was a one-baby kind of thing.*
>
> —Anya

If you are blessed with another baby, this can help to boost feelings of competence and worth. Dara talks about how relieved and reassured she felt: "That we could have a healthy baby was a big thing. With Laurie, the relief was the greatest, being able to have a normal female."

Unfortunately, as some of these parents discovered, having a healthy baby—or especially another set of twins or triplets—isn't easy or even possible. If this is the case, you may feel terribly disheartened. Do remember that whatever happens, you are a *mother* or a *father*, and more specifically, *the mother/father of a daughter or son* or perhaps *the mother/father of twins*, and that can never be taken away from you.

Also remember, having another baby or set of babies isn't the only way to ease a sense of defeat and acquire some faith in yourself again. There are a number of ways to reinforce feelings of competence and boost your sense of self-worth.

- Engage in activities that let you express your talents or fulfill your responsibilities.
- Talk to someone who is supportive—your partner, a good friend, a clergyperson, or a counselor who can accept your

feelings and reassure you that you are still a good parent and a good person.

- Practice self-compassion, which allows you to feel good and worthy for just who you are. As a mother, practice forgiving and accepting yourself and your body, faults and all.
- Recognize that you don't have to align yourself with how others might view what happened. Dismiss the assumption that failure on your part brought on this terrible misfortune. Anne describes rejecting faultfinding medical terminology:

*No wonder many women retreat even further into their shell after a miscarriage (which is a word I dislike, as it distances and desensitizes what actually happened: **your baby died**). They are told that this wasn't really a baby. Just tissue. Then told it was just a miscarriage. I looked up "miscarriage" in the dictionary, and it says, "failure." I understand what it means, the act in and of itself. But, still. Come on. Really?*

—Anne

You can also try doing "The Work," a mindfulness inquiry and reframing technique covered in chapter 4. It can help you examine the thoughts that form the basis of those feelings. When you question the thoughts created by your mind, your thinking can shift to thoughts of self-compassion, such as, "I did the best I could in that moment" or "I loved my baby in many ways that he could feel." These are the thoughts that can reduce suffering and lead to healing. (See also "Doing 'The Work,'" "Mindfully Reframing Your Thoughts," and "Practicing Self-Compassion" in chapter 4.)

Self-compassion also means recognizing that bad things happen to good people without stripping them of their goodness. Regardless of what has happened to you, you are still a good mother or father and a worthwhile person who deserves the best life has to offer.

ANGER

I have experienced anger like I have never felt before, and pain, like my heart will break into a million pieces. Uncontrollable crying and a yearning for Adisyn that is hard to put into words. I feel cheated that our experience of pregnancy and childbirth has been changed forever.

—Emmerson

Anger is a powerful and valid emotion that may consume you at times. It may accompany various kinds of distress—mental, emotional, spiritual, physical, and social. You may be angry at medical technology or the doctors and nurses. You may have thoughts like, "Could they have prevented my baby's death?" "Why did they keep critical information from me?" You may be furious with the injustices of the world, fate, God, the Universe, or Mother Nature. "Why did this have to happen to me and my baby?" You may be angry that nature makes you lactate even though your baby has died. You may be irritated by people's insensitive remarks. You may feel generally aggravated with pregnant women, especially those who appear blissfully naive or careless.

It was my first pregnancy and I didn't know, I thought my labor was starting. I called the hospital and said, "I'm getting really weird pains. I think maybe I should be checked. I don't know what's going on." The doctor said, "Don't worry about it." And I still am mad about that because I think, "If I would've gone in, they would have seen the stress and they would have gotten her out."

—Cindy

My husband had gone to check on Nicholas in the NICU and the nurse was charting. There was only my daughter and me. She lay peacefully in the incubator and I was comforted knowing we were together. Then the nurse gave me some morphine for pain—I did not want it. I'll never forgive them for giving me that. While I drifted in and out of sleep, the funeral home man came for my sweet Jessica. When I awoke—she was gone! Didn't they know, I could handle the physical pain, it's the emotional pain that is unbearable?

—Sheila

I'd see or hear about moms that smoke and drink too much when they're pregnant and they have these perfectly healthy babies. I had a perfectly healthy pregnancy and I ate all my proteins and my vegetables and vitamins, and Stephanie wasn't here. It seemed so unfair.

—Sophie

You may also resent parents with healthy babies if you think they are not being as kind and nurturing as you imagine yourself to be. You may wonder, "Why do other parents get to keep their babies when I am equally or more deserving than they are?" You may even feel anger at your baby. As Erin admits, "Sometimes I'm a little resentful toward my baby for doing this to me. It wasn't very fair of her." Indeed, it *is* unfair to carry a baby—whether for two months or nine or into infancy—only to be cheated, denied from keeping him or her.

Thanksgiving came and I was screaming mad, saying, "What do I have to be thankful for!" because I had lost David, then had a miscarriage and then I wasn't pregnant and was having trouble getting pregnant and I felt there was nothing to be thankful for. I had lost my baby and that was the cruelest thing ever.

—Bess

I could not hold a baby. I didn't want to be around babies and anyone that had a baby. I wanted to shoot them. It was a terrible feeling. That's why I think having Robin has helped a lot because now I've got another baby, and now other people can have babies too and it's okay, but back then it wasn't.

—Martina

If one or more of your babies died from a multiple pregnancy, your anger may focus on the lost chance for the special experience of raising babies together. And since people notice and celebrate twins, triplets, and so forth, you may feel surrounded by tributes to successful multiple births.

I look at all those people who can have twins and it's maddening. And it seems like it's popular now to have twins. They're everywhere, on TV; all these famous people are having them. Or that woman who lives nearby, she had five babies and they're just fine. Why not me?
—*Shannon*

You may also feel angry at the circumstances that surrounded your baby's death when you think about the inadequate medical care you received, the lack of information, or the fact that you were not encouraged to hold your baby, or weren't offered more time, or did not receive a certain photograph or other mementos. Someone may suggest that you bring a lawsuit against the hospital or the doctors, but most parents agree with Desi: "That's not going to bring the baby back."

*I was very angry—boy was I mad. I bet I was **nothing** but mad for like a week. I was just furious. I was furious at everything. I was furious at the weather. I was so mad about this particular thing, beta strep [Group B streptococcus]. Two years before my son was born they decided to stop testing for it routinely because it was statistically insignificant, the number of babies who got that. That made me so mad, I just kept getting madder and madder, and I was just so sad. It was just awful. It was the worst thing I've ever gone through.*
—*Sara*

One way to handle anger is to accept and embrace it as a way of knowing when you need to assert yourself. Unfortunately, many people squander potentially valuable anger by swallowing it, letting it explode, or simmering it. As a result, they take on a self-perpetuated victim role, in which they see life as unfair, preventing them from getting what they need. To shed this victim role and become a victor, let anger energize you. It can be the fuel that prompts you to

- recognize that there is an imbalance or injustice,
- stand up for yourself when you've been hurt or wronged,
- say what you want and what you need,
- change what isn't working in your life, and
- acquire a soothing sense of compassion.

By using your anger to fuel self-awareness, assertiveness, and positive change, you cultivate self-respect *and* respect from others. When anger is triggered, you can go with it, harness its power, and express it in ways that are nondestructive *and* productive. For instance, be clear with people about what is okay with you and what is not. To specific people or institutions, respectfully make constructive suggestions based on what you want or what would've worked better for *you*. (As in, speak only for yourself, instead of weakening your position by generalizing about others.) You needn't tell them what they did wrong, as this merely provokes defensiveness and argument. Make your suggestions and requests in writing or in person, whichever method would help you make your points with clarity and strength.

> *On my insurance bill, which I received four weeks after delivery, it had the word ABORTION, written in capital letters. That was a slap in the face.* **Please** *do not categorize a miscarriage as an abortion. I was not given a choice. My baby died. I will fight this, probably until the day that I die.*
>
> —Anne

But what if you're angry at the Universe, injustice, or God—or the innocent pregnant woman? How do you vent that? Contrary to outdated advice, it is unproductive and unnecessary to be explosive or scream into a pillow in order to "get it out." In fact, outbursts only encourage more anger. This stands to reason, as you won't put out a fire by lighting a match, much less throwing gasoline on it. Brain research backs up this view, showing that calming the core brain, which triggers your fight, flight, or freeze mode, is far more effective for managing and reducing anger. Here are some tips for soothing your brain and defusing this powerful emotion:

- Cultivate awareness, so that you can be a nonjudgmental observer right when you're triggered and before you get to the boiling point.
- When anger is triggered, mindfully observe where it settles in your body. Is your jaw clenched? Are your arms or hands tense? How about your neck and shoulders?
- Focus on your body and watch the tension dissipate. The stress reaction will be over in ninety seconds or so if you don't feed it with destructive ruminating, such as, "People are doing this to hurt me" or "If only I'd gone in sooner" or "I hate feeling this way." Instead, remain focused on your body.
- To soothe your stressed brain, daily do what calms you and releases tension, such as vigorous exercise, getting outdoors, meditation, yoga, massage, and especially getting adequate sleep. Proactively soothing your brain can ward off fits of anger. (See also chapter 4, "Mindfulness-Based Coping Strategies.")
- Write in a journal or seek out writing avenues online. *Capture Your Grief* is a structured thirty-one-day journal for bereaved parents, with mindful, creative, and healing elements, in which you can tell your story, explore your grief, and reflect on all aspects of your journey.
- Foster emotional connection by talking to your partner or a friend who can validate your anger. Let them know you don't want them to fix it, but to just listen and commiserate—and that you so appreciate this kind of support. Verbalizing why you're angry can offer you insights and the companionship is soothing.

• Talk about anger with other bereaved parents. Besides soothing validation, you can see you aren't the only one to be angry and you can share tips for overcoming the thoughts that take you there.

You can also try doing "The Work" with angry thoughts. You may find it very effective to question the thoughts that give rise to anger, examine their basis in truth, and see if the turnarounds are truer. Many times, the turnaround can help you adopt a more compassionate thought that dissolves the anger. (See also "Doing 'The Work'" in chapter 4.)

> *When I see pregnant women, which still shakes me to some degree, I remind myself that I don't know their stories. Everyone has one.*
> *—Abby*

These methods have helped many parents cope with and move beyond angry feelings. You may find your own effective, productive ways to explore and soothe anger. By productively dealing with it, you can perhaps loosen its grip on you and move closer toward forgiveness. Forgiveness comes when you can understand another's frailty, impotence, or harshness in the face of your baby's illness and death. Forgiveness comes when you can accept someone's fear, ignorance, or inadequacy in the face of your grief. Your anger is valid, but you also deserve the peace that comes when you can release it. (See also "Mindfully Restoring Calm to Your Triggered Brain" and "Mindfully Reframing Your Thoughts" in chapter 4.)

> *I have followed complaint procedures and I have forgiven. I also have to accept that I cannot change what has been and that I did the best that I could at the time.*
> *—Karen*

> *Forgiveness doesn't mean that what happened is okay, and it doesn't mean that person should still be welcome in your life. It just means you have made peace with the pain, and are ready to let it go.*
> *—Emmerson*

(See also "Is It Normal to Feel So Irritable or Frustrated?" in chapter 5; "Anger" in chapter 10.)

GUILT

> *I felt as though either I had done something to deserve this baby dying or I had done something physically to cause her death or that there was something wrong with me that they hadn't noticed. . . . I felt the guilt any parent feels when something happens to their child. I felt like I had fallen down on the job.*
> *—Jessie*

Guilt is a mixture of anxiety, sadness, and anger: anxiety that you failed, sadness that you didn't measure up, and anger at your own self. Guilt arises from your belief that you should be able to protect your children.

Mothers can be especially prone to feelings of guilt. Because that baby was inside your body or under your protective care, it is only natural to feel primarily responsible for your baby's well-being. When you are pregnant, you strive to take good care of yourself in the belief that if you are healthy, follow your doctor's advice, avoid consuming dangerous substances, and monitor your baby's every move, you will deliver a healthy baby. When you do have a healthy baby, you vow to comfort and protect this child for as long as you live.

Fathers too can feel guilt intensely. You may feel angry with yourself that you aren't able to protect your baby. You may search for answers in an effort to uncover how you were at fault or worry about not knowing what you could've possibly done to prevent this tragedy. You want to believe you are powerful, not powerless!

It is normal to wonder if there was something you did that may have contributed to your baby's problems, or to have thoughts about what you might have done to prevent them. When you assume you are in complete control of your destiny, it is easy to hold yourself responsible.

Guilt. Although the doctors have told me numerous times that there was nothing I could have done to save her and that umbilical cords accidents are no fault of the mother, I struggle with feeling a sense of responsibility. If I had slept differently or been more alert to her movements or had not laid on my back that time, that she would be alive.

—*Daniela*

*My initial reaction was, of course, "What did I do? I know I must be responsible for this and what could it have been?" So I felt guilty, but I didn't know quite how to focus that guilt because I didn't know what I had done. I had a wonderful pediatrician who actually called me a month and a half later to make sure that I wasn't feeling guilty. And the neonatologist and obstetrician kept laying facts in front of me, and saying, "There is **no way** that you were responsible for this. You couldn't be responsible." They helped me through that.*

—*Sara*

Even when your doctor reassures you that there was nothing you could have done differently, or even if you *know* that your baby's death is not your fault, you may still have nagging feelings that there was something you should have done differently or that you let your baby down in some way. Especially if you tend to get angry with yourself over things that go wrong, you are likely to feel some guilt about your baby. Some parents feel guilty for ever being aggravated with the pregnancy or the baby. Some think they are getting paid back for "bad" things they've done in the past. Both parents may feel guilty because of difficult life-and-death decisions that had to be made. (See also "Living with the Decision" in chapter 9.)

You may even feel responsible for bringing tragedy into your family, letting them down, or burdening them with terrible sorrows and grief.

Unfortunately as a mama lion, I feel like I've let them [my other children] down and I'm responsible, even though I've had no control of these life events. Life has thrown a lot at them and their innocence was stolen. I should have been able to protect them and I couldn't. I do realize it's an unrealistic expectation to protect them from everything but I can try, can't I?

—Karen

I felt very guilty and still do to this day. My body let those boys down and my husband never got to hear his sons call him "Daddy."

—Fleur

*By wanting to be the mom of Sam and Oren and Miriam, not that it was my fault that they died, but . . . this is where my guilt was—in how I had brought this **SAD** to my family.*

—Tanya

Because guilt is directed at yourself, it can be self-destructive. It doesn't allow you to feel good about yourself and can be a source of chronic depression. It may even make you wonder if you deserved this tragedy. But, of course, nobody deserves the tragedy of having a baby die. Unfortunately, bad things can happen to anyone, without warning. We cannot always avoid tragedy or know ahead of time the right course of action.

Releasing feelings of guilt can be difficult, as you might be tempted to hold on to guilt as a way of holding on to a sense of control. You might also be tempted to hold on to guilt as a form of self-punishment. But holding on to guilt, for whatever reason, only increases your suffering and does not make you a better person. You can release guilt in any of the following ways:

- Consider that *feeling* guilty is not the same as *being* guilty.
- See your guilt as what it truly is: an emotion caused by a self-condemning thought you have. When you have a thought and feel a pang of guilt, mindfully and nonjudgmentally observe them as they pass through you. Notice where the pang lands in your body, and without feeding it self-blaming thoughts, let it dissipate. (See also "Mindfully Restoring Calm to Your Triggered Brain" in chapter 4.)
- Let yourself off the hook by accepting that you did the best you could with the support you were given at the time.
- Remember that you made the best decisions you could based on information available.
- Express your feelings and concerns to your doctor or midwife, so they can reassure you that you are not to blame or that you did the best anybody could.
- Talk to others who can compassionately listen to you express your feelings of responsibility and offer you alternative views that are reassuring.

- Write a letter to your baby, explaining your guilt and regrets—and any other thoughts and sentiments you wish to convey. Then write your baby's response.
- Practice self-compassion by telling yourself what you'd say to encourage another parent who was wrestling with terrible feelings of guilt.
- Accept that you cannot always prevent bad things from happening.

You want to control things. You feel like you should be able to control things. Did I do something wrong? People would tell me, "If you lift your arms above your head, it's supposed to choke your baby" or something. And that was a bunch of . . . that was so stupid. But all those things went through my mind. Did I ever lift my arms up? Did I ever bend over wrong? You know, "what did I do?" And I didn't do anything. It took a long time and I just realized she would have died regardless of what I did. And me rolling around on the floor is not going to tie her cord in a knot.

—Cindy

I think that you feel out of control with almost any death, when you realize that we don't have control. I mean, that we do and we don't. I go back and forth on that. . . . Right after Heidi died I'd been confronted about my guilt over her death, and I go back and forth between wanting to take responsibility and saying, "Hey, come on, I did not cause this, this cannot be my responsibility."

—Holly

I wallowed in guilt for a long time. I elicited feedback from other people to the contrary—my therapist, my husband—and I commiserated with other mothers from the support group who understood that feeling. I still feel guilty every once in a while. I think that I've mostly let go of it because even if there was anything I could have done, and I think that right now I feel like there was, but that's past history and right now it's not going to do me any good—or my baby any good—to stay stuck in that place.

—Jessie

Even if you have a strong feeling that you did something wrong and feel terrible about it, you can still get to a point where you accept the fact that you made a mistake, an error in judgment, and forgive yourself for being imperfect. You may also find it very helpful to do "The Work." When you examine the self-destructive thoughts that are at the root of your guilt, you can question their validity, entertain who you would be without those painful thoughts, and you can turn it around and entertain other, more valid views of reality, such as, "My baby was fortunate to have me for a mother/father, because here are all the ways I showed my love." This may seem like an insurmountable task, but the reward is great. You and your baby deserve a bond full of love and joy, not suffering and regret. While you are entitled to your guilt, by releasing it, you can live peacefully with yourself and honorably with your baby. (See also "Doing 'The Work'" in chapter 4.)

They were going to disconnect the life support and asked if we wanted to be there, and I said, "No." What a LOUSY decision that was, but I did the best I could. . . . But for two years I beat myself up for that a million times over. For probably a good year and a half, I didn't even really deal with my guilt. It was so painful to me that it wasn't until way towards the end of my real grieving time that I was even strong enough to cope with that. It was just admitting to myself that I had done this stupid thing. It was awful. . . . I probably worked on it for six weeks in therapy, where I was finally able to let myself off the hook for it. Now I'm able to objectively say I did the best I could in that situation. I would never do it again and a part of me still wishes I hadn't done that.

—Sara

I felt guilty at first. It took me a long time to work through that. I was very active and at times I've felt like, "Gee, if I had REALLY rested and if I had really stayed in bed, this probably wouldn't have happened." To this day I could probably say to you that I still feel maybe if I had followed the rules a little bit more, I probably wouldn't have lost the baby. But, you know, I feel that that was me at the time, like it was a different person back then and she could have probably done a lot of things to make the pregnancy better but she didn't, and I forgive her.

—Elaine

I kept thinking that I did something to cause what happened to Dayani. Maybe it was the hot dog I ate, the tea I drank every morning, something. Deep down I know it's irrational, especially when I see living children whose moms take drugs and alcohol on a regular basis during pregnancy. So I remind myself to stop putting myself on trial, as it leads to nowhere.

—Destrida

Even though we had lost Kate, I naively thought something bad couldn't happen again. So with Zac, I will always regret that I didn't go to the doctor sooner. They have reassured me over and over that it would have made no difference but I can't help but wonder. With time I have been able to make peace with this, but initially, I struggled with this enormously.

—Melanie

Some parents release their guilt by eventually turning their anger away from themselves and toward someone else, making their anger less destructive to their self-esteem. Many parents turn their anger toward the lack of support or information, their obstetrician or pediatrician, fate or God.

I felt guilty. But the only reason I blamed myself was because I was the only person who had contact with the baby, so I must have been the reason why he died. . . . I couldn't blame God because I needed Him too much to lean on, so then finally after going to the support group I got to where I blamed the doctor, and that's where I've stayed.

—Desi

This wasn't one of those cases where everyone could agree that there was nothing that could have been done. Because Thor, in fact, could have lived. In the months following the stillbirth, I had to consider, very seriously, the possibility that I had made a fatal mistake in my health care choices. I had to consider the possibility that my midwife had made a fatal mistake in her care for me. I had to consider the larger context of American maternal health care—the ways economics and politics and culture sometimes combine in toxic ways. My partner, Glenn, tortured himself about his role. Although there's an urge to find a single culprit, it's usually not so simple. There were many different moments, many different decisions where, if any one of them had gone differently, Thor would be alive today. I spend a lot of time on the question of responsibility, or how things might have gone differently. And I keep coming to different conclusions, because in a situation with many possible culprits, the one you choose depends partly on who you're pissed off at, in the moment.

—Elizabeth

A statesman recently said that no one was to blame, yet all were responsible, and that is how I perceive it.

—Victoria

Remember, whatever reasoning you come up with, *you did the best you could at the time.* Like most parents, you are incapable of knowingly endangering your baby. You couldn't know then what you know now. Releasing feelings of guilt involves realizing that you cannot always prevent tragedy from happening and you cannot always avoid making mistakes. Some parents embrace a spiritual or philosophical outlook that comforts them.

I used to be hard on myself but I don't dwell on these regrets any longer. I now accept that I did the best I could under these traumatic, life-changing circumstances and with very little effective guidance from my caregivers.

—Lori

Even if I had come in after noticing less movement, I sometimes wonder if they really could have done anything. I feel like them saving him at that point is a hopeful thought but not very likely.

—Jolie

At first, when Oren died, I thought that maybe somehow I had caused it because of my interest and work around death. My midwife told me that I couldn't have caused Oren's death because I wasn't that powerful. I heard that but it still didn't make sense to me. Then Lavender told me that she thought my soul knew that I would lose a baby and that somehow I started doing work to prepare for that almost twenty years before. That was a profound comfort to me. Whether it could possibly be true or not it took away some of my feelings of responsibility.

—Tanya

We humans naturally gravitate toward feelings of responsibility and guilt, especially when it comes to our children. Even when we know we are not to blame, many of us would rather blame ourselves than feel vulnerable and helpless. Helplessness can be such a terrifying feeling to face. So if feelings of guilt are persistent, you can benefit from mindfully observing and accepting your tendency for self-blame. Without judgment, be a witness to your guilt and see it as a way to rail against helplessness. In fact, whenever feelings of guilt are triggered, ask yourself whether you're feeling particularly helpless and vulnerable. Then mindfully, nonjudgmentally, become a witness to that.

VULNERABILITY

Alex's death highlights the fact that life can change in an instant. It's a high wire.

—Victoria

Like many people, you probably thought that with enough foresight and good judgment you could avoid tragedy. Perhaps you believed that living well, being a good person, or devoting yourself to religious faith would protect you. Then, when your baby died, you were naturally overcome with questions: "How could this happen?" "What did I do wrong?"

At first, you may be reluctant to accept that the cause of your baby's problems is unknown or that they couldn't be prevented. You can't believe that nothing in particular should have been done differently. You search for the answers to questions posed by your spiritual distress. Questions like, "Why did God let this happen? Did I do something to deserve this?" Or, "Now that I know bad things can happen to me, how can I have any trust?" Jolie agrees: "I developed an irrational fear of dying. Which I still have, and after losing Judah *and* my dog *and* a miscarriage, it doesn't seem too irrational, to be honest."

As the futility of trying to control destiny sinks in, you will discover that you were powerless to alter your baby's fate. Maybe there were things you would do differently, and yet hindsight is the only way to see this. Alas, it is not possible to have twenty-twenty foresight. And even if you could go back and do it over again, it's quite possible that the outcome would be exactly the same. Such is fate.

The truth is, Judah probably wouldn't be here no matter whether I was induced or not. But those feelings are there nonetheless, and I do battle with them.

—Jolie

The independent report has been formed, and nothing "negligent," thank God, came out of the obstetricians' findings. Okay, some things could have been improved, but whether they would have changed the outcome, probably not. Nobody will ever know.

—Victoria

In the early days of my grief I asked my boss, with whom I am close personally, "Why is life so unpredictable?" He said it's always been this scary and unpredictable, but I now choose to see and acknowledge it, instead of denying the reality by controlling everything around me.

—Destrida

Gradually, as you begin to let yourself off the hook and accept the imperfections and limitations of medicine, science, other people, and yourself, you will shed the belief that you should have total control over what happens. You will realize that life is unfair and that you are vulnerable to tragedy. This can feel quite unsettling, aggravating, and anxiety provoking, to be at the mercy of random chance, or in Hannah's terms, "It felt like a bolt out of the sky."

It was very sad and stressful for us both. Our dream of a baby was slipping through our fingers and we had no control over it.

—Fleur

I was suffering from terrible anxiety. I was convinced I was going to die and not see my kids grow up and this was all-consuming. It was the idea that life was so fragile and you have no control over it and this rocked me to my core. I would wake up in the night with my heart racing, convinced that if I went to sleep I was going to die. One day I just couldn't turn off that dread that something bad was going to happen and I was almost shaking with agitation.

—Melanie

While this vulnerability can be frightening to contemplate, eventually you can accept it as a simple fact of life.

If you think you're protected, it's a real comforting feeling but you're naive. Some people go through their whole lives without anything bad happening to them. It just means they're lucky, and when something bad does happen, I guess people try to interpret it a million ways but I think it just happens.

—Rose

I know some people consider this callous or too fatalistic, but I really think that everybody picks a number and when your number is up, it's up.

—Terri

When I asked, "Why me?" I don't know that I ever got an answer. At first I blamed the doctor because he didn't care. Now I just feel like it was fate. You don't know what to think, but that's kind of where I've left it.

—Erin

In your search for answers, you can also practice not taking this tragedy personally. Death does not seek you out, nor does it mock or thwart you. Death is simply a fact of life, unavoidable, and not always under our control. You can simply come to accept that, sometimes, horrible things happen—while taking comfort in the fact that most of the time, good things happen. You can balance fear with appreciation. And you can be intent on controlling only what's controllable.

> *When it first happened, I was terrified of the future. I couldn't stand the thought of bad things happening in my life. Well, now that it's been four years and nothing bad has happened, I have Leslie now, and everything's been positive. That makes it much easier to deal with it. But I'm still afraid.*
>
> —Bryn

> *After Finley died, part of taking control and the first thing I did was to make a timetable. I literally programmed into my day time to eat, what to eat, times to drink water, time to dress, time to wash, time to go for a walk, time to read. This helped to add structure to the long days and nights. I literally ticked off what I had done that day.*
>
> —Mel

As you heal, feelings of vulnerability can become less frightening. For one thing, you realize that if you can survive your baby's death, you can survive anything. Armed with this sense of confidence, you can also acquire the sense of peace that accompanies "surrender." Surrender means casting off the idea that life requires you to stay on guard, cover all your bases, and be in charge of everything around you. Surrender means understanding that life merely requires you to control yourself, as in, do your best and roll with the unexpected. Surrender also means you stop regretting the past and you fear less for the future. You practice taking each day as it comes and cherish the time you have. Surrender means you worry less, not more. As you practice accepting your vulnerability, your feelings of failure, anger, and guilt can melt away and you can take feelings of helplessness in stride. (See also "Accepting *What Is*" in chapter 4; "Acceptance, Peace, and Gratitude" in chapter 17.)

> *You really feel like you don't have any control anymore, and there is a real loss of ego there. For a while I just felt like I shouldn't make any plans because something could happen and it could just wipe everything away. Now I feel more confident. I feel like I might as well make a lot of plans and if they don't work out, at least I had the enjoyment of making them.*
>
> —Rose

> *We have our faith, as not everything in life is within our control. It really is so true. We as humans demand answers, but life is too complicated to offer all the answers.*
>
> —Victoria

POINTS TO REMEMBER

- Feelings of anger, guilt, and failure arise from the belief that you are or should be in control of your destiny.
- If you feel a sense of failure, question the thoughts that give rise to your pain and adopt alternative views of reality that point to your worthiness.
- If you feel angry, it can fuel your ability to assert yourself and fix the fixable. When it's not fixable, there are many mindfulness strategies to soothe yourself when anger is triggered.
- If you feel guilty, you can question the self-blaming conclusions you've drawn. If you continue to blame yourself, you can practice self-forgiveness. Nobody is perfect; nobody can predict the future.
- Early on, these feelings of failure, anger, or guilt can shield you from feelings of deep sadness or vulnerability, but eventually, holding on to them can become destructive and only adds to unnecessary pain and suffering.
- Do whatever helps you to go with the flow of your grief and mourning. Going with the flow enables you to release your distress—including failure, anger, and guilt—and attain a sense of healing.
- You can practice accepting human vulnerability. Tragedies occur, and we don't have control over everything that happens to us. That's simply reality; it's just the way life is. You benefit enormously from accepting *what is*.
- Eventually you will find a balance between maintaining control over what's controllable and accepting what's not.

8

THE JOURNEY OF HEALING

It has taken me a long time to see grief as a companion instead of the overpowering, all-consuming beast it once was. I had dark, dark days and moments where I would drop to my knees in tears as the reality of not having my baby at home would hit me like a ton of bricks.

—Abby

At first, and perhaps for many, many months, you may feel ravaged by grief. Processing your experiences, acknowledging your losses, and thinking about your baby can be heart-wrenching. Managing and surrendering to your distress can be exhausting. Balancing mourning with the rest of your responsibilities can be supremely challenging. But as time passes, you adapt and make adjustments, and your grief changes, becoming softer and more pensive. Instead of being wracked with deep emotion or agitated and restless, you become reflective. Instead of fighting it, you come to accept the fact that your baby is gone. By accepting *what is*, you can integrate your baby's life and death into the larger tapestry of your life. Instead of it being your whole life, it becomes a pivotal point in your life.

I'm at a point where I am comfortable with Elizabetta's death. I still think of her every day and I have days where I cry, but my heart smiles when I think of her now and I focus on how blessed I've been to have had the privilege of being her mother and how much I have learned and grown because of her.

—Karen

Someone told me right at the beginning that the size of your grief never changes and it doesn't go away, it's just that life gets bigger around it and that resonates with me now.

—Emmerson

Healing does *not* signal an end to grief. You may always feel twinges of longing and sadness. Eventually, though, these feelings can mellow to the point that you can feel peaceful when you remember your baby.

Maybe you could call it healing, but I'm not sure that I could say the grief journey has been finally trod. I think the journey has just become woven into the fabric of living. Somehow, over time, I have learned to live with the absence of my lost daughter. But also, I sometimes yearn for her so strongly that it feels like my heart is being rebroken.

—Nathan

It is true about grief being circuitous. I am certainly learning that it runs alongside me and I am thankful that it doesn't shroud me, as it once did.

—Victoria

I'm not really sure if it's a sense of healing so much as it's a sense of peace, I guess.

—Ben

Unburdened by the ravages of grief, it's not that you've "moved on" but rather that now you can "move with." Your bond to your baby can remain strong, and instead of being stuck in grief, you can journey into your future with your memories and your bond intact.

I find the terms "move on" or "move forward" don't apply to me. My understanding is that it means I have to move away from Finley or leave him behind. I won't do that. He is every bit a part of my life, he is my son. He will remain a part of my life. I actually consider finding a way for him to be a part of my life means "acceptance." I have accepted the circumstances of his death. I have accepted that he is not physically with me. So I choose to integrate my new beliefs and Finley into my life.

—Mel

Emotionally, I'd say I held tight to Emma throughout both of the next pregnancies. Whether that was talking to her, writing to her, or finding little signs of her surrounding me. She helped me on some of my hardest days . . . beautiful, huh?!

—Abby

It is always there, and I don't think that feeling of loss and grief will ever leave. It is not as deep as it once was, but Blake and Rylee are always there, in my mind and in my heart.

—Sonya

As grief mellows over time, you'll feel more and more relief from distress. Healing enables you to feel a sense of peace and live your life in healthy, functional ways. You can find happiness, reinvest your energy in satisfying relationships and pursuits, and feel a renewed sense of hope for the future.

At first, it may seem impossible that you'll ever feel a sense of peace or accept and integrate your baby's death into your life. In the midst of overwhelming despair, it is difficult to imagine being able to think about your baby and the circumstances surrounding the death without great suffering. But, as the intensity of grief fades, acceptance can feel comfortable and you cannot help but integrate this experience into your life. This acceptance and integration and the peace it brings—all are evidence of healing.

*I can honestly say that I have now reached that deep healing. But, in the beginning, I could **never** have imagined being able to do so.*

—Lori

Just gradually over time it felt for the most part that I could accept it, I could live with it, it was not nearly as painful. It's something I feel sad about and I have regrets that it happened, but it's not anything I feel angry or guilty about anymore. It hurts, but it's okay—an important point to get to and it's not a point I could have understood, I think, before she died, that something can hurt horribly but it's all right.

—Anya

There are parents who hold on to their grief as a way of giving their life meaning, or as a way to hold on to the baby. Some parents worry that if they stop feeling angry about their baby's death, then somehow they're admitting defeat. Others believe that if they are not despondent, they are being disloyal or desecrating their baby's life. By holding on to these grieving patterns, some parents feel reassured that they will never forget their baby.

It is important to recognize that you can remember, love, and miss your baby without grieving continuously. You can go ahead in life and live well in honor of your baby. As Desi puts it, "You don't have to be miserable to remember."

Walking up the driveway towards work I was nervous, anxious, scared. I couldn't stop thinking, "What if I forgot Beau? What if I didn't have time to remember him and think of the memories I created with him when he was home with us?"

For the first hour it was hard . . . but after an hour, it was okay . . . I knew I was going to be okay and I was enjoying being back at work, doing something I loved. I deserved to do something I loved. I had worked so hard for it. I will always have Beau around my neck in my beautiful necklace and I hold him whenever I think of it or without realizing. I miss him so much it hurts to think about it but I achieved another milestone.

—Courtney

As far as my grief journey with Judah goes, I feel like I don't think of him nearly as much. I feel like I don't have time to and maybe even more so, I feel like I don't need to. That is hard to even admit as I type this, because that thought is accompanied by such guilt, but my head knows it's okay. It's okay to feel a little more whole. It's okay to be living life without my loss of Judah being the center of it.

—Jolie

How Long Will It Take?

I wasn't sure how long the worst of the grief would last, but it wasn't really long for me. At the time this was all happening, I think being so open with everyone and sharing our story helped to lessen the pain. As time went on, the rough edges became softer.

—Shellie

Although there is no definite time frame, the tough part of your healing journey can take several years. Within the first year or two, many parents report that the initial hard edges of pain gradually soften. Over time they notice that they don't cry as easily or they are able to look at infants or pregnant women without acute envy. As sad as it is, this experience becomes something to live with on a private, interior level. Martina found that it became less difficult to think or talk about her baby. She remarks, "When I think about him it's not something that is so bold like it was before, that when you start thinking about him you just have to stop everything because you're in a daze for a week." Sara noticed that instead of focusing on her baby's death, it became a part of her history, a part that will always exist but one that no longer occupies center stage. Peg agrees: "It fades a little bit to the background. I still think about the twins quite a bit and I'm sad and I wish that it hadn't happened, but it just doesn't hurt as much as time goes on."

> Sometimes I feel happy or proud, and other times just sad. It's all mixed. I can have good thoughts about her, kind of a resolved thing. Even when I feel grief it's not a desperate feeling, it's a comfortable feeling. I know she's dead and I can't get her back. I don't have those **Oh–I–can't–stand–it–get–her–back–here!** feelings, as if I could pull her out of the air if I had enough faith, if I gritted my teeth hard enough or whatever. I can't describe exactly how I feel because it's always up and down, but resolved means I can look at her picture and not burst into tears. . . . She's just one of my daughters. The subject is pretty much closed. . . . But it's definitely not like I've put her in a closet and closed the door.
>
> —Rose

> It's a relief. I feel peaceful. I know he's with God and my tormenting is over, but I still love him. He's not forgotten.
>
> —Desi

When your grief ceases to tear at you and the intensity of longing lessens, your sense of acceptance is coupled with letting go of *what might have been*. Meryl remarks, "The yearning, the little bit of grief will always be there, but I don't feel it that much anymore. I feel at peace, it's just accepted, it's okay." You also no longer feel lost and confused. You regain your footing and create a new normal. And you feel transformed—you've become better instead of bitter—and you can have happy thoughts about your baby's life. Jessie notes, "Now it feels like an unfortunate event that changed me forever. I'll always remember her and be sad that she's not living with us, but happy that we had her for a while."

Alas, the road of healing transformation is a bumpy one, and there are no shortcuts. The softening of grief and the acceptance of your tragedy don't always progress in a smooth, steady fashion. There are ups and downs and heartache all along the way. You need time to let your grief flow and to move through your tasks of mourning, whether it takes several months or several years. Anya remembers the first day she didn't cry for Rachel—seven months after her death. She admits, "I never would have thought it would take that long." Cindy remembers the first year as the worst: "The depression, the ups and downs, probably lasted three years. . . . Then, as the years go on, it gets easier. People would tell me it gets better with time, but that first year I was sure I would feel that way until I died." Abby agrees: "I miss her every day. And working through grief is hard, painstaking work. It hurts, and takes a long time to feel 'better.'"

Liza also remembers feeling much better after the first year, but still distrusting the ups because, "As soon as I'd feel really good one day, then almost for sure I'd be right back as bad as ever the next day. It took another year before I felt like there was any plateau." Even so, in the third year, she notes, "I could have a good month and then something would happen, and I'd feel like I was right back again." Bryn remembers it took her a full three years before she could be happy for pregnant friends or see newborn babies. Sara, five years later, can finally enjoy watching "tearjerker" movies again. She says, "The crying stops when the sad part is over. I can cry again and not be afraid of crying . . . just tears for fun." Maiya, also five years down the road, describes her experience this way: "Grief is like working on this giant jigsaw puzzle. You work very hard to put it together, and every now and then it feels like it's thrown up in the air and it comes down in pieces. Again, you put it back together, but it's not as bad as starting over, and you may even put it back together a little better."

Mourning is not for the faint-hearted. It takes courage, persistence, and a certain amount of faith that you will feel better, eventually. The road may be winding and long, but the rewards are great and far-reaching.

Is It Okay for My Grieving to Feel Prolonged?

Oh, absolutely, I have felt stuck. It took me about eighteen months after losing Oren to really start feeling like I wasn't completely crazy. Being stuck felt hopeless, depressing, overwhelming, and isolating.
—Tanya

Some parents experience prolonged grief because they are raising a surviving baby from a multiple pregnancy (see next section). Others simply feel unable to set aside sufficient time for grief for whatever reason. Still others are suffering from the aftereffects of trauma and need to seek brain-based therapies. But for many parents, grieving feels prolonged simply because it is exhausting, and requires the passage of more time than they ever thought possible.

With that really bad period of depression, I was getting subtle—and not-so-subtle—hints from people that it was time to get on with things, and I didn't feel ready to get on with things. I think I only heard that

from people who hadn't experienced any kind of death of anyone close. Mostly I avoided people who made me feel that way.
                                                                    —Jessie

If you are unable to find a sense of healing, you may simply need more time. Your grief may be too fresh for you to feel at peace. Or perhaps you resist "accepting" your baby's death because, as Bess says, "*Accepted* means you go along with it." Bryn agrees: "I did not want to accept that this bad thing had happened and that I was going to have to live with this terrible thing for the rest of my life."

In spite of what people may tell you, there is no hard evidence to support the idea that "prolonged grief" is bad or pathological or unhealthy in itself. True, many professionals consider grief lasting longer than six months or a year to be "prolonged" and cause for concern. But the vast community of bereaved parents would laugh at that yardstick, as for many, six months to one year can be a time of the thickest grief, after which it gradually gets better over the next few years.

What matters more is that you go with the flow of grief and release it as it flows through you. If you can do this most of the time that grief calls on you, and if you feel you are making progress as time goes on, then you are grieving, *and* you are also healing. In this way, continuing to grieve is a relatively healthy state of affairs, because you are facing grief instead of hiding from it; you are in the midst of your tasks of mourning instead of circumventing them. It may take several years for your grief to transform, but in the meantime, life goes on and you gradually reinvest in it.

I have found it an incredibly intense and exhausting process, trying to put all the pieces of my broken self back together. I guess I can liken it to a maze. It is a maze of emotion and sometimes you reach a dead end where you get stuck for a while until you conserve the energy again to move forward.
                                                                    —Emmerson

It also matters that your quality of life remains good. You may be miserable part of the time, but if you can also do what needs to be done to keep functioning, if important relationships are staying afloat, and if your emotional, mental, and physical health aren't deteriorating, you're on a good path. So although your grief may seem prolonged and you may even wish you could feel better, by going with the flow of grief, you allow your journey to transform you.

As hard as it is, I have embraced my grief. Meaning, I do not push it away, as hard as it can be at times. I want to go through it all, so I do not have it "crop up" later in life. I mean, it will always be there. But this powerful, raw stuff that happens in the first months, I have to go through it all. I want to be changed. The other option (pretending it never happened) is not an option for me.
                                                                    —Anne

It's so very hard to believe that healing is possible at the beginning of this deeply painful, devastating, soul-wrenching, and heartbreaking experience. Truly the only way to get through something as painful as this is to actually make grieving a priority. It's not something to avoid or run away from. Grief is a normal, healthy, human response to losing a much-loved baby. Grieving is also how we humans can heal! Feel your feelings and then express them . . . and do it OVER and OVER and OVER again . . . it's all truly a part of the healing process!

—Lori

In contrast, if your quality of life is suffering, you may feel stuck in a grief that remains constant. Lauren and Holly feel this keenly:

I feel like there's a fire-breathing dragon in a box and I'm tossing drops of water on it and trying to force the lid shut. I'm fighting grief, not at peace.

—Lauren

It is frustrating to me to think that although I know the pain or the caring never goes away, in a sense I think it should be easier for me now, or I wonder, "Am I hanging on to this and being more negative or sad than is healthy or than I should be?"

—Holly

Many parents have times when they feel "stuck," and sometimes being stuck is simply part of the journey. To ensure that being stuck doesn't become a habit, here are two keys:

1. Have realistic expectations. This can reduce self-imposed pressure to "get over it already" and help you take your time, trust the process, and go with the ebb and flow of this unpredictable, complex journey.
2. Stay connected to your body and whenever possible, allow your grief to find its expression. This can help you grieve as it arises, instead of consistently denying it or saving it for later.

Once you have this foundation in place, you may find yourself actually setting aside time for grieving—whether that means immersing yourself in feelings or activity—and accomplishing your tasks of mourning without feeling too overwhelmed (see "How Do I Acquire a Sense of Healing?" later in this chapter).

You can also benefit from getting assistance. For example, having information about grief and healing can shed light on this sometimes dark journey. Mindfulness practices can grant relief and build your confidence. Companionship can boost your resilience. Counseling can give you more support and coping tools. Rarely can anyone grieve freely without the benefit of such resources. If grieving feels too prolonged, you can benefit from a dedicated focus on doing what you need to do to heal, and getting both the additional support and tools you need.

My relationship with my grief is constant right now. I can't escape it. It speaks loudly and sometimes it is all I can hear. But I acknowledge it's a process and a journey that will take time—the result of the deep yearning and love I have for our baby girl.

—Emmerson

Absolutely, I got help. I cried a lot. I wrote often. I also ran and practiced yoga, both activities that brought me healing and my mental health.

—Abby

It helped so much to seek out other moms/parents. As much as I hate that there are so many of us, it helped me to not feel alone, and that was invaluable and it still is to this day. To have someone you can openly talk to is key, and if it's someone who gets it, that's even better!

—Embry

*Eventually, I found the supportive balance that I needed, between family members, a few close friends, and the support group, plus constantly journaling my thoughts and feelings, over and over and over again. Plus, I read **many** baby grief books too, and anytime I came across some "nugget of wisdom" in these books I would write it down. I did not want to forget the things that I was learning or that really resonated with me. All of these things combined were such a therapeutic balance for me to eventually discover much healing.*

—Lori

WHAT IF I HAVE A SURVIVING BABY?

I don't really cry anymore but I can't believe I'm over it. I still feel bad and I think about Jeffrey, but I don't cry. And normally I'm very sentimental and cry very easily. I cried a lot the first month while Bradley [the surviving baby] was still in intensive care. But once he came home, and for the past year, I've been forced to move on. It's so strange because you're so busy and tied up with the other one. Having Bradley doesn't give me the opportunity to dwell on Jeffrey.

—Shannon

Typically, parents who are raising a surviving baby or babies from a multiple pregnancy are distracted from grief. The time and energy required to parent your surviving baby(s) can put grieving on a back burner. Particularly if a survivor is struggling, you may put aside your grief completely until the health of that baby is assured.

Perhaps you think and talk about the baby or babies who died, but it doesn't pack the emotional wallop that you think it should. Perhaps you are hounded by feelings of sadness or anger, but are afraid to see their source. Perhaps you harbor vague but nagging feelings of dissatisfaction with your life. As Shannon reveals, "I feel unsettled. Should I go to school, have a job, get a career, or what? My life has changed so much in the past year and it's not that I'm unhappy, but . . . maybe this *is* because of Jeffrey."

You may even wonder whether you are delaying your grief. You probably are, and this is normal and okay. Anya recalls, "Because I had Kim to focus on, I put off working through some of my feelings about Rachel, so I think it dragged out for a longer period of time." As your surviving baby gets older, your emotional priorities will shift and you'll deal with it on a deeper level when you are ready. In the meantime, as long as you can think and talk about the baby(s) who died, you are dealing with it to an important extent.

Do remember that, like any bereaved parent, you can benefit from setting aside some time and space to grieve. Having a survivor does not take away your need to do so. And going with the flow of your grief will not harm your little one(s). It's the *suppression* of grief that harms your emotional availability and capacity to nurture your baby(s). The key is to find a balance between grieving and parenting, month to month, day to day, hour to hour.

Because babies require lots of attentive care, it can be especially critical to bring a friend, relative, housekeeper, or favorite babysitter on board to help you so that you have more energy to meet your baby(s)'s needs. Just as each baby who died deserves to be mourned in his or her own special way, each baby who lives deserves to be celebrated, held, and cherished like any other newborn. Enlisting the aid of others is a nurturing support to both you and your baby(s).

Even if you don't have a lot of help, you can get into the daily routine of setting aside some time to do tasks of mourning, such as letting feelings flow as they come up, seeking support from other bereaved parents of multiples, and honoring the memory of the baby(s) who died. Going with the flow of your grief and mourning promptly will benefit you—and your little survivor(s). (See also "Anniversaries and Other Reminders" in this chapter.)

How Do I Acquire a Sense of Healing?

I allowed myself to grieve these past almost three years because I did not want to act like it did not matter, and put on a mask, only to fall apart years from now. It mattered, and it still matters. And I will always think about Emily and Michael for the rest of my life. But I have accepted that this is my life story, and my reality.

—Anne

Engage in the Tasks of Mourning

To acquire a sense of healing, you must mourn. A primary task is grieving well, which means mindful awareness of your feelings as they come up, and letting them flow through your body by *feeling what you need to feel* and *doing what you need to do*. There are also a number of other "tasks of mourning" first listed in chapter 2, and detailed below. Mourning is what enables you to gradually come to terms with your baby's death, adapt to the changes, and adjust to a "new normal." As you grieve and mourn, you also heal, bit by bit.

Bereavement experts have recommended engaging in certain tasks of mourning over the days, months, and years after a loved one's death, in order to successfully find peace and healing. These are not tasks to accomplish or complete, rather they are tasks to engage in, explore, and master. They are practices that are ongoing, rather than goals to finish.

You might consider these tasks to be a set of guidelines or a roadmap to healing. If such a list doesn't appeal to you, it is not necessary to study or abide by it. However, if you're ever feeling stuck in numbness or misery, you can refer to this list for what you can do to get unstuck, recover yourself, and live more fully. Here are the tasks, tailored for parents mourning the death of a baby. For information on "how to," turn to the chapters referenced with each task.

- Affirm your baby's existence and importance. Have you been able to name your baby (even informally), and do you consider yourself to be your baby's mother or father? (See chapter 6, "Affirming Your Baby.")

- Acknowledge the reality of your baby's death. Do you have an explanation of how your baby died that you can accept, whether it can be proven or not? (See "Finding Comfort in Spiritual Philosophies" in this chapter.)

- Identify your losses (of self, identity, dreams, faith, control, etc.). Have you been able to realize the different ways you and your life have been affected by your baby's death, so that you can find ways to adapt and adjust? (See "A Traumatic Bereavement" in chapter 1.)

- Reflect on your experiences and memories, and create a clear account. Can you describe the events that unfolded or do you have a clear sense of what happened, so you can integrate your baby's life and death and this journey into the larger tapestry of your life? (See "Mindful Journaling" in chapter 4; "Memories" in chapter 6.)

- Be aware of your distress, staying connected to your body, and going with the flow. Are you connected to your body, or are you numbing your pain or hiding behind a veneer of anger, guilt, or failure? (See "Invisible Grief" and "Going with the Flow" in chapter 10; "What if I Try to Avoid Grieving?" in chapter 5; and chapter 7, "Painful Feelings.")

- Grieve in ways that are consistent with your internal experiences of grief. When you feel grief welling up in your body as emotion, do you have effective ways of releasing the emotional tension of grief? When you feel grief welling up in your body as restlessness, do you have productive activities you can engage in to release the mental and physical tension of grief? (See "Grieving According to Your Nature" in chapter 2; "Understanding Your Blend of Grieving" in chapter 10; "Grieving Styles" in chapter 11.)

- Implement adaptive strategies that ease your suffering and promote healing. Have you found adaptive coping strategies that provide comfort or improve your level of functioning in your life and relationships? (See "About Trauma and Suffering" in chapter 3; chapter 4, "Mindfulness-Based Coping Strategies"; chapter 7, "Painful Feelings"; "Counseling" in chapter 13.)
- Seek out and accept the compassion of others who can be supportive as you mourn. Have you found any friends, family members, bereaved parents, and/or a counselor you can rely on for compassion and support? (See chapter 13, "Support Networks.")
- Honor and keep your bond to your baby, moving from a relationship of presence into a relationship of memory and/or spirit. Have you been able to find ways to feel connected to your baby, or ways to remember or honor your baby's life that offer comfort *and* free you to invest in other relationships and activities you enjoy? Can you feel gratitude for the time you got to spend with your baby during the pregnancy or after? (See chapter 6, "Affirming Your Baby"; "Acceptance, Peace, and Gratitude" in chapter 17.)
- Accept *what is*, and let go of *what might have been*. Have you been able to acquire a sense of peace, forgiveness, or acceptance around what happened and where you are now? Have you modified your dreams and expectations? (See "Accepting *What Is*" in chapter 4.)
- Reflect on and adjust to the changes in beliefs, worldviews, roles, relationships, and ways of being that rise out of your experiences. Have you been able to make adjustments in how you make your way in the world—adjustments that accommodate wisdom you've realized or discovered since your baby's death? (See "Can Our Relationship Survive?" in chapter 11; "Friends" in chapter 14; "Your Healing Transformation" in chapter 17; "Making Sense of Tragedy" in this chapter.)
- Search for meaning and explore spiritual/philosophical foundations (that are perhaps new) for living your life with a renewed sense of purpose, mastery, and gratitude. Have you been able to recognize the positives, restore your sense of purpose, regain your confidence, recover some sense of control, practice gratitude, and generally reinvest in relationships and activities that enrich your life? (See also "Mindfully Embracing Positive Experiences" in chapter 4; "Vulnerability" in chapter 7; "Recognizing the Positive" and "Spirituality and Religion" in this chapter.)

In the early months after your baby dies, you can only expect yourself to have engaged in some of these processes. You can think of these as tasks to strive toward, or you can check this list every few months to get reassurance of your progress. Eventually, if you notice that you have engaged more thoroughly in some but not all of these tasks, this list may help you focus your energy on those aspects of mourning that you think might be hindering your adjustment.

What Does Healing Feel Like at First?

I find that I don't cry as much as I did in the early months of losing them . . . although I still choke up a little if I have to tell someone who doesn't know what happened.

—Kylie

It has become more manageable over time. I no longer cry at the drop of a hat, though little things like quotes, words, sentences, or flashbacks still do that to me.

—Destrida

My grief is easier to manage but I still miss my boy every day. Just contributing to this book has made me cry. But now I do not have the physical pain I had at first. Just tears now.

—Lorna

My grief is no longer all-consuming, I'm letting life back in. I think "comfortable grief" is the term I'd use. I acknowledge that it is there but I'm okay with it day to day. It might sound weird, but I actually get a feeling of warmth when I connect with my grief and think about Elizabetta; it's not acutely painful and the memory of her can make me smile.

—Karen

For many parents, healing appears on the horizon when thinking about the baby is less painful. Eventually, happy feelings are more prevalent than sad ones. Identity isn't focused on being a bereaved parent. Feelings of peace and acceptance creep up, and perhaps silver linings can be appreciated. Sophie feels a glimmer of healing: "I don't think I'll ever completely accept it, but it has mellowed. Sometimes I feel sad and other times I can feel peaceful about it all and look at the positive effect she had on me."

I think I got to a point where I thought, "My baby died, that's the way it is, and I can't change it and I better quit wishing it would change. It can't; it won't." So I have to deal with it, go on.

—Cindy

I began to realize that love isn't limited. The more you give away, the more you have. Instead of being angry at everybody else because they didn't die when he died—that's the way I felt, that the whole world should've stopped—I began to see that other people have pain whether I think it was as great as mine or not. There were a lot of selfish feelings, like, "Nobody has ever gone through something like this," but I began to realize that it's a universal thing and to really feel more love for people because of that. Once you have a little resolution you start to see what the rest of the world is going through.

—Liza

Making Sense of Tragedy

So much goes through your head when this happens. I should have insisted on being seen sooner. I should have insisted on having that C-section. Maybe I was sleeping on the right side that night. You try to make sense of something so senseless . . . try to see how it could have been prevented.

—*Helen*

Gathering Information about What Went Wrong

After any traumatic event, it is normal to want information—about what happened, how, and why. When your baby dies, you may want all kinds of details about what went wrong. You may want to know more about the procedures that were done to you or your baby, and about tests, drugs, surgeries, and other therapies. You may want information on the causes, origins, and physiology of your or your baby's condition. You may want vivid color photographs.

Since the relevant topics may involve illness and deformity, your obsession may receive less approval than say, an obsession about baseball. Some people, or you yourself, may consider such interests prurient, morbid, and a sign of serious maladjustment. However, just as dwelling on memories helps you come to terms with your baby's death, dwelling on details can help you come to terms with what happened.

Having information also can help you feel less vulnerable. If you can have some answers, you can make sense of your experience and feel less victimized by forces beyond your control, or the twists and turns of fate. Having information can also empower you, making you feel that you can try to avoid or surmount these problems in the future.

Finally, poring over this information can give you a sense of mastery over the trials or tragedy you've experienced. Gaining a better understanding of what probably happened and possible causes can help you make sense of your vulnerability and put some fears to rest. Even if no one is sure what happened or what the cause was, you can still benefit from learning as much as you can so that in your own mind, you can settle on an explanation, whether it can be proven or not. Or you can mindfully accept your status of "not knowing," which can reduce your suffering.

It may be a while before you are ready to delve into details, or you may want them right away. Do expect your interest to last a long time, if not a lifetime. Since the limits of medical science are ever changing, you may feel drawn to staying current with a particular condition and its treatments. But if a "cure" is eventually announced, particularly if this happens within a year or so, don't berate yourself for not pursuing that option. Remember, it was unavailable when and where you or your baby needed it.

To find reputable information, ask your doctor, midwife, or genetics counselor to refer you to organizations or online resources or give you copies of pertinent articles and book chapters. If you live near a medical school, you can use their library. Or your local public library should be able to arrange interlibrary loans with medical school libraries. Use the resource librarians—they are familiar with all kinds of requests for all kinds of information. If you want more information, you'll find that having it is empowering.

Why Me? Why My Baby?

Another way to try to make sense of it all is to figure out "Why me? Why my baby?" Aside from autopsy reports and medical theories about *how* your baby died, you may need answers about *why* this had to happen at all.

> *The doctors said that it was just some stray molecule of bacteria in the air that Rachel breathed, and it gave her meningitis, like she was at the wrong place at the wrong time and breathed the wrong breath. What are the chances? Why did everything come together so wrong?*
> —Carolyn

Eventually you may find acceptable answers. Upon getting pregnant so easily after Scott's death, Kelly decided that perhaps there was a divine plan at work in her life. Jane simply accepts that God gives her the children he wants her to have, enabling her to accept the fact that "this baby was for me to have, but not the one He wanted me to raise." Originally, Jessie wondered what she had done "to deserve such a horrible thing," but now she believes that there was some unknown purpose. She says, "Maybe her soul wasn't ready, maybe that was just as long as she was supposed to be with us. I do believe that it changed things, that because of her, Kent and I really developed our relationship and stayed together. So it helps me to think that maybe that was part of the purpose."

Perhaps you believe there is no plan, no single purpose. Maybe we are victims of random events in an imperfect world. For instance, Bess believes that David's death "was purely an accident of nature," while Martina concludes, "I don't think you ever find out why it happened. You just know it did and you've got to live with it." Sara has decided to stop asking, "Why me?" because "it doesn't get you anywhere."

> *One thing that has helped was a story told at our support group. In despair a woman had cried out to God, "Why me, Lord? Why did my baby die?" The reply was "Why not you?" I was moved by this powerful story. "Why not you?" is a brilliant reply. Why did I think that I should be beyond suffering or that I was special? I am human like everyone else and mortality is the gift/curse that accompanies my life on earth. And even if my children had exceptionally short lives, I did the best I could to love them and protect them.*
> —Tanya

Whatever your conclusions, you will probably acquire some understanding of why this happened, even if it's realizing that you aren't meant to understand. (For more thoughts on this, see "Spirituality and Religion," next.) You may also discover the freedom that comes with letting go of trying to make sense of what is essentially senseless, and simply accepting that *it is what it is*, and *what will be, will be*. Accompanying this letting go is the realization that you don't control your life as much as you thought you did. While this can be an unsettling thought, you can learn to live with it. (See also "Vulnerability" in Chapter 7.)

SPIRITUALITY AND RELIGION

When parents are trying to make sense of their baby's death, they often turn to religion or spiritual philosophies. Religious frameworks and spiritual ideas can offer comfort, meaning, and answers to the big questions. Spirituality or religion can play an important role in your transformation *and* healing.

> I am grateful that we had faith in something beyond us and our life on Earth; we were able to lean on that faith for strength in tough times.
>
> —Shellie

> I visit Emily and Michael weekly [at the cemetery] and just pray and talk with them. With God too.
>
> —Anne

If you have religious beliefs, they may help you cope with your grief, or they may make you more confused or angry. Even if you consider yourself devout, it is normal to question your beliefs and even modify them according to the lessons you learn about life and death. Indeed, questioning and modifying can be beneficial and key to your healing transformation. Rose notes, "It hasn't lessened my faith in God. I know He's there. But it has changed my perception of what He is and how He reacts to this world." Janet agrees: "I used to see God as all-powerful and rewarding, but now I see Him as no more in control or better than me."

> I often wonder about what I have done to make God so angry at me or dislike me to have done this to me. My husband does not like it when I talk like this, but I know he also has the same feeling, just maybe not to the extent that I do. We have been very slow going back to church. In fact, six weeks ago was the first time since Blake was born that I had been able to sit through a sermon without running out crying, and I have only been able to sit through one other time since.
>
> —Sonya

IT'S NORMAL TO STRUGGLE WITH RELIGION

Many parents struggle with the idea that God took away their baby. It is especially difficult to find comfort in the rationalization, "God needed a little angel." As Bess says, "That made no sense to me whatsoever—that now I had my personal angel in heaven, that I should be glad for that. I told the hospital chaplain that I needed David here, and he said God needed him more than I did, and I just disagreed with that!" Kim concurs, "You'd think after a million years of human evolution He'd have enough little angels." Lena notes, "I was so angry at God that I just told Him to get out of my life. It took a while to get back to the church."

I did talk to the minister in the church right after Blake's funeral services. I talked to her about this anger I was having, and she told me that the anger was okay. She encouraged me to continue to talk to God, even yell at God, just don't stop the conversation with God. . . . Deep down I truly do know that God is not doing this to me on purpose or because he hates me. I do know this, but it is sometimes really hard to remember.

—Sonya

Particularly if you're not religious or as observant as others, you may find it unhelpful when people try to soothe you (and themselves) with their own religious platitudes. You can't relate, and your own concerns may be summarily dismissed. Indeed, some people push platitudes because they are uncomfortable with your grief. So regardless of your religious leanings, this can rub you the wrong way.

I have a hard time with "God's plan," or "Everything happens for a reason," and "Trust in God," as this doesn't provide me with comfort in the same way that it might for someone who is a strong believer in God. The same with "Your baby is an angel now." The angel symbolism does not resonate with me. It also hurts when I am reminded to be grateful for the family I do have, as of course I am, yet this doesn't take away the pain of my losses. One of the worst is, "It was just not meant to be." Why?

—Tanya

If you're lucky, your religious friends and relatives will simply let you know you're in their prayers. This is their way of saying, "I'm thinking of you."

I'm a completely nonreligious person, but when religious friends told me they were praying for me, I didn't think they were being insensitive—I thought they were doing what was, for them, the most meaningful and loving thing they possibly could do.

—Elizabeth

FINDING COMFORT IN SPIRITUAL PHILOSOPHIES

Even if you are struggling with your religious faith, your speculation about what happens after death can be a comfort to you. If you believe that people or souls exist after death, you may hope to see your child again someday. Spiritual philosophies about the purpose of life and death can also help you make sense of it all. Perhaps you believe that what happens in your life is part of a divine or universal plan. Believing that someone or something is in control can help you feel a little less vulnerable. Seeing that we are "all one" can also be comforting.

Ultimately over time, God and the hope of Heaven has gotten me through this. The hope that Jed is being taking care of in a beautiful place with a Heavenly Father that loves him. And I believe I will get to see him again—that sometimes was the only thing that made me take steps forward.

—Embry

I believe in an afterlife, so I don't believe Jessica is completely out of my life. I don't believe she's hovering around or anything, but I believe she is somewhere, in a place, and eventually, someday, when I die, that I'll be in the same place.

—Rose

I am not an overly religious person. I do not believe in God per se . . . more that I believe we all go somewhere, and where we go, we are the person that we are supposed to be in the form we are meant to be in.

—Sarah

I used to feel uncertain about what happens after someone dies. I feel certain now that our souls are bundles of energy particles; death scatters those particles so that they become a part of everything. The body itself decomposes into the earth, being reborn in a million ways into a million possibilities.

—Lavender

Since having Finley, I have totally shifted my own belief system about death, life, and what makes us people. I know exactly where I believe him to be and what I believe his reason for being here for such a short time was. I would completely go along with his spirit being in the clouds, or free, or trotting off to do some important work.

—Mel

I may not have always believed in God, but I have always believed in an afterlife and I strongly believe that Judah, if not always with me, is always somewhere nearby.

—Jolie

I believe we have Angels around us protecting and guiding us through. Something will happen, be it even small, and I think to myself, "Hmmm, someone is watching over me today."

—Fleur

I believe that everything has a purpose and that we can learn so much from everything that happens to us. We just have to look at the opportunities given to us.

—Karen

A good friend reminded me that Miriam's death was not only my loss. It was a loss for the whole world. That was enormously helpful. I was grateful that it wasn't just about me.

—Tanya

I've accepted that what happens is God's will. I felt very strongly that the baby wasn't meant to be. After I'd questioned everything, I came to that conclusion and I had to live with that.

—Jane

Maybe God decided that Nicole was too good to be on the earth and go through the things that we go through. Maybe He needed an extra angel in heaven and He took her. Maybe He knew that I was going to get divorced and maybe He figured that two kids would be too much for me to handle. I don't know. I just know that He knows what He's doing and maybe He thought, through this experience, I could help other people.

—Cindy

I feel like God allows everybody a choice of what their life is. You don't know it after you're born, maybe, and it's not predestination, but I feel like we chose and Daniel chose and for some reason we were his parents, and I would rather have had him for three days than none.

—Liza

Part of what I believe is that we exist as a soul or whatever, as an entity, before we are a body. We decide how and when and to whom to be born and what kind of life to lead, which is not to say it's all predestined and cast in stone, because we make changes as we go, but that we have a purpose for being born, almost like something or some things we want to accomplish. And when those get accomplished, then we usually die. Some people accomplish these quickly and some people take a long time, and I had the sense that Stephanie had some particular things that she wanted to do in this lifetime and she had some things to help us learn and she had a reason for being here. . . . She needed to know that she was loved, and she knew that the whole time I was pregnant, and she knew that the five days she was here and that she wanted to share that love with us, and then she didn't need to stay around any longer. I also had another sense about her—I have a real issue with letting go, of all the way from trivial things to people and relationships, and I think one of the things she was here to teach me was how to let go.

—Sophie

While I was at the children's hospital with Dayani, the chaplain took the time to comfort me. While she was very caring and kind, I needed to hear from someone with my religious background. So she had one of the neonatologists who happened to be a Muslim come speak to me. She gave me the religious and spiritual perspectives that I was looking for. The first question I asked her was if Dayani's condition was a punishment from God, for my marrying outside our religion. She chuckled and said, "Why would the Almighty play this game of tit for tat with you?" She comforted me in ways that no one else could. She gave me her perspectives as a neonatologist who often sees poverty and babies dying due to fatal syndromes and diseases and how she reconciled this reality with the religions. She reminded me that everyone has a life and time on earth preordained. Some live only in the womb, some live for a few hours, days, or weeks; some live long, but however long that time is, there is a purpose to be served. She told me that God does not need a ventilator to make miracles, and that he is there for me to give me strength to go through what I had to go through. She comforted me beyond what words can describe. She was the first doctor who really soothed my soul and I will never forget her. I truly believe that the wisdom and lessons she gave me made it easier for me to let Dayani go, two days later.

—Destrida

Spiritual Growth

Most parents report that their baby's death has spurred spiritual growth, whether they consider themselves religious or not. Some explore new ideas, replacing old ideas or adding them to how they think about death and the meaning of life. Some walk away from organized religion or their family's idea of "God," but with contemplation, refine their spirituality, and their faith becomes more nuanced. Many parents develop a whole new appreciation and a deeper understanding that "God" is simply a mystery, unknowable, and incomprehensible. They can see the senselessness in trying to make sense of the senseless. And when they accept that they aren't always meant to know *why* or *when* or *how*, they find comfort in the *not knowing*. Instead of trying to control the uncontrollable, they embrace the journey and accept that it's unfolding as it should. They come to have more wonder and faith, less fear of the unknown, and a clearer vision of their priorities.

My faith helped, above all. Although being a Christian has always been part of me, it was only after his death that my faith grew, my interest developed, and my philosophies have been enhanced.

—Victoria

Whatever our beliefs, having faith and belief in something bigger helps tremendously. I do not know where we would be without our faith. My husband agrees, and says the same thing.

—Anne

I will say my relationship with God has changed. I would consider myself more spiritual than religious. And a dear friend helped me realize that God doesn't point a finger and say, "Ben and Abby's baby is going to die." We live in a broken world and he didn't intend for that, but what he does do is take our hand and be there for us through the pain. That helped me a lot to feel that God was there, guiding me and softening, when possible, the pain.

—Abby

My belief in God and religion has become looser and stronger at the same time. I used to believe that bad things happen because in some ways I had displeased God. But now I don't believe in a vengeful God, but rather, a compassionate one. He was there for me in the presence of the people whose love and prayers carried me through the most difficult times of my life. Also, I used to feel that life owed me something. I see now that life owes me nothing. We are not in heaven or hell where people only get what they deserve. We are on earth where things happen. But they happen for you, not to you and there are lessons, not trials. One thing in life is guaranteed—nothing is permanent, and you have to reach for happiness, it's not given to you. Life does not owe you anything.

—*Destrida*

Even if you do not consider yourself to be religious, or if you reject organized religion entirely, you may discover some spiritual philosophies that give you answers and help you cope. (See also "Accepting *What Is*" in chapter 4.)

Honestly I found it helpful to try to ask "what now?" instead of "why me?"
—*Tanya*

Recognizing the Positive

Although from the outside it is a tragic event to hold your baby and watch her die, in many ways it was actually a beautiful experience. Other family members in the room agreed that there was a certain sacredness to being in that room together with Ashley—watching a new life come into the world and then peacefully go surrounded by our love. I had never felt the presence of God so directly before as I did during that time; I don't imagine I will ever feel that way again. For me, that aspect of the experience was completely unexpected, that although we were obviously very sad to say goodbye to her, there was also a joy in the room.

—*Shellie*

I found that very quickly I was able to see the ways that Finley had changed my life. I made a point of thanking him for them; I wrote about them a lot. This helped. It made it feel as if there was a higher purpose, a reason for what had happened. It was not a useless waste.

—*Mel*

I'm thankful for everything we have gone through because it's all led us to where we are at today.

—*Ben*

After your baby dies, recognizing something positive is way to make meaning out of enduring this tragedy. At first, you may be too distraught or too angry to even consider anything positive. But when you start to feel better, you can try to assess the salvage from the wreckage.

Unfortunately, some people may try to help you find a silver lining by saying things such as, "At least the baby died before you were too far along . . . " or "It's a blessing the baby died because . . . " or "Be thankful that at least you know you can get pregnant." This method of comfort may seem cruel to you, but people are simply anxious to help you feel better and hasten you along with well-meaning speeches.

Other people might get philosophical, offering that "things happen for a reason" or "whatever happens is for your higher good." But finding the positives and applying philosophies are tasks that only you can undertake, when you're ready, and not when you're in shock, infuriated, or in the depths of despair. Plus these sayings are more easily applied to trials such as taking two years to find a job, when, in the end, you land the perfect position. But a long job hunt is not a traumatic bereavement. There is just no comparison. Bryn agrees: "I led a very lucky life. I always had the philosophy that, 'Hey, everything works out for the best.' I cannot have that philosophy anymore, because I will never be able to say it was best that he died. I can *never* say that." Of course you'll forever protest the notion that you've traded your baby's life for the blessings you'll appreciate down the road.

> *I have not found any meaning behind why I must lose my daughter, and I hope I never will. I exhausted myself looking for such reasons in the beginning and could not come up with one—I felt such a failure then. People kept telling me that one day I'd see the reason why I must lose my daughter. That's like saying I am promised riches and happiness in the future at the cost of losing my daughter. I sure as hell pray that this is not the case!*
>
> —Destrida

> *That kind of stuff made me really cranky. I actually found it offensive: the idea that writing* [Ghostbelly] *or some life lessons could redeem the death of my baby. There's no redemption for a dead baby.*
>
> —Elizabeth

> *I can sort of accept that it was a learning process and that you grow through pain and all that. But I just don't think anybody needs that learning process.*
>
> —Holly

Indeed, recognizing the positive never means you're therefore "glad" your baby died. The positives don't make up for the heartache. And you can certainly reject the idea that your baby had to die so you could experience growth. There is not a blessing in the world that answers the question, "Why?"

Recognizing the positive is not meant to be a platitude. It's part of the tasks of mourning that entail growth, adjustment, and making meaning. And it's important to remember that you're not reaping positive rewards or experiencing growth and transformation because your baby died, *but because you've been forced to deal with great tragedy.* In other words, your baby's death doesn't improve your life. After all, you could've merely suppressed your grief or crawled into a cave, and there'd be nothing positive in that. Instead, *you created a positive outcome*—by facing adversity head-on, embracing grief, engaging in mourning, and leaning into life again. Instead, give credit to your resilience and fortitude. Credit your willingness to ask the big questions, ponder new ways of being, and search for meaning. That's what brings new positives into your life.

> *I am grateful for the many gifts that came out of this experience. I think it's helpful and healing to try to take meaning away from difficult experiences. We really tried to do that, in part to honor Ashley's brief life.*
> —Shellie

Recognizing the positive is a hallmark of your resilience—that life after tragedy can become good again, that you've risen from the ashes. It's a way of acknowledging that your life isn't defined by what happens to you but rather by what you do with it. When you think about it that way, the blessings you discover give meaning to your baby's life, not your baby's death. This mother explains:

> *The blessings are of course my daughter, her memory, and the lessons she taught me. She had to come the way she was in order to bring in the wisdom and compassion that were bestowed upon me by family, friends, and strangers.*
> —Destrida

Eventually, when you are ready, you can recognize the positives you've acquired from the experiences surrounding your baby's brief life and your journey of surviving your baby's death. Perhaps you will find you have a strengthened marriage, deepened friendships, increased personal awareness, greater confidence, more maturity, or a better understanding of and willingness to help others who experience the death of a child. You may even have a new baby, who might not have been conceived if the other baby had lived. These positives do not make up for your baby's death, nor do they provide reasons why this happened, but you may derive some small comfort from them. Your own philosophies and outlook on life will determine what positives you notice.

> *I had to come to grips with some pretty intense things about myself and I ended up liking myself and learning things about myself I probably never would have learned had I not lost Jamie. People shouldn't have to learn those things that way, but I learned a lot of strengths that I had. Had someone told me my baby would die, I would've said, "Well, I just couldn't handle anything like that." Well, yes I could, I can, and I will again if I have to!*
> —Sara

> *Something good has to come out of it, because I don't want her death to be totally in vain. I don't want it to be totally meaningless. So*

I try to use every opportunity to talk about her and help other people who are going through the same thing. I have a desire for something good to come out of it. I know I'm a better mother than I probably would have been.

—Rose

Yes, it is sad and horrible and people don't understand how I can deal with it—but it has made me become who I am and that is not a bad thing!

—Sonya

Recognizing the positive is central to your search for meaning, which is one of the tasks of mourning. Recognizing the positive helps you find meaning in your suffering, which grants you a new or renewed sense of identity, purpose, or mastery in your life. You still realize how little control you have, but seeing the positives, you can restore a sense of control over what's controllable—which is how you choose to be and how you live your life. And when you think of the positives, you can practice gratitude for what you were able to gain in spite of what you lost. Gratitude itself grants you a sense of peace and acceptance, another hallmark of healing. (See also chapter 17, "Living in Remembrance.")

ANNIVERSARIES AND OTHER REMINDERS

I remember it was raining hard just like our tears flowing as we sat in our car after the scan appointment in total disbelief. Our world had changed forever with the news that there was something wrong with our baby. The following months were dark, cold, windy, and wet—it was winter but I think this also reflected our emotions—the shock, sadness, despair, fear, and helplessness. I will always remember the red throw that my bump and I snuggled under on cold winter days and how my rain jacket got tighter and tighter as she grew. I'm not sure how I will feel about this season next year, most likely mixed emotions, but I know that every time I have to wear my jacket because of the cold or rain or as I snuggle on the couch with our throw blanket, I think of her.

—Emmerson

Soon after your baby dies, you may notice that you feel especially blue or unsettled at a certain time of day, or on a certain day of the week. As time passes, you may feel depressed or grief-stricken on a certain day of the month and then certain times of the year. It's as if your body remembers and associates the position of the sun and seasonal weather with your baby's life and death. Daniela reports, "I always think I'm going to be fine, and then a tidal wave of sadness overcomes me."

I found out that Oren died in the evening. Most days it seemed like my grief would start to overwhelm me after dinner and push on through until the wee hours of morning.

—Tanya

In October, I'm real mellow and mopey, and on her birthday it's like, we know it's that day. We take the time to remember that she was with us at one point. It's just like a signal in your body. And I'll break down and cry over nothing. October is like a lead balloon.

—Erin

November brought a mix of emotions. I've been having flashbacks from last year, particularly from the day of her cremation. There are times when things seem to be a lot harder to bear.

—Destrida

I think the mystical bond between mother and child is what makes grief so intense at different times . . . even the seasons changing can cause grief to come for a visit when you weren't expecting it!

—Laura

These "anniversary reactions" are normal. Even years later, when you feel a solid sense of healing, you may experience anniversary reactions one or more times a year—around your baby's due date, birth date, death date, or certain holidays and family events. There may be a block of time full of anniversaries. You may feel particularly forgetful, disorganized, clumsy, or even be prone to accidental injuries, so use extra caution during these stressful times.

We are coming up on anniversaries, first Rylee, then Blake. In some ways, I like having the anniversaries so close together—one bad month rather than having to relive [it] several times a year. But it is hard, starting midway through October to the last of November. So many memories of appointments, hopes that I had, hospital stays, and just remembering what we lost. I definitely have hard moments during the holiday season. It's also hard in late February, since both children were due then (actually one day apart).

—Sonya

This baby was born on Christmas Eve, and the first year I was anxious about it, but I think, really, for the first three years, Christmas was very hard. I think when Thanksgiving hit I just immediately tightened up. I knew I had to manage these things and I would work even harder to get my Christmas stuff done, and as Christmas approached it got worse and worse and worse. I just don't like that time of year anymore.

—Meryl

Well, I feel like wearing a shirt that says, "I Survived February." And all of those anniversary dates for Emily and Michael.

—Anne

You may even feel sad on your own birthday or wistfully think about how old your child would have been on the first day of every school year. For many mothers, Mother's Day is one of the hardest reminders of *what might have been.*

Ronin's first day of school would have been his fifth birthday, and I was so sad the week leading up as I was missing out on taking my boy to his first day and standing at the gate, waiting for him to run out of school and to tell me all about his new friends and what he had done.
—Lorna

Mother's Day. Honestly, I feel relieved that this holiday is over. Nothing went wrong today—there was no major meltdown or any interactions that rubbed me the wrong way, but just the underlying feeling that it is Mother's Day, and I am a mother, but I am childless.
—Jolie

It's normal to worry about anniversaries that loom in the distance. In particular, if your baby died during the pregnancy or was born prematurely and died, the first due date can be the most dreaded. As Yolanda put it, "I'm afraid that after my due date it will really hit me that I don't have my baby, because that's when I should have him in my arms. I'm bracing myself." But many parents notice that the anticipation is harder than the actual day. If you engage in a ritual, you may even feel buoyed by this gesture of honor and remembrance. Anniversary dates can be painful *and* special.

Adisyn's first birthday was quiet and reflective, I ordered flowers, we lit candles, we had a beautiful cake, and we released a balloon with messages. I shed tears, lots of tears with the wonder of what would have been, who she would have been.
—Emmerson

On the first anniversary of Oren's death, we had a good visit at the cemetery. We all sang songs on our way there and then we used many flowers to decorate his grave. We tried to make him wings out of flowers. It was cold with snow flurries when we arrived but the sun came out as we were leaving. I think the hardest moment was leaving the cemetery. I honestly wanted to lie down on the ground to be close to him and stay there.
—Tanya

On the anniversary date of his birth, we always try and do something together as a family. I remember on the day that would have been his third birthday, being struck with the fact that there will always be somebody missing. There will always be one less child in my life.
—Sara

The days and weeks before the first anniversary were worse than the day itself. I wasn't sure how to celebrate it at first, but for sure I wanted to acknowledge it. I went to the post office the day before to post something. I then saw some balloons for sale, and immediately I decided to buy one with a Winnie-the-Pooh picture on it. The next day, the morning was bright and sunny. After breakfast, my three-year-old son Tom and I went into our garden and let off the helium balloon. I told Tom that it was "something nice to do to watch the balloon go up, up, up high into the clouds, into space and up into heaven." Tom thought it was exciting, and I thought as the years go on, I could explain why we release that balloon each year. Naturally, it was sad and I cried, but at the same time it was nice. I lit my candle (which I do every Sunday) and burned the dried olive leaves my mum gets from the Greek Church. I felt "uplifted" in a peculiar way.

—*Victoria*

Anniversary rituals can also give you the comfort of integrating your baby into the family. But as Victoria experienced, you needn't make elaborate or advanced plans. Stay in the moment, go with the flow, and let it unfold. Victoria did indeed repeat the balloon release each year. Two years later, she writes, "It is Alex's third anniversary—I like to call it his birthday. The fact that we talk about him freely and Tom is fully aware of his little brother who died, makes it so much easier and has meaning that Alex was/is part of the family." (See also "Rituals" in chapter 6.)

If your baby's birth or death happens to fall on a date that is meaningful for your family, this can also add special significance, such as how Destrida feels about her baby Dayani dying on her father's birthday. Winnie experiences this too.

I didn't realize this at the time, but my baby miscarried on the fortieth anniversary of my paternal grandmother's accidental and untimely death, which happened before I was even born. I discovered this about a month afterward when I accompanied my dad to his hometown and we visited the cemetery. I was stunned and touched. I'd always missed the grandma I never knew, and I took great comfort in the spiritual connection implied by that coincidence. Now I remember them both every year on that day.

—*Winnie*

If you have a surviving baby or babies from a multiple pregnancy, birthdays and death days may coincide or fall close together. Every year at this time you may wrestle with mixed feelings. While you want to be happy, your accompanying sorrow can dampen any festivities. You may feel disloyal since you're unable to devote yourself entirely to either celebration or mourning. While this can seem impossible to resolve, you can find ways to honor all your babies. Set aside time and make plans, however public or private, that accommodate your feelings and recognize the special ways each child had touched your heart. Accept that this will be a bittersweet time.

A surviving baby also provides constant poignant reminders of what might have been. You may feel "up to here" with baby things along with the most vivid reminders of what you are missing. If you know that a survivor is identical to one who died, these reminders are particularly graphic. Even with fraternal multiples, they were still *chronologically* identical and you may frequently envision the sibling(s) who would have been doing similar things at similar times. As Shannon points out, "When Bradley is doing something adorable or getting into something or making a mess, I look at him and think, 'Can you imagine *two* of them?'" Just the fact that you aren't as busy as you'd thought you'd be is a poignant reminder.

There is nothing so horribly un-busy, too-peaceful than that first year or more. . . . One baby is just not a totally full-time deal. When you expected to be flat-out all the time with twins, every little bit of peace and quiet or spontaneity is so awful because you know you wouldn't have had time to think about it or do this or whatever, if they were both here.
—Jackie

Even without the factor of a multiple birth, at times you may catch yourself thinking or wondering about what might have been or what your baby would be like now had he or she lived. Or your grief may be triggered by reminders as simple as seeing an advertisement that has a baby in it, or the first day of school when you know your baby would've been the age when children enter kindergarten. Initially these thoughts and reminders about *what might have been* can be painful, but as your grief softens, your reactions can take on a feeling of wistfulness or curiosity. You may feel this curiosity when you see children who were born at the same time as your baby who died, or in a pensive moment with a subsequent child as you ponder the experiences you are missing with the child who died.

I do see Bodhi in the kids sometimes. It'll be a sideways glance or a profile look and it shoots me back to the night with him. I sometimes just wonder what Claeson and Paige are thinking and then go off wondering what Bodhi would be thinking about those two at that moment. I wonder what kind of dynamic an older brother would add and how he would teach Claeson, like Claeson teaches Paige.
—Ben

We think mostly about what he'd look like and what he'd be doing now. Every year when school starts and at Christmastime I think about how old he is, and I've thought that I'll be thinking about that when he would have graduated from high school, that he would have gotten married, maybe gone to college.
—Martina

I'll always grieve the "firsts." What would have been the first step, the first word, the first day of school.
—Cathryn

Naturally, there have been moments, such as meeting children in playgrounds, my older son Tom playing with the younger kids and being gentle, etc., etc. I try to make the shift and think of what might be, not what should have been.
—Victoria

Anniversary reactions and reminders can be discouraging, especially as time goes on and you feel as though you're putting your life back together. You may be surprised by the reappearance of grief. But remember, even healing will not spare you from occasional sadness. Some call this "shadow grief"—the dull background ache that stays with you; anniversaries simply bring that ache to the foreground.

Reactions to anniversaries and other reminders can be unpredictable. It is important to go with the flow and give yourself permission to have bad days or tearful moments whenever they appear. You are entitled to your own special pattern of grieving—and healing.

When the leaves fall from the trees and the moon rises earlier in the day I will remember all of the cherished time we had together, the wintry walks, the magical moments, and the incredible bond of mother and child that will forever be ours.

—Emmerson

I don't think that we ever really get over losing a child, but we do somehow get through it.

—Ginger

Keys to Survival

The simple passage of time may prove to be one of your greatest keys to survival. Another key is to rely on the variety of resources available to you, such as your partner, your family and friends, other bereaved parents, books, faith, hope, self-compassion, favorite interests, creativity, giving back, and an inner strength that you may have only just discovered through this tragedy. To best utilize these resources, be assertive in telling people what you need, and pursue what helps you cope.

I'm not afraid of grief; I'm happy to let it be a part of me. I have forgiven, I have allowed myself to feel and cry. I've also written a whole lot of poetry, a journal of those first weeks, articles, and I gave myself a new purpose and fund-raised for a Cuddle Cot for the hospital. I also find it healing to make things for others and make blankets for the memory boxes and burial gowns.

—Karen

Time for myself. The ability to back off of caretaking for everyone else in order to give myself the help that I need. Creativity and gardening. Finding mindfulness and stillness. Spending time with babies and little kids. Being playful.

—Lavender

I believe that learning from bereaved parents who have experienced healing was key for me in getting ideas on how I could heal my suffering. I personally tried just about every suggestion I came across. A lot of the suggestions I learned from other bereaved parents did not seem like things that would be helpful to me. But, I tried them all anyway, just to see. And I can honestly say that everything I tried had some healing benefits to it.

—Lori

*Faith is what helps me here. Till I can talk to God, I probably will
never totally understand. Maybe when I do hold a child of mine, I will
begin to understand and forgive, but . . . I just don't know. I just have
to go back in faith that He will bring me and Randy the child we are
meant to have as our family.*

—Sonya

The hope of someday having a healthy baby may help you to look
ahead. Peg elaborates: "I'm sure that if I hadn't been able to have one that
I'd feel entirely different about the whole thing. Having a baby has helped
me to deal with it." If you have other children, you might derive comfort
simply from their existence. (See "Your Other Children" in chapter 12.)

If you are raising a survivor from a multiple birth, you may find it
exceptionally challenging to grieve for one or more babies while trying to
nurture another or others. But having a surviving baby can be a source of
healing too. Anya notes, "I don't know what it's like to lose a baby and
not have another baby there too. I did have a baby to hold. I've never had
a pregnancy and nothing to show for it."

The most significant key to your survival may be a conscious choice
to get through your grief without letting it destroy your life. You can decide whether you will triumph over tragedy or cave into it. Many parents
mention reaching a point where they just decide to stop wishing it didn't
happen and start learning to live with it.

*I want to be a good healthy example for our daughter even though she
is no longer here with us, and I know that to leave a legacy for her I
need to work at putting my pieces back together. It's the only way.*

—Emmerson

*Just not avoiding it helps. Reminding myself that grief is the reality
and if I don't deal with it now, I will have to deal with it way down the
road and it will be a lot harder then.*

—Embry

*We never wanted people to say things like: "They never got over the
loss" or "They've never quite been the same." It wasn't because we
were particularly concerned about what anyone thought (indeed grief
is good in that way, it strips away concerns about other people's
opinions), it was more about us doing the best we could do for
Willow's sake and for her memory.*

—Nathan

At some point, even as you are healing, another key could be to consult
with a professional counselor. Perhaps you'd like some help with coping
and adjusting to a certain aspect of your baby's death, or you think your
relationship with your partner could use a boost. Or maybe healing seems
elusive, or you feel as though sufficient time has passed and you still have
intense emotional reactions or intrusive, painful thoughts. You may decide
on counseling simply because you want more support for making progress

through mourning, getting along with others, or effectively functioning in your life. These are all excellent reasons to go. Certainly, counseling can facilitate your healing transformation. (See also "Counseling" in chapter 13.)

> *For a long time I thought this was as far as I could get, that's just how it was for me. Now, I feel like I need to get to a different place, need to move on. It doesn't feel like I want it to be, like, a part of my life. It's still too painful. I want to go to a better place, be at peace with it. So I'm back in therapy.*
>
> —*Lauren*

> *I am still seeing a counselor and attending a support group. I need all of these things to get me through this. The grief process is a long one.*
>
> —*Anne*

Remember that as you grieve, you are healing. As awful and tragic as your baby's death will always be, you can adjust to your new path. As you continue down this path, you'll discover your strength, gain more confidence, find success, own your style, and acquire wisdom about life, yourself, and those around you. You'll realize how resilient you are, and you'll know that you can survive anything. (See also "Advice Bereaved Parents Would Have Given to Themselves" in chapter 4.)

POINTS TO REMEMBER

- Healing is demonstrated by acceptance and integration of your baby's life and death into the larger tapestry of your life. Intense grief mellows into bittersweet or peaceful feelings.
- Healing also includes a continuing bond with your baby, retaining memories, and occasional sadness. It also involves a feeling of being transformed into a changed person.
- The journey of healing transformation takes time and includes engaging in many concurrent tasks of mourning.
- There are many ways you can boost the quality of your mourning, including having realistic expectations, going with the flow of your grief, and seeking assistance.
- If you have a surviving baby or babies from a multiple birth, it can be a challenge to balance mourning with parenting your newborn(s). Having extra help with any of your responsibilities can better enable you to go with the flow of your grief, which can free you to be more emotionally available to your little one(s).
- Making sense of your baby's death includes gathering medical information about how your baby died, what happened, and why. Many parents conclude that they cannot fully make sense of something so senseless.
- Religion or spirituality can be a source of comfort, meaning, and answers to the big questions. Find philosophies that help you cope.
- As part of your transformation, eventually you can find meaning and recognize the positive that arose from enduring tragedy. This does not make up for the heartache, but it is an indication of your resilience.
- Anniversary reactions and reminders can trigger grief, which is normal, even many years after your baby's death. When grief is triggered, this does not undo your healing.
- Keys to survival can include many resources, including support from others, faith, hope, creativity, giving back, and your own newly discovered inner strength.

9

MAKING PEACE WITH AGONIZING DECISIONS

A Note to the Reader: This chapter supports parents who had to make life-and-death decisions for their baby(s); it also affirms their decision, whatever it was. If this does not describe your experience and you hold fast to ideas about what you consider to be morally "right" and "wrong," or you think hearing about these heart-wrenching decisions would disturb you, then it is your responsibility to decide whether to read on. For whatever reason, if you decide to read on, you are invited to do so with an open, compassionate heart.

Every parent quoted in this book mourns for a much-loved and wanted baby. And while all of us have the right to imagine what we'd decide for our own babies, none of us have the right to dispute others' decisions for their babies. In fact, as the parents in this book can attest, none of us truly have a clue until we are thrust into this heart-wrenching position. Many surprised even themselves, as the complexities are only revealed when we are actually faced with making such a profound decision. Welcome to their world.

In our culture, there is considerable social pressure to reach for medical miracles. There is a strong bias toward "having faith," saving every life, and employing the most technology possible. Parents are lauded for withstanding severe pregnancy complications, attempting to carry mega-multiple babies to term, or pursuing extremely invasive intensive care for their critically ill newborns. These moves are considered selfless, courageous, even heroic. And the general public finds inspiration in the sunny outcomes that happen "against all odds."

Unfortunately, most people don't stop to consider that for every sunny outcome against all odds, there are hundreds of babies and families who suffer terribly for naught through these ordeals. Many people also accept the general consensus that it's wrong to make the opposite decision—such as terminating or reducing a pregnancy, inducing labor early, or refusing intensive medical intervention and enlisting hospice care. As a result, the parents who choose these so-called wrong options often feel judged, isolated, and unsupported, in spite of the fact that their decisions are more aligned *with* the odds.

> *Many people believe modern medicine can "fix" everything, but it can't. They may wonder, "Why wouldn't parents let medicine intervene to save their child?" Even family members may question this decision. But it is simply impossible for medicine to "save" all babies.*
>
> —Shellie

In fact, parents who've been down this road—whatever their decisions—can assert that their situations were far more complex, risky, costly, and painful than is usually portrayed. And they *all* discover where heroism truly lies: it's in *making* these agonizing decisions for their loved, wanted, and precious babies.

Of course, there is heroism in taking on a risky challenge, doing a full-court press in the NICU, or trying to defy the odds. But there is *also* heroism in preserving the mother's health, questioning the virtue of trying to save every life, and having the sensitivity and wisdom to know when to align with the odds and let go. Indeed, it takes as much, if not more courage to meet death head-on. And miracles can still be found in places parents never expected—often in their own healing transformation. (See also chapter 17, "Living in Remembrance.")

> Some people told us they wished for a miracle. While we knew in our hearts that there would not be a "medical" miracle for Ashley, there certainly was a miracle the day she was born and died. We have been so, so richly blessed by Ashley. She will be our daughter until we take our last breaths.
>
> —Shellie

> There was always room for a miracle but there was going to be a miracle no matter what . . . she would be healed, or we would survive saying goodbye to her. Every day we are walking in a miracle because our hearts are better because she came . . . we know what it is like to live in the shadows and what it is like to live in the sunlight.
>
> —Laura

If you faced such decisions—whether you chose to continue your pregnancy *or* intervene, whether you chose to enlist medical technology to the fullest extent *or* go with hospice care—as a now-grieving parent, you may require extra support. As you know, making these decisions is agonizing, which only adds to your trauma. The aftermath can be agonizing too, as you may wrestle with doubts, second-guessing, and a profound sense of responsibility. It is simply the nature of life-and-death decisions that they will weigh heavily on your heart, compound your grief, and perhaps become central to mourning your baby's death.

This chapter offers you compassion and additional support for what may be a most challenging aspect of your journey. It also offers this bottom line: *Your decisions were the best ones you could possibly have made for the situation you and your baby(s) were in.* As the parent, you were also the best person to make these private, delicate, nuanced, and heart-wrenching decisions. You—not doctors, not judges, not juries, and certainly not your relatives, your nosy neighbor, or the general public—*you* were in the best position to determine what was best for your baby(s). And no one has the right to doubt your endeavor to hold the best interests of your baby(s) at heart.

It was at our twelve-week scan for our darling poppet that we were told, "There is something wrong with your baby." Further along in the pregnancy there were more complications but she was a wee fighter and we had "hope." Our main, in fact only, concern was for her, and so long as she was not suffering . . . if all that I could ever do for my daughter was to carry her for as long as she decided then that was what I would do. We made the decision to let Adisyn decide. That was what felt right for us.

—Emmerson

I think what was particularly difficult was that our case was quite borderline. It wasn't something particularly life-threatening or something for which the baby would have been in objective pain for its life. No, it was something whose manifestations are quite variable. So the next days were really painful as we made up our minds about what to do. Making life-or-death decisions, literally. Yes, there are treatments, surgeries, therapies, but the more I read, the more I decided that I would not want my child to go through this.

—Annalaura

Before birth, we did have to decide about intervening. But we decided pretty early on that there was not a surgery or other medical intervention that could "fix" the many things wrong with her. So we didn't want her to suffer and spend her short life on a machine. We just wanted to hold her and let her go peacefully. I came to a peace with that during pregnancy once we made the final decision, and I would not change anything.

—Shellie

Decisions Parents Face

If you had to make life-and-death decisions for your baby, you likely found yourself in one or more of the following situations:

- **Severe pregnancy complications:** Although rare, complications in the mother's body can be life-threatening to her and her baby. When there is no good option for the baby, choosing which path to take can be heartbreaking.

  For my health, the decision was made to induce labor at twenty-two weeks. I knew this was way too early for my little girl to survive, but this is what had to occur, as sad as it was. My hope was that she would not suffer, but I also wanted to meet her, hold her in my arms, and tell her that I love her before she went to Heaven.

  —Sonya

- **A pregnancy with multiple babies:** Multiples carry a higher chance of complications for the mother and babies, and can lead to arduous decisions that attempt to balance risks and benefits. When only some of the babies survive, parenting is bittersweet at best.

After years of infertility and then losing a baby to SIDS, I knew that at forty, this was our last try to have a child. We were thrilled to discover that IVF worked. I was pregnant at last, only to find out that I was carrying four babies. The odds were overwhelmingly against me being able to carry all of them, even to viability, much less near term. For us, the choice boiled down to having two or having none.

—Louisa

- **Prenatal diagnosis:** When a baby is diagnosed in utero with a fatal or disabling condition, parents feel torn between their desire to hold on for as long as possible and their desire to protect their baby from suffering.

My husband went with me for my CVS [Chorionic Villus Sampling]. We saw the "fetal material," "beginning of the pregnancy," and all the other clinical terms the medical personnel use when viewing an ultrasound. However, what my husband and I saw was our baby. Following the procedure we took home a photo from the ultrasound to show off and to hang on the refrigerator. Waiting for the results, I assumed I would feel relief and could relax with my pregnancy, knowing very early that everything was fine. Two days later I was informed that my baby, a boy, had a syndrome.

—Avery

- **Delivery after prenatal diagnosis:** It can be supremely complicated and heart-wrenching for parents to decide when (soon? later? let nature determine?) and how (surgically? labor induction? spontaneous labor?) to deliver the baby. This decision includes weighing the risks, wanting to reduce their baby's suffering, and determining the value of increasing the chances that the baby will live briefly after birth.

Both Josh and I threw ourselves into planning to meet Pearl. Driving around cemeteries, keepsake planning, creating birth plans. The planning made us both feel like there was something we could do for her. Planning for her birth and death was something we could control.

—Laura

- **Deciding between intensive care or hospice care:** Sometimes, the doctors are uncertain as to whether a baby will do well with intensive care or not. That's when parents are drawn into shared decision making. The doctors can explain what they know and what they don't know, and it's the parents who weigh the risks and benefits and decide for themselves whether the baby should be put through the rigors of intensive care, or be allowed to live a natural life, however short, nestled in their loving embrace.

Choosing comfort care can be a very difficult decision. For our daughter, we knew it was the best way to love her and parent her in the short time we had. She was going to die no matter what, so she could either spend her last breaths snuggled in our arms and surrounded by her loving family, or she could be subjected to tubes and machines, never feeling our presence. A pediatric surgeon that we spoke with very wisely said, "Just because we (medical staff) can do something doesn't mean we should."

—Shellie

- **Deciding when to start hospice care:** If intensive care is only prolonging dying, the question becomes when to stop further treatment or when to disconnect mechanical support. Sometimes families continue intensive care as they want more time to spend with their baby, or the mother is still recovering from giving birth, or they want friends and relatives to come. Other parents want hospice care immediately, so that their baby can be held unfettered in their arms. Whatever their reasons for choosing the timing of their baby's death, it's an agonizing decision, made with love. However and whenever parents decide to let go, they must overcome a powerful urge to hold on.

At first the doctors said one day we would have to make decisions for her. We were just buying time. But after a couple of days, the attending physician told us there was no hope or cure for Dayani. She was not able to breathe on her own and had to be on the ventilator. She was deteriorating every day and that we should enjoy our time with her since it looked like she would make her own call.

—Destrida

The doctors were unable to do anything to save him. We knew that Blake was going to die. We decided to unhook him from most of the monitors and stop all other invasive means, in order for both my husband and myself to hold our son. He died in my arms.

— Sonya

Whichever of these situations you experienced, you had to absorb the terrible news that your baby's prognosis was grim and decisions had to be made to ensure the least amount of suffering. Then, to make a truly informed decision, you also had to take in a lot of unfamiliar medical information about various interventions and treatments, risks and benefits, quality of life issues, the doctors' best guesses as to outcome, as well as the emotional, spiritual, financial, and logistical challenges of each option. Naturally, it can be difficult and confusing to gather and sort through all of the facts, guesses, and details. You may have also felt rushed, making it even more difficult to think clearly or quickly. Weighing options can be supremely trying, especially when you're in shock. (See also "Survival Mode" in chapter 3.) These challenges are why many parents continue to wrestle with decisions long after they are made.

WRESTLING WITH DECISIONS MADE

With hindsight, like most parents, you may continue to review the options and question your decisions. You may experience a crisis of faith in medical authority, modern technology, or God. You may resent being put in the position of "choosing death." You may wish you could have felt more certain before you gave your final answer. You might worry whether it was reasonable to rely on your gut reaction or your doctor's advice. You may wish that God had decided for you.

Every night before we left the hospital, my husband and I would sing "Twinkle, Twinkle, Little Star" so many times. We kissed Dayani all over and said our goodnight. It was very difficult to say goodnight, as we did not ever know if there was going to be a good morning the next day. Every night before I left, I asked her to talk to God and decide what they wanted to do, and we would accept everything.

—Destrida

It is important to remember that whether you had two minutes or two years, emotional turmoil would accompany whatever decision you made. In fact, the decision-making process doesn't end with a decision. It is *afterward* that you can deliberately comb through all the facts, come to terms with it, and gain confidence. There is no deadline for the post-decision part of the process. Making peace with regrets is simply part of any life-and-death decision-making process. Your struggles are a natural part of your grief and mourning.

MAKING THE DECISION

As part of finding peace, you may find it helpful to review your decision-making process, particularly acknowledging the gravity of your baby's situation and the impossibility of choosing between unbearable options. Indeed, even as you balanced the rational arguments, your decision was also personal, emotional, and heart-wrenching.

I asked my husband what he wanted to do. In his anguish, he told me to let her go. I knew this was the right choice but I did not want to hear it. I started screaming at him saying he could not be serious! He took me to see that Dayani had turned purple. I started wailing. The doctor stood in front of me, looked at me in the eyes (his sad red eyes looking straight at me will be forever imprinted in my brain) and said, "Your baby's lungs are very sick. She has been fighting so hard. She is trying to tell you something." When he said that, something snapped in me. I realized the question I had been asking every night was being answered.

—Destrida

For many parents, the choice boils down to two questions. First, which do they fear more for their child: death or a severely challenged life? Annalaura was so torn about what to do, but remembers, "I was particularly struck by the letter of one patient who mentioned that his life wasn't all that bad, that he had been fortunate in life, but nonetheless felt SAD. That made it for me." Ted recalls, "For me, the decision crystallized and I knew it was right, when the doctor pointed out that *there are some fates worse than death*." Second, how much suffering should this child's life entail? Molly recalls, "I remember walking into the intensive care unit where they put Peter on monitors until we made our decision, and seeing him all hooked up, I *knew* I couldn't do that to him." Claudia agrees: "We were haunted by the possibility that if we chose surgery, Jacob might die without much knowledge of our love for him. He might have died without being held for any length of time by us, and just having known and been cuddled by machines. I felt that if we could hold him and be with him, then at least if he died, he would know that we loved him."

For parents who receive a prenatal diagnosis of a life-limiting condition, their baby will die no matter what, so the question for them is how to ensure the least amount of suffering. Do they cut the pregnancy short? How short? Or do they just let nature take its course? Ethically, there are no absolute "right answers," so parents are left to determine for themselves what's "right" for their baby and family.

> When we were finally seen and had another more thorough ultrasound, we were given the formal diagnosis, which meant our baby Pearl was going to die. The doctor immediately asked me if I wanted to go upstairs and "take care of this." Josh didn't know what that meant . . . when I explained it to him he turned pale and said, "No." We both said no at the same time. We let the doctor know this was our baby and we were going to treasure each moment we had with our baby. He told us he would give us a little bit to think about our decision.
>
> When I think back to the decision . . . there really was no decision to be made. We knew she was ours to love for however long we had her, we knew that there was going to be a goodbye in our future, but we wanted to be able to say goodbye without any regrets. We wanted a story instead of a secret. I knew this wasn't going to be easy, and the second we walked out of that room, everything was going to be different. But, we were going to soak in each moment and press into the pain, knowing hope was on the other side.
>
> —Laura

Above all, you chose what you believed was best for your child. Rightly so, you relied on your values, intuitions, and projections to guide you. Only you could weigh all the factors, the risks, and the benefits according to your basic philosophical or spiritual beliefs. While you may worry that you were under too much stress to make a good decision, your emotional duress actually played an important role in your judgment. It enabled you to make the decision with your heart and gut, not just your mind. Indeed, the heart and gut are wiser, with the help of your core brain making snap decisions based on loads of information you may not even be consciously aware of and coming up with a decision that "feels right." It's your mind—the thinking brain—that can sometimes get in the way, analyzing and reanalyzing, trying to make sense of something so senseless as being put into this impossible position of having to choose between "terrible" and "horrible." Your decision was right for your baby.

> *Though all of the facts and logistics were important, what guided us most was an innate, gut-level sense that human beings are not machines, that our body parts are not indiscriminately interchangeable, that our society spends too much of its resources in flight from death, and that there are times when death, no matter how painful it may be, how unnatural it may seem, must simply be met. We felt that a heart incapable of functioning was one of those cases.*
>
> *—Claudia*

It can also help to listen to other parents talk about their impossible decisions. When you hear the love and concern that was held for their babies, you know that they did the best they could, and cannot be faulted or accused of failure. As you extend compassion to them, you can also extend compassion to yourself.

> *I get very sick when I'm pregnant and with my last pregnancy, I was the sickest. I threw up every fifteen minutes around the clock. They tried IVs but I was so dehydrated, they couldn't get them in. Finally at nine weeks, I felt like I was dying and they really couldn't give me any answers and they didn't know if the baby would make it. So the doctors and my family really pressured me into terminating the pregnancy. I wish that they had given me a little more time to think about this decision, but they started things going right when I said, "Well, maybe we should. . . ." But as time passes and I get more information, I can see that I may not have survived this pregnancy with the treatment I was getting. The way things were, how could I expect to keep going?*
>
> *—Ruth*

> *I focused on the fact that selective reduction was a way to save two little lives. Still, I was bonded to all four babies and enduring the reduction was an absolute nightmare . . . an absolute nightmare.*
>
> *—Louisa*

> *I had always been a "right-to-lifer." I knew I could never have an abortion. That is, I knew until I was put into the position of having to choose between keeping my baby, knowing he had a syndrome, or aborting him. . . . The most helpful information in choosing abortion was the information I received from a friend of mine. Her first child had the same syndrome and died at age four. I called Ann to share my grief and to ask her advice. She reminded me of the "ripple*

effect" of keeping this baby. She said, "I loved my little girl, but with my next two pregnancies, there was no question that I would have aborted had the tests shown another baby with that syndrome." Ann's honesty gave me the strength to abort our baby boy. I am so thankful that I could talk to someone who experienced it firsthand. My mind was made up before my husband came home. . . . As my due date approaches, I miss our baby Jeffrey so much, but I am sure deep in my heart that I did what was best for our baby, my family, and for me.

—Avery

I went to medical school because I wanted to be a neonatologist. But after a couple of rotations through the NICU, I was horrified by the suffering of these tiny babies. So I switched my specialty to family practice. But here I was, ten years later, faced with the prospect of delivering a multiply handicapped baby to a NICU. I KNEW I couldn't do that to her. I just couldn't. To protect her from suffering, I had to let her go.

—Kaye

For quite a while I wondered if we did the right thing taking Steven off life support. I thought, "Gee, could he have been saved and lived a normal life?" They said most likely he would be mentally retarded and have cerebral palsy and he'd be a sick little child all of his life. Part of it was a little bit selfish—I didn't want to deal with that all my life. I do often wonder though what would've happened. But I wouldn't change that decision.

—Lena

The most important factor in our decision was Jacob's welfare. We tried to do what we thought was best for him. We did not feel that the life of pain and uncertainty offered by the surgeries was one that we would choose for ourselves, and we did not feel comfortable choosing such a life for him.

—Claudia

I wanted Kristina's death to be natural and out of my hands. I wanted to protect her, love her, and get to know her before and until nature said, "It is time." This waiting to see how things will turn out was the only decision I felt I would be able to live with for the rest of my life.

—Maria

I had to think what was best for him. I firmly believe James would have fought for his life if that is what I wanted, but was that the best for him? Was forcing life on a body that was so incomplete the best I could do for him? I wanted him to be happy and free. . . . He was a kind, peaceful person who gave peace to all who knew him. I didn't want him to lead a long, unpeaceful life of struggle. I couldn't ask that of one so small. The best I could do was to let go. The hardest thing I could do was to let go.

—Grace

FACING DEATH

The unknown of what might happen when she is born was a little scary. We didn't want her to suffer. We didn't want to second-guess our decision to not intervene. We were excited to meet Ashley, but at the same time sad to meet her because we knew then our time with her (at least physically) would be over.

—Shellie

Even when parents are absolutely certain about the decision made, death is so difficult to face. If there is any uncertainty (as there often is) the task of facing death can be agonizing. As Maribeth recalls, "It's so hard to hold your baby in your arms knowing you've chosen not to do everything possible to save his life. I will never forget that feeling."

It was days and hours of saying goodbye forever to a baby I loved who would never be. It was willing James to live, fearing he would die; fearing he would live, willing him to die.

—Grace

When the baby might die after birth, it's only natural to feel frightened about witnessing this. Fears about the baby suffering are also paramount, but it's extremely rare for a baby to show any signs of distress, and a hospice and palliative care team can step in, just in case. Still, the apprehension and uncertainty can be unnerving.

I was scared of what she would look like, I was scared of "losing it" in the delivery room. . . . I was scared of a lot of things. The worst time in my life was walking into that hospital knowing it was time to say hello and goodbye. . . . Looking back I would have grabbed her right away to feel her life. Kristina did move a couple of times in my arms but she spent her first five minutes in the warmer before we held her. I was afraid of death but I'm not now.

—Maria

I was so scared that Ashley would suffer and her death would be painful to see, but the neonatologist assured us that Ashley's passing would be just like she was going to sleep. The neonatologist was right—it was very peaceful and not scary for us at all.

—Shellie

While waiting for death can be an agonizing time, it is also a time for cherishing your child's existence. Whether you had a few seconds, hours, or months, before or after birth, nurturing your baby can be an important way to cope with the fact that death is coming. As Shellie notes, "It was a time of enjoying our little girl, even before she was born. Ultrasounds and appointments took on special meaning." Barbara recalls, "My husband is afraid Virginia suffered, but for me, it was twenty-three days I got to be with her and hold her." Mahalia agrees: "I saw a little person in my arms . . . and it helps knowing that I protected her till she died."

As soon as she was in my arms, I knew all the pain was worth it. I began to play with her hair, feel her soft skin, and tried to memorize each part of her body . . . her long skinny fingers, her daddy's toes, her perfect little lips. I smelled every part of her and washed her with my tears. In those moments, I was so thankful that I had not been able to imagine what it was going to be like the first time I held her in my arms. Imagining the time with her would not have done the actual moments justice . . . the moments were more than I ever could have asked for or even dreamed of.

—Laura

It was my husband's birthday. My husband had been worried all week, "What if something bad happens on this day?" So when they asked who wanted to hold her first, my husband put his arms out. After a few minutes, the nurse asked if I wanted to see her face, I said yes. You see, I had not seen her face in its entirety—the tubes had been there since the first time I laid eyes on her. I started crying as they removed her tubes. I thought I was going to lose myself. The neonatologist came by my side and whispered, "You should tell her how proud you are of her, she was very brave. She stayed for one week. Tell her that you love her." Suddenly I stopped crying. I realized I could cry for the rest of my life but at this moment, she needed her mother to tell her how loved she is and how proud I was of her. So we held her, sang so many songs. Her official time of death was 11:59 p.m. She did spend the day with her daddy.

—Destrida

Alas, not all parents have the chance to nurture their infant before death. The baby may be stillborn, or so sick or die so quickly, there is little opportunity or time. Sometimes the mother is recovering from complications and cannot get to her baby before death does. And sometimes the parents don't get the support they need.

Making plans for my child's upcoming death is a notion I would have embraced if it had only occurred to me during the frenzy of our son's short life. I never realized having the baby near me twenty-four hours a day, getting the opportunity to bathe and feed him and certainly arranging to be with him when he died could be important later on. Only after did I learn I could have taken more control over these sorts of "details."

—Rachel

Particularly with pregnancy termination, labor induction is not always an option that is offered, resulting in missed chances to be with the baby and collect memories. As Teryn tearfully suggests, "I would've liked more choices laid out, maybe the option to have the baby vaginally so I could touch the baby. I don't have that peace, because our baby was terminated; no memories, nothing to hold on to." This too must be grieved.

Unfortunately, some health care practitioners don't understand the emotional trauma involved in interrupting or reducing a wanted pregnancy.

As a result, parents are not always encouraged or able to collect keepsakes and hold their baby, memories that are so important for grieving and healing. If this happened to you, you even may not have been encouraged to mourn. You may find yourself only thinking in terms of "we terminated the pregnancy" rather than "our baby is dead." Teryn reports, "We were told it was the 'best choice' without anyone acknowledging that it was a *child.*"

As such, it is particularly important for you to affirm your baby in the ways you can. It's never too late to name your baby, create memorials, perform meaningful rituals, and collect mementos. These small acts can help you find a special place in your heart for this child. (See also "Remembering Your Baby" in chapter 6.)

It's also never too late to talk to your doctor or midwife about what you think would've helped and comforted you. Doing so is optional, of course, but it can be a healing task to voice what you've been wishing for in a way that could make a difference for the parents who will come after you. (See also "Educating Practitioners about Your Needs" in chapter 13.)

LIVING WITH THE DECISION

I have seen death

I have held it gently in my arms

and I have kissed it goodbye

with tear-stained cheeks

To know this pain was my choice

adds a new dimension

It brings peace; it brings guilt

I want to lay it aside

and just grieve for my son

but the guilty verdict pounds

in my soul

It will take time . . . time.

—Maribeth Wilder Doerr

You will not necessarily find death easier to accept just by virtue of having "chosen" it. Having a choice doesn't lessen your grief. After all, you did not want your baby to die; death was simply the only way to secure what was "best." And you are left behind with your doubts, perhaps some guilt, and a heavy sense of responsibility.

If you chose to continue the pregnancy, you may wonder whether this option subjected your baby (or babies) to more suffering. If you decided to utilize medical intervention, you may feel like you walked a fine line between trying to give your baby a chance to defy the odds without prolonging an unduly dismal or painful life. Even if those around you applaud your decisions, you might still second-guess them.

The Doubts

While some parents believe that there was only one way to go, many others feel torn. Either way, it is quite natural to harbor some doubts. You may continue to mull over the options, considering and reconsidering how every option was terrible and how impossible it was to choose. And you mourn.

Since you feel so badly, you may wonder: *Would another choice have been better?* But really, you feel badly not because you made a *bad* decision, but because you had to make a tough, *painful* decision. Moreover, none of the options offered total solutions. Each one held its own risks and created its own problems. The alternatives were equally or even more grim, not better for your baby. Most likely, you would feel equally bad or worse if you had chosen an alternative.

> I never want to have to make a decision like that again. What were the choices? Let her die slowly of heart failure in utero? If Joy was born alive, watch her die by inches and be tortured in the NICU? Sometimes I torture myself with the knowledge that I cooperated in her demise. I only know it was an act of love.
>
> —Kaye

You may wonder later, *If I had more time, would I have made a different choice?* But even with all the time in the world, you probably would have made the same choice. You made the best decision you possibly could—under terrible stress—weighing all the information at hand and balancing many factors, including the welfare of your baby, your marriage, yourself, your other children, and even your future children. If you felt pressured by the biases of your health care practitioners, relying on their judgment is still a reasonable way to decide. If you feel that the decision wasn't all yours, you can still come to accept it. (See also "Accepting *What Is*" in chapter 4.)

If you were pregnant with multiple babies, you may be particularly prone to doubts and second-guessing, as it may have been supremely difficult to weigh the options. You may not have been fully informed of the risks of either the multiple pregnancy or the reduction procedure, not to mention the emotional toll of relinquishing much-loved and wanted babies. You may be haunted by media images of families with multiples, and think to yourself, "I could have done that." To top it off, whatever your decision, you'll never know for sure how it affected the outcome.

To be in this position is terribly difficult. Even if you would not change your decision, you may regret that it could not possibly have been a truly informed choice, simply for the understandable lack of controlled studies and reliable statistics, and not being able to know how your individual profile measured up, anyway. These decisions are so agonizing because of the lack of information and guarantees. You did the very best you could with what little there might have been to go on. Remember that media tend to idealize multiples, belittle the risks, and gloss over the harsh realities in the NICU. And only rarely do parents or babies "beat the odds." The very nature of odds is that you are far and away most likely to *not* beat them.

Whatever your situation, you may feel obsessed by "What if?" for a while. When your doubts arise, use your favored mindfulness practices. For example, mindfully become a compassionate witness to those thoughts. Practice being in the present moment and staying connected to your body, rather than disappearing into the past with regrets. See your thoughts as harmless while letting them pass through your mind. Let your body metabolize any emotional reactions without buying into them and spiraling ever deeper. (See also chapter 4, "Mindfulness-Based Coping Strategies.")

It can also help to view continued mulling as a natural part of the grieving process. Wrestling with your doubts can be a way for you to evaluate, solidify, and embrace the beliefs and principles that guided your decision. While second thoughts can be unsettling, they are normal and can help you come around to accepting that the decision you made was right for your baby.

> *Much of my own healing has come from learning of families who chose aggressive alternatives. I see our philosophical differences and this has become a source of comfort. Their feelings about "life at all costs" are not right for me; my "do nothing" choice is unthinkable to them. And we are both right. Each family must determine what is right for them.*
>
> —Rachel

THE GUILT AND ANGER

Guilty feelings are very common in parents who employ selective reduction, interrupt a pregnancy, or refuse or withdraw aggressive medical intervention. While many pregnancy losses and infant deaths are regarded as "accidents of nature," the act of *choosing* to let a baby die can lead a parent to blame themselves.

It is important to remember your decision did not cause your baby's death. Your baby's condition, which presented those options, was the cause. And you did not enter into this decision lightly. You made the best choice you could, after searching your heart and soul for the answer. And you could only decide what was best in that moment, for this baby, with the information and support at hand. Even if you've heard about other parents who "went for it," this does not undercut the validity of your deci-sion. Your decision, not somebody else's, was right for your baby's situation.

Another source of guilt is reproaching yourself for not being able to face the prospect of raising a chronically ill or disabled child. Try to keep in mind that parents who already have firsthand knowledge of what that's like tend to feel far less guilty about deciding to let go. Whether they have prior experience parenting such a child or were raised with a disabled sibling, their experience has taught them about the hardships and suffering that can occur. They can be more certain that letting go is an act of kindness for the child. As one mother admitted, "I love my kids, but I hate this life."

If you employed selective reduction, you may feel particularly angry with yourself for not trying to carry all your babies. Or perhaps you refused selective reduction and you're angry that you didn't consider the risks of multiple gestation seriously enough. Try to remember that whatever your decision, you were trying to guess what route would lead to the best outcome, without any definite signs or medical guarantees to show you the way. In making your decision, you did reach for a greater good. Also remember, your decision came from how much you loved and wanted those babies, not the opposite.

It can also help to remember that guilt is a nearly universal feeling among bereaved parents. A large part of your guilt arises from the simple fact that you could not prevent your baby's problems. It is normal to *feel* guilty; this does NOT mean you *are* guilty or that you did anything wrong. Instead of being angry with yourself for the decisions you made, be angry that you were put in the position to make a choice between "terrible" and "horrible." (See also "Guilt" and "Anger" in chapter 7; "Doing 'The Work'" in chapter 4.)

Early on I was very stuck. I couldn't get over what we did to our baby for a long time. I was angry at God for giving us this decision. Feeling like we killed our child, we saw a therapist for many months and we went to a support group for people who terminated pregnancies (hugely helpful); I wrote lots of music. Lots of very angry songs.
—Julie

I absolutely do not believe I chose to end my pregnancies—I feel like I was forced. The doctors were great and informed me of all the options, and of course they were trying to save my life first; and we obviously went with those decisions, but I was forced to make those decision by . . . (and I will just say it) I feel that I was forced into this situation and forced to make these decisions by God. I am angry! Very angry! I am angry at him for doing this to me. I wonder why he did not intervene to help me and my children.
—Sonya

Mindfully observe your thoughts and feelings of guilt and anger, with compassion and no judgment, as you let them pass through you. Stay focused on your body and let it metabolize any emotional response without feeding it more distressing thoughts. (See also "Mindfully Restoring Calm to Your Triggered Brain" and "Doing 'The Work'" in chapter 4.)

THE RESPONSIBILITY

Because these decisions deal heavily in matters of the heart, parents are the most appropriate decision makers. It is a burdensome responsibility to bear, but your baby would want you, not strangers, to decide.

> I told my mom, "I don't want to have to make this decision. I'm not God. I'm not qualified to make this decision." And she said, "God doesn't call the qualified. He qualifies the called."
>
> —Kaye

> For me, it was a huge relief when a friend pointed out that my decision was based on my intuitive knowledge of Jacob, what he was like, what he could tolerate. This made the decision right for him. I might have made a different decision if I'd carried a different baby for nine months.
>
> —Claudia

There are several reasons why you, the parents, benefit from making your own decisions:

- Every situation, every parent, every baby is unique. What may be right for another baby or another family is not necessarily right for yours.
- In the midst of tragedy, you may feel terribly helpless and ineffective. Being able to decide what happens to your baby can help reinstate a sense of control.
- Making important treatment decisions is central to being a devoted, nurturing parent. This was your chance to be your baby's best advocate.
- It is you, not the health care practitioners, who must live with the decisions that are made, for years to come.

Although you may wish someone could have made these difficult decisions for you, parents who are not given choices often regret it. Even now, some hospitals do not let parents have many options. What happens instead often depends on medical staff opinions, bias, and preferences. Fortunately, this is slowly changing, and many health care practitioners now realize that instead of being told what to do, parents need to be offered all available options, as well as enough information, unbiased support, and time to make the right decisions for their baby(s) and their family. Although these decisions are agonizing to face, parents benefit when they get to examine their own hearts and minds and choose the best options for their baby(s), rather than having disagreeable options forced upon them.

Indeed, if you had been barred from making these decisions, you would probably feel even more angry and depressed. Faced with this possibility, Grace recalls, "It was unsettling to think that even if I believed in letting nature take its course, the medical ethics committee could overrule that decision and do extraordinary things to James if they felt his life was worth saving."

Also, consider this: you were responsible—not irresponsible. This was probably the most serious, complex, intense, and far-reaching decision you'll ever have to face. No one else could have been more agonized and soul-searching with regard to this baby. The urge to hold on to your baby at all costs can be so strong, and yet your sense of *what is best for my child* prevailed upon you. This takes a lot of courage and faith. And as John points out, "I really view it as probably the most unselfish thing that I've ever done."

As the parent, you tuned into your baby and let your baby lead the way. And for a different baby, you might have made a different decision. No one else could have been attuned to your baby as carefully, thoughtfully, purposefully, and solemnly as you were. You were the right person to make those difficult decisions.

> We didn't want to let go of this baby, we just got him, we just met him, we just found out how much we love him, we don't want to let go. But to be good parents, to look after his needs, maybe this is what's best for him.
>
> —Claudia

It can also help to remember that ultimately, you're not responsible for death taking your baby. Death comes because that's what nature or God intended. Death comes when modern medicine cannot cure a fatal condition. Death comes when fending it off demands a terrible price, which you wisely decide that your baby and your family are not willing to pay. Embrace your sense of responsibility—and how well you fulfilled your duty.

COPING WITH HARSH JUDGMENT

However you decide to say goodbye to a much-loved baby, you may worry that some people will judge you harshly. You may avoid sharing your experience, but this only exacerbates feelings of isolation and distress as you then mourn alone. And even if you try to keep it a secret, most social and family circles exchange information freely. As a result, it may be impossible to completely avoid judgment and harsh remarks.

> There was one instance where someone felt we had "murdered" our son and that hurt. This person had never walked in my shoes. Even though every other person felt we were courageous and right to do what we did, this one instance stays with me . . . the one comment I can't forget.
>
> —Maribeth

Not being able to share what came about further compounded the depression. Not everyone would agree with the step we took and so I found myself being vague about the loss of my child. But in this way, I could not have people relate to the added torment of having had to be the one to make the decision, to literally take your child's life.

—*Annalaura*

We felt judgment from those who thought we should terminate our pregnancy because of their own ignorance and lack of understanding. Since Adisyn's passing, we suspect some may view our grief as something we asked for or deserve because of our decision. Others suggested that Adisyn was suffering, when she couldn't have been any more safe where she was. This darkness made me question people, their motives, and the relationships I have with them. I felt myself building walls to protect myself and our baby.

—*Emmerson*

So how do you face everyone? Eventually, as your grief softens and you come to accept that the decision you made was best, it will be easier to be around others and talk openly about your experiences. In the meantime, however, you needn't withdraw until you resolve your doubts, anger, or guilt. You only need to practice surviving others' comments. To do this, try the following suggestions:

- Gather insight into what drives those who judge you harshly. Many judgmental people are limited by simplistic thinking or their own emotional issues. They may cling to a black-and-white view: *Life is good and death is bad.* Or, *terminating is the only reasonable choice and continuing the pregnancy is just crazy.* There are others whose capacity to reason shuts down when they hear the word *baby*. Remembering these shortcomings can help you ignore or deflect harsh comments. (See also "When Friends Turn Away" and "Unsettling Remarks" in chapter 13.)
- Reframe your thoughts. Especially in the thick of your grief and doubts, it is normal to be upset by unkind remarks and take them to heart. But it can help to recognize that others' judgment is most distressing when you yourself harbor similar thoughts. When a remark stings, take the opportunity to be a witness to your feelings, examine the thoughts behind them, and mindfully replace them with alternatives that are more accurate and compassionate. Over time, as you unload troubling thoughts, you won't take others' judgment so personally, for it no longer sets off an echo of remorse inside you. (See "Mindfully Reframing Your Thoughts" and "Doing 'The Work'" in chapter 4.)
- Practice self-compassion. Self-compassion is the best antidote for dealing with a lack of compassion from others. When you are able to counteract harshness with your own internal source of

kindness, you can become more skillful at disregarding others' judgments. (See also "Practicing Self-Compassion" in chapter 4.)
- Remember, you don't owe anyone a list of justifications. You don't require anyone else's approval or forgiveness. And you needn't try to change others' views—just insist that they respect yours. You can also reassure yourself by saying, "It doesn't matter what they think. It wasn't their body, their baby, their family, their decision." Even if some people don't accept your decision, they can refrain from being hurtful to you. If necessary, avoid them while you heal. (See also "Educating Well-Meaning People about What You Need" in chapter 13.)

Whatever your decision, there will always be people who disagree, judge, or cannot understand why you made the choices you did. Some will avoid talking about it all together. But there will also be people who can agree, accept, understand, and listen. So you might consider casting a wide net and telling people openly. Your openness invites those who've traveled this road to step forward and allows others who can support you to offer their companionship as you mourn. In short, your openness can make your journey less lonely. If you're fortunate, you will have friends and family members who can support you, without judgment.

I wish I could have known the outpouring of love and support we would receive. Even people who may not approve of abortion for themselves, they respected our decision. The flowers, food, cards, notes, and visits were so loving and so appreciated. Also, many women "confessed" to me their abortions from their pasts.

—Avery

We talked through the best way to tell people about Pearl, and each time we had to tell someone, we found ourselves comforting them. At times that was exhausting, but good for us to be reaching out and even finding people we could borrow hope from, when our hearts were especially weak. When people asked why we would continue with this pregnancy, we asked them, "Why not?"

—Laura

I Wanted So Much for You

For Kristina

I wanted so much more for you, my sweet little baby.

I wanted to change your diapers, not my life.

I wanted to nurse you, not my grief.

I wanted to dress you up, not bury you down.

I wanted to hear the sounds of you crying for me at night,

    not my own sounds of crying for you,

    my innocent, misconceived baby.

I wanted to see you grow, not the grass upon the grave.

I wanted to see you asleep in the crib, not in the casket.

I wanted to give you life, not death.

I wanted to show you off, not alone go on.

I wanted to comb your fuzzy hair, not save a lock of it.

I wanted to pick up after you, not put down my dreams for you.

I wanted to hold you in my arms, not this doll.

I wanted to walk you late at night, not my fears.

I wanted so much for you,

    my newly born, newly gone–child.

I wanted so much more

I wanted so much

I wanted

I wanted you.

—Maria LaFond Visscher

Points to Remember

- Although there is considerable social pressure to reach for miracles and save lives, there can be wisdom and heroism in letting go. Some fates *are* worse than death.
- Having a choice does not make death easier to accept. Making a decision only gives you the illusion of having control over the death of your baby. In reality, your baby died because of problems over which you had no control.
- Rightly so, you relied on your values and projections to guide you. Your baby would have wanted you, not strangers, to make this decision.
- Your emotional duress played an important role in your judgment. It enabled you to make the decision with your heart and gut, not just your mind.
- It is the nature of making life-and-death decisions that they weigh heavily on your heart. It is normal to wrestle with doubts, second-guessing, and a profound sense of responsibility.
- Mindfulness-based coping strategies can help you manage painful thoughts and feelings.
- Feeling badly does not mean you made a bad decision. It means that you were thrust into a tough situation with painful decisions to make. Had you made the other choice, you'd probably feel worse.
- Deal honestly with your deepest feelings of doubt and guilt. Facing your feelings will allow you to come to terms with them and to feel less defensive with other people.
- Instead of being angry with yourself for the decision you made, be angry that you were put in the position of having to choose between "terrible" and "horrible."
- You were responsible—not irresponsible. This was probably the most serious, complex, intense, and far-reaching decision you'll ever make. No one else could have been more agonized and soul-searching. You were the right person to make that decision.
- Whether you decided to fight death or accept it, your decision was right for your baby, you, and your family.

10

ESPECIALLY FOR FATHERS

On the second day of summer, our daughter was stillborn. Her name was Willow Blue Lotus Ariel Oldfield. I'll never be able to articulate the pain and despair of our grief journey. It was so impossibly dark and bleak and cruel.

—*Nathan*

Both mother *and* father must grieve in order to come to terms with their baby's death. However, most couples are struck by the differences between their grieving. While individual differences are to be expected between any two people, the gulf between men and women tends to be consistent and wide.

This gulf occurs partly because of biological differences between the "typically male" and "typically female" characteristics in our brains. But there are also differences in the social expectations placed on males and females, as well as differing cultural pressures to conform to certain ideals. For example, men are especially expected to "keep a stiff upper lip" in the face of great tragedy, whereas women are expected to be more emotionally expressive as part of their "inherently hysterical nature." These attitudes have stifled men and demeaned women.

Fortunately, there is a trend toward uncovering popular myths about men's grief and shedding those limiting values, manners, and rules of relating. As we begin to accept emotions as intrinsically human and essential to decent civilizations, we are starting to view men expressing emotions—even tears—with compassion instead of derision. As we become more enlightened, we respect the man or woman who grieves exactly according to his or her nature.

This chapter examines the father's grief and considers the traditional pressures and expectations our culture places on men. Some mothers will also identify with these pressures to clamp down on their emotions. Provided with these insights, fathers and mothers alike are encouraged to question social expectations, claim their grief, and express it as their individual natures intend.

MYTHS ABOUT MEN'S GRIEF

Everyone's expression of grief is affected by the interplay of a complex set of factors. Grief itself is a biological, brain-based reaction, but since early childhood, we learn about expressing grief by what we've been told, what we've observed, and what's been expected of us, both in our families and the surrounding culture. These social influences have shaped each of us according to our sex and our personal predispositions toward certain emotions, emotional sensitivity, and expressiveness. Social expectations have led to several myths about men and grief that create unnecessary suffering for bereaved fathers.

Myth #1: Men aren't supposed to express emotion or need support.
For men in many cultures, tears are generally frowned upon. Crying in particular is considered the opposite of masculine ideals, such as being in control, brave, rational, independent, and productive. From very early on, many boys are taught to be ashamed of expressing need, crying openly, feeling bereft or afraid, and even having affection for other males. "Real men" aren't supposed to weep or lean on others.

Myth #2: Grieving requires expressing emotion.
Most people assume that true and healthy grieving is expressed only by the outward display of emotion and talking about it. But as discussed in "Grieving According to Your Nature" in chapter 2, many people experience grief, not as intense emotion looking for expression, but rather as an urge to "assess and do what needs to be done." And for many men, this activity-oriented grieving is a primary inclination.

Myth #3: Men's grief is (1) inexpressive, (2) mild, and (3) brief. (1)
Whether a father is primarily inclined toward activity-oriented or emotion-oriented grieving, his grief demands expression. (2) For a father who tends to be emotion-oriented, he too can be grieving deeply, but is subdued as he conforms to social expectations. (3) A father who tends to be activity-oriented can, in fact, be grieving when he is immersed in activity. To the untrained eye, he may appear to *not* be grieving (see myth #2), when he *is*. So when a father's grief appears inexpressive, mild, or brief, this does not necessarily indicate the true depth of his grief or its expression.

Myth #4: Men don't need support.
When it appears that the father has done his manly duty and snapped out of it in short order (see myth #3), people are unlikely to offer much in the way of condolences or support. This myth might not be much of a problem for the father whose natural grieving style is primarily activity-oriented. He might be skilled at dosing his grief in manageable bits and expressing grief through meaningful activity, and if he also happens to be a self-reliant introvert, he might not even care if people don't inquire. But for most fathers, this lack of support can be isolating, hurtful, and detrimental.

Myth #5: Men find it easy to conform to social expectations.
A father cannot possibly conform, as social expectations put him in a bind. If he tends to be emotionally expressive, he may be admonished for lacking control of himself and his life. But if he tends to be emotionally

*in*expressive, he may be admonished for being out of touch with his emotions and unable or unwilling to express them. Either way, men are often faulted for "not grieving right," and it is the rare father who feels completely affirmed that his grief is natural, supported, and finding healthy expression.

It is always unfortunate when cultural pressures discourage anyone from experiencing or expressing the very feelings and behaviors necessary for mourning. If your grief and its expression don't line up with social expectations, you may feel inhibited, disoriented, and unsupported. Most unfortunate is that these myths put fathers at risk for avoiding or suppressing their grief, which brings on unnecessary pain and suffering.

> *Because I'm a man, society has decreed that I should put this matter behind me and get on with the business of life. In trying to do just that, I denied myself the due process of grieving which, in hindsight, more than likely did more harm than good.*
>
> *—Ron*

While you cannot change society, you can benefit from a social circle that grants you the freedom to express your grief authentically, trusts you to find your path, values your strengths, and offers compassionate support. For you, this might translate into having solid family support (including your partner), a group of friends who "get it," a network of bereaved parents who understand, or any resource (a counselor, other fathers' written or spoken stories of grief) that can reassure you that your grief and its expression are normal and just right for you.

> *I was searching everywhere for someone or something to support my husband. I found Kelly Farley's book* Grieving Dads. *And that was about it. I ordered the book for my husband, because the average guy isn't going to go to the bookstore and seek out a self-help book on grieving. I got my husband to start reading the book one night, and he never stopped until he finished it. He told me about the other stories of bereaved fathers and I know that he found comfort in reading it.*
>
> *—Jolie*

> *It makes it seem more real—knowing that other grieving dads are out there.*
>
> *—Charlie*

INVISIBLE GRIEF

When a father's grief is invisible, where does it go? Underground. But it doesn't go away. Grief that's suppressed still demands expression, so it will be indirectly expressed in the father's behaviors, mood, and health status. Stan operated this way. When he was eighteen, he lost his grandmother, an uncle, and his father. After that, he vowed he'd never grieve again. Ten years later when his baby died, he said, "Stuff happens. That's the way it is. You tolerate it and move on." Unfortunately, he needed everyone around him to have the same attitude so that he could keep the lid on his grief. He became very controlling and angry, particularly with his wife who felt entitled to her feelings. He also started to drink heavily, a common anesthetic for men like this.

Another father may keep most of his grief in the back of his mind. He knows he has it but finds it too overwhelming or painful to face. Nick was like this. He filled his days with working overtime and justified it by pointing to the extra money he was making. But rather than feeling a sense of accomplishment, he felt empty and frustrated. And he stopped taking care of himself—no more working out or watching what he ate. His feelings of grief did come to the surface now and then, especially at night. Sometimes he brought them out, but usually he was ambushed. Nick felt like he was losing control over his life, and he often felt isolated as others around him failed to acknowledge his pain.

For men, as Stan and Nick help illustrate, suppressed grief commonly shows up in three disguises, which are often intertwined and result in unnecessary suffering:

1. Silence
2. Anger
3. Numbing

Because of the stifling nature of social expectations, men commonly suffer in silence. And many men, unaccustomed to dealing with intense emotions and lacking social support, fall into anger and numbing, which can include addictions. Men who have emotion-oriented grief are particularly prone to these indirect expressions of grief. Stan fell mindlessly into silence, anger, and addiction. Nick was aware that he needed help, and was referred by his doctor to a psychiatrist (an MD who can diagnose psychological problems and prescribe medication). He was diagnosed with depression, but because the psychiatrist offered no compassion or engagement, Nick couldn't be sure the medication prescribed was really what he needed.

Incidentally, these three disguises are not for men only. Both men and women are influenced by a culture that values emotional stoicism and places judgment on grieving. This section focuses on men and the social conditioning that pushes fathers away from their grief and toward silence, anger, and numbing.

All I wanted to do is isolate myself and be alone. Not talk to anyone. Try not to think about it. Not feel the pain and emptiness inside.
—Charlie

SILENCE

This is silent and painful. I can't tell of my wife's gallant labor or how beautiful our son was. Only those who have experienced loss want to know.

—Fred

From infancy, many boys are shamed, rejected, and reprimanded when they express needs, want affection, or show fear, sadness, or disappointment. "Big boys don't cry." "Don't be a sissy." "Buck up, buddy." These are just a few of the sayings proffered to boys. Boys are even encouraged to cut themselves off from physical sensations such as when athletic coaches scold shivering boys to quit being wimps, get out there, and *play*! Is it any wonder, then, that many fathers have lost touch with the emotional sensations in their bodies, and cannot acknowledge, identify, or explore their internal experiences? Some avoid feelings to avoid the associated shame.

Even if a boy's family allows expression of a wide range of feelings, he quickly learns that his peers are not so accepting. Also, he may notice how other men in the family tend to keep feelings private. Both boys and girls are affected by a family that denies emotions, and many adults have learned to suppress or keep feelings to themselves.

By withdrawing into silence and avoidance, you protect yourself from any unacceptable feelings associated with grief. Feelings such as yearning, anxiety, fear, despair, and insecurity are kept at bay, and you may even be convinced that those emotions don't exist. Since friends and family generally don't ask how you are doing, your silence is reinforced. Unfortunately, by burying your feelings, you place yourself at risk for any of the health and emotional problems associated with suppressed grief. (See also "What if I Try to Avoid Grieving?" in chapter 5.)

Some men may appear silent, but grief is expressed privately. You may set aside time for visiting the grave or writing in a journal, but you may try to cover up your whereabouts. You may wait for opportunities to be alone, and then you open up and cry. While this can work really well for you and is far healthier than silence accompanied by avoidance, you may miss out on the benefits of social support, recognition, validation, and wise counsel. If you think you'd find support helpful, do reach out. (See chapter 13, "Support Networks.")

ANGER

It is common for fathers to get stuck in anger. Tied to assertiveness and aggression, anger is considered masculine and therefore acceptable to display. So for fathers who need emotional release, anger allows them to maintain an image of strength.

Anger is a valid response to your baby's death, but when sadness is what's begging for expression, anger doesn't really fit the bill. When anger is a habit, it's also easily triggered—and easily mismanaged—making it become hurtful to you and others. As a result, you may find yourself easily frustrated when even trivial things don't go as you've planned. You may overreact to petty annoyances and find yourself slamming doors or throwing, pounding, or swearing. You may be easily irritated by people you care about, and behave in ways that you later regret. You may experience back, neck, or shoulder pain, indigestion, or headaches. Anger turned inward can result in depression—feelings of hopelessness, worthlessness, powerlessness, or fatigue that won't budge. You may feel less effective at your job or in your relationships. Sarcasm, cynicism, paranoia, or forgetfulness can be indirect expressions of anger.

Anger can also be a way to recover from profound feelings of helplessness and loss of purpose, which many men experience upon their baby's death. But for some men, anger becomes a way to suppress deeper feelings of grief, including sadness and fear. (See also the introduction to chapter 7, "Painful Feelings.")

Although anger can make you feel powerful, you pay a high price for avoiding feeling broken. You may become aggressive, pushing people away instead of inviting them to support you as you tend to your grief. You may become self-destructive too (see following section). And when you run away from grieving, you also run away from healing. Instead of coming to terms and moving on, you hold on—to blame, revenge, resentment, bitterness, and ultimately to your pain. In these ways, anger merely exacerbates brokenness. (See also "Is It Normal to Feel So Irritable or Frustrated?" in chapter 5; "Anger" in chapter 7.)

NUMBING

After your baby dies, feeling numb is a normal reaction to the trauma. Numbness is a result of stress hormones surging through your body and brain, and the part of your brain that processes emotions shuts down. Unfortunately, if the trauma continues or if the original trauma is more than your brain can resolve on its own, you will remain hyper-reactive, your stress hormones will keep being triggered, and you'll remain numb—and stuck.

Numbness can also be self-inflicted, as a way to circumvent the pain of grief. Particularly if any of your grief calls for emotion-oriented grieving, you may view the emotional pain as too intense, too threatening, or too scary to handle. Numbing can be a way to avoid this pain.

Here's how numbing works: because your grief is held in your body, in order to avoid your grief, you must avoid being aware of your body. So you engage in behaviors or activities that keep you disconnected from yourself and what's going on in your body, physically or emotionally.

Common numbing behaviors include:

- neglecting self-care, such as overeating, eating poorly, sleeping too little, staying up too late, poor hygiene

- habitual use of alcohol or mood-altering drugs
- compulsive behaviors, such as gambling, sexual activity, extreme sports, obsessive religious practices, spending too much time on electronic devices

As you can see, numbing isn't a viable long-term plan because there are many undesirable consequences to these behaviors. For example, one dad, when asked if he had strategies to cope with the death of his baby son, replied, "Healthy ones? No. I ate." In fact, he gained forty pounds by not caring about what he ate and compulsively overeating.

When numbing behaviors are habitual or compulsive, they can be difficult to stop. That's because they keep you disconnected from your body, what's truly good for you, and what you truly want. Some behaviors can also provide distraction from grief by immersing you in a drama that keeps you disconnected from your true self and what's really important to you.

Some numbing activities look good, even admirable from the outside. Exercising many hours a day, working overtime, devoting many hours to a charity, becoming an expert online poker player—these activities can enhance your life . . . unless they serve to disconnect you from yourself and your body. Any activity can become destructive when the push to excel or the urge to do it takes you away from your relationships, any of your responsibilities, your health, and, of course, your grief and mourning. With sports, you may find that you cannot take a break, even if it means risking or sustaining serious injury. Overtime at work can win you fame and fortune, but your family and friends become strangers. Charity can bring you praise and recognition, but true charity begins at home. The Internet can expand your horizons, but done to the exclusion of *real life,* your horizons are actually only as broad as your screen. And by engaging in numbing behaviors and activities, you stay stuck in mourning and saddled with suppressed grief. Numbing helps you avoid grieving; it does not help you adapt or find peace. And by avoiding your grief and mourning, you are essentially avoiding your life.

These three methods of disguise—silence, anger, and numbing—can result in a number of harmful consequences, including:

- withdrawal from your partner, your other children, family, and friends
- relationship difficulties, including conflict, feeling isolated or unsupported
- spending more time away from home, or being reluctant to leave the house
- dropping out of activities that are good for you
- behaving recklessly, aggressively, and/or violently
- trouble sleeping, including nightmares, insomnia, oversleeping, exhaustion

- financial instability
- chronic pain, tension in the body, frequent or chronic illness
- declining mental or physical health
- depression, anxiety, feeling hopeless and empty
- decreased ability to feel emotions, including positive ones like love and joy

If you see yourself in any of these consequences, or if anyone else is telling you that certain ones describe you, this is not evidence that you have failed. This is evidence that you are suffering unnecessarily from your baby's death, and you could benefit from support and perhaps professional assistance in getting your life back on track. Also, your struggles could be due to the aftereffects of trauma, in which case you could benefit from a brain-based treatment such as EMDR (Eye Movement Desensitization and Reprocessing). (See also "About Trauma and Suffering" in chapter 3; "First, a Note about Trauma" in chapter 4; "Counseling" in chapter 13.)

It's possible that just reading down the list of consequences could motivate change. If you are engaging in a numbing behavior, you might try mindfully slowing down and comparing what reward you expect with what you actually experience. Doing this lets you (and your brain) realize that what you thought you wanted to do is actually the source of unnecessary suffering. This exercise can inspire you to refuse to fall prey to the hollow short-term reward that leads to long-term pain and boost your willpower to pursue long-term gains. The book *The Willpower Instinct: How Self-Control Works, Why It Matters, and What you Can Do to Get More of It* by Kelly McGonigal, PhD, explores the science of willpower and offers many insights and practical suggestions for working with your brain, instead of against it, to achieve your goals.

All this being said, grieving need not be done perfectly. It's only necessary to do it well enough.

I didn't do it well all the time: I was angry, sometimes I drank too much wine on my own, or hid too long in my man cave, or didn't answer calls from well-meaning friends, or just emotionally shut down. I failed plenty of times. But I also tried hard to make things work.

—Nathan

This book is full of ideas that can help you take charge of mourning and ensure balance and healing in your life. The rest of this chapter provides specially tailored ideas and support for claiming your grief and your right to grieve your way. Instead of suffering from suppressed grief, you can grant your grief the expression it demands. You can also take charge of integrating grieving into the flow of your life. Then you can reap the benefits of the resulting transformative, healing journey.

CLAIMING YOUR GRIEF

My heart is still broken as we just delivered a baby boy, Adam John. A cute little kid who looked full of mischief and couldn't wait to get in trouble with his older brother. Splash in mud puddles, pull the dog's tail, eat cookies before dinner. . . . I will never be able to teach him how to shoot a hockey puck, or douse a spinnaker sail in a yacht race, or scare Mom with a batch of night crawlers, or to teach him about more important things like "I'm sorry" or "I love you."

—Fred

One of the hardest things I've faced yet is having to write my son's name on his death certificate.

—Ben

You may already have considered that the traditional images of manhood need revision. Whatever your grieving style, you may resist the social pressures that put men in a bind. Especially if you are confronted with intensely painful feelings of grief, you may see the value of rejecting the constraints put on men's emotional expression. But forging a new identity that balances strength and gentleness can be difficult. If you're used to burying your emotions, then shedding the in-control, aloof, rational, and independent veneer can be a frightening prospect.

I wouldn't know how to get a guy out of that way of coping. How would you stop doing something you're so accustomed to—especially how you deal with emotions? No one wants to be seen as weak—especially not a man.

—Charlie

Realistically, before you can shed old ways, you must acquire new ways so that you can manage the grief that comes up. Here's an analogy: Although it may be in your best interests to move out of a dilapidated old house, you must first find a new house to move into so that you're not left completely vulnerable to the elements. So it is with your emotional life. It is only fair to expect yourself to give up old ways after you've begun to master, trust, and find strength in the new ways. Do take heart—by simply deciding on change, you are more than halfway there.

IDENTIFYING YOUR STRENGTHS

While society, culture, and upbringing can stack the deck against males when it comes to grieving, you are also encouraged to acquire certain strengths, which can come in handy when you are facing adversity. These "masculine traits" actually translate into adaptive strategies that can benefit you, whatever your grieving style. Here are some of the strengths you might already have or perhaps you strive to cultivate:

- having self-reliance
- being a team player
- being a contributing member of a community
- being a mentor
- knowing the importance of courage
- protecting your family
- assertively standing up for yourself and getting what you need
- bonding with others through teaching, humor, storytelling, and shared activity
- controlling when, where, how much, and with whom you express emotion
- solving problems
- remaining productive
- having a sense of purpose
- being physically active

You may have learned and applied many of your strengths in sports, business, leadership, and work. And some of your grief will likely find expression in meaningful, skilled activity that restores functioning to your family and purpose to your life. (See also "Grieving According to Your Nature" in chapter 2; "Jumping into Action" in this chapter; "Grieving Styles" in chapter 11.)

> *Although I recognize that racing isn't nearly as important as "real life," I do know that there are some similar lessons. One of the most important of them is to know that it's most important how we respond to adversity. Do we stop and feel sorry for ourselves, or do we surge up that hill into the darkness with all we have?*
>
> —Ben

As society opens up to diversity, men are also claiming those strengths traditionally cultivated in females, such as verbal ability, expressiveness, emotional sensitivity, empathy, and nurturing. Any of these may come quite naturally to you, and they too can translate into adaptive strategies, whatever your grieving style.

If you find that you are struggling so much that you can't call up your strengths, you will likely benefit from more support than you're getting. *No parent should suffer too much despair, nor do this alone.* Although asking for or accepting help may seem like it only confirms your weakness, it actually falls under the masculine strengths of "assertively standing up for yourself," and "getting what you need," and "knowing the importance of courage." A good place to start is to ask one person to assist you in getting the support you need. Possible sources of support include your partner, a support group, a friend, a family member, a mentor, another bereaved father, a clergyperson, or a counselor.

The Challenge of Getting Support

A lot of people would ask me, "Is there anything I could do for you?"
So badly, I wanted to say, "Yes. You can ask my husband how he is
doing." I have so much to say about this issue, as I'm sure my husband
would as well. It is so important to give fathers the attention they need,
and so deserve.

—Jolie

Many fathers notice that people tend to offer support only to the mother,
as if he is unaffected. Charlie agrees: "Attention is pretty much 100 percent
focused on the woman." It's easy to feel left out when friends and relatives
inquire only about the mother's condition. You may flinch when others
compliment your ability to "hold up," when inside you feel so torn down.
You may be expected to return to work without any drop in productivity.
You may not have male friends who can listen to you talk about your deeply
held thoughts, feelings, struggles, or even your experiences. Francisco notes,
"I feel emotionally isolated from my male friends, in contrast to my wife
whose female friends talk about this stuff so freely."

It's true how lonely a guy feels—how lonely I feel. Men are so
different. They basically act like nothing happened. Even one time
when a friend took me out to get my mind off of stuff, it was just that—
to get my mind off of it. It wasn't even mentioned—maybe just briefly.

—Charlie

Back at the office, nobody said anything. No "Congratulations!" No
"I'm sorry." I was on my own. Oh sure, the company president said,
"It must be God's will to have something like this happen to you." I
might try that the next time we lose a large account.

—Fred

Ironically, people may hesitate to inquire how a father is doing, knowing
that many men find it difficult to verbalize their grief. And if you *are* able
to verbalize or express deep emotion, people may judge you as weak or
"not handling it." It can help you to remember that if you and your grief
go against social expectations, others' cluelessness or disdainful opinions
only reflect social bias, not unfitness or error on your part.

As my office became electrified with this new father's story about
his daughter's birth, I feel strange. We just had a child and nobody
cares. They said he should take some time off to help his wife. They
thought that since my child is dead I should get back to work. How
unfair. My wife needs support and I would like to be there for her.

—Fred

Sometimes a father doesn't even get much acknowledgment from his
partner, the mother. For many couples, this happens partly because she is
so distraught, and partly because he is so worried about her that he dives

into the role of being her main support. Especially if his partner is strongly inclined toward emotion-oriented grieving, he may easily step into the role of holding her up and putting his own grief on hold.

> *In the beginning, he gave me courage when I had none, the strength and confidence to carry on when all I wanted was to stop, and reassurance that I needed constantly to help manage my anxiety and fear.*
>
> —Emmerson

Being your partner's bedrock can make you feel useful and may be immensely appreciated by her. But as a result, your grief may become invisible even to you, and understandably remain a nonissue to your partner. As time passes, if this role prevents your grief from finding appropriate expression, it will wear on you. If you are unaware that this is happening, you're likely to abandon your partner in frustration rather than shift your focus with care. In order to shift with care, be aware of when you need a break and share this information with your partner. Your partner is likely to be relieved that you grieve too, and willing to offer support or give you space to tend to your own needs.

> *I felt bad for my husband. Before I got treatment for postpartum depression, he did not really get the chance to grieve, as he became my nurse and had to worry about me—and whether he was going to come home and find his wife dead.*
>
> —Lorna

You may be fortunate to have a partner who can be sensitive all along to your need to grieve, even if it finds expression in ways she doesn't understand or expect.

> *After Zac died, I tried really hard for us to keep the lines of communication open by always asking how he was doing. I think often everyone asks about the mum but rarely about the dad. They are suffering just as much as we are.*
>
> —Melanie

If you wish you had more support than you're getting, here are some suggestions:

- Go online and search "grieving fathers" and the like. You will find stories written by dads—even videos—and networks to tap into that can help you feel less alone and more affirmed in your grief and how it finds expression.
- See a counselor. This can provide you a "safe space" to explore your experiences, express thoughts and feelings, and even release your tears. Fathers who feel little permission to have intense feelings can find this kind of support invaluable. Counseling can also assist you in overcoming emotional numbness, reducing suffering, and learning new coping strategies.

- Attend a local bereaved parent support group or a men's group. These kinds of groups generally accept and encourage exploring issues and emotions that may never see the light of day out in the "regular" world. If you want but cannot find a fathers group to attend, you can ask for a special "men only" meeting of a parent support group. This meeting can be a natural opportunity to launch a regular fathers group. You can also find "grieving dads" support networks online.
- Do an activity that you can share with certain friends whom you think you can count on for support. Many men notice that talking and emotional expression about difficult or sensitive subjects can happen when they are busy working together. It's as if the physical and mental task before them helps to regulate intense emotion and ease social interaction.

Men don't really know how to sit in circles and unload, or meet in a café with a friend and debrief. We tend to do our best talking while engaged in activity: hiking to the surf, fixing a car, going on a road trip, campfire beers once the fire has burned down low.

—Nathan

Also gauge whether the support you're seeking is comfort, reassurance, and emotional support, or more along the lines of practical support, like help with running your household, advice about your marriage, or referrals to quality online resources. Even if you want to remain private about your grief and mourning, you still benefit from companionship.

And so I made this little surfboard, then I shared it with my friends. Everyone who rode the board in the film understood what it was about. They rode the board to honor Willow. I can't really remember anything specific that anyone said, but sometimes they came back to shore after surfing, with tears in their eyes and a hug on the beach.

—Nathan

UNDERSTANDING YOUR BLEND OF GRIEVING

How your brain and body react to your baby's diagnosis, dying, and death is a function of your core brain's response. In other words, you don't have control over the grief you experience. What you do have control over is how you handle it.

I believe there are different seasons of grief: numbness, rage, despair, withdrawal, confusion, loneliness, resentment, dullness, guilt, darkness, hopelessness. It's important to sit through each season, to neither cling to them nor reject them, but just to accept them as part of the process. Of course, that's so much easier to say in retrospect.

—Nathan

The key is to match your grieving with your grief. In other words, when your grief feels like a general restlessness welling up in your body, and when you are energized by assessing and doing, and you can only think about your baby in manageable doses, go for it. That would be activity-oriented grieving. And when your grief feels like an emotional energy welling up, and your heart yearns to dwell on your baby and immerse yourself in grieving emotions, go for it. That would be emotion-oriented grieving. If your grief changes by the hour or by the season, go for what expresses and releases the welling-up energy *in each moment.*

While you may favor one style over the other, the vast majority of people are actually a blend of both styles, sitting somewhere on the continuum between extremes. As a result, you will likely benefit from expressing your grief in both ways over time.

I cried a lot, whenever or wherever I needed too. I talked about my loss and my heartbreak. I tried to sleep as much as I could. I said no to extra responsibilities at work. I constantly communicated shared grief with my partner. I went into the great outdoors whenever I was able. I expressed my grief creatively. I prayed, fasted, meditated.
—Nathan

Being able to detect "what your grief feels like" requires that you be connected to your body and its sensations. If you're feeling disconnected from your body, you might benefit from one or more of the mind/body or brain-based therapies listed under "Counseling" in chapter 13, as well as mindfulness practices that can cultivate self-awareness. (See "Simple Mindfulness Practices" in chapter 4.)

JUMPING INTO ACTION

I began making this little surfboard as a way of rising from the ashes and learning to live again. To use my hands to build something.
—Nathan

Many fathers are primarily activity-oriented grievers, whose grief finds expression largely through taking action. You too may notice the benefits of moving your body, scanning your world for problems to solve, planning projects, and accomplishing meaningful tasks. Even if you tend toward emotion-oriented grieving, being activity-oriented at times can release the physical and mental tension of grief. Moving your body literally releases tension. It also keeps you connected to your body, which keeps you connected to your grief. Solving problems or keeping projects afloat can release the tension of helplessness, depletion, and disorientation by making you feel helpful, fulfilled, and purposeful. "Doing" can give you a sense of making progress through the quagmire of your baby's death. "Doing" doesn't have to become a way of suppressing feelings or thoughts about your baby's death. You can be aware of the quagmire. You can even think about it and feel about it, and if you're routinely able to have an abiding sense of accomplishment, this reassures you that you won't get lost in it.

I'm a doer. I don't sit there feeling bad about it and about myself. I go do something and push it aside in my head to focus on other things for at least a little while. I don't ignore it, but I've learned that I can't just feel bad about it, because it doesn't help me get on with life.

—Ben

Making this board was a gift for me during the darkest time of my life, because it kept me busy, gave me some focus, helped me believe that there could be a future beyond the hard, sharp ache of those early months of grief.

—Nathan

Feeling productive also restores your sense of worth, which might take a hit when your baby dies. You may even dedicate an endeavor to your baby or acknowledge that you've taken a different path because of this baby's life.

His death caused me to reevaluate everything I did—my career, my life, and what I was going to make of everything. I quit my job about six months later to pursue some business opportunities, and I haven't had a full-time employer since.

—Ben

There are many ways fathers jump into action. Perhaps you researched information on your baby's condition or the status of the pregnancy. Perhaps you were involved in making medical decisions. You may have advocated for yourself, your partner, or your baby; orchestrated the funeral arrangements; or pored over autopsy results. You may keep the household running, engage in physical labor, or become deeply involved in a hobby, sport, or project at work.

I made some phone calls to family to let them know what was happening and then went back into the room with Amy. We decided right then that we were going to go ahead and take the opportunity to go through the labor, at a normal pace, learn from the experience of having our firstborn, and be there for each other and Bodhi. They induced Amy and it was on.

—Ben

The day our baby started miscarrying, our cat disappeared. We knew we couldn't get our baby back, but by golly, Mark was going to find that cat. He took a week off from work and was consumed by making phone calls, canvassing the neighborhood, distributing fliers, and searching through animal shelters. I really believe that because of the sheer force of his efforts, our kitty was returned to us by kind strangers. And that was his way of dealing with our baby's death.

—Winnie

Jumping into action can be a great way to counteract feelings of helplessness and reestablish feelings of competence. Being active is a way to feel in control. Being in charge, taking up projects, and making decisions are ways to strike back at the unfairness of the universe. To be competitive at work and at play is a way to fight back the feelings of fear and vulnerability.

And, yes, jumping into action can distract you from feelings of grief. Particularly when you're being "a doer," people around you may question whether you're "grieving right." They may wonder if your activity level is healthy. They might conclude that you're avoiding or suppressing feelings. You may wonder about this too. But as mentioned earlier, if your activities are constructive, healthy, meaningful, and keep you connected to your body, then these activities are likely serving as adaptive strategies.

> *I'm grateful for not developing the "avoid reflex." Avoiding anything, from work to feelings, just delays the inevitable.*
>
> —Ben

DIVING INTO EMOTION

> *The midwives let me deliver her myself. After a day and night of grief and labor, I at last received Willow's warm but lifeless body as she slipped silently from between Eliza's legs and into my waiting trembling hands. I buried my face in our Willow's tiny, still, exquisite body and I covered her with tears and kisses and tender words and anguished groans that came out of such a strange, deep place in me, that I hardly recognized them as my own.*
>
> —Nathan

Many fathers have a strong or moderate tendency toward emotion-oriented grieving, with activity-oriented grieving playing a secondary role. But these fathers might have a harder time than fathers who tend more strongly toward activity-oriented grieving. This is partly because emotion-oriented grief is considered unmasculine, partly because it is indeed more emotionally painful than activity-oriented grieving, and partly because many men are unsure about how to manage it. If you're feeling overwhelmed, you may worry that your feelings will be detrimental to your family and other relationships. You may fear losing others' respect. Perhaps your biggest fear is that you will fall apart and lose control of your emotions, your mind, your life. Nathan shares more about the moment Willow was born into his hands.

> *In that terrible and beautiful moment, I felt my spirit being torn apart. I can remember the feeling quite clearly. In that moment I recognized that some essential part of me had in that very instant been broken irreversibly and utterly and completely. It is a brokenness that I will never hope can be restored in this life.*
>
> —Nathan

Whatever your style of grieving, you'll likely have moments when grief demands expression as emotional pain, and it is normal to perceive this pain as too intense to handle. You may feel ill-equipped to deal with your grief, as you may have been largely conditioned to shut down any painful emotions you have. Unfortunately, if you buy into this socialization and consider it unacceptable to feel broken, you may deny your grief the opportunity to flow, and suffer the consequences of suppressing it.

Still, it is normal to feel wary of emotion-oriented grieving. As John H. says, "I think men are into production and with grief, there's no product. You go through it, you're miserable and what do you have in the end? Nothing! It's like, why even bother?" Ron recalls his response around the birth of his twins, one of whom had died many weeks before their birth:

Over the last few weeks I had been so careful not to allow myself to think of this moment, and when it came, I found myself quite unprepared for it. And the tears flowed—the uncontrollable sobbing brought on by a loss I never felt before.

—Ron

Indeed, emotion-oriented grieving demands you shed, to some extent, traditional masculine ways of dealing with emotions, and open yourself to feeling vulnerable. This may be yet another frightening prospect.

It may help to try putting catastrophic thoughts into perspective. While opening up may lead to a flood of pent-up emotions from your present as well as past losses, grief is not a bottomless pit. Instead, imagine a tunnel. It may be dark and cold inside, but there is a light at the end, where the rest of your life is waiting for you. Milling around at the entrance can keep you from getting on with your life. You can't go over it or around it. You just have to go through it. If you get stuck in the middle, it isn't quicksand. You are the one who controls whether you move forward. Getting through the tunnel does ask you to go with the flow of your grief and its expression, but you can find safe ways to do this. You certainly are not required to do it all at once or to become completely submerged—unless you are called to, and even then, *submersion is temporary.* However you do it, going with the flow of your grief helps you to regain control over your life. Eventually you'll feel transformed and able to function even better. Your relationships will benefit, and others will respect how emotionally centered and healthy you are. You'll also acquire a sense of peace and healing. By looking at grieving this way, you might even agree that it's the brave thing to do.

It's good to know that falling apart is temporary—that you won't cry or hurt forever.

—Charlie

Your baby's death changes you whether you grieve or not. If you let yourself grieve, you can change for the better, rather that succumbing to the pitfalls of suppressed thoughts and feelings. You can even play an active role in your grief. There are many suggestions throughout this book on ways to facilitate your mourning process. (See also "How Do I Acquire a Sense of Healing?" in chapter 8.)

The next few sections are a primer on emotion-oriented grieving. While you will find many emotion-oriented suggestions throughout this book, these sections are tailored for fathers. Remember: even if you are primarily an activity-oriented griever, you are secondarily an emotion-oriented griever, meaning you may harbor some grief that demands emotional expression. These sections are for you too.

MANAGING FEELINGS

As mentioned earlier, emotions are always manifested somewhere in the body. Anger might be experienced as a tightness in the jaw or fists; fear as a queasiness or knot in the stomach; sadness as a lump in the throat; shame as a flush of heat in the face. So a first step for getting in touch with feelings is to be aware of the sensations in your body:

- **Scan your body.** When you feel emotion welling up, it's actually the sensation of a constriction in your body. Mindfully observe, breathe, scan your body, and take note of the sensations you feel.
- **Find the words** to express the feelings you have. Even if you simply describe the sensations you're feeling in your body, this will help you become more aware of your physical experience. (See also the next section, "Finding the Words.")
- **Let the sensations dissipate.** Whenever a feeling is triggered, the chemicals coursing through your body will dissipate within two minutes if you don't fuel them with negative thoughts. Stay focused on your body, relaxing into your breath, putting your attention on your abdomen as it rises and falls.

This mindful awareness of your body can actually reduce your emotional distress by calming your core brain, which may have become hyper-reactive due to your experiences around your baby's death. (See also "Mindfully Restoring Calm to Your Triggered Brain" in chapter 4.)

If you find yourself resisting the idea of sharing feelings or eliciting support, entertain the idea that no bereaved parent is expected to suffer alone. Even having just one person in your corner can reduce your suffering markedly and boost your ability to put your life back on track. Counseling can be key. Even champion boxers have professional support in their corners.

We couldn't have gotten this far without all the support we have, and for that I am very grateful.

—Ben

FINDING THE WORDS

After Jacob died, it just seemed so hopeless to talk about. I couldn't find the words, so why try? There was no handle; it's just a nonverbal hurt.

—*John*

To this day, I don't like talking about it much because I don't like the feeling of that pain.

—*Charlie*

It's always hard to find the words.

—*Nathan*

Many men find that words don't come easily. Men who tend to be activity-oriented grievers especially might do better if they don't verbalize it or think or talk about it too much. Some of these fathers will set aside time for themselves to think about it, and then the rest of the time, they stay focused on other activities. This adaptive strategy is common and helpful for many men.

But if you're feeling overwhelmed by intense feelings at times, it can actually help you to find the words. When you verbalize emotions, you're activating a part of your outer brain that regulates the emotions that rise up from your core brain. Labeling emotions can also take a giant, formless ball of pain and render it into smaller chunks that are easier to manage. Even if you can't find the words to identify emotions, you can identify where in your body you feel the tension or other noticeable sensations.

Once you have the words, you are able to talk or write about your emotional experiences—both activities can be therapeutic. If you think it will help you to have someone to talk with, find a safe, supportive person who can listen to you. You need someone who is nonjudgmental, patient with your grief, accepting of whatever you say, and unafraid of anger or tears. A counselor can be ideal. You can also try journaling, blogging, or attending a bereaved parent support group or a men's group.

I also had a kind of desperate need to want to tell Willow's story. My father's heart wanted to scream to the world that I had a beautiful little daughter, brown-skinned and raven-haired and perfect, and I lost her.

—*Nathan*

SHEDDING YOUR TEARS

You may not have any more tears to shed, but many men do—and are understandably reluctant. Social expectations and limiting ideas about self-image can come into play.

Women are generally more prone to crying than men, but after the death of a loved one, men and women are equally likely to shed tears.

Still, in some cultures, when someone gets misty eyed, it's often assumed that they have lost control of everything, not just their tear ducts. But this attitude continues to change as mounting research shows that crying has many health benefits. It serves primarily as a release valve for emotional stress, and calms the body in several ways:

- Emotional tears contain stress hormones, whose buildup is washed away when tears are shed.
- Crying reduces blood pressure and heart rate.
- Crying boosts levels of feel-good hormones, making you feel relieved and even more content afterward.

In contrast, holding back tears can be bad for your mental health, contributing to depression and emotional distress. Your physical health can also be compromised, as fighting tears exacerbates high blood pressure, allergies, ulcers, colitis, headaches, and cardiovascular disease.

In fact, some people notice that when they need a good cry, tension builds up in the head and body. If this describes your experience, you can find release by setting aside private time to think about your baby and your memories, perhaps going through photographs, visiting the grave, or as you work on a memorial project. Or it might work better for you to just accept the tears as they come up. Charlie has found his own way for going with the flow.

I can't set aside a time to cry like my wife does, because I would have to be thinking about it all day to get that emotional buildup for a release. For me, crying is sporadic—maybe when I hear a song or I'm watching a movie. It's not planned or expected.

—Charlie

Not every man will be moved to tears, especially after the first few weeks, so if you don't find yourself ever crying, this in itself is not cause for concern unless you're harboring tears and feel too inhibited to spill them. Particularly if you have been taught that crying is foolish, or if you feel too overwhelmed as they well up, you may try to squash them. But if your internal experience of grief includes intense or deep emotions, crying is a normal, even necessary expression. If you deny them, you may be embarking on a journey of repressed grief and unnecessary pain and suffering.

The tears have stopped now but the pain lingers on. If I could turn back the hands of time, I would allow myself to open up and realize it's all right to be scared and feel totally out of control. . . . Never again will I be a victim of the silent crying.

—Ron

Many men do have tears and it's a benefit to shed them. Even though you may feel helpless while you're crying, you'll notice the benefits afterward. Crying also makes you feel better in the long run, as it biochemically aids your emotional recovery. And you can always pair crying with a meaningful activity that boosts your activity-oriented grieving as well.

> *I couldn't help but make that surfboard and the film. My close friends knew what I was making in the shed under my house, and some of them came to help, or watch, or just be. Most of the time, though, it was just me in my man cave, probably internalizing too much, wrestling with despair, keeping the wolves of hopelessness at bay however I could. I did a lot of crying over that little length of foam and fiberglass.*
>
> *—Nathan*

If you are afraid that once you start crying, you won't be able to stop, your fear is unfounded. No one has ever cried forever. It is more realistic to expect yourself to cry until you are relieved of the pressure of welling emotion, which for many people usually means two to six minutes, max. This may seem like forever, but it isn't, at least in the grand scheme of your entire life. Also, you may feel like you are crying "all day," when in reality you are crying for short periods of time, off and on all day. Whatever your pattern, rest assured that crying jags will lessen in frequency and duration over time. And whenever you shed tears, you are keeping company with plenty of other fathers.

ACCEPTING YOUR BLEND OF GRIEVING

As a man, beware of falling into the trap of thinking that being activity-oriented is the way men are supposed to grieve. Nor should you expect yourself to be completely, stereotypically activity-oriented even if that's the style you favor. The only kind of griever you can be completely and authentically is *your kind*. Your brain's grief reaction is what it is, and whatever your blended experience of grief, that's the optimum blend of expression. However much you benefit from jumping into action or diving deep into emotion, this is determined by your unique brain and your unique mosaic of grief, not by your will, your image management, or social expectations.

To follow the lead of how your grief and its expression naturally flow, stay connected to your body and the sensations of grief that will either well up as emotion or appear as restlessness and the urge to "go do." Nathan provides a great example of how to follow the lead of grief. Below, he reports his grief reaction upon writing his narrative for this book, clearly demonstrating (1) his blend of emotion- and activity-oriented grieving, (2) how he remains connected to his body, and (3) how he answered his grief's demand for expression:

> *Ah, I had a big cry revisiting these days. My heart aches. I am going to go and jump into the sea.*
>
> *—Nathan*

GOING WITH THE FLOW

Just like racing, life can be a cruel and humbling creature. One minute you are cranking along full speed, and the next you double flat and break your chain.

—Ben

Your baby's death is tragic. You're experiencing many sorrows and challenges. And grieving can be debilitating. Going with the flow is a daunting prospect. But it is far more debilitating to stem the flow, for this silently cripples your strength, drains your energy, injures your health, and sabotages your happiness. Suppressing thoughts and feelings turns them inward, increasing their power to control you. The more you try to avoid grief, the more it runs your life, because every move you make has to keep you detached, tough, or in denial. In fact, men pay a high price for pushing grief aside and maintaining a stoic front.

I realize the ways my grief surfaced—in anger, numbness, and avoidance, and then the effects were rage, anxiety, nightmares, losing interest in taking care of myself, and having a new baby and being afraid that she is going to die.

—Nick

For me, when Eli died, I had all these feelings that were hard to identify and incorporate—generalized feelings of anxiety and anger, and none of the books talked about that. I was a wreck. Finally I realized it all boiled down to powerlessness and fear—that my life was being torn apart and there wasn't a damn thing I could do about it. After that realization, it seems like I settled down and coped a lot better.

—John H.

Even if you think you cannot afford to take the time or energy to grieve according to your true nature, once you do make a conscious effort to devote yourself to this endeavor, you'll realize that *your grieving actually frees up more time and energy for living your life.*

There really are benefits to letting it out, and that kind of assigns a purpose to the grief.

—Charlie

Still, you might be skeptical or fearful of "going with the flow," as the flow might feel like it would be akin to a dam bursting. But even if the flow is great at first, that high rate and large volume only lasts a short time, settling down into totally doable whitewater. And you can navigate it better than you think.

You just don't know how you'll get through it. But, you bear down, jump back on, and keep going.

—Ben

In fact, it may be helpful to see your grieving as a powerful river that is uniquely yours. Your outcome will be far better if you keep your eyes open and proceed downstream with the flow. And like many fathers, you may be surprised at how well equipped you actually are. Grieving itself never killed anybody—it's only the fear that does people in. Grieving is simply a necessary passage; it is not your enemy. By ignoring or fighting it, you rob yourself of the opportunities this passage grants you. In surviving it, you'll learn a lot about yourself and what you're made of. It's a hero's journey, and *you are the hero.*

It is much too hard to believe that it has been ten years today that I first and last held you in my arms, our dear lost daughter, Willow Blue Lotus Ariel Oldfield. Today hurts as it always does and the ache is as fierce as it ever was. Yet somehow I dance for you and with you forever, you who are etched always on my skin and also as you are so much more profoundly and perfectly scribed into the most intimate and private corners of my heart, forever and ever and always, my beloved, deep to deep.

—Nathan

HALF MOON PASS

Here I am again
　　　on top Half Moon Pass
Warm sleeping bag awaiting me
　　　some distance behind
Half Moon—a good place
　　　to be alone
　　　six months after tragedy
Half Moon—a good place
　　to scream and holler
　　into noisy wind
　　　and deafening quiet
Half Moon—a good place
　　to see forever
　　as if a vast expanse
　　　were a help
So I sit here alone
　　except for myself
　　and the Keeper of this Vista
And I comb through tangled
　　and flowing memories

Looking to tend the wound
> looking for a place
> where it stops or starts
But grief is playing that familiar trick
> and the only thing to touch or feel
> is a bucket full of numb
So with exasperation climbing
> I undress
>> to the freezing touch
>> of unattending wind
And in bitter angry madness
> I pass sentence on grief itself
> "If you will not feel the pain,
>> I'll match you numb for numb"
The sun is giving up her reign
And I'm floating in a sea of goosebumps
> feeling righteous
> and of one accord
I spy a place where lightning has struck
> ten miles between me and the growing faraway
> fire–going to work
Watching, waiting–numbing it
A question lurks its way
> to the surface of my mind
>> "John, would you rather freeze or burn,
>>> Which death would be most kind?"
I can't decide tonight
So I elect my sleeping bag
> and the arms of solace there
Believing tomorrow wiser
> in this battle with despair.

—John E. Hicks
In Memory of Eli

Points to Remember

- As a father, you may feel overlooked. When others around you fail to acknowledge your grief, you may feel isolated, misunderstood, and feel compelled to keep your grief silent.
- Grieving is how you come to terms with your baby's death.
- Grief starts in your brain and is held in your body. To get relief from the tension and energy build-up of grief, stay connected to your body and aware of its sensations, so you can give your grief the expression it seeks.
- When you're going with the flow of your grief, your journey is made easier.
- If you or your grief go against social expectations, remember that others' disdain is only a reflection of social bias, not unfitness or error on your part.
- No parent should have to suffer too much, nor grieve alone. Even if you want to remain private about your grief and mourning, you still benefit from the company of other people.
- Find other parents to talk to, if you think you'll find this supportive. Men's support groups may be particularly affirming for you. Reading fathers' narratives is another way to feel a sense of community.
- If you are feeling stuck, numb, or have signs of avoided grief, you might benefit from counseling, perhaps including a brain-based treatment for trauma.
- Seeking professional help is a sign of your courage and willingness to seek positive change. Even champion boxers have professional support in their corners.

11

You and Your Partner

When it was time to check out of the hospital, we were ready to just get home. We packed our things, said our "thank-yous," and it was time to leave. I stopped Amy, looked at her, and said that this whole experience could make us stronger or destroy us. Then we walked out the doors and drove home.

—Ben

All couples notice that their relationship is affected after their baby dies. Some feel closer and draw together in sorrow. In the process, they learn more about each other's sensitivities and strengths, and their intimacy and mutual support may be enhanced.

I know the stress of a loss, let alone multiple losses, can ruin a relationship, but our losses have strengthened our relationship. We are rock solid. That's not to say we were all roses. Many times we were at polar opposites in terms of our grief, and I can't imagine how hard it was for my husband holding it together when I could not. But it has only acted to solidify how much we love each other.

—Melanie

At times losing Judah made us weak in spirit, but it made us stronger as a couple. What an intimate, deep experience to go through with your spouse.

—Jolie

Most couples pull apart at different times, as grieving often demands that you withdraw into yourself. And many couples withdraw temporarily into blame, hurt, displaced anger, and misunderstandings. For some, this tragedy becomes a catalyst that breaks up an already troubled relationship. For many couples, a baby's death drives a needless wedge into an otherwise healthy partnership. But whether you stay together or go your separate ways, your adjustment to your baby's death can spur personal growth, enabling you to make peace and create a better relationship.

Lilly Marie's father and I are not together. Sadly, after a few years of drifting along, we realized we were happier apart so we separated. We are still friends. I still hold the same love for him now as I did then. It has just morphed into something new. He and I will always be connected because of Lilly Marie.

—Sarah

We knew right away that it could take a huge toll on our marriage, which is another reason we fought so hard to grieve in a healthy and timely manner. We allowed each other personal time to process and then also made sure we were constantly checking in together. In the end, because of how we did it, our marriage came out even stronger and more mature than it was.

—Embry

It is normal to alternate between intimacy and isolation. This may be the first tragedy you've faced together, and you may discover new ways of being there for each other. "Being there" can even include taking time-outs, which can be soothing to both of you—and your brains—enabling you to come together in calmer ways. But sometimes, the stress of grieving can make you so needy individually that it can be difficult to be there for each other in any way. Many of the grieving emotions, such as anger, guilt, and sadness, make being supportive too much of a challenge. Often you will grieve very differently from each other, making it hard for you to empathize or accept each other. That's why one of the most important strategies for your relationship is to find support outside of it, including good friends who will listen, a parent support group, *and counseling*. There is no reason why you should try to do this by yourselves.

We both needed support outside of our partnership. I found this through the Bereaved Parents' Support Group, a few close friends, and therapy. She has been finding support with her work in the gardens, a few close friends, and a new therapist. Our relationship grew stronger when we starting looking for support in other places.

—Tanya

Nurturing Your Relationship

Glenn and I were incredibly lucky: we just didn't experience the strain that so many couples face. This may be a good place to point out that we were a bit older, and that we'd both been around the block when it came to relationships (perhaps obvious from the fact that I had a sixteen-year-old with a woman). We'd accumulated a bit of experience and wisdom. We didn't have any expectation that we'd handle things the same way, grieve on the same schedule, or want to do all the same things to remember Thor. But I think it only worked because we both did grieve. I think if one of us had had the impulse just to shove it under the rug, then we'd have been in big trouble.

—Elizabeth

Some couples take bereavement in stride, some will go their separate ways, but many will stretch and grow their relationship. Certainly, the tremendous stress of grieving can push you apart. You may not even realize how much you've drifted away from each other, particularly if your baby's death is followed by the stress of a subsequent pregnancy or two and you're also adjusting to having a new baby (or two). When the dust finally settles, you may be looking at each other across a chasm.

Paramount is making room for each of you to do the grief and mourning you need to do. Plus, there are a number of activities, approaches, and skills you can try on to see which ones ensure your relationship survives and even thrives. Many strategies can fit under the themes of *connection, sharing, acceptance,* and *reassurance,* which are ingredients that can help any relationship flourish. Skills that can come in handy include resisting the urge to "fix it," navigating sex and intimacy, and managing conflict.

CONNECTION

We loved our Emily so, and in the days that followed, we were going to need a whole lot of love and patience for each other. We taped "Love Is" from Corinthians to our bathroom mirror, as a reminder.
—Anne

When you're depleted by the stress of grief and mourning, your connection may falter. It is common for grief-stricken partners to have trouble finding each other. It is normal to drift apart.

Maintaining a caring connection even in the best of times requires ongoing devotion, energy, and communication skills. Like any living thing, your relationship will thrive better when it's nurtured by activities that demonstrate a basic sense of connection, such as
- keeping the lines of communication open,
- discussing tough topics skillfully,
- dealing with the feelings that come up,
- offering each other warmth and positive support, and
- spending quality time together.

If your relationship could use some mending along any of these lines, putting your efforts there can improve your connection, even in the worst of times.

It can also help to remember that before you were bereaved parents, you were friends and lovers. Hold on to that sense of care you have for each other—care about what each of you is feeling, care about what each of you needs. Also hold on to a sense of caring about your relationship, and consider it a lovely creature or a kingdom that also needs the right kind of attention to thrive. For instance, there are a number of simple pair-bonding activities you can do that will nourish your partnership on a brain-chemistry level, releasing the feel-good hormones oxytocin, dopamine, serotonin, and endorphins. Besides boosting feelings of connection to each other, these hormones reduce feelings of stress and grant a sense of well-being, even as you mourn.

See which of these activities appeals to you, given where you are on your journeys. Come back to this list down the road and add more to your repertoire when you're ready.

- Engage in physical affection. Even just casual touch begets feelings of closeness and devotion because it releases oxytocin, which is the feel-good hormone of bonding. It is also calming to your brain and body, reducing blood pressure and lowering levels of stress hormones. So mindfully reach out for each other by holding hands, sharing twenty-seconds-long hugs to get the oxytocin flowing, and affectionately patting each other as you pass by.
- Set common goals for your relationship. What qualities do you want to cultivate in your partnership? Pick one or two to work on in a collaborative effort, which can enhance feelings of closeness and release oxytocin.
- Make eye contact. Get your eyes off your screens and put them onto your beloved. Doing so releases oxytocin as well.
- Laugh together. As part of your therapeutic respite from the ravages of grief, see a funny movie, watch your favorite sitcom, listen to stand-up routines, or watch online animal videos. Doing so releases endorphins, which can reduce the feelings of stress and spur a sense of well-being.
- Do something new together—try a new restaurant or a new recipe each week; create something meaningful in memory of your baby—art, architecture, landscaping; join a support group for bereaved parents; go into couples counseling; get out of town on a weekend. Novelty releases dopamine in your brain, which motivates you to explore in anticipation of reward.
- Pay it forward. Make a donation of goods or services to a worthy cause. Giving activates the parts of your brain associated with pleasure and social connection, and releases endorphins.
- Move together. Whether you're dancing, riding bikes, or walking, the physical exertion enhances mood and releases endorphins.
- Get outside. Have a picnic on a balcony, spend the afternoon at a park, comb a beach, climb a mountain. Being out in nature will release serotonin, which boosts mood and your partnership.
- Hold tightly to the concept that, especially on this most difficult leg of your larger journey together, you are allies, not adversaries.

SHARING

Right after the baby died, there was this honeymoon period where we felt, "We're alive, I love you so much, we'll try again soon," and then you start drifting apart into your own grief and grieving so differently, and that incredible closeness goes away.

—Clara

Like many couples, it can appear that you will walk similar paths, sharing thoughts and feelings as you go. But as each of you settles into your own unique grieving style, you will probably part ways. It takes energy to communicate, and you may wish your partner could just read your mind or understand you with minimum effort. You may wish you could speak freely about your baby without raking up your partner's pain. You may want reassurance that you're not the only one in pain or thinking about your baby. Communication in a relationship is normally challenging, and after a baby dies, the stress of grieving can add tension.

> *I used to be able to tell him what I was thinking and how I was feeling. He would be feeling the same or would acknowledge how I was feeling. But recently, our friends—who were pregnant at the same time and went on to have a little baby boy born only a few weeks before Adisyn's due date—celebrated their baby's first birthday and that really affected me. When I told Ben, he didn't seem to understand and looked at me like I was crazy. This I find a hard road to navigate.*
>
> *—Emmerson*

Many couples find themselves at odds. Misunderstandings can flare up easily. For instance, you may find it difficult to cope with your partner's displays of emotion because it worries you, or because you are struggling to manage your own intense feelings. Or perhaps one of you finds it helpful to share thoughts and feelings, but the other finds it supremely challenging to understand or absorb what's being said. This isn't for lack of effort or caring, but simply that your grief demands that you grieve accordingly rather than trying to match up to something that doesn't fit. If you expect each other to grieve out of alignment with your own experiences of grief, this only deepens your rift.

> *We grieved very differently, which most bereaved parents know will happen, but it's a lot harder to live it. Initially we were strong, he was my rock and my everything. I didn't want to do much if it didn't include him. But as time wore on, he couldn't be that anymore and he wanted and needed his wife back. I can see that now, and in the moment I reacted in a way of pulling myself together for us. But I also went inward more and stopped sharing with him things I should have. It was not and has not been an easy road.*
>
> *—Abby*

> *Often all I want is acknowledgment of my feelings. When he doesn't acknowledge my feelings around our precious baby girl, I feel even more isolated and alone.*
>
> *—Emmerson*

Many couples experience the dynamic of one parent wanting to share and talk more than the other. Both of you may need affirmation and validation of your experience, but one of you may need far more than the other.

Charlie needed to be affirmed, but in a more simplistic way than I do. For example, I need to know, "Am I a bad mom when I did/said/ thought/felt this? What about when I did this? What about now?" Charlie's fulfilling of affirmation was straight and to the point, like it seems like everything else is for him: "Am I grieving wrong? No? Okay, good."

—Jolie

There were times when I just needed that time by myself, time just for whatever. I needed to not be pressured about talking about it. I needed a break from that.

—Charlie

If sharing thoughts and feelings lessens the pain for one of you but burdens the other, what you *can* share is a mutual respect and concern for each other. Check in and talk about what you're looking for in terms of support, and agree that *you don't have to get everything you need from each other.* It is perfectly reasonable for you to reach out to other people and use other resources, especially when you're both already running on empty. Other outlets might include close friends, other bereaved parents, support groups, online communities, counseling, journaling, or writing a blog. By sharing a mutual concern and supporting each other in seeking what you need, you can enhance each other's coping.

I stopped talking to him about how I feel, which seems to work better for him. And I see a counselor, which he doesn't know about because he wants to believe I am okay. He supports me by just letting me do whatever I need to do.

—Karen

I feel like at the beginning I was constantly trying to pull stuff out of my husband and I totally didn't understand how he was grieving or coping (or if he even was!), but once I fell into that kind of "comfortable" space in my own grief, I didn't feel the need to prod and pry anymore. I just realized he was grieving as Charlie—as a male, a husband, and a father.

—Jolie

Once you find out what kind of support your partner is looking for, you only need to give what you can. For example, many a mother is focused on the *loss of relationship*—with the baby and perhaps her partner—and she tries to maintain connections. So mothers can be immensely comforted by partners who can simply share the fact that they think about the baby too. This lets the mother know she is not the only one, and it helps her feel less alone. In turn, many a father is focused on the *loss of purpose,* and is trying to regain a sense of mastery and meaning. As such, he may feel supported by being able to have alone time, and not being pressed to talk about it. Typically, thinking about the baby and grief may not even be a verbal experience.

As you learn about what each of you finds helpful to give and receive, you can both acquire realistic expectations to fend off disappointment in each other. You can also choose which small but meaningful gestures will make a big difference for your partner without draining the life out of you. You may even find nonverbal ways of sharing and offering support.

> There are certain bands and songs we listened to in the days that Emily and Michael died. And we really listened to the lyrics. It was amazing how close the words came to how we were feeling in those days. It was like we did not even need to tell each other the pain we felt. Sometimes it was just too hard. When these certain songs played, we could just see it in each other's eyes, and know.
>
> —*Anne*

> A wonderful thing Lavender did was to help change the traumatic energy of a special item of mine. She took the expensive bathrobe she had bought me, which I had worn for labor when Oren was born, and dyed it indigo with a butterfly. This was very touching, as I'd felt sad every time I wore this bathrobe. Now it was beautiful and I could have a new relationship with it.
>
> —*Tanya*

If you prefer not to talk about your own feelings but you don't mind lending your ear, you can be supportive by quietly listening to your partner express feelings as desired. Being there to listen—without trying to "fix" or offer solutions—is a wonderful skill that can take practice, especially when you hate to see your partner in pain or you're intent on problem solving. It can also help to remember that expression of intense feeling is okay—it's how your partner goes with the flow and finds relief and healing. If you find it challenging to take in all the words, just let them wash over you. Simply by being a caring presence and letting the waves come, you can be a tremendous support.

> I never felt like I was burdening him with my tears. I needed to talk about it and I needed to cry about it, and he never left me feeling like he didn't want to hear it. Other people tire of hearing your problems, but he never gave me that feeling. He always was willing to listen no matter how many times he heard it.
>
> —*Sara*

If you find it challenging to share thoughts and feelings with each other, that's okay. The bottom line is that you can still build trust and strengthen intimacy by sharing a mutual respect and concern for each other.

ACCEPTING YOUR DIFFERENCES

> I connected with a few key people, but mostly I savored solitude. My wife, on the other hand, who is much more socially oriented, found

solace in a few deep close friendships. . . . I think the key is creating the space that is necessary for you and your needs.

—Nathan

No two people will grieve or mourn alike. Distinct styles can be attributed to normal variations in personality, socialization, family history, philosophical bent, emotional tendencies, coping style, and postpartum hormonal changes. For instance, after giving birth, the mother's hormones will make her more likely to cry and to feel certain physical symptoms. Parents also vary on what bothers them most, what they struggle to cope with, and the changes they undergo.

Accepting your differences can be easier if you know why they exist. For many couples, many of their differences can be explained in terms of their connection to the baby, grieving styles, and the dynamics of taking turns.

CONNECTION TO YOUR BABY

Amy had been so close with Bodhi for twenty-four weeks during the pregnancy and I felt [like] a supportive bystander.

—Ben

His pain does not seem as raw anymore, but perhaps that is the difference between men and women, given that we carry our babies and when they die, a part of us dies too.

—Emmerson

Partners experience different degrees of bonding to the baby, and this naturally colors their experiences with grief. During pregnancy, the mother usually feels a closer connection with the baby. For the father (or nonpregnant partner), the baby is more abstract until birth. This may be particularly true when the baby dies early in the pregnancy; the mother may feel a *much* greater bond. But as the pregnancy progresses, the father can see the growth occurring, feel fetal movements, and, especially after birth, the fatherly bond deepens and so will his grief. Even so, it is okay and normal for each parent to feel a different connection with the baby.

Since this baby was full-term, this was the first pregnancy that my husband could identify with. The others were miscarriages, and as each miscarriage occurred, it became the norm to him, I think. He was always concerned about me, but he never ever mentioned the pregnancies. He could never identify with me as to how I felt. All these losses I was on my own, and it was something he could never understand, but with this one, he did.

—Meryl

GRIEVING STYLES

There are always little sections in the books I read about how losing a child challenges a marriage. Of course it does. We grieve differently

*as a mother and father, and as individuals. But once we figured out
each other's "grieving style" and how to decode that and give each
other grace, life got a lot easier.*

—Jolie

*My husband and I thankfully talked a lot during that time, and we
grieved in similar ways. I think it would have been much more difficult
for me if he wasn't willing to talk about it and cry with me.*

—Shellie

It is common for parents to be in similar straits during the first days or even weeks after their baby dies, as both of them are reeling from the shock and stress. It can be quite comforting to keep such close company. But after this initial period, each of you will settle into your long-term, natural grieving styles, which might still be similar, but are more likely to be quite different.

As discussed in "Grieving According to Your Nature" in chapter 2, there are two basic styles of grieving:

1. Emotion-oriented grievers focus on feeling and expressing.
2. Activity-oriented grievers focus on assessing and doing.

Neither style is better than the other, and nearly everyone experiences a blend of both. And because everyone's grief is a unique mix, you and your partner will likely differ, not only in how you experience and express grief, but also in the adaptive strategies you choose to implement. As a result, you may rarely see eye to eye.

Fortunately, successful grieving is largely a solitary endeavor, and does not require you be in sync with your partner. Where couples tend to run into trouble is when they misunderstand each other's differing styles and adaptive strategies—especially if they have strong inclinations toward opposite directions.

*My husband says I scare him because I grieve too intensely. We try
to find a happy medium where we can talk about it without frightening
each other.*

—Rosemary

*I hated my husband. I felt like he wasn't sympathetic and he wasn't
grieving like I thought he should be. I didn't really see him for about
six months because he was trying to bury himself by keeping busy,
school and work, thirteen hours a day.*

—Rose

*I often felt like I needed to tone down my desire to go out for a long
ride. While I wanted to just get out and do my thing, ride, push
myself, and just go, I didn't. I didn't bring it up, I didn't ask. I just
stayed home because I could tell she would get the feeling that I
wasn't showing the same emotion as her.*

—Ben

If you tend to be an emotion-oriented griever and your partner is primarily activity-oriented, you may worry that your busy partner is unfeeling, uncaring, and has forgotten about your baby. You may feel angry at this seeming callousness, and feel isolated as you intensely grieve alone. It's hard for you to imagine how your partner could possibly be grieving when he or she is so busy *doing.* The reality is that your busy partner can actually be busy *grieving.*

- Grievers who are primarily activity-oriented tend to experience grieving emotions as relatively less intense, and they are adept at regulating them—so perhaps after the first week or so, or most of the time, it is simply unnecessary to "have a good cry."
- They may appear to be "over it" too soon, but actually, they let grief flow by being meaningfully active, thereby restoring a sense of purpose and mastery.
- When they sense the tension of grief building—often a generalized feeling of restlessness in the body—it can be helpful to get busy with activity, or even purposely look for problems to solve and projects to do.
- Indeed, they express attentiveness, caring, and love for their babies through actions, which to them speak so much more loudly than words.

Just because we didn't carry the baby, and just because we don't show it as much, doesn't mean we don't grieve as intensely.
—Charlie

If you tend to be an activity-oriented griever and your partner is primarily emotion-oriented, you may view your intensely emotional partner as dwelling too much on the baby, unnecessarily bringing on tears, and going too deeply into mourning. You may feel impatient, wanting your partner to snap out of it and be more functional so you can do activities together and life can proceed. It's hard for you to imagine how your partner could possibly ever climb out of this hole and recover.

The reality is that your emotional partner is actually experiencing the emotional distress of grief more keenly.

- Grievers who are primarily emotion-oriented tend to find grief's intensity to be energy depleting, making it hard to get tasks accomplished, and everyday life seems so shallow and useless anyway.
- They may appear "too mired" in grief, but actually, they let grief flow by airing feelings, thereby releasing them.
- When they sense the tension of grief building—often an ache in the chest or a lump in the throat—it can help them to give in to a crying jag, or even purposely trigger one by, for instance, going through baby photographs and keepsakes or visiting the grave.

- For them, this deep expression of emotion is a testament to their love and devotion to their babies.

I would go into Judah's room, I would put on a song, I would hold my weighted bear, and I'd look at his picture while I rocked in his chair. I knew these things would make me cry and ultimately make me feel relief.

—Jolie

As Jolie and Charlie, above, demonstrate, couples can be at opposite ends of the spectrum in terms of their outward expression, but they can find common ground in how intensely they grieve for their baby. Ben, too, provides a great description of the contrast and common ground between him and his wife, Amy:

*The sadness is more because I'm sad for Amy and her ongoing way of going through it. She'll have the aches of sadness from time to time . . . when the kids mention him or she thinks about him. I haven't really broken down or "had a good cry." It just doesn't do anything for me, I guess. I feel like that's weird sometimes, but then my brain says to me, "Crying isn't going to do anything." I'm focused on **doing**.*

—Ben

As you can see, Amy experiences grief as an ache of sadness, whereas Ben experiences grief as a physical restlessness. Whereas she'll have a good cry, he'll have a good ride. And here is the common ground that they share: Both are *connected to their bodies*. When the energy of grief builds, they each sense the tension and seek the kind of release their bodies are demanding. Amy feels an ache in her chest, perhaps a lump in her throat, and tears well up in her eyes. Crying is a full-body activity, with paroxysms releasing tension and tears flushing stress hormones from the system. Ben feels a restlessness in his body and senses the urge to hit the trail on his mountain bike. When he's on a ride, he focuses on how his muscles, strength, coordination, and breathing are powering him up an incline or expertly weaving him down a winding single-track. For both Amy and Ben, their outward grieving expressions match their inner experience of grief, and they each experience a healthy release of tension, each going with their own flow. And for a blended griever like Nathan—he'll have a good cry *and* a good jump into the sea. (Read more about Ben and Nathan in chapter 10.)

So rather than trying to get your partner to grieve your way, it is far more productive to understand and accept each other's tendencies and preferences, and support each other's healthy ways of grieving. Also remember, you both *want* each other to be true to your internal experiences of grief, because key to healing is that *the avenue of expression is in line with the internal experience*. So when your partner experiences grief as an emotional challenge and intense feelings, accept this emotional expression. Likewise, when your partner experiences grief as a mental challenge or physical restlessness, accept this assessing and doing. See the validity of each other's experience of grief and the value of each other's expression. And appreciate your common ground of staying connected to your bodies.

We are open and honest with our communication, and try not to judge or criticize. I know that my husband loved and still does love our babies. Our daughter. Our son. And was and is sad that they died. And that is all that matters.

—*Anne*

It can also help to remember that the traits that first attracted you to each other—such as being emotionally sensitive, expressive, active, athletic, purposeful, a problem solver, relationship-oriented—may be evident in the ways you each grieve. If you valued those traits before, rather than finding fault now, you can mindfully continue to value them.

Taking Turns

Often I wished we were grieving the same. I recognize that if this had been the case, our family would have fallen completely apart as I was barely hanging on at times.

—*Tanya*

My husband has been amazing. He held everything together when I was falling apart, and he did it while grieving himself.

—*Melanie*

There are advantages to grieving differently. If your grief finds expression through feeling, you'd be fortunate to have a partner who is busy doing, because he or she will keep the ship sailing. And if your grief finds expression through doing, you'd be fortunate to have a partner who is busy feeling, because you'll have more than enough activity to keep you engaged. Still, most couples find that they benefit from taking turns at the wheel, as this can give the activity-oriented partner some breathing room to attend specifically to grief and mourning, and can give the emotion-oriented partner a break from nonstop despair.

At first, I never saw him cry. I'd talk and talk about the baby and he'd hold me and I'd ask him, "Why don't you cry?" and he'd say, "Well, it's over with, he's dead, what's crying going to do?" And finally one night about three or four months after, he cried and then I was better. I could be strong for him. I just held him and let him cry. It was a big relief to see that, gee, he does care, he is human, because I couldn't figure out why I was so depressed and crying when he was handling it just fine, which he really wasn't.

—*Desi*

If you're both primarily emotion-oriented and grieving in sync, you can put out your sea anchor and stop sailing for a little while. You can benefit from feeling and talking together. But eventually, somebody has to go back on deck—the bills need to be paid, work has to be done; life does go on. Many couples take turns, switching off who's sailing the ship and who's below deck tending to their wounds. When one of you is deep in "feeling" mode, the other can become immersed "doing" mode.

Sometimes couples find themselves switching off daily, sometimes weekly or monthly. Other couples don't switch until a year or so after the baby dies.

In one sense it has drawn us closer, but we've been so focused on self-survival that we've grown apart. He denied his grief for quite a while and wanted me to move on. Then it hit him hard a year later.

—Holly

Taking turns can happen naturally when the most intensely emotion-oriented partner starts to have more "good days." That's what tips the balance and grants the other partner the opportunity to have some "bad days." If you've been carrying the lion's share of emotion and want to mindfully grant your partner the time and space to tend to his or her mourning, you can simply decide to be more functional. Whenever you can take a turn at handling more responsibilities, your partner has more room to go with his or her natural flow. By striking a balance, you can collaboratively share the load of keeping your ship upright and sailing.

When Zac died, I made a conscious decision to not go to bed when my husband got home. I needed to be there for him. It was not fair for him to carry all the load again. He was grieving just as much as I was. And I feel terrible thinking back that I was not able to be there for him when we lost Kate. I was just so heartbroken.

—Melanie

The Path to Mutual Acceptance

If you and your partner can understand where your differences come from, you may feel less threatened by them, and even able to talk about them. Acceptance is also easier when you remember there are no right or wrong ways to grieve.

It is also important to avoid judging each other or making assumptions, for instance: "Since he feels this way, he must not care much about the baby" or "She will never get over this if she keeps feeling that way." Be mindfully aware of your thoughts and question their validity. Be aware that overgeneralizations, assumptions, and pessimism are often unwarranted. And avoid emotional reasoning—when a thought makes you feel an emotion, this emotion does *not* prove that your thought is true.

Instead, focus on acceptance. By simply accepting your partner's grief and ways of mourning, you are acknowledging that he or she is entitled to his or her feelings, just as you are entitled to yours. Remember, accepting another's feelings doesn't negate your own. You may not share your partner's feelings; you may not always understand them. You may even feel angry or disappointed at your partner's reactions. But by accepting each other's silences and tears without judging or placing blame, you encourage nonthreatening communication. You also provide the kind of support and understanding so necessary to promote healing and enhance your relationship.

My relationship with my husband has become better. We are and have been grieving differently. I think that has been hard, but we realize we are different. I think it is important to bond in some way through your grieving. Our way has been through music.

—Anne

Many couples discover that counseling or attending a support group can help them understand and accept each other's journeys and open lines of communication. By listening to other parents, you can be reassured that both of you are reacting normally to your baby's death. By listening to each other share thoughts and feelings in a group or with the help of a counselor, you can get insights about yourself, your partner, or your relationship.

For instance, Carolyn remembers the time her husband casually mentioned to the group that he thought about their daughter Rachel while he painted the house. Although to an observer this may seem unremarkable, he had never told Carolyn about this, and she found it comforting and reassuring to discover that he *did* think about their baby. (See also "Understanding Your Blend of Grieving" in chapter 10.)

I felt like my husband should be grieving and showing his grief exactly the same way that I was. That if he were grieving, that it would somehow lighten my load. When I heard another parent in group say these same things, then I started realizing it was just absurd. I was expecting him to do the work for me and angry at him for not being an identical twin.

—Liza

Our counselor suggested writing a letter, telling our baby everything we wish we could have said to him and done with him. I remember reading Charlie's and reading something about him having guilt about not being able to protect him. And that was very surprising to me because I never realized Charlie ever felt guilt about the situation.

—Jolie

Couples are often dismayed to discover that they each grieve differently. But differences are not a sign that your relationship is doomed, that your partner doesn't care about what you're going through, or that your partner is suffering more or less than you are. Differences simply confirm that you are different individuals, and that everyone's path is unique. A mutual willingness to accept your differences can be an invaluable quality in your relationship.

REASSURANCE

Before your baby died, your relationship may have been relatively effortless. Unfortunately, grieving can create chasms that can easily widen, and you may fear that your partner will abandon you. Ironically, these concerns can make you withdraw even more as you try to protect yourself from the hurt. Or you may try to protect yourself with blame and anger, using these emotions to push away your partner. Unconsciously you may operate on the principle, "I'll quit before I'm fired" or "I'll leave you before you can leave me!"

> *We had mostly grieved at a similar rate and style for the first couple of months, and then it seemed as though I felt a lot more alone. Kent was handling it in his own way and I was handling it in my own way, and it was becoming a problem in the relationship.*
>
> —*Jessie*

> *I expected John to be the one person I could hang on to in the storm. But through the thick of it, we were both staggering under our own burdens and we couldn't possibly pick up another pound. As a result, we each staggered alone for a while.*
>
> —*Claudia*

Grieving alone, although necessary at times, can be difficult and sometimes frightening. Do try to build bridges, not walls. Reassuring each other of your love and devotion can guard against fears of losing each other. It is reasonable to ask your partner if she still cares about you or to ask if he blames you. In turn, you can reassure your partner that you still love her or that you don't blame him for your baby's death. You both need to be sensitive to each other's needs for this kind of reassurance.

> *It really helped that my husband kept telling me that I was important and kept telling me that we were there before the baby and we would still be there after the baby.*
>
> —*Bryn*

> *We kept hearing that everybody who said they'd lost a baby said they split up and we thought, "Oh, we can't do that! We've lost something already." So we got a lot closer.*
>
> —*Martina*

> *Overall my relationship with my husband has strengthened. Knowing that we are the only people on this earth who lost Dayani as a daughter and going through what we went through, while it sounds obvious, that helped us keep it together when times were the darkest.*

There were obviously missteps and misunderstandings, as we grieve differently. But my husband assured me that we will stay together no matter what.

—Destrida

RESISTING THE URGE TO "FIX IT"

After your baby dies, you will change and so will your partner. Many of these changes can give rise to conflict. Emerging differences can put a strain on your relationship. Experiencing these rough spots does not mean there is something wrong with you or your relationship. Growing pains are part of mourning. They are also part of any partnership. There is no way to make either one smooth or painless. Terri remembers when someone told her that life's upheavals were *supposed* to be hard. Just hearing that affirmation helped her let go of her struggle to eliminate the conflict. Only then could she ease into learning how to handle it. When you are in the middle of a lake, instead of trying to bail out the water, you're better off learning how to swim.

Also, it is natural to want to help ease your partner's emotional pain. But remember, just as you appreciate it when others *don't* try to fix or smooth over your feelings, your partner will appreciate it when you simply listen and accept. While you may believe you have some answers, remember that these answers may not work for someone else. Resist preaching your insights, perspectives, and attitudes to your partner. If you do share what has helped you, speak personally and without being directive: "I did this and it really helped me." Or, "For me, it helps to look at it this way." Avoid being prescriptive and presumptuous, as in, "You should try this because it helped me." Also never underestimate the soothing power of just listening and saying, "That sounds really hard. I'm sorry."

Keep in mind that your partner may not embrace your ideas or follow your path, even if it's working wonders for you. What is right for one person can be counterproductive for another. The best help you can offer is to be a nonjudgmental sounding board. This will encourage your partner to find his or her own special path of healing and growth.

SEX AND INTIMACY

For some couples, sex provides the intimacy and reassurance they need from each other. However, for many couples sex becomes a tension point. When a couple is drained emotionally and physically, when they feel depressed or angry, or when communication breaks down, sex may be the last thing they desire. For many parents, the link between sex and conception is painfully obvious. For others, the association between sex and affection makes them feel hurt by their partner's lack of interest or desire. Bereaved mothers must also cope with natural postpartum physical and emotional changes that can make them less responsive and less eager. Their lack of eagerness is compounded by the distress of grief and the stress of mourning. Many a mother also struggles with body image issues. The trauma of a difficult childbirth and the death of her baby can make her feel self-conscious and uncomfortable in her body, and less willing to be vulnerable and intimate. She may feel awkward and anxious at the prospect of sexual intimacy, and discourage her partner's interest.

Negotiating your sexual relationship requires more sharing, acceptance, and reassurance. Be sensitive to your own and each other's needs during this stressful time. To cultivate understanding and caring, explore and share what meaning sex has for each of you. For instance, it is common for the father to find lovemaking a source of support and relief, whereas the mother may be struggling with feelings of reluctance, fear, and a biologically based disinterest. By talking, listening, and holding each other, you can maintain feelings of affection and intimacy without the pressures of sexual activity. You may find comfort in spending quality time together, including dinner for two, going for long walks, and sharing other activities you enjoy. In time, as your grief becomes more manageable, your sexual relationship can become more comfortable. (See also "Sex and Contraception" in chapter 5.)

MANAGING CONFLICT

The key to managing conflict is getting in touch with what you truly want, and expressing it in ways that will be heard and respected. Here are three skills to master, based on the work of Julia Colwell, PhD, author of *The Relationship Ride*:

1.   Practice managing your painful feelings. As when grief is triggered, mindfully observe and identify where you sense constriction in your body. Name the feeling (silently or aloud), breathe deeply, and remain focused on your body as your physiology calms. This mindfulness can help you recover your equanimity, so you can reengage with your partner in ways that build your connection instead of undermining it.

2.   Identify what it is you really want. As calm returns, in simple terms, express what it is you truly want. Not "I want you to stop acting like an idiot," but something true about *you*—and basic, bottom line, such as, "I want to feel understood" or "I want to talk about our baby" or "I want to spend time doing things we *both* enjoy." This invites your partner to better know you and your needs, which builds connection. This also invites him/her to help you get what you want, which leads to more satisfaction. When this endeavor is mutual, you can invite each other to express your hearts' desires and work out ways for both of you to get what you want. The result is a more rewarding partnership.

3.   Avoid stating what's arguable. Making arguable statements only leads to arguments. Examples of what's arguable: "You always . . ." or "I never . . ." or "You're so . . ." or "You're just trying to . . ." or "My way is better"

or "You did this" or "I said that." Criticisms, judgments, assessments, even observations and memories of what just happened—all arguable. These statements will not get you what you want—unless you actually *want* an argument. Instead, only say what's unarguable. Unarguable consists of (a) sensations in your body, which indicate your feelings, and (b) what it is you really want. Your body doesn't lie, and what you want is simply *what you want.* (See skills #1 and #2.)

These three skills are simple, yet powerfully effective for building connection and satisfaction in a relationship. If you and your partner can commit to working together on these, you can't lose. But acquiring them is easier said than done. Old habits are hard to break, and new habits require lots of mindfulness and practice, with mistakes inevitable along the way. Patience is key. So is attention to detail. And practice slowing down and taking breaks when you are triggered into reactive mode, because *nothing good comes out of your mouth when your stressed-out core brain is in charge.* (See also "Survival Mode" in chapter 3.) Celebrate small improvements in communication. Rest on the assurance that you *both* can get what you truly want. Enjoy fewer arguments and more positive moments.

CAN OUR RELATIONSHIP SURVIVE?

Many couples experience ups and downs after their baby dies, and in spite of the downs, their relationship survives.

> *The first month or so after Stephanie died, Cal was very supportive and did as much as he could to help me physically as well as emotionally. But there was some point after a month or so—maybe he had deferred some of his grieving because he was so busy taking care of me—where he kind of lost his patience and there was a lot of tension between the two of us. We got some counseling at that point. And it went through my head that events like this either really cement a marriage or blow it out of the water entirely: "Which one are we going to do?" So then I'd get scared that my marriage was also falling apart, but then I began to understand that Cal was dealing with his own grieving and his own stress. He'd been so super-attentive to me that he finally was worn out and couldn't do it anymore.*
>
> *—Sophie*

> *We never really blamed each other for what happened, but there was just stress. There was so much unhappiness for having lost the baby that I think we took it out on each other. Then he, trying to handle grief his way, would go elsewhere sometimes, and that was very, very difficult. I became very dependent on him and then when he wasn't there, it hurt me more and I became very angry with him. I remember that spring I asked him to move out of the house, and then we got back together and went to counseling.*
>
> *—Bess*

For some couples the stress may break apart an already floundering relationship or create problems that seem too big to overcome. Poor communication habits that existed before the pregnancy may flare up and ignite smoldering long-standing issues such as sex, money, and relatives. Mira recalls, "After Matthew died, we simply stopped talking and we had nothing in common anymore. We lost each other." Anya remembers how she and her husband drifted apart: "My husband never talked about her, ever. He never showed his feelings, never held her, did not want pictures, never cried."

> As soon as we got home he said the cruelest words a person could say: "If you hadn't gone skiing, we'd have a healthy child." I felt so guilty. I thought I'd murdered my own baby because I'd gone skiing. That was the beginning of the end of our marriage.
>
> —Lena

It's common for couples to retreat into their respective corners for a time, where they can learn more about themselves and what they need. Many couples come back together with new skills, better understanding, and more maturity. Just know that reuniting can take patience, courage, persistence, mindfulness, and commitment. Sometimes it's a hard road back to each other. But if you are both determined that your relationship will survive this tragedy, it probably will.

Many couples benefit from counseling. A therapist can help you understand why you are withdrawing or what triggers quarreling, and can coach you on game-changing skills. Improving your relationship can be a challenge, but the payoffs of strengthened communication, warmer connection, and deeper commitment can make the struggle worthwhile. Faith advises marriage counseling for anyone having trouble: "It saved my marriage. And after my baby died, the last thing I needed was a divorce, to lose my husband too!" (See also "Counseling" in chapter 13.)

> I was so unwell from the grief and depression. My husband felt as if he had to take care of me, so instead of being my partner, he treated me as a client. In the end we had to go to relationship counseling and work though what issues we had from our grief. I am very lucky that we have worked through it and are still together.
>
> —Lorna

> We have certainly been challenged and we have grieved differently, especially as time goes on. My grief is still very raw [whereas] Ben seems to have taken it to a "numb" place. Continuing to see our counselor has been a huge help; she knows us and has walked the entire journey with us.
>
> —Emmerson

> Thanks to therapy for both of us, we are strong again and moving through life together, not separately, as we were for a while after Emma died.
>
> —Abby

For many couples, their baby's death is a clear wake-up call and catalyst for doing the inner work and relationship work necessary for them to weather the storm of grief and mourning. Their transformation is part of their baby's legacy.

About two months after Miriam died, Lavender and I both started doing intense therapy work. Things were at rock bottom already and we really needed help if the relationship was to last. We both identified areas in which we needed to do our own work as well as how to survive as a couple. Now a year and a half later, Lavender and I have been doing really well overall, separately and as a couple. It totally turned our world around.

—Tanya

This was a huge challenge for us. After the prenatal diagnosis, when we decided to terminate the pregnancy because our marriage didn't feel strong enough to support our daughter, we decided to commit fully to making our marriage stronger and better. We didn't know if our marriage would survive, but we did it and we are still together. We had a lot to learn to get to this point but we came out stronger.

—Julie

Many couples are reassured by the fact that they came through this experience feeling closer than ever. You may have opened up new lines of communication or discovered aspects of each other that enhance your intimacy or dedication. You may even realize a sense of accomplishment—if your relationship can survive this, it can survive anything.

We have shared twice the most horrific thing any parent should have to experience. He was there for me when I was so heartbroken I couldn't function. I could barely breathe. I was so consumed by grief. We have seen each other at the very worst points in our lives and still wanted each other. I cannot put into words how grateful I am to have him and how much I love him.

—Melanie

It was wonderful for our relationship. It's an awful thing to say, but it's really true. It brought us so much closer together and we've managed to keep close. It was a real binding kind of thing, finding strengths we didn't know each other had.

—Sara

PARENTS WITHOUT PARTNERS

If you are a widow or widower in addition to being a bereaved parent, your sorrow may feel too deep to comprehend. You may feel confused, not knowing who your tears are for, or you may feel disloyal when you cry more for one loss than the other. You may long for the understanding hugs of your baby's other parent as you grieve your baby's death; you may long for that baby to be safe in your arms, so you could hold on to a piece of your partner's living legacy. As if dealing with one or the other death isn't unbearable enough, for both to die can seem especially intolerable and cruelly unjust. Be sure that you get support for both of your losses by talking about each one, reading books specifically for each, or attending support groups for each.

If you didn't have an established relationship, you may long for the commiseration of your baby's other parent. You may feel isolated and lonely as you grieve. You may also feel like the accommodations you made in preparation for being a single parent were all for naught. You may feel you are being punished for your decisions or being denied the chance to prove that you could succeed.

If your relationship ended by separation or divorce, the pain you feel as a bereaved parent can bring up grief you may have experienced during the breakdown of your partnership. After your baby dies, you may feel a greater bond to the other parent. You may consider reconciliation as he or she is a tangible connection to the baby you miss. You may even have fantasies of achieving another pregnancy with this person in an effort to recapture what you've lost. Indeed, the desire for another child can make your single status a huge source of frustration.

To add to your isolation and frustration, others may fail to offer you the sympathy they might offer an intact couple whose baby has died. Attitudes such as "being a single parent is tough to manage" and "children are better off with more than one parent" can make people see your baby's death as "a blessing in disguise." Or you may project those attitudes onto others when they act uncomfortable around you.

If you are single, don't fall into the trap of idealizing grieving within a partnership. Grieving is something that you must do largely on your own, whether you are in an intimate relationship or not. Isolation and loneliness are common feelings for any bereaved parent. Remember that even in a normally close and sharing marriage, partners will grieve as individuals, often incongruently and at a distance.

Do seek out support from others. Support groups can help you feel less isolated. Bereaved parent support organizations have access to the vast network of bereaved parents and can put you in touch with others who are in similar circumstances. Having friends or a therapist to talk to can be key to your healing.

POINTS TO REMEMBER

- As a couple, you may notice that your baby's death affects your relationship—sometimes for better, sometimes for worse.
- You may hope to grieve in sync and feel validated by traveling the same path. At first, this may be the case, but most parents settle into very different grieving styles.
- Tolerate, accept, and be unthreatened by your differences. They are normal and necessary.
- It is normal to drift apart at times as you grieve. As you each retreat to your corners, support each other's efforts to focus on your own healing so you can reunite stronger than ever.
- Even though you can expect to grieve differently and drift apart at times, you can still have a harmonious relationship.
- It is wise to seek additional support from others so that you don't deplete each other further.
- Key ingredients to help your relationship survive include nourishing a caring connection, sharing a mutual concern that you each get what you need, accepting your different grieving patterns, and reassuring your partner that you are committed to the relationship.
- Understanding and having empathy for each other's grieving style can help you avoid misinterpreting each other's behaviors and intentions.
- Partners often have very different needs for sex and intimacy. Keep the lines of communication open, and find ways to feel connected that are comforting to both of you. In time, as your grief becomes more manageable, your sexual relationship can become more comfortable and easier to navigate.
- Listening and resisting the urge to "fix it" will build intimacy and strengthen your relationship.
- Constructive ways to resolve conflicts involve awareness of your own physical and emotional reactions, identifying and voicing what you want, and saying only what's unarguable—as in, what you feel and what you want.
- If you are both determined that your relationship will survive, it probably will. If you think couples counseling might help, try it.
- If you are without a partner, seek out support from others. Support groups and bereaved parent organizations can put you in touch with people who are in similar circumstances.

12

YOUR FAMILY

YOUR BABY'S GRANDPARENTS

The hardest thing was making the phone call to my family, to tell my mum my son was dead.

—*Lorna*

Not only do I grieve the death of my grandson, I grieve for my daughter. I don't want her to have any pain because she's my baby, and I can't make it better.

—*Pearl*

My mother, who was a preschool teacher for many, many years, read Oren a story that she had found in the hospital waiting room. That was a real tearjerker. One line in the book read, "Hola means hello. Adios means goodbye." It was very fitting.

—*Tanya*

Many grandparents endure a double sorrow. They grieve for the grandchild who will never grow up and they grieve for you, their child, who suffers the death of a baby. They may also feel as though they've lost you, so immersed are you in sorrow. Your parents may feel very helpless or inadequate because they cannot lessen your suffering. They may feel the same anger that you experience and may want to blame someone for their grandchild's death. If they have ever lost children of their own, they may relive that pain now. In any case, you may feel as though you have to protect them from your despair.

My mother cares so much, I feel like I can't give her a whole lot of my problem. . . . She'll just feel so awful herself. It's not that I couldn't say anything to her, but I just thought, "Why?" It won't help me, it won't help her, and I'll feel like I have to take care of her.

—*Meryl*

It's easier to talk to somebody who's unrelated because relatives have so much emotion themselves. I felt I had to protect them, you know; my mom lost a grandchild. We didn't talk about it that much. They were there, but no one really talked because we didn't know what to say to each other.

—*Erin*

At a time when you want to depend on your parents for emotional support, they may not be able to give it for one reason or another. They may withdraw, frightened by the way your baby's death forces them to face their own mortality. Some simply do not understand the grieving process you must go through. If they have trouble dealing with emotions, they may try to smooth over your feelings of despair. Others may have lost babies of their own, but if they were not encouraged or allowed to grieve, acknowledging your grief would require them to examine their own. For many, that's too painful. Instead, they may try to belittle your baby's importance or try to talk you out of your feelings in order to protect themselves from their own sadness, and you from yours.

I think the death of our unborn baby girl may have awakened suppressed emotions in the people surrounding us, namely our close family members. There was an expectation that we too would suppress our emotions, but that didn't happen and then the disconnect truly began.
—Emmerson

My mother-in-law was furious that we sent out announcements of our baby's death. She said, "It wasn't even a baby you lost." It turns out she had a miscarriage but never grieved and was told, "Just have another baby and forget it."
—Clara

The relationship I had with my parents was rocky before I found out I was pregnant. It has gotten worse. I stopped making the effort as it was too forced and only one-sided. I have people in my life who were like parents to me and I have a lot of support from them.
—Sarah

Even more difficult, some grandparents may not readily recognize your baby as a grandchild, particularly if there are other grandchildren. If your baby died during pregnancy or early infancy, they may not have had a chance to develop a grandmotherly or grandfatherly bond. While they may feel sorry *for* you, you may wish they could feel sorry *with* you. You may be very hurt when they make comments that appear to discount your baby's life, or when they don't say anything.

My family has been great about it, but my husband was hurt as some of his family did not acknowledge Ronin's death or realize the impact that his death had on us.
-—Lorna

My mother came in the hospital room and was trying to be real cheerful and happy and perk me up and make me feel better. She didn't really let down too much around me. She did with my sister. With me she was trying to be the "good mommy" and that kind of stuff. I felt like she didn't have to do that. I cried when anybody came into my room, and they did too, and she didn't need to be so . . . The crying made me feel better!
—Hannah

The Christmas after my first baby miscarried, I was fifteen weeks into another pregnancy, but I was consumed with thoughts of the baby who should have been a couple months old, cradled in my arms that holiday season. My parents were focused on the new baby and gave us a couple of baby gifts, but I had my husband open them because I couldn't bear it. . . . To commemorate this baby, I hung a special ornament on their tree, without saying anything. I didn't want to "spoil" the celebration, even though I really felt like screaming.

—Winnie

When your parents aren't supportive and you want to say something, avoid telling them what they are doing wrong—criticism is rarely productive. Instead, make suggestions for what they can do to help. Emphasize that you find it most comforting when people listen and let you cry without judging, advising, or fixing. Remind them that they can't, nor should they try, to ease your pain. Point out that your grief will last a long time and that you'd appreciate their sensitivity. You can do your part by forgiving any misguided efforts when you know they mean well. (See also "Educating Well-Meaning People about What You Need" in chapter 13.)

Still, you may be afraid to tell them what you need for fear they won't respond, and then you'll be even more disappointed. However, you have a right to at least try. If it is difficult to talk to them, you could write a letter, buy them a "grieving grandparents" booklet, or send a photocopy of a chapter or article on supporting bereaved parents.

Sometimes grandparents become more supportive if they are included in acknowledging the baby's life. Show them your mementos and any pictures you have. Invite them to the funeral or send a formal announcement. Ask them to memorialize your baby in their own way, perhaps by making a donation, planting a tree, lighting a candle, or including the baby in their prayers. If you've made requests and invited them in and they still cannot be supportive, focus on friends or other family members who can be there for you.

Many grandparents are able to be supportive without much prompting. Your parents may be educated about grief or may naturally react sensitively and compassionately to your needs. Or they may be responsive to your suggestions.

My mother and father came to the hospital to meet Bryce. My mother held him, talked to him, and she even requested that the nurse take a picture of her holding him. It very much surprises me that she seemed to instinctually know to do these things. I am so impressed by her inner wisdom.

—Lori

My parents were uncertain if they wanted to see her. My dad in fact had told me that he did not. I respected his decision. I guess he changed his mind, because they all came in the room and each one of them held our baby girl, with tears streaming down their faces too.

—Helen

My family was amazing and still is to this day. My parents did everything they could and more, and everyone knows how important it is for all of us to talk about Emma.

—Abby

OTHER RELATIVES

You may feel close enough to some of your siblings, cousins, or even aunts or uncles to consider them friends. If you normally rely on these family members for companionship or support, you may be able to count on them being there for you.

While some relatives will surprise you with their sensitivity, others may disappoint you with their callousness or evasiveness. Differences in emotional outlook or religious and philosophical viewpoints can drive a wedge into a relationship. After Avery interrupted her pregnancy, her sister was openly critical and their relationship sadly disintegrated. Winnie and her cousin suffered miscarriages within a month of each other but the circumstances were so different that there was no common ground. Winnie says, "We've always felt close, but this was not something we could share. Her pregnancy was her fourth and unplanned. Already having three small children, she felt relieved and relied on her strong religious faith, so she could say, 'Oh, well, it's for the best.' This was my first baby and I was in utter despair."

Also, in many families, babies are born concurrently and you may be desperately envious that your sister has her arms full and yours are so empty. If you find it difficult to be around or talk about other babies in the family, do let those parents know how sad, envious, or resentful you feel. Chances are, they want to know how to handle this difficult subject when you are around. If you bring it up, they'll probably be eager to hear what you have to say. (See also "Friends" in chapter 13.)

YOUR OTHER CHILDREN

Having Lisa made me feel very much better. If I had had a miscarriage before having her, I probably would have thought, "I'll never have a baby." But I had one at home to come home to. I was so thankful to have her. I felt empty inside, but I didn't feel like I was empty-handed.

—Jane

There were many times when my older son was my only motivation to get up in the morning and make the choice to keep going. I wanted to continue to be a great mom for him because I knew he deserved the best no matter what and especially because of what we were all going through together.

—Embry

When I was spending time with [stepson] Ayden, I loved the moments I had with him when he would play with my hair or lay his head down on my chest. I crave the emotions that those tiny gestures give me. They truly make my heart feel full. It is so odd to think of how pathetic and vulnerable those emotions make me feel—like I am right on the verge of begging a three-year-old, "Please cuddle with me! Please let me hold you until you fall asleep!"

—Jolie

Having other children at home can be such a blessing, and yet, this also brings concerns. You may wonder what to tell them about the death of their baby sibling. You may worry about how they will react. Their responses will depend on several factors, including
- their level of understanding about death,
- their relationship with the baby,
- their reaction to the parents' grief, and
- the support and reassurance they receive.

CHILDREN'S UNDERSTANDING OF DEATH

I thought it was a good idea for the girls to see Zac but my husband wasn't so keen on the idea. I talked about it with my midwife and she felt that it would be a good idea, as children take everything at face value.

—Melanie

Lavender's sister, mother, and Derek were all able to hold Oren. I think those few moments when Oren was in Derek's arms changed his entire life. They took away some of the fear around death and they gave Derek a chance to realize that his brother had lived and now was gone. I believe that his grieving process would have been entirely different if he had not met his brother.

—Tanya

We both agreed that we wanted the boys to meet their sister. We explained that our baby was not going to look like they might think a baby would. That she would be turning red. And would be really small. They both said, yes. Matthew had a hard time with it. Ryan was making kissing noises and motions, and wanted to kiss our baby. But I did not want them to grow up not having met or seen her. My husband and I, we are both glad that we did show them her body.

—Anne

How well children understand death depends on their level of intellectual development. Until adolescence, many children struggle with abstract concepts like death. Dead is not something they can be for a little while to see what it's like. Death is not something they can do to see how it works. As a result, children have difficulty understanding death the way adults do—that death is when the body is no longer alive, that it is irreversible, and, depending on beliefs, the person either ceases to exist, the spirit goes to heaven or to another plane of existence, or the person goes on to be reincarnated as another living being. (See also "As Your Children Grow" at the end of this chapter.)

Most children acquire an inaccurate understanding of death, but this is not necessarily a problem. They may simply have a unique way of looking at it, a way that causes them no concern. Other children may have some misconceptions about death that frighten them. Rather than focusing on how accurately your children understand death, try to address any concerns or fears they may have. (See also "Providing Support and Reassurance" later in this chapter.)

Explaining Death to Children

Tom talks about Alex freely and has mentioned him to close friends and teachers. I have told Tom to tell whomever he wants to. My friend with the stillbirth has a son in Tom's class. They are friends and often talk about the babies they never met.

—Victoria

Many parents are uncertain about how to discuss death with their children. They may want to protect their children's innocence or spare them from sadness or grim realities. They may be tempted to tell their children stories such as "Grandma went on a long trip" or "Spot went to sleep and won't be waking up again" or "God needed another angel." Unfortunately, this may only add elements of fear, rejection, or anger to the sense of loss. A child may wonder, "Why did Grandma leave me without saying goodbye and why can't I visit her? Doesn't she want to see me?" Or, "If I go to sleep, will I be able to wake up?" A child may be fearful or angry toward a God who takes loved ones away forever. In these attempts to spare children the pain of grief, parents may unwittingly intensify disturbed feelings.

Instead, children can cope better when they are informed. Informing your children, however, can be difficult to carry out if death has been a taboo subject in your family. Even if death was always handled openly and appropriately in your family, talking to your children can still be hard. You may worry about adding to their suffering. There may be tears. But children are typically far more upset by being left out of important family events and conversations than being included, even during the saddest times. And the lessons learned can be invaluable.

One of the hardest things was telling the girls about what happened. Greta especially was so looking forward to the baby coming. She just cried and cried and cried. We said that the baby had decided not to come and had gone to the sky to be a star. So we have been out on the deck to light some sparklers and wave to Kate the baby star.

—Melanie

I think for both of our other children, our openness makes them see that death is a part of life. Hopefully it happens when a person is very old, but for our family it wasn't like that. We don't dwell on it, but they know that things can happen so we need to appreciate each day and love each other.

—Shellie

I was mortified the first time I heard my girls playing pretending to be pregnant and asking if the baby in their bellies was alive or dead. But this has been their reality. My oldest daughter was already quite a sensitive child and losing Kate and Zac heightened her sensitivities.

—Melanie

Here are some tips for talking to your children about your baby's death—and death in general:

- Find children's books and stories about death, dying, and grief. The ones that are gentle, simple, reassuring, and respectful can make death seem less mysterious, frightening, or gloomy. Reading them yourself can help you find the words to talk to your children. Reading stories together can open up discussion, making it easier to broach the topic and talk together.
- Observe your children's play. Children often weave themes of death, grief, and babies dying into their play. This is how they explore concepts and feelings, and you need not intervene unless you see it as an opening to share ideas and feelings.
- Don't try to find the perfect words. There is no perfect way to explain death to children.
- Speak honestly, informatively, and age-appropriately. Accurate information they can understand empowers your children to master their ideas and feelings.
- Answer questions directly and simply. Instead of offering complicated, elaborate explanations, let the children ask more questions so you can see where their line of curiosity is going and address specifically what they want to know.
- Accept and honor their curiosity. If your children know they can ask questions and get honest answers from you, they will learn not only about death, but also that they can confide in you. This in turn will encourage them to ask more questions about whatever they find worrisome or confusing.
- Clear up confusion. When your children ask questions or make confusing or false statements about death, take the cue and answer, clarify, and reassure them.
- Follow up with ongoing discussions. If the time or place isn't right, tell them you'd like to discuss this at a better time and then make sure you bring it up again within a day or two. This shows it's okay to talk about.

After the twins were born, my daughter (age four) saw Bradley and kept asking, "Now, when are you going to have the other baby, Mom?" The first thing that came to mind was, we'll just tell her the doctors made a mistake but then we thought, "No, because we don't want her to have a mistrust of doctors." So we just told her that when Jeffrey was born he was too small and too sick and he went up to heaven. She seemed to handle it okay, "Oh, all right." Even now (one year later) she'll say, "Isn't it sad that Jeffrey has to be up in heaven and can't be with us?"

—*Shannon*

An open attitude speaks volumes. If you are not afraid to talk about death, they will not be afraid to hear about it. You will not overwhelm your children if you take into account their need for information *and* reassurance.

Our kids were amazing with me . . . Such sweet moments with them, and I am so thankful that we embraced the pain and didn't try to hide from them or pull away from them. That pain made our family stronger and we always talk about how brave our family is because we can do hard things!

—*Laura*

Attending the Funeral and Other Rituals of Mourning

I am grateful that my mom brought my son Derek to the hospital to see and hold Oren; Derek was reluctant, but I think he was glad in the end.

—*Lavender*

Matthew and Ryan also saw their baby brother. I know it was probably a lot to take in at such a young age. But again, I did not want them to regret not having seen or met him. I felt like there could be more damage not having met our babies than seeing them.

—*Anne*

In the past, many parents felt that siblings should be spared from seeing the baby or attending the baby's funeral or graveside services. However, children who are not allowed to participate in these rituals may feel excluded from the family at a time when they need to be surrounded by loved ones. Being a part of the family, seeing how others grieve, and hearing others talk lovingly about the baby are comforting and help them sort out their feelings about the death. They may also gain understanding about where and how the dead are buried or ashes are spread, instead of being left to think about scenes from cartoons or horror films about skeletons rising from dusty, crumbling graveyards. If you can explain to them what the baby's funeral or service will be like, you may be able to encourage them to attend. You may be able to encourage them to go to some family gatherings and to forgo others. It is generally better to err on the side of allowing children to be a part of rituals and family gatherings, rather than excluding them. It's never too late to include them in ongoing rituals, like visiting the grave or memorializing your baby during special holidays and anniversary dates. Whether your older children got to meet their baby sibling or not, you can also share photographs, keepsakes, and memories to make your baby's life seem more real, answer their questions, or satisfy curiosity.

Understanding Your Children's Sense of Loss

If your children knew there was a baby but the baby never came home, they may wonder where the baby went. But children vary widely as to how much they look forward to a new baby. If they looked forward to helping or playing with the baby, they may feel sad or disappointed. Older children will be able to grasp many more layers of loss, and may grieve deeply.

> *Derek was devastated. He had been excited about the baby. He had practiced swaddling dolls and watched videos on baby care.*
> —*Tanya*

If your baby lived for several months and your children had time to develop a bond with the baby, they'll likely grieve. Even so, your children do not share the same anticipation or fantasies as you and will not grieve as intensely. In fact, your children may have harbored some resentment or jealousy as they watched you fuss over the baby or the nursery. Your children's apparent lack of concern for the baby after a few days may strike you as callous. But if allowed and encouraged, your children will grieve according to the unique sense of loss they feel.

> *Derek often thought about Oren. He made two art projects at school in Oren's memory. He wrote a few pieces for school about losing his brother. . . . We were super proud of his courage to talk about his brother's death.*
> —*Tanya*

Providing Support and Reassurance

Whether your children are older or very young, they will respond to the family disequilibrium caused by the baby's death. The disruption of familiar routines and the changes in you—from playful, responsive, and easygoing to sad, withdrawn, and irritable—can be very distressing to them. Even if you try to hide your feelings, children are perceptive and may become more confused and anxious by your reticence.

> *Our older daughter Claire was only two and a half years at the time. . . . I think it was hard for her to understand why Mom and Dad were so sad. It was hard for her to understand why the baby couldn't come home.*
> —*Shellie*

It is normal for children to struggle with this family tragedy. Struggles are often revealed through changes in their behavior. If your children are upset you may notice signs such as a regression in abilities, stronger resistance to change, or increased emotional sensitivity, irritability, fearfulness, perfectionism, restlessness, or withdrawal.

Whenever your children are acting out, there is an underlying problem that needs to be addressed. Common underlying concerns around death and grief include concerns about how the baby died, fears of sleep, concerns about dead bodies, and fears of separation or abandonment.

Concerns about How the Baby Died

Your children may ask many questions about the cause of death. While children are naturally curious, their questions usually arise from a need for reassurance or to master a confusing or scary topic. Even as adults, we want to know the cause of death when we see an obituary for someone who died relatively young. By knowing the cause we can vow to avoid it or be relieved that we don't run that particular risk. Similarly, your children will benefit from honest answers. Answers can reassure them that they are not in danger of dying too.

If your baby died from an infection or other illness, your children may equate sickness with impending death. You may notice repetitive questions about illness, disease, germs, health, or why the baby died. They may express concern about getting sick, being around sick people, or other loved ones (including you) falling ill.

Give your children as much information as they need, including details about the baby's illness or birth defects. Even if you don't know the cause of death, you can still answer that somehow the baby didn't grow right, or was born too early, or that the body didn't work properly. Avoid simplistic explanations such as, "The baby had a bad tummy ache," or your children may fear for their lives the next time their stomach hurts. Emphasize to your children that it's obvious they are growing just right, were born right on time, and that their bodies are working beautifully. Emphasize the difference between weak, little babies and big, strong, healthy kids like them and grown-ups like you.

> *Luke asked tons of questions about what made his brother die. I think he was worried that the same fate might befall him. So I assured him that babies aren't as strong as older kids, so he decided that for a baby to survive the first year, to make it "past zero" to one, was very difficult, but that since he was four, he was out of danger. He would reassure himself by saying, "It's hard to make it past zero."*
> —Cathryn

If you made life-and-death decisions for your baby, even though your role as decision maker may be paramount to you, be careful to emphasize that the baby died because of severe illness or deformity and offer those details. If they ask why the doctors couldn't fix it, you may explain that doctors cannot fix everything. You may even broach the fact that letting go was the only way to protect the baby from suffering. You can gauge how much to reveal by the sophistication or simplicity of their questions. Older children might want to know about the entire matter of difficult decisions, and appreciate the ethical or religious dilemmas.

If your baby died in an accident of any kind, you may want to postpone revealing what happened until your children are old enough to handle the information without feeling scared or vulnerable themselves. If you decide to conceal certain details, you must make sure that others respect your wishes, and that your adult conversations are in private. You can still explain in broad terms why the baby died. Cathryn, whose baby Kevin died in a particularly frightening situation, talked generally to son Luke about why death occurs. She told him that Kevin died because his body stopped working—no more beating heart, breathing lungs, or thinking brain.

Fears of Sleep

Particularly if your children hear people equating death with sleep, or if they have a chance to see the baby after death, they may conclude that death is similar to sleep. There are several signs that your children may be confusing death and sleep.

- They are restless at nap time or bedtime.
- They wake up in the night and can't get back to sleep.
- They ask you why the baby won't wake up.

To reassure your children, you can explain that death and sleep are totally different, that sleep is necessary for a healthy body, and that your body stays alive when you sleep, and then you wake up. In death, the heart and breathing stop, and then the body dies and can't become alive again. Your children may have difficulty understanding it all, but the message that sleep and death are completely different should sink in.

Concerns about Dead Bodies

If children resist seeing the baby or attending the funeral or graveside service, or if they seem preoccupied with dead bodies, burial, cremation, or afterlife, it is important to help them sort out their fears. For example, are they concerned about the baby suffering? Are they afraid the body may burst out of the casket? Do they worry about skeletons and ghosts? Your children may acquire scary ideas about death from movies, television, comic books, or friends; children are prone to misinterpreting what they see and hear, to confusing fantasy with reality.

You can reassure your children by answering questions honestly, giving whatever details they require. Let their questions be your guide and keep in mind children's need for reassurance that death is a natural end of life and a quiet, peaceful existence. If you decided on burial, you can talk about the body returning to the earth; if you chose cremation, you can talk about the body returning to the air. Some children are satisfied with the idea that the physical body stays in the earth or turns to ashes while the spirit goes to a peaceful place. Your own personal beliefs can provide a comforting framework for your children, even if the abstract idea of "spirit" is hard to grasp. For younger children struggling with the concept of death, emphasize that a dead body cannot move or feel anything, including loneliness or pain. Talking to your children about these stark realities may be difficult and sorrowful, but you may also benefit from these reassuring reminders that your baby is not suffering.

> *I remember that Derek had been all into zombies when Oren died, and one night he came to ask us if we were sure that Oren had been dead when we buried him. We assured him that he was and that we would never ever have buried him if he had been alive. We also told him that he could not come back as a zombie and that this was a good thing.*
> —*Tanya*

Fears of Separation or Abandonment

When a new baby arrives, most children have trouble dealing with this separation from mother and all the attention given to the baby. When a baby dies, siblings have to deal with the physical separation *and* a change in both of their parents. Plus, children may wonder, "If the baby can go away, then what's to prevent Mommy and Daddy from going away?"

During this difficult time, your children need reassurance that you can still take care of them, that you still love them, and that eventually you will feel better. You are your children's main source of emotional support, and they need you to be there.

When children have fears of separation or abandonment, they tend to act out in ways meant to elicit your prompt attention, such as regressing into infantile behaviors or becoming more annoying, fearful, clingy, aggressive, or sullen and withdrawn. They aren't trying to manipulate you. They are trying to regain the safe feelings of earlier times, when you were more available and attentive. Be alert to any of these signals, and even when your children are irritable or annoying, a hug or a gentle reminder that you love them may be soothing and ward off more troubles. With your comfort and empathy, they will regain confidence and security sooner than if you ignore these bids for attention or insist that they "act their age" and be as independent or well-behaved as they were before the baby died. Even if your children seem self-reliant, they may still need extra reassurance that you are available.

*Derek wants to fix me. He wants me to be who I used to be. I get it.
Sometimes I want that too. We did have a really good conversation
last year. I explained that my relationship to Oren was different than
his and that I would never be "over" my grief. I told him that it comes
from my deep love for Oren and that if he (Derek) were to die I would
feel similar. I also told him that even though I was different now, I still
loved him. Things have gotten better as time has gone by.*
—Tanya

Unfortunately, when you are in the depths of grief, it can be very difficult
to be a responsive parent. It is hard enough to deal with your own grief, let
alone the day-to-day needs of your children. Ultimately, by taking care of
your own emotional needs, you will be able to reinvest in nurturing your
children. So, when parenting becomes overwhelming or draining, rely on
your partner—or other adults your children enjoy—to take up the slack.
Or find someone to help you with the mundane chores so you can be more
available to your children and able to spend relaxing, enjoyable time with
them. (For suggestions, see "Calming Activities" in chapter 4.)

*Perhaps the best gift I gave to my other children and myself after
Teddy's death was to grieve as wholeheartedly as I was able and to
seek as much support and help with this process as was available. It
was very hard to do, yet very necessary.*
—Lisa

*After William died, I found it very difficult to be a nurturing mother
to my girls. I was grieving so much that I had nothing left for them. I
felt guilty about that, like I wasn't a good mother, but I pretty much
left their care to my husband for the first couple months. And then,
eventually, as I felt better, I was able to be an attentive mother again.*
—Eva

TELLING TEACHERS AND CAREGIVERS

Be sure to alert your children's teachers and other caregivers that a baby
sibling has died. This knowledge can help them to be more understanding,
patient, and sensitive to your children's needs for extra attention, guidance,
and reassurance. You might even ask about or share written materials on
talking about death, children's grief, behavior changes, and how to help
children through this tough time. If you are tempted to make suggestions,
remember, you'll be more likely to make an alliance if you are sympathetic and offer written information in the spirit of helping them gather
insights—"I know my child has been a handful lately with all that's going
on. I hope this helps make your job easier." Also let them know how much
your family appreciates their support.

*My son was rather upset that his baby sister had died. I told him
he was allowed to talk about his sister whenever he wanted to. I*

informed his teachers at school as well as his youth pastor and scout leader that I had told him he could talk about Lilly Marie whenever he wanted to, and gave them any information they needed to be able to talk back. His dean at school called him into his office to talk about her and told him he was welcome to talk anytime he needed.

—*Sarah*

SUPPORTING YOUR CHILDREN'S EXPRESSION OF GRIEF

I think it has been good to teach them it is okay to cry. That if they are upset they don't have to hide it. My girls would often find me in tears and I would say I am really sad that baby Zac or Kate has died and I really miss them. Often they would give me a cuddle and tell me they miss them too. So it gave them many opportunities to talk about Zac and Kate and how they were feeling.

—*Melanie*

Like you, children benefit from letting grief flow. Whether they are seeking emotion-oriented or action-oriented expression, you can guide them toward talking and sharing or engaging in physical and creative activities. By encouraging a range of expression, you are helping your children cope, and this will reduce their need to act out in destructive ways. (See also "Grieving According to Your Nature" in chapter 2.)

There are many ways to encourage expression. You can try sharing some of your thoughts and feelings to initiate a dialogue. Some children may be able to talk about things; resist the temptation to push those who are reluctant. It is also important to provide opportunities for drawing pictures, painting, sculpting clay, writing stories, dictating letters, or playing out emotions in dramatic scenes with toys. Encourage physical activities to let off steam. Read children's books about death and grief—this can help your children clarify ideas, understand emotions, and feel less isolated or abnormal.

When my son sees me cry and asks why, if it happens to be because I miss Dayani, I tell him so. It lets him know that it's okay to miss her and talk about her.

—*Destrida*

If your children cry, let them sob as much as they want. Remember, you needn't fix it. Resist saying things like, "There, there. Everything's okay. Don't cry." While this is considered comforting, children hear it literally and get the message to buck up and swallow their sentiments. Try something affirming like, "You have lots of tears today, don't you?" If you allow tears, your children will know that you also allow feelings. If they worry that they don't feel like crying, reassure them that this reaction is fine too. People can be sad without tears.

Expressing Anger

Young children tend to see their parents as all-powerful. If you promise a baby, you should be able to bring one home. Your children may reason that you did something wrong or somehow sabotaged this promise.

To direct their anger away from you, explain that the baby's death was a cruel twist of nature, that no one is to blame, and maybe that you are angry too. You can help your children express their anger and disappointment by encouraging them to draw pictures, talk about their feelings, move their bodies, and practice soothing themselves when triggered. (See also "Simple Mindfulness Practices" and "Mindfully Restoring Calm to Your Triggered Brain" in chapter 4.)

> *We kept telling our six-year-old son that it was okay to be angry, but then when he would get mad, we'd tell him to stop it. So, finally, he regressed to wetting his pants and biting, and I realized that not only did I need to allow him to express anger, but I needed to give myself permission to express anger.*
>
> *—Ami*

Expressing Guilt

> *It was really hard on my ten-year-old daughter. She had been wanting a brother or sister, but then when I was pregnant she said, "I don't want a brother; they're mean." So when Gregory died, she blamed it on herself. So next time I was pregnant, she said, "I don't care what— if you have a monkey, Mom, that's fine."*
>
> *—Martina*

Children often believe that things happen because their actions, thoughts, or wishes are powerful enough to cause things to happen. This normal egocentric thinking may make your children feel responsible for the baby's death, particularly if they ever felt competitive or resentful or wished that the baby would never be born, or would go away forever. When the baby dies, your children may worry that their thoughts were indeed powerful enough to cause the baby to go away forever. They may feel horribly guilty and yet be unable to admit it.

This self-centered thinking may also lead your children to feel responsible for your grief. When you are feeling sad or mad, your children may naturally assume that they did something to disappoint or irritate you. To compound this, your children may worry that you are upset because you have figured out that their wishes caused the baby to die.

To help assuage feelings of responsibility, you can provide assurances that nobody is to blame, that thoughts or wishes or unrelated actions cannot make bad things happen. Your children may also benefit from repeated explanations of the possible or definite physiological reasons for your baby's death.

Also let your children know that they are not responsible for your grief. You needn't share your private, overwhelming grief with them, but if you can explain why you cry or get away or go do stuff, you can reduce their confusion or anxiety. As Anne explains, "When they ask why I am crying, I say, 'Because I miss Emily and Michael. And it is okay to cry when you are sad.'"

Your children may have other fears or worries about death not covered here. If you become concerned by any behavior, it may be helpful to talk with a family counselor who is knowledgeable about how grief affects families and can help you figure out what your children need to get through this family crisis. (See also "Guilt" in chapter 7.)

His whole life has been affected by the loss, but I think as far as my grief, I'd like to think that really only affected him initially when I was in the immediate raw stages (that first six to nine months for me). We have always made it very clear that we are very sad about losing Jed, but that it doesn't change how we feel towards him and that nobody did anything wrong or made Jed die.

—Embry

AS YOUR CHILDREN GROW

As time goes on, children may seem to have recovered from the baby's death, but memories of one kind or another may still surface. As children grow older, they become more sophisticated in their ability to understand death, and the death of a younger sibling may take on new meaning. For a three-year-old girl whose baby brother died, the typical questions are: "When is the baby coming back?" and "Where did he go?" and "Why can't we see him?" When this girl is older, she may ask more detailed questions concerning the physical and spiritual nature of death, and she may be concerned about the rituals of burial and cremation. As an adolescent, she may have thoughts and questions about how her life might have been different if her brother had survived. As children acquire new understanding about death and the meaning of having a sibling who died, they benefit from continuing support and information from their parents.

As he's gotten older and continued to ask some of those questions and new ones, we have continued to give him more and more information and made it age/maturity appropriate for him so now he knows most of the details of the story and can wrap his head around it better.

—Embry

You too will continue to grow as you adjust to your baby's death. At first your own raw feelings of grief and vulnerability can make parenting seem like a daunting task. But as you heal, you see how this experience transforms you into the kind of parent you want to be.

In the beginning it was difficult for me to let my son out of my sight. My counselor helped me by saying that I need to choose what Dayani's name is synonymous with in our house. Fear shouldn't be one of them. I don't want my son to say ever since his sister died he couldn't do anything that normal kids do because his mom became a scared person.

—Destrida

My parenting style has been greatly affected, I think. I do not get "hung up" on the silly things. I remember when Matthew (our first) was a baby then a toddler, mothers would get into this comparison game as to what their child was doing. Or wasn't. It really is silly. My thing is, are they happy? Are they healthy? Are they kind and nice human beings? That is what matters.

—Anne

I'm a better person in so many ways; I'm sure I'm a better parent too.

—Julie

POINTS TO REMEMBER

- Grandparents often carry a double sorrow, as they grieve for their grandchild and for you, their own child.
- Many grandparents have difficulty supporting their grieving children. It may help to include them as much as possible in affirming and memorializing your baby.
- If you are close to other family members, you may or may not be able to rely on them for support. If there are other babies in the family, be honest about your feelings so that their parents might be more sensitive to your needs.
- Children grieve according to the loss they feel. Young children in particular are primarily affected by your grief and the family imbalance resulting from your baby's death.
- You may feel immensely grateful to have other children at home, but it can be difficult to be totally attentive when you are grieving. Have others help you, particularly with household tasks, so you can be more available to your children.
- Children need information and clarification about death and grief. Otherwise, they can fear death or feel responsible for your sadness or even for the baby's death. By being honest and by sharing some of your feelings, you can help them understand and cope.
- Children often need help expressing themselves in constructive ways. Try to be a good example; children learn a lot by watching you handle your own grief.
- Children need reassurance that you are still there to love and take care of them and that you are upset because the baby died, not because of something they have done.
- If you feel unsure about what to tell your children about the baby, err on the side of honest disclosure. In general, secrets are more damaging than the truth.
- As your children grow, they will acquire new ideas about death and the meaning of their sibling's death. As a result, they benefit from continuing support and information from you.

13

Support Networks

Friends

My relationships have been affected for sure. That is just the nature of going through something very life changing. Some will be there for you. Others won't. I tried to focus on those who were being helpful.

—Anne

The most supportive friends are those who recognize that your baby's death is a significant and tragic loss. They try to understand what you are going through, they listen whenever you need to talk, and they accept your behavior and your emotions without being uncomfortable or judgmental. Perhaps most importantly, they affirm your baby and the fact that you are this baby's mother or father. Having this kind of support can help you mourn your baby's death.

What I found that I needed most was not to be fixed, but to be listened to—to have my pain and loss validated, and for Bryce to always be included and remembered as my forever son. His memory was not to be tiptoed around or forgotten ever! The Mama Bear in me wouldn't have it, I guess.

—Lori

The biggest help came from those who held me, listened to me, gave me their time or a small gift—like Sam's orchid. It came from those who honored me as a mother.

—Tanya

You may even find that the support you get from friends or even acquaintances is more soothing or affirming than what you get from your partner or family members, who may be immersed in their own grief. As Shannon points out, "I lost a baby but my husband lost a son and my mother lost a grandchild. So, it doesn't feel like they can be real helpful to me. It feels more helpful to have sympathy from a friend or a nurse—someone I can *lean* on. It seems special too, because it's someone who doesn't necessarily have to care, but they do."

My students! I'll never forget one of them coming up to me as my first Mother's Day approached and wishing me a Happy Mother's Day. A sixth grader! That class will forever be extremely special in my heart.

I brought them all pennies when I visited them after Emma died and some of those students still have them. Warms my heart.

—Abby

In particular our babysitter was amazing. She rocked around a few days after Kate was born with a massive bag of lollies and said she didn't know what to say or what she could do for us, but lollies always made her feel better, "So I hope this helps." She was only eighteen but just so wise beyond her years. She is such a special soul and I so appreciated her ability to just be real and in the moment.

—Melanie

Friends who are able to say or do just the right things are always good to have around. Even if you tend to handle things by yourself, you may feel better just knowing that someone else sympathizes and cares.

My sister and my friend Sally, they were just always there and I could act how I wanted to act, be distracted, things like that. Just to know they were aware of things. Like when we went out to eat, Sally would tell people what happened so they wouldn't come rushing up and say, "Oh, what did you have?" She just did anticipatory stuff that turned out to be real helpful.

—Hannah

A comment that helped and meant the world to me in a sad but also sweet way was a friend of mine telling me "Congratulations" at Oren's funeral. She explained that she knew it was a strange thing to say but that she recognized that probably no one would say that word to me. She was right. I had grown and birthed a beautiful baby boy and no one had congratulated me. It was another loss not to celebrate his birth.

—Tanya

I have been very lucky with my work. The outpouring of support through prayers, cards, donations in Dayani's memory, phone calls from domestic and abroad were just overwhelming. It humbled me. I was so honored. My return to work after maternity leave was made easier because of this. I can freely talk about Dayani to almost anyone anytime, and I was given a lot of time to adjust, especially in the first month of my return.

—Destrida

You may discover the true meaning of friendship, as some friends stand by you through thick and thin. Sadly, some friends won't align themselves with your sorrow, perhaps because of their own discomfort. However, you may be touched by the kindness of casual acquaintances, and even strangers, particularly those who have experienced loss and grief. You may even form long-lasting bonds with these people, who can turn out to be more supportive than old friends. Victoria remarks, "Alex's death gave me the opportunity to build a very close friendship with a friend who also had a stillborn baby.

And yes, we talk about our babies freely, we buy gifts, and just get on as friends with two boys who are in the same class as each other!"

You learn who your real friends are. The ones you think are going to be there for you aren't, and the ones you least expect to be are the ones who step up to the plate.

—Fleur

Some friends did some hurtful things and I made the conscious decision to not have them involved in our lives. Then there were others who were amazing, and I will be forever grateful for those who helped us through the worst times of our lives.

—Melanie

Many elderly women have spoken through their tears about their losses, which has been a privilege. The most beautiful gift was from a woman who tearfully told me she had an earlier loss, she knew it wasn't the same, but she was there to talk if I needed.

—Karen

We have been surprised by the support we received from some people, perplexed by the behavior of others, and overwhelmed at times by the true kindness of strangers.

—Emmerson

WHEN FRIENDS TURN AWAY

Most people don't seem to understand that I delivered a baby, and for some reason grieving a miscarriage or having a funeral is not seen as "normal."

—Karen

To us she was real, but to others Claire was just "stillborn." I think people just brush her off as insignificant.

—Henry

It is amazing how many people think that if they don't mention your baby, you will "get over it" quicker. And I will always be amazed by the judgments people make when they don't even bother to have a conversation with me. We love talking about Adisyn and her tragically short life. It hurts us more when people pretend like she never existed.

—Emmerson

Unfortunately, supportive friends can sometimes be few and far between. You may discover that many friends do not recognize the importance of this baby. Or they may be supportive at first, but soon wonder why you aren't "over it" yet. Holly recalls, "There's that period where everybody's very attentive and then they all fade away and people expect you to be better or they don't want to bring it up." In particular, you may sense these attitudes from people who are unfamiliar with this type of bereavement. You may find it sad or frustrating that some people don't even try to understand. Victoria adds, "It became very apparent the friends who were genuine and friends who were not."

Sometimes, people turn away because of their own discomfort due to inexperience and not knowing what to say. Others may avoid you because of their own painful history and, as Emmerson puts it, "to ensure their own comfort and save themselves from exploring places that are too frightening for them to visit." Some of the people closest to you may withdraw because of their *own* grief for your baby. You may withdraw from people too. Still, it is normal to feel hurt by others keeping their distance. Elizabeth observes, "In my experience, that's the worst thing. . . . It makes the bereaved person feel contaminated or unwelcome. I'd rather have someone say something slightly awkward than nothing at all."

> Chris and I have concluded there is not a magic word that can take away the pain. There just isn't. I think others around you are searching for this answer, and sometimes give up on it and say nothing at all. Which can be very hurtful.
>
> —Anne

> Abandonment and denial were certainly not helpful at all. While we understood some of the behavior (we had a therapist to help us with this), it didn't stop the hurt and disappointment we felt and still feel. I still have love for [these] people but the trust is gone and I now keep a safe distance from them to protect myself. I am, as my counselor encourages, "respectfully aloof," no longer as naive or forgiving.
>
> —Emmerson

> I kept the concrete friends, and lost the weaker ones, the ones who couldn't deal with it. For example, a friend who found out she was pregnant and lied to me. I was so cross. I thought, "I don't need this sort of people." Alex's death has highlighted not only what is important, but also **who** is important. So our relationship is finished. All I want from family and friends is truth. Yes, I would have been upset, but grateful for her to tell me the truth.
>
> —Victoria

It is normal to feel hurt or disappointed when friends don't come through in ways you'd like. If they are dismissive, you may find it best to keep your distance. But many people mean well—they are simply cautious, inexperienced, or overwhelmed at the prospect of interacting around an emotionally sensitive subject, or mistaken about what you'd find comforting. Some will be open to learning from you about what you want or need from them. You can also ease your suffering and cope with others' awkwardness or dismissiveness by being a mindful observer, accepting what is, and expecting less from those who have little or nothing to offer.

Most importantly, focus your attention on those who can support you. Rely on them, so that you won't even feel the urge to rely on those who are unsupportive.

One way to soften feelings of rejection is to have compassion for those who fall short. Expect people to be however they need to be. Just as you want them to accept you as you are, you can start by accepting them as they are. As always, having compassion will reduce your suffering. (See also "Educating Well-Meaning People about What You Need" later in this chapter.)

> *The family and close friends who didn't know how to support us, I just tried to give them grace thinking maybe it was so hard for them to be supportive because it hit them so close to home.*
>
> —Embry

> *Some of our friends didn't know what to do and our relationships have changed with some, but that's okay. I have no bitterness about that. It's life, we will all deal with tough times and those who stick through it are your people.*
>
> —Abby

UNSETTLING REMARKS

> *Some of the comments have been nothing short of shocking. I have been told to just get on with it and have another, as if Adisyn can somehow be replaced by another baby.*
>
> —Emmerson

> *Somebody asked me, "Why did you name him? It was just a miscarriage!"*
>
> —Kelly

Like most bereaved parents, you may endure insensitive, rationalistic statements from well-meaning people who are trying to erase your pain. Some may make light of your baby or your sorrow in a misguided effort to help you snap out of it.

> *One well-intentioned friend said she didn't consider Sam to be a baby yet. I think she was trying to help by minimizing the loss. This was after Oren and Miriam too, and she made it clear that in her mind only Oren was a baby. But Sam and Miriam were babies to me, and even if I only thought of them as "an embryo" and "a fetus" (which I didn't but some people do), they were my embryo and my fetus and I was their mom.*
>
> —Tanya

Alas, it is a common reflex for people to try to boost your spirits. Some may look for silver linings or count the "blessings in disguise." Some may want you to feel less alone by pointing out others' tragic losses—or happy fortunes in similar situations. Many people voice the first thought that pops into mind and have no clue that it might sting.

> *I had my share of insensitivity. An elderly neighbor said, "Isn't that funny, this other lady could have quadruplets and you couldn't even have one."*
> —Bryn

> *When the twins were born prematurely, somebody told me, "Well at least you have two extra income tax deductions for this year."*
> —Anya

> *Someone said to me, "Don't worry, I know a woman who had thirteen miscarriages before she had a baby." I thought, "Oh God. I don't want to hear that!" She was trying to help, but that was not really the right thing to say.*
> —Peg

As Camilla testifies, platitudes like "It's all for the best" fall flat even when a baby has severe problems. There may be much suffering and heart-ache during the baby's brief life. And parents have so much love and care invested that their baby's death is still very difficult to bear.

> *When Kacey died, many, many people said, "It's better this way." They didn't take care of my Kacey—they didn't stay up with her all night, they didn't take her to sometimes three or four doctor or therapy appointments a day. They didn't hold a screaming baby— knowing there was nothing that could be done but to love her and make sure she was as comfortable as possible. She will always be in our hearts. Don't ever tell a grieving parent "It's better this way."*
> —Camilla

When you are met with unsettling remarks, depending on your source, your first impulse might be to go silent or walk away. Or perhaps you feel like lashing out in anger or dissolving into tears. This is another opportunity to practice mindfulness and become a compassionate observer. If the person is someone important to you, or if you're simply in the mood for it, you might consider responding in a way that will plant seeds of change. Here is a small sampling of unsettling remarks, and how you might *gently but firmly* respond in order to have your say.

"You're healthy, young. You can always have another baby."
But I want *this baby.* [Use your baby's name] is who my heart yearns for.

"Well, since you know what went wrong, you can fix it or fend it off and try again."
But I still grieve for my baby who died and another baby won't erase my sorrow.

"Be thankful that you already have a healthy child."
Unfortunately, children can't replace each other.

"I know just how you feel. My dog died last summer."
I'm so sorry. I too know the grief of losing a pet. And I can assure you that there is simply no comparison to the death of my baby.

"Your baby is a little angel in heaven."
But I don't want a little angel. I want my baby in my arms.

"This is nature's way of weeding out the defective ones."
Even though my baby had problems, s/he was perfect to me.

"I've known other people who have handled this well, never cried."
Actually, handling this well means expressing my grief with tears, not repressing it.

"You're lucky it happened now instead of six months from now."
I'd give anything for an additional six months!

"At least you know you are fertile."
It is hardly a comfort to know I can conceive but perhaps I cannot keep my babies.

"At least your loss was final. When our house burned down, for months we kept remembering more things we were missing."
No loss is ever final. I too keep remembering more things that I'm missing, like the first smile, first tooth, first steps, first word . . .

"It's all for the best."
I'm sorry but my pain is too deep for me to see any blessings at this point in my journey.

You may come up with your own responses that will stop people in their tracks and set them straight. If you can be assertive with grace and compassion, you may even spur a conversation that goes deeper, allowing you to share your experiences and garner support.

While most people have good intentions, there may be some who are abrasive or malicious. Try to remember that these people have significant problems and push blame or resentment or denial on you as a way of avoiding their own pain. They may make remarks such as, "What did you do to deserve this?" Remind yourself that you certainly do not deserve their incrimination for something beyond your control! If they insist that your baby's death isn't a big deal, you'll know not to expect their support. You need to take care of yourself by avoiding people who cannot be compassionate.

I have learned through our experiences that you cannot change people. You grow closer to those who are supportive and let you grieve. Those who are not there for you, you just say, "Oh, well."
—Anne

Some relationships I think are made naturally, like the sand dunes, and others created, like the sand castle. Both can be eroded by the

waves, which represent things that happen in life. You make a choice to protect or rebuild, or you can leave them as they are, accepting that nothing can make things change. I read this quote today: "Some people come in your life as blessings. Others come in as lessons."
—Emmerson

WHEN FRIENDS FOCUS ON THE SURVIVING BABY

Parents who experience the death of a baby or babies from a multiple birth may endure especially awkward moments, particularly if they are able to bring a baby home. When you have a surviving baby or babies, it is natural for you to be happy about this. People will be happy for you, but they may be unsure of how to react toward your baby(s) who died. Shannon points out, "I don't blame people for being happy for us because it was such a mixed thing. I think people find it hard to say, 'We're sorry about your baby and oh, congratulations, by the way!'" In addition, others may refer to "the baby" when to you, she or he is "one of twins." "The twins" to others will always be "the triplets" or "the quads" to you.

Unfortunately, some people may expect or encourage you to relish the survivor(s) without mourning for the one(s) who didn't make it. They may encourage you to consider yourself lucky. Or they may think that the baby or babies who died were simply a nice bonus that just didn't work out. Others may even express relief that you've been spared the emotional, physical, and financial challenges of raising multiples. If you have battled infertility, people may chide you to just be grateful for any children you might have. This lack of sensitivity and support can leave you feeling isolated, misunderstood, and angry.

People focus on the fact that we have Bradley. That's so frustrating. I never really respond except to say, "Yes, we thank God." But what I want to say is, "Yeah, we are really lucky but we also have two cribs sitting up there, we'd gotten excited about the idea of two babies, and we were looking forward to two babies. We still lost a baby!"
—Shannon

Sometimes people treat us like our triplets were not real because they were not with us for very long. . . . No one knows what to say to us. Our older son is our greatest comfort—but having him doesn't make us feel any better about losing Cory, Carly, and Allex. I love my son more than anything, but don't tell me "At least you have him."
—Georgia

If one or some babies survive, there is often pressure from all sides to focus on the living. You may receive little acknowledgment of the babies who died, and minimal patience for feelings of grief or attempts to remember the dead. Others may also lack appreciation for the efforts and challenges involved in caring for the survivor(s) as you grieve.

As such, if you are raising one or more survivors, it can be especially helpful to remember that people mean well, and they think they are being kind when they encourage you to forget and move on. They simply don't know that it's important for you to remember and honor the baby or babies who died. You can be open and tell them why you resist the pressure to forget, and what kinds of support you appreciate most. This can encourage some people to step up and support you. For those who don't, ignore their judgments on how you are doing. Surround yourself with people who understand and appreciate what you are going through. Tap into the many supportive online resources and networks for parents like you. (See also "Internet and Social Media" later in this chapter.)

EDUCATING WELL-MEANING PEOPLE ABOUT WHAT YOU NEED

This has been a real learning experience for both of us, to find out that all the supposedly comforting things we used to say to our friends who had miscarriages, those are really some of the worst things to say.

—Mark

Friends and family truly want to help support us bereaved parents but they don't know how. Sadly, but at the same time understandably so, it falls upon us, the traumatized, heavily grieving, to train those around us on how they can best help. And, of course, what we need is constantly changing, as we grieve and heal.

—Lori

It's easy to feel isolated or angry when the people close to you don't know how to comfort you. Naturally, if you interpret your well-intentioned friends' actions as uncaring, you will feel even more upset and uncomfortable sharing your experiences with them. It can be easy to fall into cycles of misunderstanding.

You may be able to avert these cycles with many people by giving them the benefit of the doubt. Until they prove otherwise, assume they have good intentions. It's also important to have realistic expectations. After all, what you need is a supportive listener who is quiet, compassionate, and wise, granting you sufficient space and time to air thoughts and feelings, to grieve uniquely, to fall apart and come together again, and to gain new insights. You deserve to have this kind of support, but that's expecting a lot from most people.

However, it is possible to maintain or restore a connection with those friends and relatives *who mean well and are up to the task of supporting you*. The first step is to identify those who are capable of being there for you. As Emmerson points out, "We could tell when someone was really trying, but the words just didn't come out right and there was no malice or offense intended."

It can also help to be mindful of your interpretation of what's going on between you. You can question distressing assumptions and try on alternatives. For instance, when your friends resort to platitudes or clichés, this can sound dismissive of your feelings. Consider that perhaps they are simply repeating common sayings in an effort to say *something*. When friends avoid the topic, it can seem uncaring. Consider that perhaps they may avoid talking about your baby in order to avoid raking up your despair. Likewise, when friends encourage you to move on, they may be expressing concern for your well-being. (See also "Mindfully Reframing Your Thoughts" in chapter 4.)

Reframing people's intentions can help you replace your anger or hurt with compassion for them, and seeing theirs for you. Even so, when you are feeling so vulnerable and sensitive, it's normal to find it difficult to tolerate their blunders. Plus, when people aren't inviting you to share, it's natural to feel awkward or afraid to talk about your baby. You may even think you have to protect them by not bringing it up, especially around friends who are pregnant or have babies, or during celebrations or the holiday season. And it is a challenge to ask for what you need when you are feeling so sad and helpless.

> *You feel so insecure you don't feel like you've got a right to stand up and say, "You know, that's really inappropriate. How dare you say something like that!" I wanted to wear a shirt that said "Please Be Nice to Me."*
>
> *—Bryn*

> *Friends backed off, and I understand that now. It was too close to home, especially for people that had little children. They acted as if, "I don't even want to think that my baby could die." So when this happened to me, it made it real to them, they backed off and they didn't come around for a while.*
>
> *—Cindy*

It is common for bereaved parents and their friends to disengage from each other. Parents often retreat if they sense that their grief is an imposition, and then they notice their friends back off even further. An irony about grief is that when you withdraw, you may need people's support more than ever, but people sense your withdrawal and leave you alone. If you feel as though your friends and family have backed off, remember, they take cues from you. Don't fall into thinking, "If they really loved me they would know what I need." They can't read your mind. Tell them how miserable you really are and how much you need to talk about the baby. Instead of waiting for them to bring it up, you can initiate conversations about how painful this is and how much you miss your baby.

Here are some other suggestions you might try sharing with your trusted friends:

- Tell them that you will cherish their sympathetic ears for listening, their shoulders for tears, their calls, and their hugs.

- Let them know it's okay to ask questions. After all, you *need* to talk about what happened. If you cry, this means they asked a very *good* question. Thank them for asking.
- Confess that you need specific, detailed offers of help because you don't have the energy to assign tasks and you don't want to impose on anyone. "Call if you need anything" is too intimidating to follow through on. It's much easier to say "Yes" to "When it snows, can I shovel your walk?" or "How about I take your kids to the park tomorrow?" or "Can I drop off lasagna and salad on Friday?" Remind them that if offers are turned down, to make them again in a few days.
- Assign dreaded tasks to friends who offer their assistance. For you, this might be grocery shopping, housecleaning, driving the older kids to scheduled activities, or sending out a mass email announcement and then responding to the replies.
- Explain how you would rather have them bumble through with honest expressions of their feelings than avoid you, cheer you up, fix things, or offer advice. Reveal that the best words to hear are the very ones they are censoring as they desperately search for the perfect thing to say. The best—and most honest—words are things like "I can't imagine how awful this is for you" or "I want to say the perfect thing to make you feel better but I'm not sure what that can possibly be" or "I'm so sorry your baby died."
- Ask them to use your baby's name and to acknowledge your baby on anniversaries and holidays. Remind them that even if you get pregnant again, your focus may still be on the baby who died.
- Tell them that you'll appreciate their patience and support as you find your own way through grief.

Even though it can be difficult, you do have the right to let well-meaning people know what helps and what doesn't. You can give them something to read (including this book), write them an email, or tell them in person. It takes energy and courage to confront people, but sometimes that is the only way they will know how to support you. Friends and relatives are usually grateful to know what you need. Those who truly want to help will appreciate your guidance. Surround yourself with people who can be responsive and compassionate, with or without your coaching.

> *It was about three to four months until I saw my family, and they obviously didn't want to bring it up and it was never really discussed. Looking back, that's something I would do differently. Now I'd probably say, "Hey, look, I want to talk about this."*
> —Dara

> *I say to my friends, "I feel like everybody is tired of listening, but I still need to talk." When I say that, it makes them feel like they aren't one of those people, and they want to listen.*
> —Claudia

I want to tell my friends, "Just say you're thinking of us, that you care, put your hand on our shoulder, don't probe, don't try to make us feel better, don't stay long, maybe drop off a meal and leave. It just helps to know you're thinking of us."

—Kim

It's also important to remember that sometimes friends will think about what they've said to you and wish they could take it back. But they might not want to bring it up, maybe out of embarrassment or being fearful of conflict or not wanting to hurt you even more. But if you can bring it up, it can clear the air and even improve your relationship. One mother recalls, "I got pregnant by accident, in a relationship that wasn't going to last. When I miscarried, a good, caring friend said, 'It's probably for the best.' At the time, that really stung. Months later, when I wasn't feeling so fragile, I was able to tell her, 'You know, I really wanted that baby. It didn't matter about the relationship.' And she actually apologized for saying what she said. The whole time, she'd been wishing she could take it back. I'm so glad I brought it up. It was such a weight lifted off both of us."

Internet and Social Media

Social media's whole format of status updates invites "friends" to comment and "like" what someone has written; a complicated path to traverse for the bereaved parent. And yet, sometimes just knowing that people "like" what you have written may help you feel that you have been heard.

—Tanya

I have been fairly open on Facebook, mostly on a private page, but some on my main page, particularly on his first birthday. I asked people to light a candle or release a balloon for him and give us a picture. A couple dozen people did this with us and it meant so much.

—Embry

As technology continues to develop and change, so will the landscape of the Internet and social media. Many parents have benefited from what this technology offers, such as

- the efficient ease of communicating with far-flung friends and relatives, including the ability to post photographs of their babies;
- tools to help people organize themselves to provide help to the bereaved friend, relative, neighbor, coworker, or community member;
- overcoming constraints of remote location, mobility, time, and money that might otherwise impede connection with loved ones or a community;
- round-the-clock, wide-reaching access to online support, resources, information, and communities of similar need, culture, and interests;
- the ability to connect with other bereaved parents, including forming invaluable one-on-one connections;

- access to a wide variety of bereaved parents and stories of grief and healing;
- access to medical research and information;
- platforms from which to advocate for better awareness, bereavement care, and parent support;
- opportunities to participate in memorial walks, candle lighting, and other local or worldwide events and awareness days;
- a way to find information, resources, and support groups, as well as organizations, books, blogs, and magazines that offer what parents are looking for;
- a way to view and purchase products from compassionate companies that offer everything from caskets to weighted teddy bears, from memorial jewelry that can contain ashes to portraits made from photographs; and
- creative ways to memorialize babies who've died, including online memorial sites, collections of narratives, videos, and photographs, and projects that invite parents to share thoughts on grief and healing.

Online (and in-person) grief communities are places of incredible creativity, as people find ways to commemorate a loss for which there's no established ritual.

—Elizabeth

Unfortunately, there are also pitfalls. The quality of information and support can vary widely. The ease of communication also means that you are exposed and perhaps judged by others who don't understand your need to tell your story or post pictures. You are also vulnerable to being triggered by the happy pregnancy, birth, and baby news in your social circle, or as Tanya says, "Everyone's happy baby pictures kick you in the gut a little." Some parents solve this problem by going off social media for a while.

Here are some pointers for navigating the mixed blessing of online information, communication, and social media:

- Be cautious and discerning when you visit websites that contain information on topics such as cause of death, medical ethics, grief and mourning, bereavement care, or parent support. Not all websites are created by qualified people or based on credible sources. Bad design can be off-putting, but does not necessarily mean bad-quality material. Likewise, a good design and big claims do not necessarily reflect high-quality or sound practice. Be a smart consumer.
- Email and status updates can be misunderstood or limiting, as they can lack the emotional depth and connection that speaking to someone in person or over the phone can provide. Well-meaning friends may interpret your words in ways you don't intend, such as presuming that you are "staying strong" or

"a total wreck" based on a few sentences, when neither is an accurate reflection of your journey.

- Be mindful that social media isn't really set up for accommodating grief and mourning—unless you're posting on bereavement pages and sites.
- Accept that you are exposing yourself to scrutiny if you "go public" with posts about mourning or photos of your baby. It's important to remember that some people might feel uncomfortable and make insensitive comments. On the other hand, posting is a way to affirm your baby, and some people will be supportive. Ignore, delete, or block the insensitive ones and bask in the compassion offered.
- Accept that you'll be triggered by reminders that the world is moving on without you, or by celebratory compilations of posts and photos—even of your own—declaring what a "wonderful year" it was.
- It's okay to take a break from email and social media in order to protect yourself from people's discomfort or to spare yourself from the everyday goings-on.
- When you join or explore an online community, remember that you needn't fall into "groupthink," as in, feel pressure to conform or feel excluded when you're an outlier. Although bereaved parents share much emotional common ground, everyone's path is still unique, and it's important to make room for differences rather than thinking there is a "better" way or a "right" way to mourn. Instead, by everyone staying true to themselves, you can learn far more from each other.
- If you feel like your situation, experience, or culture isn't reflected at all, expand your search for community. Whether you feel represented or not, you can enrich your journey and healing transformation by seeking out a wide variety of bereaved parents and their stories, music, poetry, videos, coping tips, and spirituality.

Most unfortunate of all, when meeting bereaved parents online, you have to keep up your guard and your radar, because although rare, there have been a number of documented cases of disturbed individuals posing as grieving parents in bids for attention, sympathy, or to feed an obsession or compulsion. To protect yourself, use these common sense guidelines:

- Trust your intuition. Intuition is a most valuable tool for sensing when something is "off."
- If any interaction makes you feel the slightest bit uncomfortable, back away. Or if a person's story seems extreme, over-the-top tragic, or not quite "right," it could be a hoax. Report your suspicions to site moderators. Chances are good that your

intuition is not the only one to sound an alarm. Silence only entrenches the problem.

- Don't send photographs of yourself or your baby to individuals who ask for them. You have every right to maintain privacy.
- Don't divulge your full name, address, or even your general location, as individuals have been known to track down phone numbers with this information.
- If an individual wants to set up a face-to-face meeting, use utmost caution. This could be a nefarious bid for information about your location or personal details.
- Rather than tapping into general social groups or online marketplaces, use the websites and pages of established parent support groups or organizations—although these still pose some risk, at least you have moderators who can handle problems and the backing of a wider community, should a dishonest individual come along.

In spite of the need to practice reasonable caution, do remember that the vast majority of people are honest and caring, and you can benefit immensely from all the good offered by the Internet and social media.

Parent Support Groups

In the days after we found out Emily had died, I just wanted to talk with anyone we knew who had experienced this. I wanted to know, "How are we going to get through this? And through these days ahead?"
—Anne

Meeting other bereaved parents face-to-face truly helped me to feel less alone in this. I also learned coping ideas in this group and was able to express my thoughts and feelings in this very safe environment too. Bereaved parents could truly understand what I was going through . . . because they were going through similar things and experiencing similar thoughts and feelings as well. It was so comforting somehow!
—Lori

We have attended a support group and met other people who have had a similar experience to us. The connection we have gained from that is hard to describe at a time when you feel so isolated and alone. In the face of such loss and grief comes a wonderful closeness and understanding of each other.
—Emmerson

Slowly, I didn't feel alone in my pain anymore. I had met other mothers and fathers who have felt the same, who were survivors just like us. This was the beginning of the healing. Every session, I would come out of the group devastated with pain but also stronger. One of the "positive" sides of having gone through this ordeal, if there are any, is that this tragedy put me in contact with fellow parents who have had similar tragedies and the bond we established is quite unique.
—Annalaura

A support group can be a valuable source of comfort for parents who have experienced the death of a baby. Other bereaved parents, unlike many friends and relatives, can be sensitive and knowledgeable.

Attending a support group is comforting in many ways. In a positive, accepting group atmosphere, you can share your grief with others who truly understand. You can talk openly about your baby, your experiences, and your feelings. Others can validate how significant and painful your losses are, reassure you that your feelings are normal, give you insights on coping, and help you discover that you are not alone in your experiences.

> *It felt like a lifeline, knowing others were surviving this devastating loss. It was a place to talk, and that helped me work through the guilt.*
> —*Jessie*

> *It helped, just being able to air out some feelings and just the fact that I was doing something positive, was getting out, just somewhere to go every other week, being a part of something. I would have been a lot more desperate if it wasn't for the support group and friends made there, if I couldn't have had anyone to talk to.*
> —*Rose*

> *The group just made me feel normal in a state where you don't know what to do. I felt like no one could possibly feel this bad, and then I would sit there and hear these people saying the same things that I was thinking myself. It was an incredible comfort.*
> —*Liza*

> *I just needed a supportive forum in which to voice feelings of anger and isolation, to know the feelings I had were typical. And it's helpful if you go for a period of time to watch people work through their grief and know that there is a point when things begin to improve.*
> —*Holly*

Support groups also provide a forum where you can share difficult feelings and ask difficult questions, and there is no judgment. You can learn from other parents' hard-won wisdom, and share your own. Even if your situation or experience is unique or very different from the majority of the parents in a group, you still share much common ground in terms of the emotional aspects of grief and mourning. You can trade effective coping strategies and hear about other perspectives and different ways of being. You acquire hope as you witness others' healing transformations. And perhaps most important, a support group provides a community of people who are willing to companion each other along the mourning journey. Tanya notes, "Who my friends are has changed over the last six years and three losses. Many of my current friends are bereaved parents themselves."

> *With Camden and Keegan, we just had the support of hospital staff, family, and few friends. Not long after we lost Keegan I joined the support group. So then with Caeden, a few hours after delivery, two*

group members came through the doors with camera, care packages, and support. The visitors didn't stop all day. We have never felt so much support and comfort in our lives—totally different from the first two losses.
—*Fleur*

This community we now belong to means so, so much to me. At a time when I am trying to work out how to be in this world and come to terms with this new, different version of myself, I have been warmly welcomed by a group of people where I feel I belong, where I am completely understood. It is safe, comforting, reassuring, and accepting of us. These amazing people give us a place to be heard, a place to talk openly and honestly about how we really feel, a place to be "not okay," a place to experience and go through our own personal grief process now matter how long it takes, feeling supported throughout the entire journey.
—*Emmerson*

Many support groups are free, sponsored by hospitals, hospices, churches, bereaved parent organizations, or mental health agencies. Whether online or in person, a well-run support group has a moderator who makes sure everyone understands and abides by the rules, and scheduled meetings start and stop on time. People are expected to be respectful and compassionate, to take turns, and to accept differences. Parents are encouraged not only to tell their stories and talk about their grief but also to also share ideas about managing, coping, and cultivating hope and healing. Most groups meet for two hours once or twice a month. Parents may attend as many meetings as they wish. Some charge a small fee or take donations. Some groups bring in speakers and then open up for discussion, while others devote the entire time to open discussion. The moderator may offer information and help guide the discussion, but parents often determine the issues by sharing the feelings they are struggling with and what they find helpful. If a parent does not wish to talk, he or she should feel welcome to simply listen.

Online support groups have their advantages: you can set your own pace and engage as much or as little as you want at times that are most convenient for you. But the missing ingredient is face-to-face contact with others, which is what our brains are wired for and our souls find so comforting. Even if you find an online group you like, you can still benefit from attending a local support group, in person, or connecting with bereaved parents nearby.

Many parents attend support group meetings without their partners. Schedules and babysitting sometimes make it possible for only one parent to attend. Or one partner may not feel a need to attend or may feel reluctant to share private feelings with others. If your partner is reluctant to go with you, you might encourage him or her to attend one or two meetings, just to observe and to support you.

Going to your first support group meeting can be scary, particularly if you tend to be an introvert. You may feel anxious, especially at the thought of sharing your feelings with strangers. It can help to go with someone—your partner, a friend, a relative. Or you can even ask the moderator to connect you with another bereaved parent who can look after you. These people know how difficult that first meeting can be.

Because grieving the death of a baby is so different, many parents who experience miscarriage, stillbirth, or infant death find that pregnancy/infant death support groups are far more helpful than general bereaved parent groups. If you made life-and-death decisions for your baby, you may feel uncomfortable about the possibility of others judging you. You could contact genetic counselors, chaplains, social workers, or psychologists in your area and ask for a referral to a support group specifically for parents who faced difficult decisions—or suggest that they sponsor such a group.

Do remember that any well-run support group will embrace and offer compassion to *all* parents, whatever the circumstances of their baby's death. Also consider that as you struggle with pangs of regret, any judgment you feel may be your own. By attending a "regular" support group, you can see that other parents cope with feelings of guilt. "What have I done?" and "What if . . . ?" are universal questions. You may find special comfort in this.

Some parents do not feel the need to attend a support group. They may feel they are getting enough support from other sources, or the idea of a group just doesn't appeal to them. Other parents may go once and get turned off by the experience. If you go only once (or not at all), however, you may not be giving it a fair chance. Most groups have open attendance, so the composition can vary from meeting to meeting. Talking and listening to other parents may be more helpful after your shock and numbness have worn off. If you feel reluctant or skeptical, you can still go a couple of times or talk with the moderator about your doubts.

We went once, two weeks after Jessica died, and I didn't like it. They had all lost their babies less recently than me. Then, at two months, my husband started school and I had no support. So I went to the group by myself and met another woman who was struggling with spiritual stuff too, so I called her. She's been my biggest support ever since.

—Rose

As Rose discovered, even if you do not like the idea of a group, it can be a good place to meet another parent to connect with. You can continue this relationship outside the group, offering each other the kinds of reassurance and understanding that are so helpful. Many parents who lack the support of other bereaved parents feel an extra sense of loneliness and uncertainty about their grief.

I never attended a support group. Looking back, I would've benefited from that. . . . It would've helped just to know that I wasn't the only person it happened to. That it wasn't this big mystery and we weren't bad people and that kind of thing.

—Hannah

To find a support group in your area, ask your doctor or contact the social worker at a local hospital, hospice, or mental health agency. Or you can contact a national parent support organization to see if there are any groups in your area. If you are too shy or overwhelmed to make inquiries, ask someone else to make the phone calls. A good friend would be pleased to assist you with this.

If there are no support groups in your area, you may get a sympathetic counselor or health care practitioner to start sponsoring one. If you live in a sparsely populated area or if a support group doesn't appeal to you, you can join a well-run online support group or forum. Or ask your doctor or midwife to put you in touch with other parents who've been through a similar experience. However you make the connection, another bereaved parent can be a lifeline. (For fathers, see also "The Challenge of Getting Support" in chapter 10.)

When I had Judah, if I'd just had another mother say, "This happened to me," it would have made a world of difference. And when I did find that mother, I was so thankful for her companionship. I don't know where I would have been without being able to relate to her.

—Jolie

Where I live there are no support groups, so there is no opportunity to meet other parents. So I've felt very isolated. But with time, I have gained more confidence to say, "We lost Kate and Zac." And particularly when we get comments from people saying, "Are you going to keep trying for a boy?" given we have four girls with us, I try to be strong and say we had a wee boy before Zara, but he died. I have tried to be honest as often as I can because I might come across someone else who has been through what we have been through.

—Melanie

COUNSELING

My midwife suggested seeing a counselor. I was very reluctant to do this. I came from a family that did not talk if there were issues. You just put your head down and got on with it. But hands down I feel like it saved my life and I tell everyone and anyone how great counseling is. Just to be able to talk to someone about all the chaos in your brain, and not worrying that you sound like a nut job. I went to her every week for several months. A lot of the time I just cried and tried to come to terms with our new reality. Every now and then it would get a little easier and then it would go backwards, but she was eventually able to help me climb out of the hole. She gave me a lot of tools for dealing with my anxiety and accepting that there is a lot in life I have no control of.

—Melanie

In addition to a support group, many parents benefit from individual counseling. Each has its own unique benefits. Whereas attending a support group can help you feel less isolated, offer opportunities to strike up supportive friendships, and let you have hope for the future by observing how others have coped, individual counseling can give you a chance to air your feelings at greater length, help you work through other personal issues that are dredged up, and offer more specific guidance. Many parents have particular difficulty dealing with the trauma, or feel overwhelmed by anger, guilt, regrets, despair, or anxiety. A counselor can directly address and treat your unique trauma and distress, and therapy is individually tailored to your needs. Family therapy can also benefit surviving children, and couples counseling can benefit your relationship with your partner.

You could benefit from counseling if any of the following apply:

- You think it might help.
- You feel stuck or worry that you are resisting grief or consumed by it.
- You feel you are falling apart or no longer in control.
- You notice that you are engaging in addictive or destructive behaviors.
- You continue to find no joy in other aspects of your life or resent others who do.
- Your feelings, behavior, or physical symptoms interfere with your well-being or your functioning (for instance, your depression prevents you from eating or sleeping, your lack of concentration produces costly mistakes, your headaches or fatigue keep you from enjoying favorite activities or fulfilling responsibilities).
- You feel isolated or want the comfort of someone who can listen and support you.
- Others, such as a friend, relative, doctor, or clergyperson, suggest that you might benefit from counseling.

Some people hesitate to enter counseling for fear they will never stop needing it. For many people, getting into therapy implies weakness, mental illness, or character flaws. Actually, it indicates personal strength, health, and courage because being successful in therapy means facing your distress, addressing your problems, and seeking growth and change. More specifically, counseling can help you to improve self-awareness, gather insights into your reactions, build your strengths, learn new skills for solving problems and communicating with others, and acquire additional adaptive strategies for grieving, coping, adjusting, and healing.

Eventually, through counseling, you gain the ability to help yourself. When you stop going regularly, your counselor can remain available for occasional consultation as needed.

If nothing else, counseling gives you a chance to talk about your baby. In particular, a sensitive counselor can be a companion who walks with you as you mourn. With that special support you will find it easier to avert unnecessary suffering, come to terms with your baby's death, and find peace and healing. (See also "About Trauma and Suffering" in chapter 3.)

Therapy was essential for me, just to be able to go in once a week for an hour and talk about Kevin and go over and over the same stuff. You don't feel like you're imposing because you're paying them to listen; that's your time to do whatever you need.

—*Cathryn*

When you're in counseling or therapy of any kind, the practitioner's compassion is necessary, but not always sufficient. If traditional "talk" therapy or medication doesn't seem like enough, there are many mind/body and brain-based therapies that are especially effective for treating trauma, stress, anxiety, and depression. Some of these therapies cut to the chase and change the way painful memories are stored in the body or brain. EMDR (Eye Movement Desensitization and Reprocessing), which is a remarkably effective at treating trauma much faster than other methods, works by digesting and integrating traumatic memories into the brain so they aren't front and center anymore. Other therapies increase mind/body awareness and calm the brain, thereby reducing unnecessary suffering. And others restore the sense of comfortably inhabiting one's body, and cultivate mind/body balance. All enable regaining one's true self. Following is a list of examples:

- Eye Movement Desensitization and Reprocessing (EMDR)
- neurofeedback (self-regulation training)
- mindfulness based stress reduction (MBSR)—an eight-week program
- mindfulness meditation
- mindfulness-based cognitive therapy (MBCT)
- Emotional Freedom Technique (EFT), commonly called "tapping"
- acceptance and commitment therapy (ACT)
- Traditional Chinese Medicine (TCM); includes acupuncture, herbs, nutrition, and holistic health care
- somatic therapy
- movement therapies that boost body awareness, such as yoga, tai chi, qigong, Feldenkrais, Pilates, martial arts, dance
- therapeutic massage, including Rolfing (myofascial release)
- cranial electrotherapy stimulation
- art therapy, music therapy

For me, EMDR has been a lifesaver. I can truly say that I am not ruled by PTSD anymore. I will always grieve for my kids, because I will always love them, but once the PTSD was under control, my grief could really begin to shift and look different. It also helped to pass those initial [anniversaries] after Miriam's death. I think of my babies every day, but often it is with happiness now, that they lived, even for such a short time, and that they lived in me. I am honored to be their mother.

—*Tanya*

These mind/body and brain-based therapies are effective because they enhance the brain's ability to repair itself following trauma and during the stress of grief and mourning. These therapies can have positive effects on many symptoms and areas of life, including pain, sleep, emotional status, and relationships. Many, including EMDR, MBSR, and mindfulness meditation, create measurable, visible changes in the brain that are in line with a reduced reactivity to stress. As research reveals more about the brain and effective treatments, promising new therapies may appear on the horizon.

I found that I could release those emotions in a way where I did not have to speak, and was supported by the other person. Reiki also helped me realize that I don't need to be sad, I don't have to cling on to those feelings as a way of holding on to Finley. I will allow them and sit with them, but let them go.

—Mel

After we lost Zac I went back to seeing my counselor again. I struggled once again with anxiety and the actual trauma of what we went through. I just couldn't turn off my brain and thinking about all the blood and how my life was in danger and what could have been good or bad. So she suggested seeing an EFT practitioner (Emotional Freedom Technique). She said there was research going on at the moment using EFT with post-traumatic stress disorder. I was once again pretty dubious about this somewhat holistic approach but I was willing to give anything a try. I think if someone had told me standing on my head all day would give me some relief I would have done it willingly. So I went along expecting nothing. But it was truly amazing. I left my first session feeling like I could breathe again. Like a massive weight had been lifted off my chest. It didn't lessen my grief, but it helped give my brain a rest from the constant churning of beating myself up and thinking about what could have been. EFT helped immensely.

—Melanie

If you decide to try any of these therapies, look for a licensed professional who preferably has experience working with bereaved persons, trauma sufferers, and/or mindfulness practices. In fact, research indicates that practitioners who themselves adhere to mindfulness practices can be more empathic, compassionate, nonjudgmental, and attuned with their clients than practitioners who don't. As a result, their clients tend to experience more relief from distress. A licensed mental health professional is also qualified to give you an accurate diagnosis, for instance knowing the difference between postpartum depression, trauma, anxiety, depression, and preexisting depression or trauma. The right diagnosis can be key to getting the right treatment.

A reputable psychological counselor can be a clinical psychologist (PhD or PsyD), licensed clinical social worker (LCSW), psychiatrist (MD), or psychiatric nurse (PMH-APRN). You can find therapist and counselor directories online, such as "Find a Therapist" at PsychologyToday.com, where you can even refine your search according to location, type of therapy, and issue (including grief). Or check your local listings under "Counselors," "Therapists," "Psychologists," or "Mental Health Services." To explore other emotionally healing avenues such as art therapy, yoga, meditation, Traditional Chinese Medicine, and therapeutic massage, locate specialists in your area by visiting the websites of professional organizations. Get recommendations from people you know, including your doctor or midwife, friends, or other bereaved parents. Referrals from people who have direct experience with a counselor or practitioner can be most valuable. In fact, finding the right therapist is sometimes more important than the mode of therapy. You also might ask the following:

- parent support group moderators
- the social worker or psychologist at a local hospital
- the women's center or parent education department at a local hospital or clinic
- your community mental health clinic
- your place of worship
- a hospice organization
- the local college, university, or medical school counseling center
- a family service agency

If cost is a concern, community, university, medical school, and training institute clinics operate on reduced or sliding scale fees, so you pay what you can afford. Many private practitioners will negotiate their fees or refer you accordingly. Most health insurance, employee assistance programs, and health savings accounts will pay some or all of the cost. It may help to remember that *you are worth it.*

HEALTH CARE PRACTITIONERS

I always say that if you have to go through such a difficult experience, if you have good care, it makes all the difference in the world.
—Shellie

We had a fair amount of support at the hospital. The doctor on call and the nurse were wonderful. Very sensitive, kind, and loving. We were really blessed.
—Anne

My husband and I were in shock. I couldn't stop blabbering, while he cried every time someone started talking to him. The nurses at the Mother and Baby floor were very sensitive.
—Destrida

After Emma was born my doctor came over and said, "I want you to remember two things: (1) This was not your fault. You did nothing wrong; and (2) People will say stupid shit." It was so endearing and SO truthful for the moment.
—Abby

Parents are profoundly affected by the treatment they receive from health care practitioners. When treated with warmth, respect, and empathy, they are comforted by the fact that someone truly cares. You may be deeply touched by practitioners who provide a compassionate, mindful presence, can share a tear with you, and acknowledge the depth of your grief. Any support where feelings are validated makes a lasting impression and reduces the effects of trauma.

> *The pastor, social worker, doctors, and nurses kept coming in to check, and I think it was helpful because it made me think, well, when you have a baby that's alive, they come in to see how you're doing and how the baby's doing, but if you have a dead one, they don't just leave you out. They treat you like you're human too.*
>
> —Martina

> *The nurse cried right along with me. You know, there's really something to someone giving validity to your feelings when everybody else is trying to make you feel better. Here this wonderful woman was crying and letting me know I had good reason to cry. She didn't try to shut me up. She wasn't in a hurry. She acted like a regular person who was really feeling sad that this had happened to me and she wasn't scared of what I was going to do next. I could be hysterical and it was okay.*
>
> —Sara

> *Our doctor was there for us in a lot of ways. He was unusually sensitive. When we went into his office just a few days after Meghan died, he said, "I want to talk to you about the emotional side of this," and he made a real point to discuss what we could expect to feel. And he was real open about his own feelings. I remember him crying the night we delivered the baby and saying how hard that was for him, that the reason he went into obstetrics was so he could bring life and not have to deal with death so much.*
>
> —Jessie

There are no words that can erase your pain. But you can be deeply comforted by the special attention you receive: your doctor's availability to just listen and be with you, your midwife's gentle touch or any special arrangements made for you. Caregivers may also help by handling some of the paperwork, gathering information on funeral homes, or sensitizing others to your special situation. Even simple, fleeting gestures that save minuscule moments of pain can make a big difference.

> *They did things to make me get well, but also be separate from the maternity ward. Since they didn't have facilities on that floor, they brought me a portable sitz bath. That they cared was real important. You need to feel that you are important and not just another one of the patients.*
>
> —Bryn

The hospital social worker was so nice, she wanted to listen and she helped us. We didn't know where to start, how to bury him or what. We had never had to deal with this, and she helped us through the whole thing. She called around and she got prices of things. You know, that's something to think about. She made you realize that you did have to think of cost and not to feel guilty.

—Kelly

My regular doctor is amazing. He turned to me and said, "Tell me all about it." He listened and knew all the right things to say. Not many girls have been born into our family; he was chuffed to know Lilly Marie was a girl. After we had chatted for nearly an hour he told me he had not been informed about Lilly Marie and he was going to ring the hospital and find out why not. He has known me since conception, he delivered me, he knows me. He cried with me for the daughter I had lost.

—Sarah

Parents will forever remember this support, and continue to derive comfort from it over the years. Kylie listed the many kindnesses received at the hospital and says, "I really appreciated it all. It made lasting positive memories of what was a difficult time for us."

I distinctively remember one midwife, Doris, who must have been close to eighty. In the middle of the night when she was checking on me she sat down beside me and said she needed to talk to my husband and me. She said that when she was young she had a stillborn baby and that her husband never spoke of this baby their entire life. She said she had ached to speak about this baby and the experience but she was never given the opportunity. And then much later in their lives when he was close to dying he spoke of this baby and she said she was so angry that he had chosen the end of their lifetime to finally talk about it. And that this was not the way for us to deal with our loss of Zac, and she made us promise that we would talk about Zac together. She wanted to make sure we didn't make the same mistake they had.

—Melanie

Honesty from your caregivers is as important as warmth, empathy, and sensitivity. You needed to know what was happening and to be told the truth about your baby's prognosis. If the doctor was perplexed, you wanted uncertainty rather than phony answers or assurances. To be prepared for the worst is far preferable to being caught unprepared.

My doctor was very good during the labor, as well as right after delivery, about keeping me informed of exactly what was happening and what the risks were and what the choices were and what things he suggested. Later he spent a lot of time talking out some of the more philosophical and emotional issues about a kid hooked up to machines. He was very open, direct, and supportive.

—Sophie

My OB was open and sincere. He was sad too, and that was very helpful. When he came in the second night—he had just gotten back from seeing the baby at the hospital—he came in and flopped down on a chair and just buried his head in his hands, and he said, "You know, I don't know what to tell you." I appreciated that he didn't come in with some big long dissertation on something. He just didn't know what to say, and that honesty was so nice.

—Sara

I feel like no one was really geared towards dealing with a death. None of them would admit for a moment. I kept trying to find out how bad it was and my pediatrician talked to me at the hospital and she kept saying, "Things look bad," but she was the only person that would say it like that and try to help me get prepared for the worst. I think everybody else was denying it more than I was. I'm very angry that the other doctors were not honest with me.

—Liza

A compassionate health care practitioner also becomes a connection to the baby who died. Not only did they see and meet your baby, they affirmed your baby's importance. You may value an ongoing relationship with this caregiver and bear another loss if either of you has to move on.

When I realized my midwife only has a couple of visits before she moves on, my first thought was I wasn't ready to let go of Elizabetta again. In some ways my midwife is one of the few external connections to Elizabetta. So I made her a scarf from yarn I was given after Elizabetta was born; it felt like the perfect project for it. I also made a card just to thank her for her support through Elizabetta's and then Nico's birth and for listening and responding to me in such a way that I felt safe and trusted her. It felt nice to acknowledge her by giving her something connected to Elizabetta and when she got a bit teary, my heart swelled to know that part of her is connected to Elizabetta too.

—Karen

The benefits of compassionate, quality bereavement care are many, including reducing trauma, affirming the baby's importance, and providing cherished memories that can aid mourning. There are also long-term benefits that have been documented, including reduced anxiety and less grief during subsequent pregnancy.

IF HEALTH CARE PRACTITIONERS TURN AWAY

Parents are very impressionable after a baby dies. If your doctors and nurses treated you as if your baby's death was insignificant, you may come away wondering if they are right. If you were treated with aloofness or evasiveness, you may feel that you are not entitled to information. You may wonder if you did something wrong to make your doctors or nurses abrasive, too busy to listen, or too uncomfortable to share your grief.

My doctor was saying things like "products of conception" and "Be grateful that it happened early. You were hardly pregnant!" I couldn't believe what I was hearing. Hardly pregnant? My baby was dead and he was telling me this!

—Mariko

I saw my doctor just standing up against the wall, so I've always felt like there was some grief there, but she just couldn't share it with me. I've always felt like if she could've shared that, it would have been a little bit easier for me.

—Liz

You may have resented your doctor's cool, clinical attitude. Charles remembers, "It was my wife and my baby Kimberlie, and the doctors were looking at it as another fascinating case." Jessie recalls, "The doctor kept calling it 'fetal demise.' I felt like he had difficulty saying 'dead baby.' That really bothered me." Rayleen feels this clinical attitude undermined her dignity: "They come in and just do to you whatever they want and after a while your body is just theirs." A clinical attitude can also lead to treating the baby more like a specimen than a baby who deserves respectful care. Even though your baby isn't suffering, it's only natural that this matters to you.

I remember going back to the hospital, and my nurse friend took me to the room where they had put the baby and then left him there for a little while. That upset me so much, not that they'd done anything wrong, but that he'd been alone. I just kept thinking he was alone in there, the poor thing, and he was cold, and that upset me.

—Bess

Educating Practitioners about Your Needs

Unfortunately, some doctors, nurses, and midwives don't know how to support grieving parents. Comprehensive grief education is not routinely included in medical training, and death is not a regular feature of obstetric or pediatric practice. Just as parents may feel like failures after their baby dies, doctors, nurses, and midwives may also feel helpless. This mutual sense of failure can make parents and their caregivers feel awkward with each other.

Just as friends and family may take their cues from you, so may your practitioners. During postpartum visits, the doctor, nurse, or midwife cannot read your mind, but if you can explain your feelings, your concerns, and what you want, he or she may be responsive to your needs. If you feel like crying, cry. If you have questions, ask them. If you feel scared, talk about your fears. By being open, you can enlist their support and perhaps inspire them to support other grieving parents too.

If your main practitioner is unresponsive to your requests or if you do not feel comfortable with her or him, consider finding another one. Changing practitioners can feel like another loss, but you deserve a caregiver who is supportive, especially if you embark on another pregnancy.

Over the past few decades, bereavement care has changed substantially due to research *and* bereaved parents speaking up about what they want and need, especially around the time of their baby's death. The Internet has also provided a forum for bereaved parents and their advocates to push for quality bereavement care and greater social awareness about the support grieving mothers and fathers need.

As a bereaved parent yourself, if you are moved to do so, you can be part of this progress by discerning what you need and insisting on getting it or expressing in hindsight what would've helped you. Doing so might be part of your healing. Doing so also honors those outspoken parents who paved the way before you—and it paves an even wider, gentler path for those parents who will come after you.

POINTS TO REMEMBER

- Sensitivity and support from friends can help you cope with your grief and adjust to your baby's death.
- Some friendships will deepen, others will be lost, and new ones will form.
- Many people do not know how to be supportive because they are unfamiliar or uncomfortable with death and grief.
- If you are irritated by the cluelessness of others, it can reduce your suffering if you replace anger with compassion for the fact that they simply cannot understand.
- Friends often take their cues from you. Tell your friends what you need. True friends will appreciate your guidance.
- Attending a support group can help you feel less isolated and can reassure you that your feelings are normal and that you will feel better over time.
- However you make the connection, another bereaved parent can be a lifeline.
- Counseling can help you manage painful feelings and recover from trauma. There are many mind/body and brain-based therapies that can reduce reactivity to stress, alleviate unnecessary suffering, and boost healing.
- Health care practitioners can make a tremendous difference by offering you compassionate, individualized care. Having their support validates the significance of your baby and your grief.
- You can be part of the change you want to see by speaking up about the postpartum care you want and the kind of bereavement care you wish you'd had around the time of your baby's death.

14

Trying Again

*We had always wanted four children, and I think if I had stopped
there I would have felt like I had empty arms for the rest of my life.*
—Melanie

After a baby dies, many parents realize that they still want a child—or a
certain number of children—and that vision didn't die with their baby.
But as a bereaved parent you've lost your innocence. Your firsthand experience with tragedy teaches you that there are no guarantees. So even if
you yearn for another baby, you may feel anxious and uncertain. And it's
complicated, as there are a number of issues you will have to face along the
way, including the emotional decision of *whether* to try again for another
child, either by getting pregnant or adopting, and if so, deciding *when* to
try again. Either trying to conceive or starting the adoption process can
be fraught with anxiety. Furthermore, if you get pregnant, you will likely
want to make careful decisions about prenatal care and testing.

Should We Try Again?

*We saw the obstetrician six weeks after we lost Zac. I had been tested
for anything and everything and I had nothing that would predispose
me to having an abruption. I said to him, "I don't understand, how do
you go from three normal pregnancies to this?" He said we have just
experienced extraordinary bad luck. There was no rhyme or reason to
it and he was confident we could go on to have a healthy baby.*
—Melanie

*I cannot get it out of my mind that our family feels "incomplete,"
but of course this has been reinforced with Alex's birth and death.
Would I have felt like this without the birth and death of Alex?
After all, Tom was our miracle. We had waited for many years; the
complications—endometriosis, blocked tubes, an unsuccessful
attempt at IVF, and finally, wham bam, Tom was conceived. But both
Mathew and I have siblings and we talk fondly of our relationships
and especially our childhoods.*
—Victoria

One reaction to the death of a baby is to shy away from having more
children. The risks may be too much to bear. Especially if you have had a
number of losses, or if your age, health, or situation increases the chances

of complications, you may simply feel it is time to move in another direction with your life. And particularly if you already have one or more surviving children, you may decide to be content with that and throw in the towel.

After Emily died, seeing our boys with this friend's baby made me really think about having, or rather, trying for another baby. I thought, "They would have been so good with Emily." It made me sad, and I thought, "Maybe we could try." Then after Michael died, a lot of people are saying, "Just have another, it will help." Maybe it will. But maybe not. I just cannot think of this happening again. And I just count my blessings of these two boys that we have here.

—Anne

At the other extreme, you may yearn for the opportunity to have another baby, especially if you're just starting your family or you feel like it's incomplete. If you think it would help you cope with your grief, you may think about getting pregnant or starting the adoption process right away to fill the emptiness and ease your sorrow.

Many parents vacillate between these two extremes month to month, or even minute to minute. One day you claim, "NEVER AGAIN," and the next day you long to feel new life inside you or hold a new baby in your arms. You may be certain you want another baby, but you need to gather your courage before trying again. Or you may be uncertain, perhaps because the baby who died was "a surprise," or you'd planned on that being your last pregnancy, and yet now, your arms feel so empty. If you have to deal with the possible recurrence of a genetic defect, pregnancy complications, or infertility, or if you're looking at adoption, you may want more information before making a decision about future children. Whether you're considering another pregnancy or adoption, feelings of anxiety and hesitation are normal.

It was a really hard decision for us. We had to weigh up, could we go through the pain of it happening again, knowing what effect this would have on our family? Because the reality was it could happen to us again. We were no less likely than before to potentially have another stillborn baby. But for me personally, I didn't want to look back and regret not doing it because I was too scared. And it was the scariest and hardest thing I have ever done being pregnant again. But the reward far outweighed the potential loss.

—Melanie

Since Johanna's heart defect was genetic, the doctor thinks there is a 15 percent chance it will happen again, so we feel anxious about another pregnancy. We'll wait until we can focus on the 85 percent chance that it won't happen again.

—Kim

Testing showed that Ashley's condition was something that just happened by chance, she didn't inherit it from one of use. So the

chance that it would happen again was very, very low. It was scary to contemplate having another child after that, but we knew we had to try.
—Shellie

Perhaps I am scared that we will be turned down for adoption based on our experience and be judged. I need just a bit more patience and just let things unfold. Having said all this, I have told a handful of people and already I can see the support network that will be there with me. I can't help to bring up the subject as it brings excitement and happiness to my conversation, but I'll try and hold back a bit.
—Victoria

If you've experienced the agony of infertility, your decision is whether to keep trying or to instead get off the fertility treatment treadmill and essentially "stop trying." The decision to stop fertility treatments is one of uncertainty and letting go. But sometimes that does result in a baby, as Fleur can attest.

Fertility treatments are so invasive and take a huge toll on you mentally, physically, and emotionally. The losses are just another kick in the guts through the whole process. It was horrible. So, no more fertility treatments and if things happened naturally, then so be it. I honestly wasn't expecting to fall pregnant ever again, as I was forty, and after struggles with infertility the odds were not in my favor. Nature had the idea and threw that curveball at us.
—Fleur

If you've experienced a number of losses, you may wonder, "How many times can I go through this before giving up?" You needn't answer that unanswerable question. Just ask yourself whether you can do it *one more time*. Whatever that answer is, that's all you need to know.

About having babies, I feel like I'm not a pro, let me tell you! The thought of having another baby, trying again, scares the hell out of me. I guess I do feel like I'm not the best baby producer.
—Cindy

At the time a lot of people said to us they could not have done what we did. But I didn't feel very brave. I really felt like a failure. I had done nothing to cause these losses but it happened inside me so I blamed myself. Now I look back and I can appreciate how brave and courageous we really were to try again.
—Melanie

After Sam, it was an easy decision. I wanted to be a mom to a baby. I wanted to carry and birth a live child and it seemed like getting the fibroid removed would make that dream a possibility. Then after Oren was stillborn, it was a harder decision. Ultimately it came down to hope winning out over fear. Now, since Miriam died, I couldn't do this again. Three losses in five years was too much.
—Tanya

After Anne's first and then second subsequent baby died in the second trimester, she felt uncertain about trying again, but her husband Chris was adamant. "He said there is absolutely no way of us trying to get pregnant again. Even though in my heart I think he is right, it is still hard to bear and accept. I still have this small ounce of hope for something different." As hard as this decision was for her, almost a year later Anne reflects on her lingering ambivalence but also demonstrates a growing acceptance. If "no more" is your reluctant decision, you too will adjust in time.

> *With deciding to "not try" anymore, there are days that I am okay with it. I am happy. My life is good, and I just thank God for our two here, Matthew and Ryan. They fill me with so much life, and are so much fun. Recently I had a thought, "Could we try one more time and go through some of the suggested treatments of blood thinners and such?" I am turning thirty-seven in a few months. Or I have even thought, "What about adoption?" I think these are normal questions to consider if you have gone through recurrent pregnancy loss, and you are nearing forty.*
>
> *—Anne*

When Should We Try Again?

> *Especially given how much our older son was anticipating a baby and our hearts still longed for more children to hold, we started trying as soon as I was "medically released" to do so (six weeks after Jed).*
> *—Embry*

> *When our marriage felt like it was on better ground, we really wanted to get pregnant again.*
> *—Julie*

> *We both know we would like to give Adisyn a little brother or sister but we have not made any decisions about when. The idea terrifies me.*
> *—Emmerson*

Your Doctor's Advice

If your baby died during or shortly after your pregnancy, there are certain physical considerations that bear on the timing of another pregnancy. After an uncomplicated pregnancy and vaginal delivery, your doctor may advise waiting three to six months, enough time for the uterus to get back into shape so that it can sustain a healthy pregnancy. If you had a Cesarean delivery or complications during your pregnancy, your body may need more time to mend. Ask your doctor about your special needs for physical healing.

Aside from the physical healing, there is emotional healing. Many doctors and psychologists have speculated that after the death of a baby, parents may encounter difficulties relating to the subsequent child. The mother may be anxious and hesitate to bond during pregnancy, she may be overprotective, or she may treat the new baby as a replacement for the dead one. Because of these concerns, many doctors suggest a waiting period of six months to a year, so that the mother can "resolve her grief" before having another baby.

However, this view is changing as more evidence shows that "resolution of grief" is an unrealistic goal. Many mothers do not feel like they've come to terms with their baby's death for four or more years, and there is healing, but the grief never "resolves." In addition, after her baby dies, it seems only natural that the mother will feel anxious about another pregnancy; it is normal for her to want to protect her heart, and she'll be protective of her children. As for bonding problems and replacing the baby who died, these concerns have proven to be unfounded for healthy mothers. If anything, parents are especially attuned to bonding issues and acutely aware that no child can replace the baby who died. Finally, parents notice that having another baby can boost coping and emotional healing. So rather than telling parents to first heal their grief, it would be more helpful to acknowledge that by seeking another baby, they are actually striving toward healing and envisioning a brighter future. And if the parents encounter difficulties, they can be appropriately referred to emotional support, assistance, and coaching on effective parenting, just like any other parents. There are many keys to successful parenting.

Still, many doctors advise their patients to wait six to twelve months. Whatever the time period your doctor suggests, it may seem like an eternity. Jessie points out, "I didn't want to wait a year to start thinking about another baby. I had all this parenting energy and nowhere to direct it." On the other hand, if your doctor tells you to get pregnant right away, you may later resent it because, as Holly says, "It sounded as if, 'Let's just write this one off and move on.' I think it adds to the demeaning of the life that was."

DECIDING FOR YOURSELF

Most mothers agree that open-ended advice and information are more helpful than a prescribed number of months. With information, you can decide what is best for you as an individual. Deciding for yourself can also restore a sense of control that may have been shattered by your baby's death.

My doctor said to wait until I felt ready. He said, "They can tell you six months or a year, whatever, but you've got to tell yourself when you're ready because some people can't handle it right away, and some people have to get pregnant because they can't handle not having that baby." I was glad he said that because I feel that every person is different. Some people need that baby right then and they want to go right back into a pregnancy—I did at first. . . . And if they give you six months or a year, whatever, you figure like that's a timeline.

If you don't get pregnant after six months or after a year, whatever, something else is wrong. If they leave it up to you, it makes you feel like you can do something right.

—Martina

Waiting six months was something I decided for myself, and that made me feel good because that was one little place I could have control. It really seems like it should be an individual decision, because you know what is best.

—Liza

We knew we wanted our older daughter to have a living sibling. Since we started grieving several months before Ashley was even born, we talked about getting pregnant with another child just a few months after her birth. We didn't want the new sibling to be significantly younger than Claire.

—Shellie

They just encouraged us to start healing and putting some of the pieces back together, made themselves available to discuss things, and told us that when/if we decided to try again, they would monitor and support us closely due to the psychological and emotional effect Adisyn's death would have on us.

—Emmerson

As these mothers demonstrate, when to try again is not just a medical decision, it's also an emotional one. Deciding for yourself lets you take into consideration your own unique needs and feelings. You may want to contemplate the following questions before making decisions:

- Do you want to have all your children before you are thirty, thirty-five, forty years old?
- Do you want your baby to be close in age to your other children?
- Are you worried that it may take awhile to conceive, so you should get started soon?
- Do you feel that having another baby as soon as possible may help you cope with your grief and your emptiness?
- Do you need more time to heal physically?
- Do you need more time to research the cause of your baby's death?
- Do you need to find a supportive doctor or a specialist who can help you get answers?
- Do you feel that waiting a while may help you feel less anxious about the next pregnancy?
- Do you feel that waiting may help you to enjoy the new baby more, so you aren't grieving for one baby and preparing for another at the same time?
- Are you anticipating any big changes in your life—school, job, moving, relationships, other deaths and births in your family?
- How does your partner feel?

One important, universal consideration is avoiding the possibility of being pregnant during the same time of year and giving birth to your next baby around the first anniversary of your baby's death. It can be emotionally challenging to mark the passing of the same seasons and then try to celebrate the arrival of one child while in the throes of a milestone anniversary for the one who died. Because "3 + 9 = 12," many parents are glad they got pregnant *after* more than three months had passed. Even several years later, a synchronous pregnancy can be a challenge, as Abby can attest, though she figured out how to take this, her second subsequent pregnancy, in stride.

> I was pregnant at exactly the same time I was with our daughter Emma. It was amazing to think that three years ago I sat pregnant with her. I chose to let it be a beautiful connection between this baby and our girl in heaven, because let's be honest, at first I was terrified. And it was hard at times to be pregnant with the same seasonal timing as her. And, towards the end, I had days that were scarier than they probably should've been because I could recall what I was doing with my girl in January, three years earlier. Thankfully I am in a better place with my grief three years out but yes, it was still difficult. Much better, but challenging too.
>
> —Abby

GETTING PREGNANT SOON

Some mothers who get pregnant within six months of their baby's death are simply driven to have a baby. For them, the pregnancy can be a very anxious, grieving time, but a healing thing to do.

> I really felt that getting pregnant soon was what I needed. I was aware of what the problems could be, and it's just hard not to. It's not like you totally have control over it. You try to comply with what you know is best—just from a physical point of view, the chances of having a healthy baby are better if you give your body a certain period of time to recuperate. So I waited as long as I could [four months].
>
> —Hannah

For some mothers, the need to become pregnant is overwhelming. They find that being pregnant fairly soon helps them deal with their baby's death and erases the feeling of failure. Some mothers report a need to "prove I could do it." The advantages of getting pregnant soon include:

- having the feeling that you're moving on toward more hopeful, joyful times
- overcoming feelings of failure, wanting to be able to "do it right"
- overcoming feelings of anxiety about possible infertility
- overcoming some feelings of emptiness (while the new baby can't replace the baby who died, you want a baby in your arms)

- beating the biological clock
- having the new baby close in age to your older child

Many mothers recognize the emotional and physical disadvantages of getting pregnant or adopting so soon, but for some the advantages still outweigh the drawbacks. They may even find it difficult to use contraception because it feels so counterproductive.

If you decide to get pregnant before three to six months have passed, there may be people who disapprove. Your doctor and your friends may express concern about your physical or emotional recovery or how you would cope with pregnancy complications or another death. But remember, it's not their decision to make. It's your recovery, your body, your heart, your pregnancy, your children, your life. It's also your decision.

> *It was okay except for the fear. It would've been a calmer pregnancy if I had waited at least a year. But then the aching for a baby overtook the fear. I wanted a baby, so forget the fear, we're having a baby!*
>
> —Cindy

> *I risked it, losing another baby at a time when I was already vulnerable. I thought I could handle it better than if I got over the grieving process, felt happy about my life, got pregnant, lost another baby. That terrified me more. I couldn't face that, whereas, I thought, "Okay, I'm at the bottom right now and I think I could handle this." I don't understand this advice about waiting a year. For me I think that would've been much worse.*
>
> —Bryn

WAITING TO GET PREGNANT

> *I was told it was best to wait anywhere from six months to a year. That all felt way too long for me. We decided to start trying again after three months. It took me seven months to get pregnant with Conner, and although it was hard month after month, I believe my body and my mind were not ready at three months to carry another child.*
>
> —Abby

Many mothers report waiting the minimum time before trying again, but they don't conceive until months later. Whether waiting was your plan or not, there are many advantages to waiting before another pregnancy, including:

- having more time to heal physically
- having more time to heal emotionally
- having time between the babies to help you appreciate their individuality and keep them more separate in your mind
- being less anxious during the pregnancy
- being able to enjoy the new baby more because you are grieving less

You may have your own special reasons for waiting a while. If you've had a string of losses, you may need a break, emotionally and physically. If you had physical complications during pregnancy, your body may need extra time to heal, increasing your chances for a healthy baby. There may be other changes in your life, and you want to feel more settled before you try again. Perhaps you have a surviving twin to care for. Perhaps you are a single mother without a steady partner.

Some mothers who try to get pregnant fairly soon end up waiting because infertility or early miscarriage postpones a successful pregnancy. Many mothers, like Abby above, concede that their bodies and minds may have needed more time to prepare for another pregnancy and another baby. Jessie and Holly finally had success after working through anger and periods of depression. Claudia notes, "When I accepted that my life is full even if I never have a child, then boom—I got pregnant." Hannah agrees: "I think your mind and body know to some extent when you're ready." Bess eventually had a baby a year and a half later, but feels "glad that it happened that way. By then I felt more positive about the future and carrying a new baby. She fit right in, and I could be happy about her."

Some mothers who get pregnant within six months wish they had waited a little while longer. They discover that grieving intensely, being pregnant, and then having a new baby is a confusing, unpleasant combination. Typical of these mothers, Sara admits, "It was just too close. It was all so blended—exhaustion, grief, hormones, being pregnant again, postpartum blues, everything. That first year was a nightmare, even after Gary was born, not knowing what was the cause for my tears that day. I was a mess."

But waiting can be very difficult. You may feel frustrated, in limbo, unable to move toward your goal of having a baby in your arms. Instead of waiting a prescribed number of months, you may want to consider your own physical and emotional needs and childbearing situation. Educate yourself about the advantages and disadvantages of postponing pregnancy and assess the situation each month. Ask yourself, "Is this the month we try to conceive?" You'll know when you're ready. Shellie remembers, "We felt emotionally ready, but nervous."

Remember, even if you wait more than six months or a year or more, having another baby can still have a healing impact.

When Partners Are on Different Timetables

*The decision to start trying was a really hard **and** easy choice to make. I felt that the decision was already made for me because I had always wanted two children and to have a small age gap. But I really needed to ask Nick whether or not he was winging to start trying again or if that was it for him. He was so different with his grief and that was the scariest bit of deciding to try again—whether Nick wanted to or not.*

—Courtney

It was probably a good six months before I craved to have children again, and my partner was keen from the beginning to give it another go as I think this was part of his way of dealing with what had happened.
—Kylie

We went back and forth about having another child. Cal wanted to get pregnant right away, and I said, "No, I'm not ready." And then by the time I was ready, we had reversed positions. He was saying, "Maybe we should wait six months or a year." So there was a lot of stress there.
—Sophie

Unfortunately, it is very common for partners to take turns feeling ready for another pregnancy. This is normal and usually an indication that as a couple, you need more time to gather up your courage. But this can be particularly exasperating if you, the mother, want to get pregnant and your partner doesn't. After all, you may think, "It's my body and *I'm* ready, so why not?" But because you will need each other's emotional support more than ever during a subsequent pregnancy, you are wise to be concerned that you are *both* ready before you take the leap.

But how can you convince your partner that it's okay to try again? You can't. Each of you has to convince your own self that it's okay. You can't *make* someone else ready. But if you're the one who's ready, here are some things you can do to help your cause:

- Instead of talking, try *listening*. By encouraging your partner to talk about feelings and fears, you may provide the support he or she needs to feel ready.
- It can be illuminating to discuss together the following questions: What is the worst thing that could happen? What is the best thing that could happen? What is the most likely thing that will happen? Any answer is valid and can give you insight on ways to support each other.
- For many couples, a main concern is for the mother's safety and well-being. Perhaps your doctor, midwife, or therapist could address some of these issues. Meeting with a genetics counselor may also offer necessary information. If the mother is feeling confident about her prospects, this can also be reassuring to her partner.
- Being patient can be most helpful. Pressure does little to make anyone adjust or work through things. By simply easing off, you may give your partner the space he or she needs to feel comfortable.
- Be aware that a common dynamic is to strike a balance in the relationship, such that the more obsessed you are with getting pregnant, the more your partner backs off. By reducing your obsession, you may enable your spouse to feel more open to

another pregnancy. But how can you stop dwelling on it? Unload your thoughts into a journal. Renew or set your sights on other interests. Tend to your tasks of mourning. Also recognize that new babies don't fix things—they make things more complicated. Another baby will not entirely fill the emptiness or banish the longing you feel. Alas, mourning is what brings you lasting peace and happiness.

When Dayani's diagnosis was confirmed and we were told she was not going to make it, I wanted to try again immediately but my husband did not. Then a couple of weeks after she passed away, my husband said we should try again whenever I was ready, I told him not anytime soon. So, we then decided to wait at least three months and if we felt in our hearts that we wanted to try again, we would. We also needed to be certain that a new baby is not a replacement, rather a sibling to my two children. So we waited, and at the three-month mark we both felt strongly about trying again, so we did.

—Destrida

CAN WE GET PREGNANT?

Chris and I prayed, but also kind of "jumped" off a cliff, holding hands, eyes half-shut. Maybe even all the way shut. And we got pregnant.

—Anne

I wanted to get pregnant straightaway, but I think that my mind and body were not ready, even though at the time I thought I was. It was after his first anniversary that I finally conceived.

—Lorna

Once you decide to start trying again, you may feel hopeful because you are doing something positive and moving forward. You may feel as though you are regaining some purpose in your life. You may feel closer to your partner.

Trying again can also be a frustrating, infuriating, and anxious time. Especially if it doesn't happen right away, you may feel obsessed with trying to get pregnant, knowing that a baby could fill some of the emptiness you feel. You may feel anxious as you know you're embarking on another journey that might be fraught with danger. You may feel sad because you know that this baby will not be the baby you're longing for. You may feel angry that you have to do this again. As Jessie recalls, "I felt like I'd put in my time being pregnant and I just wanted the baby." You may worry that if you get pregnant, you'll wish you had waited a little longer out of loyalty to your baby or out of fear that you're not ready to love another baby as much.

I vaguely remember crying after sex the first time we had officially started "trying" as I was so scared of pregnancy happening again and the anxiety starting.

—Courtney

If you are struggling with infertility, your grief and anxiety can be intensified by the invasive procedures, mechanical timing of sex, and disappointment month after month. Even if you are normally fertile, you may worry if you don't get pregnant after a couple of months. Shellie recalls, "It was tough waiting once we made the decision, as we didn't get pregnant right away."

The monthly thing of finding out you're not pregnant is a grief every month. After Heidi died, the first miscarriage set me back. Then the second miscarriage and D&C—that was like the final blow. That whole invasion of my body . . . that was probably the height of my depression, because I was still grieving over Heidi and frustrated about getting pregnant.

—Holly

It took me over a year to get pregnant after Ronin's death. I did not want a baby to replace Ronin, but having something that was so wanted taken away from me was difficult to move on from. I got to the point where I thought it was never going to happen for me, and that my one chance of having a baby was gone.

—Lorna

Trying again can be especially difficult for parents who have lost one or more of twins, triplets, quads, or quints. There is something special about raising two or more children who were conceived and born together. You may feel as if you have blown an incredible once-in-a-lifetime opportunity, as the likelihood of conceiving another multiple pregnancy can be slim. When a subsequent pregnancy is not a multiple one, you may feel added disappointment.

There's not even the illusion that the score has somehow been evened. . . . You don't get to say, "Well, I'll really grieve and then get pregnant with my subsequent twins."

—Jackie

Losing twins really bothered me more than any other loss. It bothers me just to read about twins or see them. It hurts to think about twins. I had them fixed in my mind as something special. It's something I really wanted. A lot of people think that would be too much work to have two, but I think it would be fun. I always thought it would be fun.

—Peg

Can we get pregnant? Even when the answer is yes, as you know, there are no guarantees. Perhaps a more pertinent question is, *Can we have a healthy baby that survives infancy?* Unfortunately, some parents must endure more heartache before they get to hold another healthy baby in their arms. It can take an enormous amount of courage to try yet again. Understandably, some parents decide to adjust their dreams, some turning to adoption.

All I wanted to have is a bigger family than just one child. Whilst in hospital for ten days after my operation, I mentioned this to my best friend Rose who came to visit me. She planted the seed and very clearly and honestly said, "You can have a bigger family with adoption." Although my mind has been consumed this past year with the "what went wrongs" and the "ifs and buts," that seed of adoption has remained. Despite having many questions and naturally some doubts on adoption, I am still well aware I'm swimming in the shallow end of that large swimming pool. I believe that one day, I will turn this tragedy into a positive experience.

—Victoria

If you do decide to add another child to your family, however you go about it, your parenting journey will unfold naturally, as it should, without anyone needing to force it along prematurely. As always, it helps to accept what is, breathe deeply, trust the process, and take one day at a time.

CONSIDERING ADOPTION

After losing two children to me developing preeclampsia, we have decided that adoption is the best path for us. We have lost our children, but we have not lost our hope for family.

—Sonya

If you know you want another child but cannot get pregnant or don't want to risk it, this is another grief for you to bear. If adoption is a serious consideration, your questions become, "Should we?" and if so, "How?" and "When?"

One aspect about adoption is that you have little control over the timing. It's not like you start the paperwork and, nine months later, you have a newborn in your arms. And if you're wanting to start the adoption process sooner rather than later, be aware that you may well face questions about your grief and recovery, and assessments as to whether enough time has passed for you to have the ability and emotional resources to invest in your next child.

You might feel especially concerned about how your story of bereavement and longing will be received. Indeed, social workers have some experience working with bereaved parents who want to adopt, and what they look for during assessment is that parents have acknowledged their grief and are dealing with it, and that it will not block their bonding with an adopted child. Victoria worried about this part of the assessment, but over time felt resolved that her heart was in the right place, and because of Alex, she knew she had even more love to give. In fact, many social workers know that bereaved parents identify with the grief the birth mother feels when relinquishing a child, and this empathy enriches the adoption process.

Another challenge might be that you are keenly aware that if it weren't for the baby who died and your own fertility, genetic, or pregnancy complications, you wouldn't even be pursuing adoption. For you, adoption isn't a noble gesture or a sign of altruism, but a way to add a child to your family. And even though you are making a real difference in a child's life, you realize that you're also asking this child to make a real difference in yours. Rest assured, this careful consideration is a great quality in an adoptive parent.

> *My husband and I are going to an "adoption open day," so that in the future, we will expand our family in another way. And give love and help another child in a lost situation. We can surely relate to that— to turn tragedy into something positive. After all, Alex would want that. And he or she is not Alex—he or she will enter our family as an individual, and so we can give that further love to another child.*
>
> *—Victoria*

Because adoption often takes longer than pregnancy, you may feel impatient, but you may reap the benefit of more time passing and the attendant emotional recovery. The adoption journey unfolds as it should, and you can choose to trust the process.

> *I think we'll let the process "unfold" as for sure this has helped me in my grieving process. "Unfolding" is a beautiful word, since I can visualize a flower's petals unfolding in the early morning sun. So, I shall do just that.*
>
> *—Victoria*

Four years later, after their adoption was completed Victoria noted, "It has been a real long process, but for us, the timing has been right." (For more on this process, see "Adoption and Bonding" in chapter 16.)

Prenatal Care for Subsequent Pregnancy

Collaborating with Your Health Care Practitioners

If you're lucky, you have a doctor or midwife who treated you with special care and compassion when your baby died. If so, you'll likely prefer to stay with that practitioner for your subsequent pregnancies, as you know you can count on her or him to listen and be responsive to your needs.

> *The midwife is aware and very sympathetic. I had her while pregnant with Elizabetta and felt it was better to have her again than to try explaining to someone different.*
>
> *—Karen*

> *I love my obstetrician. She wasn't Emma's main doctor but came in to meet her when she died. And then from there on she became my person. I could call her and ask her anything and I thank my lucky stars for her! She gets it and never makes me feel crazy for my questions or when I need to come in to hear the heartbeat.*
>
> *—Abby*

If you're not so lucky, you might have health care practitioners who want to shift focus to the future and dim the past. They may simply encourage you to put aside your worries and be optimistic, as if that was easy or would help the outcome. They may try to avoid the topic altogether, being uncomfortable with your tears and the intensity of your feelings. There may be times during this pregnancy that *you* might even feel uncomfortable with your feelings.

Remember, it is still normal for you to think about your baby who died. Even as you carry new life, you may long for your other baby, the "right" baby. Holding on to your memories is how you say goodbye and gradually let go. Grieving is what frees you to enjoy and bond with your new baby.

It is also normal for you to be anxious. To get the reassurance you need, you may want more monitoring than usual. It is natural to want to hear the heartbeat, check your progress, and pay more attention to details. And yet, you may be worried about imposing on the nurses, midwives, and genetic counselors with incessant calls, interrogations, and requests. It can help to remember that *tending to your special needs is their job.*

> *My doctor knows me well enough to know I need to talk things through and have her explain everything to me! That's how she puts me at ease. Just listening and explaining what's going on!*
>
> *—Abby*

> *With Michael, I asked so many questions prior to and during the pregnancy. I went to many, many doctor appointments to try and find a reason as to why Emily died and what I could do differently.*
>
> *—Anne*

If you're worried about being accommodated, you may wonder how you can ask all those questions and make all those demands without alienating everyone. How can you talk about your feelings without raising eyebrows? How can you get the reassurance you need during this trying time?

Here are some ideas for collaborating with your doctor or midwife during your subsequent pregnancy:

- Don't apologize for how you feel. Whatever you are feeling, it's right for you and you needn't change or deny your feelings to please anyone.
- Surround yourself with emotional support. Get in touch with other moms going through a subsequent pregnancy. See a counselor. Keep a journal. All of these measures can alleviate the pressure for your doctor or midwife to be your therapist too. (See also "Mindful Journaling" in chapter 4; "Counseling" in chapter 13; "Support Groups" in chapter 15.)
- Try to empathize with your medical practitioners. Remember, your relationship may feel more complicated to them. You are

a *bereaved parent*, not just another patient. Most pregnant women and their partners are blissfully naive and excited. Not you.

- Have realistic expectations. No doctor or midwife is perfect. Work with one who is "compassionate enough" and willing to collaborate with you.

- Don't expect your medical practitioners to read your mind. Go ahead and ask for what you want. Do you want reassurance? Do you want information? Do you have concerns and feelings you want to discuss? Do you want longer visits? More visits, more tests, *fewer* tests? Talk about *what you want* rather than what they "should" do. By telling them what you want, you'll inspire and encourage their accommodation of you, rather than putting them on the defensive. (See also "Educating Practitioners about Your Needs" in chapter 13.)

- Your health care practitioners can't read your body either. *If you are concerned about any symptoms or sensations, you must let them know that your condition feels worrisome and request fetal monitoring or other exams to get answers or reassurance.* (See also "Home Monitoring" later in this chapter.)

- If you can, make appointments in the practice with those you find supportive. You don't have to "get to know them all." And at the birth, should you get the doctor with the unpolished bedside manner, it won't matter much as you can make sure you are surrounded by other supportive advocates as part of your birth plan. (See also "Taking Action" in chapter 15.)

You deserve to have a compassionate doctor or midwife who attends to your anxieties, respects your feelings, and works with you to have a healthy baby. If your concerns are brushed aside, you may feel more worried or angry and less in control. A dedicated caregiver should be willing to accommodate your needs and wants, thus showing a commitment to you and your baby.

Rayleen recalls, "When the twenty-seventh week came along, I was just really bothered. My doctor said I could come in every week, every day if I had to. That helped." If complications arise during this pregnancy, you will be especially anxious and want additional care and reassurance. In Peg's case, her doctor's extra attention helped her to comfort herself and feel more confident:

When I was about thirty or thirty-two weeks pregnant with Justin, I started bleeding and I was a basket case. At that time they had already put in a cerclage [to keep the cervix closed] and I was taking medication [to stop contractions]. I remember I had a doctor's appointment that day, and I was getting ready to go and I started

*bleeding and I thought, "Okay, take a deep breath, calm down. . . .
You're farther along than you've ever been before, so even if something
happens, you're going to have this baby." And I went to thirty-eight
weeks with him.*

—*Peg*

*I had a wonderful relationship with my doctor and I went in often. She
was so gracious with her time and towards the end when I wanted to
come in weekly, then twice a week, she didn't even blink an eye, she
just made it happen.*

—*Abby*

*Doctors listening to mothers' concerns during pregnancy would be
so empowering to the moms who have a feeling something isn't right.
The mystical bond between a mother and child is so amazing and
should be taken very seriously.*

—*Laura*

If you're worried about being an imposition on your doctor or midwife,
remember that obstetric practitioners generally like working with mothers
who are eager to have the healthiest pregnancy possible. As Anne says,
"The thought of taking medicine other than vitamins created some fear
inside of me. But if a doctor said, 'Take this,' I would have."

Prenatal Testing

In this age of advanced medical technology, we often assume that the more
technology we employ, the better the outcome. With prenatal care, however,
it is important to differentiate between tests. There are tests that identify
treatable problems in the pregnancy and check the mother's and baby's
vital signs. And then there are tests that identify untreatable genetic and
developmental problems in the baby. Certainly, a test is useful when there
are remedies or actions to take if a problem is discovered. But if there isn't
anything that can or will be done, then you might consider the test useless,
even detrimental, especially if such tests rake up your anxiety. Courtney
recalls, "I'd had a rough week and my anxiety was in overdrive for the
upcoming scan at twenty weeks. I was so paranoid that something would
be wrong. I was an emotional wreck." Tanya agrees, "I hate ultrasounds.
They always show me that my babies have died."

*Once I was so anxious before a scan, I threw up in the toilet.
Thankfully the sonographer knew our history, and as soon as she
started scanning she would say something about the heartbeat.*

—*Melanie*

The most valuable tests are the ones that can make a difference to your
baby's health. They examine aspects of the mother's or baby's condition that
may be remedied if problems are spotted. Examples of valuable maternal
testing include screening for or diagnosing preeclampsia, preterm labor,

gestational diabetes, or infection. For the baby during the final weeks of pregnancy, there are tests that monitor fetal heart rate during movement or contractions, measure amniotic fluid volume, and detect the position of the baby and placenta. If problems are discovered, solutions might include bed rest, diet, medication, induction of labor, or Cesarean birth.

Your doctor or midwife may offer you a number of other tests, which are not required to ensure a healthy pregnancy and do nothing to improve the baby's health. These tests are available for parents who want detailed information about the baby. Prenatal *screening* tests detect risk factors and indicators of potential genetic or developmental problems in the baby. Prenatal *diagnostic* tests diagnose these problems, either confirming or refuting the initial screening results. Unfortunately, with current technology, getting a closer look at the baby's chromosomes or the organ and skeletal development isn't going to lead to prenatal repairs for these problems. In addition, jumping through the hoops of testing does not guarantee that your baby will be fine. These tests are meant to look for a handful of anomalies, but are not foolproof and cannot identify or rule out many other problems. Most important, these tests do not prevent certain problems; they merely identify them.

Another disadvantage to prenatal testing is that too often, it doesn't provide the reassurance parents are looking for. Even slightly abnormal development can be detected, and will be reported to you even though "abnormal" doesn't necessarily indicate that anything is seriously wrong. Your baby may simply be developing faster or slower than average, or in a position that makes for difficult viewing. However, less than perfect results can be alarming.

Even more alarming, unfortunately, screening results sometimes indicate the possibility of a problem *even though no problem exists.* Needless to say, you don't need the added and unnecessary anxiety produced by false alarms! You also don't want to unnecessarily expose your baby to the risks of invasive follow-up diagnostic tests.

> *Prenatal screening with Conner was reassuring but with this [second subsequent] pregnancy, I've had two big ultrasounds so far because this baby's kidneys were slightly enlarged at twenty weeks. As if I needed something else to fear. I thought the umbilical cord was enough! I'll go back at thirty-two weeks but they think the kidneys will correct themselves. So with this babe, screening will be reassuring too, but the kidney issue threw me for a loop.*
> —Abby

In spite of the disadvantages, there are some advantages to prenatal screening and diagnostic testing. If the results come back "normal," this can quell some of your anxiety. If you carry genetic risk factors, you might want to know if they can be ruled out. If you know that you would terminate a pregnancy after receiving "abnormal" results, this is another reason to consider testing. And parents who find out their baby has a life-limiting condition and decide to continue the pregnancy are grateful that testing provided them with knowing that they need to make the best of what little time they have with their baby, both during the pregnancy and shortly after the birth. Being emotionally prepared and able to make meaningful plans make this period a "gift of time." The alternative is a shocking, confusing, traumatic time after birth, and not being able to just love on the baby. *But,* as an experienced bereaved parent, you already know that there are no guarantees. You don't need diagnostic testing for you to mindfully consider this pregnancy "a gift of time" and think through how you would deal with difficult medical decisions and end-of-life care. If you've already experienced perinatal hospice, you already understand the advantages of comfort care.

Whether to do prenatal testing on your baby is a personal choice. Your decision may be simple and straightforward, or belabored and complicated as you try to find the right balance between technology and letting nature take its course. Even if it is highly recommended in your case, you can still decide against it. Even if you have zero risk factors, you can still decide to do it.

Your decision will be based on many things, including:
- your personal experiences with infertility and previous pregnancies
- the probabilities of and kinds of genetic risks you hold
- your desire to be reassured or forewarned about possible problems
- your beliefs about disability and suffering
- your beliefs about and willingness to terminate a pregnancy
- how your partner feels
- whether you have surviving children to care for
- your gut feelings
- your faith in science or Mother Nature or a higher order

Answers to the following questions can also help you decide:
- How high is your risk for having a baby with birth defects?
- What will each test try to detect?
- When and how are they done? Are there risks to either mother or baby?
- What are the advantages and disadvantages to having each test?
- If a screening test indicates potential problems, what diagnostic tests will be recommended?
- How much will each test cost?
- Do you have access to experienced specialists who can perform the tests and interpret the results?
- How do the probabilities compare? (Balance the chance that your baby has problems against the chance that problems will be caused by testing procedures.)
- Are there noninvasive, risk-free ways to get similar information?
- How long does it take to get results?

- How reliable or accurate are the results?
- How will you use the information?
- What steps follow an abnormal finding or result?
- Would you change course if problems were discovered?
- Which feels better to you: doing prenatal testing or forgoing it?

You may decide that screening or diagnostic testing is a way to get some peace of mind, maybe even a glimmer of hope. If your deceased baby had a genetic condition or birth defects, you may want to test for possible recurrence. As Janice points out, "At least we could rule out some things, even if we couldn't rule out everything."

The twelve-week checkup went well. Everything looked fine. We even got to see the baby moving on the screen which was a big relief! I got emotional during the ultrasound but it was expected, I think.
—Destrida

Many mothers find prenatal testing reassuring, while others find it invasive and nerve-racking. Waiting for test results is always anxiety-provoking and can seem endless, especially when one test begets another. When you're trying to carry a baby to term, it can be distressing just to contemplate the possibility of taking a sample of placental tissue or amniotic fluid and inviting the risk of miscarriage. And, heaven forbid, if screening results do call for invasive diagnostics, you'll have to decide whether to perform risky tests, or just live with the initial screening and hope the disconcerting results are false or meaningless.

Even if state-of-the-art procedures bear no risks, when you are struggling to be optimistic, testing can rake up fears and undermine already shaky feelings of confidence. Examinations themselves can prompt flashbacks and flood you with memories of the previous pregnancy and the baby who died. A focus on testing can also exacerbate the common hesitation to bond with the new baby.

Needless to say, the ensuing pregnancy was wrought with anxiety and concerns. Each day was fighting off fears of malformations, waiting for the amniocentesis's verdict, then waiting for the morphological scan, since other fellow mothers had passed the amniocentesis only to find their children with heart malformations or missing the cerebellum or other vital organs. Each day was a hurdle. I tried not to bond with the baby I was carrying. I tried not to think about him too much. One day at a time. My goal was to pass each "test," each scan, each blood test, amniocentesis, etc., from one exam to another, like in a video game, moving on to the next screen, next level of difficulty.
—Annalaura

If you're leaning away from prenatal testing, you may also feel fatalistic—that this baby's fate is already sealed and there isn't anything you can or should do about it. As Terri points out, "I figure I'm going to have the babies I'm meant to have. And I'm terrified at the thought of inaccurate results and terminating a normal baby." Winnie concurs, "I just figured I'd hope for the best and accept the rest." You may simply want to avoid having to make any decisions that come with unfavorable results.

It may also make more sense to you to simply do the prenatal tests that check the health of the pregnancy and the mother's and baby's vital signs. Winnie says, "Looking back, it helped that I had an intuitive sense that this baby was fine. I was far more worried about my body letting her down."

You can also consider doing some basic screening and no more. If you have miscarried a baby in the first trimester, an early ultrasound might be all the reassurance you need. It may feel just right to see the heartbeat and then coast the rest of the pregnancy. If you want more information about the baby but hesitate taking samples from your womb, it is reasonable to go ahead with just maternal blood tests and high-level ultrasound, which are less invasive and may offer some reassurance. If any low-level exams lead to concerns, then you can choose whether to go on with more high-level testing.

If you decide to forgo some or all prenatal testing, talk to your doctor or midwife about avoiding unnecessary exams. Ask them to support you and your efforts to focus on having a healthy pregnancy, which can be a better way to foster your hopes. If your health care practitioners are pressuring you or offering testing as if it's required, they are only trying to provide you with the most sophisticated technology. You should be able to discuss your concerns and politely refuse without ruining your relationship. After all, they want what's best for you and your baby. And what's best is for you to decide.

> I've never done prenatal diagnostic testing before. I've always felt uneasy about being faced with a life-ending decision, so would rather not be put in a situation where I would have to make a choice. I'm also hesitant to have an amnio done, which might threaten a pregnancy and I'd need to have one to confirm a diagnosis, so I would rather not. I only considered it this time because of my age (forty-three) and because I thought it might make me feel more accepting of this pregnancy if I knew the risks were low. I was pleased that the OB could see that it would just cause me concern and advised me not to do it.
>
> —Karen

> At thirty-eight years old I knew about the risks of "advanced maternal age." As a midwife I knew all about genetic testing and ultrasounds. I decided not to have any prenatal testing. I did not want to spend the pregnancy worrying about something suspicious that might be unclear on an ultrasound, or the percentage of a chance that my baby might have an anomaly.
>
> —Tanya

I felt like testing promoted the assumption that there were problems that had to be uncovered or ruled out. I just wanted to assume that this baby would be fine. To encourage myself, I'd remember that women have been having healthy babies for centuries without prenatal testing and kick charts to guide their pregnancies along!
—Winnie

HOME MONITORING

There are basically two kinds of monitoring that you can do yourself, at home: noting the baby's movements and listening to the heartbeat. Movements and heartbeat are primary indicators of the baby's well-being in utero.

I remember getting scared, thinking she hasn't moved, and I was counting time on the clock. I would count the hours. I'd lay down real still and see if the baby would kick. I remember holding my belly, holding my baby there, and I would talk to her and I just was very hopeful that things would be okay with her.
—Bryn

A common form of noting the baby's movements is keeping a "kick chart," where the mother looks for a certain number of kicks in a specified period of time, typically ten kicks in two hours. The problem with this system is that babies vary widely as individuals, and at different times, plus mothers can find it hard to know what qualifies as a kick. And sometimes they have to wake up the baby in order to count them. So keeping a kick chart can become yet another source of anxiety, along the lines of unnecessary prenatal testing.

Newer research shows it's far more productive to look for significant changes in the *quality*, not quantity, of the baby's activity pattern. In this system, obstetric caregivers ask the mother to note, keep track of, and describe her baby's typical movements and patterns, *and* trust her perception and judgment. Not only does this spur the mother to get to know her baby in utero, it creates a collaborative partnership between patient and practitioner, and lets the mother know that if she is concerned about a change she notices, she can go straight to the hospital. Getting prompt medical attention might not necessarily avert tragedy, but when the mother's judgment is trusted and she's encouraged to seek care, this eliminates the trauma of being distrusted and discouraged, and worrying about any hesitance or lack of assertiveness.

Here are some patterns of movement you can pay attention to:
- What times of day or night is your baby most active? Most quiet?
- Does your baby perk up or stay quiet when you're talking or surrounded by voices?
- Is your baby responsive to certain sounds or environmental noise?
- How does your baby respond to loud or sharp sounds? To music?

- Is your baby typically more active or less active during or following your engaging in certain activities?
- Is your baby responsive to certain foods or drink that you ingest?
- How would you describe the typical movements you feel? Jabs? Kicks? Rolls? Swishes? Flutters? Twirls? Kicks?

As you get to know your baby, you'll learn that he or she is perhaps a night owl or lark, laid back or bouncy, a social butterfly, a music lover, a dancer, or budding soccer player. This kind of assessment can enhance your feelings of connection and bonding.

Like kick charting, checking the baby's heartbeat is also controversial and perhaps inadvisable. Some mothers want to be able to hear their baby's heartbeat whenever they wish without having to go into the clinic or medical office. You can talk to your doctor or midwife about having home access to a medical instrument that will let you do this. But some mothers find that it only increases their anxiety as they become focused on *what if there's no heartbeat? I'd better check, because I can.* In this way, home monitoring merely feeds passive—and obsessive—worry. As a result, many doctors and midwives are reluctant to grant this request.

Also consider, what are the consequences if you tried to but couldn't hear the heartbeat? Are you risking unnecessary alarm? And if this baby were to die, would you be willing to discover, on your own, that there was no heartbeat?

> *A friend offered me a fetal Doppler, but I think I would spend the whole day checking for a heartbeat and it would be counterproductive.*
>
> —*Karen*

It can be far more productive—and active—for you be knowledgeable about pregnancy and stay tuned into your observations and intuition about this baby. Are you noticing troubling symptoms or changes in your body? Are you noticing changes in your baby's movement or feeling a sense of doom? If so, you're better off seeing your doctor or midwife rather than trying to make medical assessments yourself. If you can speak specifically about what you've observed or why you're concerned, you're less likely to be brushed off with, "Don't worry, everything is fine."

Also remember that hearing a good fetal heartbeat doesn't guarantee a healthy, live born baby. The heartbeat is but one small aspect of health and well-being. In fact, monitoring at home can provide a false sense of security, whereas you might be better off being observant and attuned, and seeking medical attention if you feel uncomfortable or notice changes.

However, in spite of the drawbacks, you may discern that you'll do better with home monitoring. You'll know it's beneficial if it truly helps you feel more calm, and if you are able to focus less, not more, on checking your baby's heartbeat. Still, it's even more important to have health care practitioners who listen, support you, and accommodate your needs for information, encouragement, and reassurance. For example, Jessie's doctor lent her a stethoscope so she could listen to the heartbeat whenever she wanted, but what she found most reassuring was how attentive and dedicated her doctor was.

I had the most fantastic midwife. She would come and see me at the drop of a hat. If I was worried or concerned in any way over anything she would come and put the heart monitor on for reassurance.

—Melanie

POINTS TO REMEMBER

- For many parents, the decision to try again is a difficult one.
- Give yourself a few months to think about the timing, even if you know you want to try again.
- In deciding when to get pregnant, there are many physical, emotional, and logistical factors to consider.
- There are advantages to waiting, and there are advantages to getting pregnant fairly soon. Weigh these advantages according to your unique situation and needs.
- When trying to get pregnant, you may feel anxious, angry, obsessed, ambivalent, sad, or mechanical, but many parents also feel more hopeful about the future.
- It is important to have a supportive doctor or midwife who is considerate of your anxieties and needs for attentive care.
- There are two kinds of prenatal tests: those that look for pregnancy problems that can be treated, making a difference to your baby's health; and those that look for genetic or developmental problems in the baby, for which there are no treatments.
- Whether to do prenatal testing on your baby is a personal decision. Some mothers find it reassuring; others find it invasive and nerve-racking.
- It is perfectly reasonable to forego some or all prenatal testing on your baby, and just focus your efforts on having a healthy pregnancy.
- There are two kinds of home monitoring: noting the baby's movement and listening to the heartbeat.
- Noting the quality of your baby's movements is better than just counting the number of kicks. Being able to listen to the heartbeat is not recommended for a number of reasons. Being observant, attuned to your body, and alert to any changes are far more important promoters of well-being.

15

Subsequent Pregnancy

It was completely different than my blissful pregnancy with Emma. I was terrified and so grateful, and dancing between those two emotions was a daily battle.

—Abby

Some days I thought, "I'm pregnant; the world is great!" Then other days I'd think, "I've already lost a baby. What if it happens again?"

—Cindy

When parents embark on another pregnancy, it is only natural that much of their focus will still be on the baby(s) who died—and hoping to avoid another tragedy. That focus involves anxious thoughts and complicated emotions, making for a complicated journey.

My brain is trying to protect my heart and I'm convinced that I will miscarry. It's interesting all the negative background noise my head is making. Why do I think I will get a baby? I don't deserve another. My body is older and all the statistics are stacked against me. I have six beautiful children in my home. I can't expect another. I'm almost convinced that I will be told I've suffered a missed miscarriage when I see my midwife next week. Oddly enough there is still a shred of hope, and I dare for brief moments to think ahead a little and pray and hope for the life inside me. At the moment I am learning a little about faith and trust and I will see how things go.

—Karen

To some extent, the journey is complicated for all subsequent pregnancies, not just the first one. In some ways it can be easier, as grief won't be so raw, so front and center. And if you are raising a healthy subsequent child, this can be a welcome distraction. But as Julie says, "Every pregnancy and birth brought it up again." And you may be as anxious as ever, especially around gestational milestones.

Because Emma's death was at forty weeks, the closer to term I got with both boys, the more scared I became. Each was hard. I wish I could say Jack being my third was easier, but he wasn't. I was scared.

—Abby

This emotional journey can include worry, hope, ambivalence, anger, courage, vulnerability, detachment, faith, sorrow, and distrust.

By simply accepting that it is what it is, you can reduce your suffering. Accept that the more traumatic the circumstances around your baby's death, the more emotions will be triggered. If you are struggling, you—and your new baby—deserve to get the compassionate care and medical attentiveness you need. Subsequent pregnancy will never be smooth or carefree, but you can try to make it as smooth and calm as it can be. (See also chapter 4, "Mindfulness-Based Coping Strategies"; "Counseling" in chapter 13.)

> *A doctor who gets the emotional aspect of all this is vital! I just went in two weeks ago terrified, and she made me feel completely at ease. I truly cannot imagine going through this without her.*
>
> —*Abby*

> *The sonographer was lovely, talking us through parts of the anatomy and commenting on how cute the baby seemed and joking about how it was being stubborn and not moving into a good position. I started crying when we saw images of the baby's brain, as there is a question whether or not Elizabetta's brain had developed, if at all. It was the first time that I allowed myself to believe we might get a baby, and I was surprised with how much it hurt but felt freeing at the same time.*
>
> —*Karen*

FEELING VULNERABLE

> *That pregnancy was extremely hard because I felt very vulnerable until the day I was induced. I walked through the entire pregnancy trying not to be overwhelmed with fear.*
>
> —*Embry*

> *I was so anxious that Owain would die too, if not at birth, from something else. I would be up in the night counting down how many weeks, days until he would be here, hoping that I would wake up in the morning and that it would be January and not September. It felt like the time dragged so much that I would never make it through.*
>
> —*Lorna*

Having a baby die, especially during pregnancy or shortly after birth, will probably color your experience with subsequent pregnancies, making you more anxious that something could go wrong. You don't just have abstract knowledge that babies can die. You can't hide under the assumption that it won't happen to you. It *has* happened to you, and while the chance of it happening again may be remote, you *know* it is a possibility.

> *It was scary to be pregnant again. When our older daughter Claire was born healthy, we expected it and took it for granted that this is always how it happens. Now we knew better. We were fairly confident that this wouldn't happen again, but now we weren't living in the world of "ignorant bliss." We knew that something else could*

*go wrong. Until that baby was born and put into my arms I didn't
completely believe it would be okay.*

—*Shellie*

If you don't have any living children, death is all you know. You may
feel you simply cannot expect a pregnancy to result in a baby that will
survive. Holly recalls, "All through my pregnancy I thought, 'Yes, I am
pregnant, but I don't feel like I'm going to bring anything home from the
hospital.'" Abby agrees, "I wasn't sure I could have a living baby. I had
so many doubts about my body or my ability to know if something was
wrong. So I was a basket case day in and day out."

You may feel angry or disappointed that you can't have that innocence
back and enjoy a blissful pregnancy. You may wish that you could relax,
but you can't totally ignore what happened before. You may even resist
sharing the news in order to dodge people's naive expectations. Karen says,
"I'm actually fearful of telling people because of the word *congratulations*
and having to respond positively when I don't want to. I need to start
practicing a polite *thank you* instead of struggling to hold back what my
brain wants to say."

Feeling vulnerable can be difficult to cope with. You may feel uneasy
because you know that even if you take good care of yourself—or the
pregnant mother—and your baby, death can still happen. The mother's
partner may also be worried about her health or life.

*My husband was there for me 100 percent. He doted on me, fixed
my meals, and ran all the errands. Overall, he was excited about me
being pregnant again, but he was also very quiet and reserved about
the pregnancy. He was so scared for not only our child's life but also
my life. He almost lost me during Blake's pregnancy, and he was
scared about this pregnancy too.*

—*Sonya*

Although you can remind yourself that the vast majority of outcomes
are normal and healthy, the statistical probabilities may offer little comfort.
After all, you "beat the odds" when your baby died. While intellectually
you know everything is likely to turn out fine, it can be difficult to convince
yourself *emotionally*. While you may be certain that others will have healthy
babies, you may feel sure that you won't. Knowing you have so little control
over the outcome, you have no choice but to feel vulnerable. As Martina
says, "Nothing is guaranteed. You've just gotta go one day at a time. After
you lose one, it's so hard." (See also "Vulnerability" in chapter 7.)

*I'm having difficulty separating the information I have about this baby
and my previous experiences. I'm not sure they can be seen as
separate entities, but the obstetrician does, so they think I should be
fine. They see the numbers. I see and feel the experiences, the worry
over low blood sugars, the extra monitoring, the breathing difficulties.
I already have huge emotional investment in this baby (despite my*

brain's attempts to ignore it) so I will move heaven and earth to make
sure my heart is protected. Just this time it's a little out of my control.
—Karen

*As a pregnant woman **prior** to experiencing a loss, I was quick to*
calm myself or say everything was okay. I would tell myself "women
have been having babies for thousands of years." After a loss, none
of that matters anymore.
—Abby

Your sense of vulnerability can also contribute to an ongoing animosity toward women who are pregnant or have new babies. Your resentment can feel crazy making, yet it is a common and complex reaction that makes sense.

I kind of hate how I feel around other pregnant women. I still
feel bitter around them—and that, in turn, makes me feel insane
because I am pregnant myself! Why is it so hard for me to be happy
for other mothers who are also pregnant? It is even more difficult to
see women, whom I am close with, being pregnant and having new
babies. I guess maybe it could be because I still feel "ripped off"
in combination with the underlying fear that maybe I won't get to
take this baby home from the hospital either. Maybe it is some sort
of defense mechanism, shielding me from being happy for others
until I know for sure I can be happy for myself. I really don't like it.
It makes me feel very irrational and selfish. I want to feel happy for
other expecting mothers and new mothers, but it is like the second
I see them or see a picture on Facebook, that good intention goes
out the window.
—Jolie

High Anxiety

Everyone says it was a freak thing with Beau and it won't happen
again, but the reality was I thought I was fine. I'd done everything right
and then four weeks before I was due to give birth, this happened!
—Courtney

All of those legitimate worries for an expecting mother, they have been
replaced by the worry that I might have to give this baby back as well.
—Jolie

It's going to be a long road but I refuse to let fear win over me. It's my
fear and I can control it, right? I really need to find a calm place to
just be, but it's a bit hard.
—Karen

Anxiety is *normal* during pregnancy, and essentially unavoidable for parents who've experienced the death of a baby. As such, rather than feeling bad about it or trying to get rid of it, which is impossible anyway, accept it as a natural and common result of being a bereaved parent. Just by accepting anxiety as part of subsequent pregnancy, you can actually decrease your suffering. Abby matter-of-factly remarks, "If I'm scared, I'm scared and that's okay. And if I need the advice of a nurse or doctor, I seek it."

Still, you may wish you could stop worrying, and others might reinforce the idea that you should just control your fear and focus on hope. In fact, it's only natural to try to control, ignore, or fight your fears. But controlling your fear is not an effective coping strategy, as it merely focuses your mind on your worries, and you essentially create *more* fear by being afraid of your fear. Likewise, if you try to ignore or control your anxiety, you're essentially creating more anxiety by getting anxious about it. This is how panic attacks and vicious cycles of worry are made. And trying to *not* be anxious and fearful also backfires by making your brain more reactive, which means you can't help but focus even more on what worries you. Karen noticed this when she remarked, "I know there is a risk of losing this baby and I refuse to entertain that thought, yet it is the one that most consumes me."

> *I know my underlying anxiety levels are reasonably high, as I just want to disengage from people and my tolerance for things is quite diminished. Right now I feel like I don't want and can't cope with having a baby and wish I could snap my fingers and not be pregnant (but not lose the baby).*
>
> —Karen

> *If anything I have become more scared as time goes on, just constantly monitoring this babe's movement. The fragility of life terrifies me. These little beings are such miracles and knowing something could go wrong that is out of my control makes it hard to relax.*
>
> —Abby

> *This was incredibly hard. For most of the pregnancy I could just get through the day and no more.*
>
> —Melanie

In fact, as much as you'd like to be in control, fear, worry, and anxiety are not under your conscious control. Your reactive core brain is reacting to what your emotional core brain believes or perceives as being a threat—including your thinking brain's thoughts about being doomed.

Understandably, many bereaved parents consider simply being pregnant as a threat. Other commonly perceived threats include prenatal tests—particularly ultrasounds—and being in the same exam room, labor room, or hospital. Even getting pregnant at the same time of year and reaching each pregnancy milestone during the same season can be unnerving, as you really *need* this experience to be so very different. In fact, creating and focusing on the differences can foster hope. Holly says, "I had a lot of superstitions. Whatever I did the last pregnancy, I didn't do this time. If I went swimming last time, I didn't go swimming this time. Things like that."

As painful as feelings of anxiety and vulnerability are, their managed presence can actually improve the quality of your pregnancy. You have your priorities straight. You take care of yourself and do what you can. You don't miss any prenatal appointments. Even if you're untrusting, you appreciate every bit of evidence that everything is okay. Even though time drags, you treasure each additional day.

> *This pregnancy was a happy time, but also a very difficult and scary time. I went to work, came home and put my feet up. My life was boring, but I felt that I was doing this for my daughter and hopeful we would have our little girl, because I was doing all I could to get through the pregnancy successfully.*
>
> —Sonya

The rest of this chapter outlines a number of strategies that can help you cope with your worries and calm your anxiety.

PRACTICING MINDFULNESS

Because worries are inevitable, mindfulness practices can be very helpful for calming your anxious brain, reducing your suffering, and boosting your ability to cope. (See also chapter 4, "Mindfulness-Based Coping Strategies.") Mindfulness is part of the following three-pronged approach.

- Mindfully own the worry. Nonjudgmentally observe your anxiety when it pops up; practice calming your triggered brain. Reframe the thoughts that lead to worry, such as replacing the catastrophic thought, "babies tend to die," with the fact that "the vast majority of babies are born healthy."
- Hope for the best. Envision the outcome you want; do what you can to have a healthy pregnancy and baby. Boost hope by mindfully observing that *all is well* in the present moment.
- Brace for the worst. Pinpoint what worries you, so you can obtain pertinent medical information and not waste energy on unfounded concerns. Think through the negative possibilities and come up with plans for what you'd do and how you would cope if tragedy strikes again.

Mindfulness practices can help you cope with this journey and soothe your anxious brain. Although it may seem counterintuitive, bracing for the worst and making contingency plans builds confidence in your ability to make the best of it, should that come to pass. Planning for the worst also frees you to shift some focus toward having hope, controlling what you can, and letting go of the rest. As a result, your anxiety won't disappear, but it won't be constant or incapacitating either.

> *If I went into extremely premature labor, I had a plan: I would insist on hospice care. No heroic measures, no needless suffering for the*

baby. I also kept a journal and took weekly photos of my growing belly, which I thought would be good mementos. And if the baby died for whatever reason, we would take care of the baby's body ourselves, including taking it home. With all those plans in place, I felt like, "I got this, no matter what happens." And I think I was actually able to be more hopeful as a result.

—*Winnie*

Mindfully continuing to go with the flow of your grief is also advisable. Resisting, avoiding, or suppressing it will only exacerbate your tension, which feeds anxiety. Instead be mindfully present with it. (See also "Welcoming Your Grief" in chapter 4.)

Like many mothers, you may also find it helpful to focus on taking one day at a time, instead of focusing on how the months stretch out before you. This also keeps you grounded in the present, rather than wandering off into regrets about the past or worries about the future. This worked for Abby, even in the face of waiting a month for another ultrasound after a scan raised questions. She says, "I'm fully aware of what could go wrong. For the most part I hold it together and remind myself to take it day by day."

You may also find certain spiritual practices soothing. For instance, mindfully take a "wondering" approach. Wondering how your journey will unfold lets you remain open to the possibilities rather than making desperate demands. "I wonder how this will turn out?" is far calmer than "I've got to get a baby out of this!" Similarly, you might hold on to the spiritual concept that everything will unfold as it should. Anne agrees: "I am trying to give it to God. He knows we would like this baby. So I will just do all I can to be healthy and hopeful."

If your anxiety feels overwhelming, you may benefit from a professionally administered, brain-based treatment for trauma. Abby says, "I did EMDR [Eye Movement Desensitization and Reprocessing] with my therapist, which was huge for me. I had a lot of fear behind labor and delivery, and through EMDR, I was able to advocate for myself for things I didn't even realize I would want—different lighting, room location, layout of room, music. It made my delivery so much more comfortable." (See also "Trauma and Suffering" in chapter 3; "Counseling" in chapter 13.)

Taking Action

In general, passively worrying is more painful than actively doing something. When you get lost in worry, you can stay stuck in feeling vulnerable and out of control. In contrast, by making plans and doing what you can, you gain a sense of mastery and confidence, which can help diminish feelings of vulnerability and the attendant anxiety.

So what can you *do*?

- Make arrangements with your doctor or midwife for more frequent visits, and get reassurance that you can go in any time.

Abby agrees, saying, "It's essential to have a great relationship with your doctor and to not fear going in any time. The beauty of knowing I can, it helps me so much." (See also "Collaborating with Your Health Care Practitioners" in chapter 14.)

- Talk to your doctor or midwife about tailoring your care to avoid what went wrong last time. Discuss the kinds of monitoring you want and the schedule for your visits. (See also "Home Monitoring" in chapter 14.)

- Take an active role in your prenatal care. Get coaching on healthy habits that promote a healthy pregnancy. Keep your ear to the ground for the latest research from reputable sources (for example, on the ideal sleeping position for pregnant mothers to reduce the risk of stillbirth, or causes and prevention of premature birth) and discuss it with your doctor or midwife. Educate yourself about prenatal tests, what they do, and how they are done. Become informed about fetal monitoring and nonstress tests. (See also "Prenatal Testing" chapter 14.)

- Seek information on any topic that interests or concerns you. Accurate information is an antidote to fear. You may also find that the more you know, the better in control you feel. And if it helps you to read every book and article you can find on complications that can befall mother and baby, then do it. It is not morbid; it is mastery.

- Learn about the signs and symptoms of problems that could pose a threat to your baby, so that you can get timely medical attention should you require it. Sometimes vigilance can avert tragedy (anxiety is good for something!). Not every disaster can be prevented, but you can sure try.

- Plan for labor and birth. How do you want labor managed? What kind of pain relief? (Even if you plan on none, decide what you'd like in case you deliver by Cesarean.) How much monitoring of your progress or baby's heartbeat? Do you want the baby handed to you as soon as possible, or do you want the essential health checks done first? While plans are not guarantees, they can help you feel in control.

- Make arrangements to have supportive advocates with you during labor and delivery so that you have help getting what you want and need, and support around any on-the-spot decision making. Your partner may fit the bill, but consider additional people. Perhaps you have a friend or know a bereaved mother who would be assertive and persuasive on your behalf or perhaps just a comfort to you. You might even find that people are honored to be asked, and will rise to the occasion. Destrida says, "I requested the nurse and doctor who took care of us during Dayani's birth to take care of us for Cheeni's birth, and they went out of their way to do just that. And neither of them was on duty or on call that day." You can also consider hiring a doula.

- Plan for your hospital stay. Particularly if your other baby died shortly before or after birth, you may have some strong feelings about the smallest details. Do you want the same hospital but a different delivery room? Do you want your new baby wrapped in a special blanket or the standard-issue hospital duds? Do you want to stay as long as possible or leave as soon as you can? It is normal to want to feel close to the baby you miss and yet distance yourself from the tragedy of untimely death. This can be tricky, but you can find the balance that is right for you.

- Talk to someone who can listen and accept your anxieties as normal. As Melanie attests, "I look back now and think, 'How was I ever able to cope with being pregnant again after losing Kate and Zac?' But it was having an amazing midwife and husband, and the tools I learned in counseling."

- Write about your feelings, worries, hopes, and dreams in a journal. Besides the therapeutic value of helping you untangle and express your thoughts and feelings, a journal can be a priceless keepsake of a special, perhaps agonizing, but miraculous time in your life. Reading your journal can help you gain clarity and see your own progress during the pregnancy. (See also "Mindful Journaling" in chapter 4.)

- If you have a job outside the home, keep working through the pregnancy, if possible or advisable.

- If you have older children, dive into caring for them, as this can be an active, productive, and rewarding distraction. Abby compares her first subsequent pregnancy to her second (and current) pregnancy: "I have son Conner keeping me busy this time, whereas being pregnant with him was difficult, as I consumed my time thinking about being pregnant!"

- Make fun plans and seek pleasant diversions to pass the time and boost positive mood, which in turn boosts your ability to cope. (See also "Mindfully Embracing Positive Experiences" in chapter 4.)

While attending counseling after we lost Zac, I got pregnant with my daughter Zara. My husband had suggested maybe we take our girls on a trip. But I was convinced that something bad was going to happen due to the fact that when I last went away, Zac died. I just couldn't believe that we could go away and everything could be okay. I talked all this through with the counselor and she thought going was a great idea. And in fact, it was the best thing we could have done. I really had to make a conscious effort to acknowledge that yes it could go pear shaped, but it also could be okay. It definitely helped me to have something to look forward to.

—Melanie

For even more ideas on *what you can do*, review the suggestions under "Prenatal Care" in Chapter 14. All this "doing" can also be balanced with (1) remembering that you cannot control everything (including your feelings), and (2) surrendering to the knowledge that so much is out of your hands. (See also "Vulnerability" in chapter 7.)

ACKNOWLEDGING YOUR IMAGINATION

Another calming strategy is to determine whether your anxiety is based on what you can observe or intuit or whether it is based on what you are *imagining* could go wrong. Your imagination may be fertile indeed, now that you have experience as well as knowledge and acquired fears about all sorts of things that can go wrong. If you're worried about what you are actually observing or sensing, seek medical attention. But if you're worried about what's in your imagination, you can mindfully observe it, let it go, and turn your sights toward what's going on, in reality. (See also "Being Aware of Thinking Traps" and "Mindfully Reframing Your Thoughts" in chapter 4.)

To keep an active imagination at bay and hold a firm grasp on reality, ask your doctor or midwife to outline the differences between what they can tell about this baby and the baby who died, and between this pregnancy and that pregnancy. And if you are being treated and monitored with sensitivity, let yourself find comfort in this excellent care.

> I constantly worried that something was wrong. So I would say to myself, "What is the evidence that there is something wrong, or what evidence is there that she is okay?" My husband used this as well to help me when I was really anxious.
>
> —Melanie

> When I was pregnant again with Toni-Joi, my little girl who was born just over a year after we lost Finley, I found it hard to stay positive. It was too much for me to be able to say to myself that I would have a healthy baby because Finley was healthy. We never found out why he died, so people telling me it wouldn't happen again didn't help. I couldn't believe it. So I had a series of alternative thoughts. Things like, "There is a 95 percent chance I will have a healthy baby," or "It's very rare that it could happen again," or "Almost everyone I know has had a healthy baby, therefore there is every chance I will too."
>
> —Mel

> I remember taking a Lamaze class and our instructor constantly said, "Every pregnancy is different; every baby is different." That is very true, and my situation is not what she was referring to, but it applies nonetheless. So I am able to have hope.
>
> —Jolie

Tuning into Your Intuition

Along these same lines, mothers in particular can also tune into their maternal intuition. Intuition is different from imagination, which is a creative ruminating or envisioning, or simply reacting to an association from the past and assuming it foretells the future. Intuition is a deep or gut-level knowing, often described as "the sixth sense" or "a blink," where you know something to be true but you can't put your finger on how you know it. People who consider themselves to be exceptionally intuitive tend to see it as the voice of the soul or spirit. Those who are religious might see it as the voice of their deity. Analysts see intuition as a pattern of ideas that forms as you accumulate experience and information. Brain scientists see it as your emotional core brain at work, taking in countless bits of information as it scans the environment.

Whatever the source, there is research that gives credence to the idea that a mother's intuition can be an accurate indicator of her baby's overall well-being. Like some (*but not all*) of the mothers in this book, you may have even had an intuition that something was wrong with your baby who died, either from the start or at some point. Likewise, during your subsequent pregnancy, practice tuning in to your baby's movement and position, which has the added benefit of letting you spend time focusing on your bond and the hope you have for your little one. You may also have some superstitions or rituals you heed, which is fine as long as this nurtures you and your baby. Whenever you have a sense that this baby is all right, dare to trust it.

> Part of me was so **glad** I was pregnant and another part of me was so terrified. I thought, "I can't do this again. I was a fool! Why did I think I could go through this again?" I kept trying to be positive. I did have a feeling she was going to be okay.
>
> —Bryn

> With the other pregnancies, there wasn't anything I could do about it and I just knew it wasn't going to work. This time I was more accepting, saying, "Since there isn't anything I can do to make it one way or the other, I might as well realize that there could be a good outcome, not just a bad outcome."
>
> —Meryl

Getting Past a Certain Point

> Getting past the sixteen-week check where we found out Elizabetta had died was a huge milestone. I'm not sure who was more relieved after the checkup, me or the midwife.
>
> —Karen

It's been going well so far. But I am starting to dread my twelve-week checkup as that's when things started going downhill with Dayani. I expect to feel some anxiety in each of the pregnancy milestones.

—Destrida

Ever since I found out I was pregnant with Aviana, I knew the moment I would feel relief—and the only moment—would be when I heard her cry. I would often imagine this moment while driving in my car and it would bring me to tears.

—Jolie

Depending on when your baby died, you may feel that if you can just make it past a certain point, you can relax a little. If you didn't make it beyond the first trimester, you may hold your breath until you reach the second trimester. If your baby was born too soon, you may feel more confident when you make it well into the third trimester. If past problems occurred during a certain week of the pregnancy, your anxiety may intensify then. And of course, it can be challenging if you're approaching the one-year anniversary of your baby's death, particularly if it's near the due date of your subsequent baby.

From my twenty-second to my thirtieth week I was nervous about everything, and time just went so slowly. I can remember thinking, "I have to get through one more week and one more week and one more week. . . ." You're waiting and hoping nothing happens, and that was probably the worst time. Once I reached thirty weeks, then I think I relaxed quite a bit.

—Peg

If anything I have become more scared as time goes on, and am just constantly monitoring this babe's movement. The fragility of life terrifies me.

—Abby

My doctor agreed to inducing me by eight days prior, since that's when I lost Jed, and I couldn't bear passing that mark, especially given both of their due dates fell on the twenty-second of the month, which was crazy.

—Embry

Some mothers find it hard to relax at any point. Lorna confesses, "I had anxiety all the way through the pregnancy as no one could promise me that this baby would not die." Jolie agrees, "Even though these little milestones are somewhat comforting, like getting out of the first trimester or getting to hear the heartbeat, I know there is truly no 'safe zone' ahead."

The first three months, everything's okay if you don't lose the baby, and then usually the middle months are okay, and then pray from six

*to nine that you don't go into premature labor, and then pray that you
don't have a stillborn.*

—Cindy

The due date itself can be another prompt for complex emotions. On
the one hand, you may feel very impatient for the due date to arrive so
that you can relax with the baby safely in your arms. On the other hand,
you might wish that you could just stay pregnant, the baby remaining safe
inside you.

*The whole nine months, I swore it took nine years. It was the longest
nine months I've ever been through. But I didn't want it to be time to
have her because I just kept having these pessimistic feelings, so
why hurry it?*

—Martina

*Things are getting "very real" and I'm not sure if I'm ready. Hard to
say, but this pregnancy is flying by and taking forever, a bit of both.
I'm still petrified of giving birth. The midwife has assured me that
I will get skin-to-skin contact straightaway, but I think I will lose it
completely if the baby has to go into special care.*

—Karen

*I went in for a regular checkup at thirty-six weeks and four days and
there was more protein in my urine than usual. This, in combination
with the fact that I was on bedrest for high blood pressure, prompted
my doctor to ask if I'd be interested in having the baby that day (repeat
Cesarean). We were teetering between whether the baby was safest
inside or outside of me at that point, and the protein in my urine kind of
just gave us that last nudge to go ahead and pull the trigger.*

—Jolie

And even if the new baby is born healthy, you may worry about his
or her survival during the first six months or the first year. Then, if you
embark on another subsequent pregnancy, another baby can rake up all
those anxieties again. Still, you can be heartened by each milestone passed
with flying colors. Be sure to lean into your relief and gratitude. (See also,
"Mindfully Embracing Positive Experiences" in chapter 4.)

BALANCING PESSIMISM AND OPTIMISM

*It is indeed a challenge to stay optimistic. I am not worried about
the same syndrome that Dayani had. Now I worry about all the other
things that can happen between now and birth.*

—Destrida

*It was an everyday battle to just choose to be grateful for whatever
time I had with my new child, and be excited and hopeful it would
turn out fine.*

—Embry

While vulnerability makes you worried and bonding makes you scared, pessimism only makes you suffer needlessly. Worrying about the possibility of a bad outcome is different from pessimism, which is being convinced of it. Worry leads to feelings of uneasiness. Pessimism leads to feelings of dread.

That's why it's important to balance any pessimism with optimism. Even if you feel overwhelmed with pessimistic thoughts, it is possible to have some optimism, maybe not blissful, durable, or concrete, but optimism nonetheless. Hopeful thoughts and feelings, however elusive, can encourage you and help you cope with your anxieties. You may feel that pessimism and holding back hope are useful, yet they only offer the *illusion* that you would be protected from heartache. So, if you have any thread of hope, spend some time hanging on to that.

> *I'm still waiting for someone to tell me this baby has died too, silly I know. I feel like I'm bracing for a car wreck even though the car is traveling slowly and there are no other cars on the road, making an accident unlikely.*
>
> —Karen

> *Sometimes it is easier to expect the worst than it is to hope for the best, as it avoids disappointment. I worked on dealing with disappointment and knowing I won't fall apart if things go wrong again. So it has become less scary to hope.*
>
> —Mel

Naturally, finding that balance is easier said than done. Here are some ideas to try:

- View pessimism as an attitude or frame of mind. When you go down that road, mindfully observe your thoughts and let them pass without judging, dwelling on them, justifying them, or giving them power to upset you. "There I go, assuming the worst. Interesting." And then get on with your day or the task at hand. As you practice this skill, you may notice that pessimism becomes fleeting and occasional rather than a way of life.
- Stay tuned into your body. When pessimistic thoughts make you tense or agitated, practice deep breathing, meditation, or simply do a body scan and relax any tension. A calm body helps you have a calm mind.
- Remember that your thoughts are separate from your pregnancy. Your pessimism, while normal and understandable, does not necessarily bear any relation to your baby's condition. Your emotional reality may be in the throes of horrific worry, but your physical reality—and the baby—may very well be normal and healthy.
- Especially if this pregnancy is uneventful and your baby is doing well, welcome feelings of gratitude, which will allow feelings of hope to rise up. As Destrida notes, "I am thankful for every day

that I have with her and I realize that I am at the mercy of the universe at this point. But I sure as hell hope that the odds are in my favor this time."

- Understand that "risk" just means that there is a *chance* that you or your baby will run into trouble. *Risk is not a guarantee of trouble.* For example, if your pregnancy is classified high-risk because of your history, it might actually be low-risk this time. Even if your condition is concerning, with high-risk pregnancy management, trouble may well be successfully diverted. And if you're being closely monitored for problems, this doesn't mean tragedy is around the corner. It means you're getting attentive medical care, and in partnership with your doctor or midwife, you're doing all you can to keep your baby healthy and safe.
- Resist the superstition that you will invite curses by having any hopes or confidence. Remember, optimism does not make bad things happen.

Constant pessimism can cost you dearly in terms of energy and peace of mind. So when you feel hopes rising, let them flow. Dare to dream about the soft smell of this baby's head. Permit yourself to fantasize about how full your arms and days will be. Go ahead and buy darling baby clothes. You may fear that dreaming and nesting will raise your hopes too high. You may imagine that if the baby dies, you would only be more devastated, surrounded by reminders that would heighten your despair. To the contrary, these are the very things that would aid in your mourning and eventual healing. In your darker moments, you can see how these items could be precious mementos of this baby you love. Besides, even if you don't want to allow it, you would love and miss your baby terribly whether you had a stocked nursery or not. Although you don't feel like a "normal" pregnant woman, you can dare to nest like one. If it gives you hope, do it.

When I was about seven months pregnant, I bought a pretty little baby dress. I was terrified to do it—afraid that if I did, this baby wouldn't happen. But after I did it, it felt great! It actually made me think that maybe this baby was for real and everything would be all right.

—Clara

I went back and forth between high anxiety and blind faith. When I bought some maternity clothes, I knew it was an act of faith that I'd even need them. I also found it comforting to collect cute cotton baby clothes. It gave me hope. Of course, this was balanced against reading a stack of books about prenatal testing, birth defects, prematurity, and medical ethics. Looking back on it, it was like having a split personality. But that balance worked for me.

—Winnie

Support Groups

Some parents stop going to their bereavement support group after they get pregnant again. To hear about babies dying may make them more pessimistic or anxious during their pregnancy. Jessie recalls, "That was the only negative part about being in the support group. Now we knew 101 ways that babies can die, even things we never used to worry about." For other parents, going to a support group or at least staying in touch with those parents gives them an opportunity to talk about their anxieties about the new baby, as well as their continuing sadness about the baby who died. Besides, as Annalaura explains below, it's challenging to try to fit into a "regular" prenatal group.

> At one point I realized that this was no way to live through a pregnancy. I tried to "lighten up" by taking a prenatal class. I felt this would help me live through the pregnancy in a different way, like normal mothers. I came home crying after the first class because everyone was so happy and joyful while I had this weight and sadness in me. What a difference from the bereavement support group I was coming from. In that group all we did was cry and talk about death, grief, and burial, and in this class, soon-to-be mothers were talking about preparing their baby rooms and cute baby outfits. I stuck to the class but always felt alienated. My birth plan in the end was that they could do all they wanted to me as long as the baby came out "alive and healthy." Quite different from the birth plans other moms were drafting.
>
> —Annalaura

Fortunately, some hospitals, hospices, private practitioners, and bereavement organizations sponsor organized "subsequent pregnancy" support groups for parents who have already experienced the death of a baby. These groups (often called "PALS" or Pregnancy After Loss Support groups) can help parents cope with the challenges of subsequent pregnancy, as well as connect them with others who can accompany them through this experience. To find a group near you, ask your obstetric practice, other bereaved parents, and support group leaders, or contact area hospital women's and parent education centers. You might also look for online subsequent pregnancy support groups, where you might find a community that offers emotional support, including private forums, helpful tips, and inspiring personal stories. Any well-run group can make you feel respected and listened to. Such a group should allow for and accept your grief for your baby who died, encourage you to air your anxieties *and* hopes for your pregnancy or labor and birth, help you deal with feelings of detachment, and encourage your unique process of bonding with the baby who's coming.

Points to Remember

- During your pregnancy, it is normal to feel anxious and vulnerable to tragedy.
- When you are feeling anxious, mindfulness practices can be very effective for calming your brain, reducing suffering, and boosting your ability to cope.
- Acquire the habit of noticing that, in the present moment, you can observe that *all is well.*
- Bracing yourself for the worst and making contingency plans can help you feel prepared for any outcome, boost confidence in your ability to handle it, and free you to shift some of your focus toward hope for the best.
- Continue to go with the flow of your grief. Resisting, avoiding, or suppressing it will only exacerbate your tension and anxiety.
- Instead of passively worrying, be active about what you can do, such as gathering information, practicing healthy habits, taking an active role in your prenatal care, creating a birth plan, and getting the support you need.
- Remind yourself that the fears and thoughts in your imagination are created by your mind, and have no basis in current reality, unlike what you can actually observe or sense. Let go of imaginary worries so you are better able to observe actual worrisome symptoms and seek timely medical attention.
- There is research showing that a mother's intuition can be an accurate indicator of her baby's overall well-being. So whenever you have a sense that everything is okay, rest on it.
- Let yourself be heartened by each milestone passed with flying colors. Be sure to lean into your relief and gratitude.
- Hopeful thoughts and feelings, however elusive, can encourage you and help you cope with your anxieties. Dare to nest and dream. Do what gives you hope.
- A subsequent pregnancy support group can be a great resource for helping you continue to grieve for your baby who died, giving you a place to air your anxieties *and* hopes, and encourage your unique process of bonding with the baby who's coming.

16

BONDING, BIRTH, AND BEYOND

It took a very long time to accept that I was pregnant and bond with the baby. I think I was trying to protect myself if it turned pear shaped.

—Melanie

BONDING DURING PREGNANCY

After the trauma of a baby's death, many parents hesitate to bond with the next baby. Your joy and expectations are clouded by fears and pessimism. You may not be able to enjoy milestones like the first ultrasound or the baby's first fluttery movements. You can feel totally committed to this pregnancy and you desperately want to count on having a healthy baby, but at the same time you worry about the devastation you would feel if this baby died. Parents often remain reserved because they dare not pin their hopes on a positive outcome.

In the early stages of feeling movement I really hated it as I associated it with losing Elizabetta. I had felt her move a few times, then we lost her. So every time I felt movement, and then nothing, I would feel anxious and resentful. I felt it would be better to feel nothing at all and I spent most days expecting to be told the baby had died.

—Karen

DETACHMENT

Like many parents, you may try to protect your heart. Detachment also protects you—and your brain—from the stress of constant worry. As Jolie says, "I would rather be a little detached than overprotective or constantly worried."

Your detachment also means you may resist typical milestones like nesting, naming, and baby showers. You might be avoiding the baby sections of stores, as going there triggers grief and thoughts of *what might have been*. Not wanting to feel too attached to the new baby is a common experience.

I tried to connect by buying some cloth nappies, tiny little cute ones. I thought buying something I feel passionate about for the baby might just spark a little bit of hope. It turns out it has given me a feeling of dread, not sure why. I got them in the post today and I just want to bury them at the bottom of a cupboard and not look at them.

—Karen

Part of me was also mad that I was shopping for a new baby and not Judah. That is a very tough to deal with—feeling negative emotions about a subsequent baby and pregnancy.

—Jolie

It can also be too much to bear if others express investment in your new baby. You don't want the fuss of a baby shower. You don't want them cooing over potential names. You may even resist telling people you're pregnant. And if your partner feels more connected to the baby than you are, you may feel annoyed and envious.

I am not as vocal about the pregnancy and I am not telling everyone about it. I am afraid that people will think that I have "gotten over" Dayani. In fact one person said, "I can't believe you got over your loss so quickly" when I told her the news. One person even asked me if this pregnancy was planned. These words hurt, and they come from people who were close to me during my time of loss. Imagine what I may get from strangers? So I am limiting my exposures this time to protect my heart, at least for now.

—Destrida

My husband would ask if I had felt the baby move and made comments like, "How is my baby today?" It was really sweet but I wanted to punch him and yell at him that it's too early to feel the baby move and I'm too frightened to feel it move in case it stops and how the hell am I supposed to know how the baby is if I didn't know Elizabetta had died? I felt really bad that I was not in the same place as him and I resented that he was making a connection and I couldn't.

—Karen

Your ambivalence is a normal part of the bonding process. And if investing in the new baby makes you feel guilty or disloyal to your baby who died, this only reflects your ongoing grief and a desire to protect your baby's memory. Also note that disloyalty is a common dilemma that any parent might feel at the thought of bringing another child into the family. Rest assured, your heart will expand to hold all your babies.

YOUR GROWING BOND

Over the course of the pregnancy, you will likely make more and more small gestures that reveal the growing bond you have to your baby. Thinking about names. Wondering what this baby is like. Venturing down a baby aisle. Noting and perhaps even enjoying in-utero movement, especially as it gets more pronounced. Even your concerns about bonding reflect your bond.

While he was still in the womb, I consciously would sit and pat and rub and talk, which I didn't do much with the others, but I kind of thought I'd give him a little extra advantage. It made me feel good, but I also knew that now I was feeling attached and that was hard— on the one hand being told, "Don't get your hopes up too high," but thinking, "There's no way that I can't feel something!"

—Meryl

To protect myself I rarely allowed myself to think about bringing our baby home, but I also bonded as much as I could with him/her. I took pictures of my growing belly, which was something I didn't have many of with Emma.

—Abby

With Blake Arlan, we did not share his name until I was hospitalized. At that point, we felt that we need to share his name so people would feel a connection to him as they prayed for us. As for Rylee Anne, we told the world her name. We knew that there could be some issues with my pregnancy and we hoped that all the love and prayers would be there for our little girl.

—Sonya

For a lot of mothers, preparing the nursery and collecting baby things, thinking about names, even feeling the baby move, seems too hopeful. Sara remembers how doubtful and cautious she was: "I wanted to pretend I wasn't pregnant. I packed up the nursery. I wasn't into maternity clothes or little pregnancy conversations, none of that. I was going to wait and *see* if I got a baby!" Hannah postponed baby showers and shopping until *after* Michael came home. Lena concurs, "I didn't want to go buy a bunch of stuff and have this one die too." Even after Bryn's daughter was born, she recalls, "I was afraid to buy diapers above the newborn size because, 'What if she didn't make it?' I was still just taking it a day at a time." For many mothers, superstitions add to their caution. Kitty notes, "I've always been superstitious, even with my first. I didn't want to start the nursery too early in case something would happen."

We won't buy anything for this baby until I am eight months along. It's a traditional, long-standing superstition from my husband's side, for good luck they say. We waited for Dayani as well but it didn't really help in her case. I have done it for Ishan and Dayani and will do it with this one too.

—Destrida

We had decided on her name, but unlike Blake, we had done no other planning. No clothes, no toys, no repainting of walls. We just could not look that far in the future. Though we were always praying for the best, we were both so scared of the worst because we had been there before.

—Sonya

If you have kept the nursery set up, you may be very protective of its contents. Cindy remembers not letting anyone borrow her baby things until she had a baby of her own to use them. If you put the nursery away, you may hesitate getting things out again because preparing for a new baby triggers memories about the baby who died. This may be difficult, but you can grieve for your missing baby while you look forward to another one. Dara recalls, "Bringing out all her baby things brought everything back into focus again, but it didn't feel worse."

It's important to remember that when you try to assess your bond, you are comparing apples to oranges. When you think about the depth of your bond to the baby who died, of course your bond to this new baby seems lacking. Jolie explains how she tries to keep perspective.

Being pregnant right now is just . . . different than being pregnant with Judah. Sometimes I am scared that I am not bonding with this baby, but I feel like that thought is somewhat distorted. With Judah, I was basically "nesting" for nine months. I was reading books about pregnancy, I was constantly Googling where he was developmentally, and I started acquiring baby supplies from the get-go. Judah's room was stocked and ready probably a month or two before he was even due. I feel like those events made me bond with Judah more in general. We were very much involved with that pregnancy. He was my first child.

So naturally, I think I bond less with this baby simply because we are a little more prepared and knowledgeable about being pregnant in general. I also remind myself often that I probably didn't bond much with Judah this early on either, because I could not feel or see him at this point. I think once I am able to feel this baby move, and once Charlie is able to see and feel this baby move, we will be able to bond more and enjoy this experience more. But, I am not completely in denial and do acknowledge that I am a bit emotionally detached during this pregnancy. I think it was just naturally easier to have bonded with Judah. This time, I am being patient and giving myself grace.

—Jolie

As your pregnancy progresses, your confidence can grow and you may allow yourself to feel a greater bond with this baby. Especially in the months after the birth, you will acquire the full depth and joy of maternal love.

The nursery is painted, clothes and blankets are bought, and a couple of months ago, my son nicknamed this baby Cheeni, which means "sugar" in Tamil (my husband's mother tongue), and we've been calling her that since.

—Destrida

I distanced myself during the pregnancy—we did not find out the gender and did not have a baby shower—and I think this initially affected my bonding with him. But we adore each other now and I have not let that affect our relationship in a negative way.

—Embry

I have accepted that it will take a bit of time to feel connected with this pregnancy (still hesitant to use "baby"). I figure if I keep pushing my boundaries like buying baby things—and today I went to a baby expo—then I will start to force my brain into saying "baby" more comfortably, and eventually my heart will say it too.

—Karen

What Counts as Bonding?

Many bereaved parents have found that certain bonding thoughts and activities are helpful, comforting, wise, or even irresistible during subsequent pregnancy. Many of these nurture you *and* your relationship with your partner, which lays a foundation for nurturing the baby and your bond. As you read down this list, try the ones that seem doable and shelve the others perhaps for another day. Perhaps you've been doing some of them already.

- Continue to go with the flow of your grief for the baby you miss so much. Doing so promotes emotional healing, reduces your stress, and helps you prepare emotionally for the new baby.
- Know that it's possible to grieve for one baby while you bond to another.
- Realize that happiness for the new baby does not negate your love for the baby who died.
- See this pregnancy as an opportunity to start parenting this new baby, such as taking care of your pregnant body—or supporting the mother's efforts to do so.
- Engage in mindfulness practices, as this reduces stress for you *and* the baby.
- Seek emotional and social support from friends, family, other bereaved parents, your obstetric team, and counselors.
- Nurture your relationship with your partner.
- Seek higher-level obstetric care, even if the pregnancy is going well.
- See prenatal exams as opportunities for your baby to tell you what's going on.
- Ask your doctor or midwife to tell you what they know about this baby.
- Tell your doctor or midwife what you know about this baby.
- Whenever you have concerns, call your doctor or midwife.
- Make a list of questions for your next prenatal visit.
- Think about what you'd like to happen during labor, the birth, and meeting your baby.
- Write a birth plan. Include what you want the labor and delivery staff to know about your history. Talk to your doctor or midwife about it.
- During prenatal visits, listen to the heartbeat or view the baby on the ultrasound screen.
- Ask for an ultrasound photo. Keep it in a special place.

- See this baby as a baby now, not just an abstraction.
- Differentiate this baby from the one who died.
- Journal to the baby who died about the baby coming. When you feel ready, switch to telling the baby who's coming about the baby who died.
- Meditate on and be present with the baby.
- Make note of your baby's movements, including patterns and quality. Movements are another way for the baby to tell you how he or she is doing.
- Talk to the baby. Sing. Play music.
- Lay hands on the pregnant belly. Your partner can also snuggle up and listen in.
- When you go to special places or events, be conscious of "taking the baby with you."
- Take photographs of the mother's changing shape.
- Have professional photographs taken or ask a friend to take some shots. Include the whole family.
- Think about acquiring supplies and nesting.
- See yourself as a parent to all your babies, continuously and simultaneously.
- Consider how your parenting role is different for each baby.
- Remember that your bond will naturally deepen during the pregnancy, and as time passes, your baby leads the way with a growing presence.
- Fake it till you make it by taking tiny steps along your bonding goals. Call them "baby steps" if that makes you smile.
- Surrender to your parenting instinct to bond.
- Accept that you cannot protect your heart by shutting it down.
- Know that, like other parents, you will experience a surge in your bonding upon birth.
- Rest assured that your heart will expand to hold all your babies.

Most of all, give yourself time. You will do many of the "typical" bonding activities when your preparatory instincts finally kick in. In fact, many parents wait until the last month of pregnancy or even the first month after birth to complete tasks like getting supplies and picking out names. If you force yourself to do things before you're ready or anything that makes you miserable, you're only adding to your suffering. And that's not good for you, the baby, or your bond. Indeed, *reducing unnecessary suffering is key to your adjustment and healing—and your ability to enjoy your new baby.*

> That bond which I have been trying to ignore snuck up on me and took over. At this point in the pregnancy, with just a few more weeks to go, I'm starting to feel connected, secure, and enjoying feeling movement. I want to stay in this "happy space" forever.
>
> —Karen

ADOPTION AND BONDING

*My boss, who also adopted, once joked that once you are on the list
for adoption, you are in some ways pregnant. You are planning for the
child, you just don't know what it will look like or when it will happen—
you just know it will.*

—Sonya

*It perhaps feels more removed or distant, the fact that the baby isn't
physically inside me and I don't have to go through a pregnancy and
birth process. Yet, a baby is "on its way" metaphorically speaking.*

—Victoria

Going through the adoption process is a figurative pregnancy. As such
you may experience similar trials, like being uncertain about sharing your
plans, trying not to get your hopes up, and keeping any news from family
in order to spare them disappointment. And the process is lengthy and
complex, with multiple meetings, and unpredictable waiting.

As a result, the emotional landscape can be similar too, including happy
anticipation, anxiety, fear, and guarded optimism. At times, you may feel
intrusively inspected and judged. Anxiety and uncertainty reign, as there are
no guarantees. These are all very common "subsequent pregnancy" emotions.

*Still waiting. That is the most difficult thing with adoption—the waiting.
When you go into an adoption agency, what you want is to walk out
with a baby. You are that ready to have a child in your home! It is
not like a car dealership where you just go "look around and see"
and you might walk away with a car or you might not—no big deal.
With adoption, you are ready now and the waiting up to two years is
sometimes torturous.*

—Sonya

In a sense, the adoption assessment is your time of conception. And
just as bonding begins when parents are merely trying to conceive, you
too are beginning the bonding process. And even if you held back, you'd
be devastated if you didn't attain your dreams. So you might as well enjoy
the anticipatory bonding. And remember it's normal to be anxious, feel
vulnerable, and want to hold back from completely investing in the idea.

As a bereaved parent, you might especially worry about passing all
the tests and proving your suitability during interviews. Will your grief
over pregnancy complications, infertility, and the death of one or more
babies shed an unfavorable light on you? Will you be seen as a crazed and
desperate bereaved parent, or even worse, an unfit parent who's merely
trying to "replace" a beloved baby who died? You may even doubt your
own worth or motivations.

*When a couple is picked and removed from the list, you start to
question yourself and your profile and wonder, "Why didn't they pick
me?" and "What was right about them that made that birth mother*

pick them over me?" It's hard! But you HAVE to remember that your child will come. And the right birth parent will pick you to be their child's parent.

—Sonya

We had two social workers visit us for our initial meeting. Naturally, I was very nervous. Almost immediately they asked about Alex and our grieving process. Mathew gave them a detailed description of what had happened, the length of time, the inquest, and the outcome. I sat there and I was fully aware of their thoughts and their judgment. And so the questions followed: How have you dealt with your grief? How about Tom? Are you stable enough to take on something so intrusive as adoption? Are you ready? What do you see when you see Tom? Et cetera. I have to say, they were very likable and very professional. Yet the atmosphere was not relaxed, nor free. It was time to step in. I just said it how it is, very clearly, very honestly because I really do wear my heart on my sleeve! Something on the lines of, "We have experienced something very traumatic, Alex has changed our lives, maybe for the better? We would like a bigger family, I can't have biological children for the obvious reasons, we've got a lot to offer, Tom would love a sibling and he would make a fantastic brother, our child would be welcomed into our family. Alex will always be with us, and that is something we want to celebrate, that Tom and our new child had a little baby brother, but became poorly and is now in heaven. And I would like the photos of my children to be together and proudly displayed . . . blah, blah." Well, the two social workers stopped in their tracks and just responded with, "Well that ticks that box then," and thereafter, the atmosphere changed.

—Victoria

Once you get approved and the matching process starts, figuratively that's your baby's time of gestation as you wait for "delivery." Just as you would during a subsequent pregnancy, you start to wonder about your child-to-be and perhaps start feathering the nest. It's not the same as carrying that child in your body, but the idea of him or her is carried in your heart. You may even notice your anticipation adds joy to your conversations about "expecting." These are bonding moments to relish as they give you hope and help you envision a bright future. But it's normal to feel tentative too. Here, Victoria compares the adoption process to subsequent pregnancy, and Sonya talks about how she copes with the waiting, and bonds to the future baby by making hopeful gestures.

Of course I can see some similarities too, such as the fact that our adopted baby maybe would never have existed in our lives if were not for Alex's death. I'm already thinking about his movement, his body, his smell, etc., and would Alex's have been the same?

—Victoria

Still always hoping and dreaming for the baby to come, and I know it will happen in due time and I just have to be patient. Sometimes I do get down and frustrated on the process, but then I get a "baby fix" by buying a few small items. Knowing that a child of mine will play with or wear an item makes me surprisingly feel a little better. It helps with the pain of not having my babies here. It also reminds me that we will have our family someday. Yesterday, I bought four small toys and two books. It is not the total cure when I get that aching feeling, but it helps.

—*Sonya*

Looking Forward, Looking Back

I proudly tell people it's my third pregnancy even though they're confused looking for my second child. When asked, I then say she died at birth and she'd be two and a half. This is how I carry her and this new babe.

—*Abby*

I'm trying my hardest to keep Beau close and make sure that I don't ever forget him but it worries me. What will happen if I suddenly forget him when I'm busy with the new baby?

—*Courtney*

Many parents find it emotionally challenging to prepare for another baby while grieving for the baby who died. Friends and relatives might be relieved to hear that you're pregnant again or adopting, and assume you're "all better now." Others believe it is best to move on to the future without looking back, and may have little patience for your ongoing grief. What they may not understand is that avoiding grief thwarts emotional needs and can make parents less capable of emotionally nurturing their new baby. Others might believe that the subsequent baby can somehow replace the one who died or erase the need to grieve. But, as Clara realizes, "Being pregnant is great, but it doesn't fix everything; it doesn't banish my grief."

Imagining the baby's arrival is another issue that invites looking forward and looking back. You may struggle with how to balance staying connected to the baby you miss so much, while also tentatively connecting to the baby who's just starting to show on your radar. The balance you strike will depend on the day or even the moment, and whether you're looking forward or looking back. It's an emotional time. As usual, go with the flow.

Having to change Beau's room and make it the new baby's room scares me. We have such a small house and I wish that I could keep his room "his room" forever, but over time it's going to have to change and be the new baby's room. That both scares and excites me.

—*Courtney*

One thing that is starting to come back is the memory of that feeling you get when you finally give birth and you see your baby for the first time. I want that so badly, it hurts. It also triggers a lot if grief and guilt for not having that when Elizabetta was born. I think there is a lot of crying still to do, happiness and sadness rolled into one, and maybe I should stop trying to run away.

—Karen

Although challenging, it is possible to manage these competing feelings—to express hope for the future *and* grief for the past. Continuing to mourn also brings you along your journey of healing, which benefits you and your relationship with the subsequent baby. (See "How Do I Acquire a Sense of Healing?" in chapter 8.)

Merging the babies in your mind is another normal experience during pregnancy. You may imagine the new baby will be similar to the baby who died, as the hope that this baby survives merges with the wish that the other baby had lived. You may even feel that the baby who didn't survive is reborn in some way with the new baby. Rayleen notes, "When I was pregnant, I did think about Christopher. I never thought it was the same pregnancy, but it was hard to believe it was another person, another child. It was really hard for me to imagine there could be two of them. I *knew* it was another, but I know I thought about him."

Intellectually, you know it is not the same baby, but especially before the birth, it is easy to believe that your subsequent baby holds the essence of your other baby. As long as you can appreciate the unique biological and spiritual identity of this new child, imagining similarities can be a harmless way to hold on to the baby you miss so much. After this baby arrives, you may imagine or even notice similarities, but as you become acquainted, you will find it easier to keep the babies separate.

*Before Charlie arrived, when the social worker said, "Would you like to see the photos of Charlie?" it was **this** I was nervous about. They showed him as a real baby and I kept on returning to the last photo, which was taken a few weeks back. He was sitting upright on the carpet, staring with his big blue eyes at the camera. He didn't look like Tom, he didn't look like Alex—he looked like "Charlie." That was reassuring and that was what I was scared about. I also tried to imagine myself looking at a girl and it didn't feel right. As a boy, he just seemed to "fit in" with his own cheeky face and character.*

—Victoria

Wishing for a Certain Gender

Many parents have a strong preference for the sex of the new baby. If your only daughter or your only son died, or if that baby's gender fit nicely into the makeup of your family, you may hope to have another of the same. You may feel disappointed if you don't get your wish. If you do get your wish, you may feel very grateful, even redeemed.

After Jenni died, when I got pregnant I really, really wanted another little girl. Then I had Dustin, and I love him dearly, but I had my heart set on a girl. I think about trying again, having another baby, but with no guarantees, it doesn't seem like the thing to do.

—Maiya

I had done everything. I had known when I was ovulating, so there was no doubt in my mind it was a girl. Even through the whole pregnancy I was telling people it was a girl. When Chris was born, I remember feeling disappointed and I felt like a jerk because I thought, "You're disappointed in the sex of your child?" But you wonder, "If I hadn't lost the other baby, I would've had a girl."

—Elaine

We wanted a girl, not just because Melanie was a girl, but because, you know, the perfect family, a boy and a girl. For some reason I didn't think I was going to have a girl, so when I did, I was just really happy. It took me a couple days to really realize that I had a normal healthy baby and it was a girl, everything I wanted.

—Kitty

I was happy when I had Max, because I really never thought I'd have a boy. I always thought I was going to just have girls, that I wasn't meant to have a boy.

—Jane

I am known as "the woman who lost three boys." The number of people who would say to me, "Oh well, it's natures way of telling you, you obviously can't carry boys." What joy I had when my living baby, after my losses, was a boy, to prove them all wrong. I can carry a boy and he is the highlight of my life.

—Fleur

Or perhaps you hope your subsequent baby is the other sex, in order to keep them separate or avoid feeling as though you've replaced the baby who holds a special place in your heart. Bryn observes, "I think maybe it's good that I had a girl. If I'd had another boy, I wonder if maybe my memories would have meshed into one." Martina agrees: "We didn't want a boy because we were afraid we'd try to put the boy in Greg's place." You may also wonder if having a baby of the same sex would trigger a stronger sense of being faced with what you've been missing—and some parents think it has that effect. Embry believes that having another boy added to her grief, but, as she says, "Just having another sweet baby brought into reality exactly what we had been missing for those two years."

Many parents have mixed feelings, in a way relieved, but also disappointed when they find out the sex. After all, there are many reasons to prefer one or the other, and some reasons will be at odds with each other.

I was thrilled she was a little girl. It was nice because I immediately saw that I couldn't go through with my little fantasy, that if it was a little boy, it would be the same little boy. And that would've been pretty strong because at birth she looked so much like him. . . . But sometimes I wish I had another little boy so that I'd see a little bit more of what he would be like.

—Liza

I found out we are having a boy. I was unprepared for the overwhelming sense of relief but also the immense loss that I felt at the same time. Obviously my head thinks I'm better at making boys, but I guess to a certain extent I'd hoped to be able to do some of those girly things that I'd lost with Elizabetta. I've been trying to explore my thought processes and work out why it is such a huge secondary loss. Was I hoping for a "replacement"? Would I have pretended this baby was Elizabetta? None of that makes sense. I think a big factor was how much Zafira has wanted a sister and how much she mourns for that loss of female relationship.

—Karen

As many of these mothers illustrate, it is very common to be especially disappointed when a daughter dies and then to give birth to a son. This may have to do with the mother's "loss of self" being less repaired when a son instead of daughter is born. Or it may be the fear that she has forever lost her chance to have the special relationship that mothers and daughters often have.

Like many women, you may believe that mother-child intimacy is best achieved with daughters. In our culture, it is commonly held and practiced that mothers must push their sons away, starting when they are barely out of diapers, in order for them to reach full masculine maturity. It may help to remember that with the changing image and role of men in our society, there will be less pressure for mothers to do this—and you needn't bow to that pressure, in any case. We are beginning to recognize that when a boy is close to his mother, he is better prepared for the trials of life, better able to express emotions, and better able to have strong, respectful relationships with others. Both boys and girls need attentive caring and guidance into adulthood, and the mother-child bond can be powerful and enriching with either sons or daughters.

Is it a good idea to find out the sex before the baby is born? There is no right or wrong answer, so you need to intuit or discern what's best for you. On the one hand, knowing means you know another detail about this child, which may enhance bonding, naming, and your ability to differentiate your babies during the pregnancy. On the other hand, knowing the sex can also color your bonding if you're going to be upset by this baby being either a boy or a girl. Sometimes, it's better to meet the baby in person so your heart can melt, whatever the sex. And then you don't have months to stew about being disappointed or nervous. Either way, finding out during pregnancy or at birth, the news is likely to bring up strong emotions. Janice, Holly, and Destrida all found out during their pregnancies; Embry waited.

I am having a hard time accepting that I'm having a boy. I've been trying to realize my motive for wanting a girl and it's really because I want Carolyn, and since this baby would not be her, I'm getting used to the idea of a boy. But I would like to have another daughter someday.

—Janice

I had an amnio so I knew it was a girl, and I did that specifically for two reasons. One, I wanted to be able to say there are problems I know this baby won't have, and two, I wanted to know the sex because I had always wanted a girl, and I knew that if it was a boy I was going to have that sense of loss to deal with, and that if it was a girl I was going to have to work on separating her from Heidi. I remember when I got the results, being excited it was a girl but being really frustrated or sad and crying for a long time. The doctor said, "Well, you have a healthy baby girl." But I was thinking, "Why couldn't it have been Heidi?"

—Holly

How do I feel about having another girl? It's bittersweet. I am happy for this baby but sorely miss my other girl. This past Tuesday was exactly seven months since Dayani left us. Being so close in timing, I thought I would transfer some of my feelings for Dayani to this baby but it doesn't seem to be the case, at least so far. It is amazing how the heart is able to expand to make distinct individual spaces for all three children.

—Destrida

We didn't know the gender of the baby until he actually arrived into the world! Holding him while he was all warm, alive, and thriving on my chest was so emotional, and when I found out he was a boy it became even more emotional as all the reality came flooding in.

—Embry

If you're adopting, you may struggle with whether to request a preference. Knowing you can actually have some say can make you second-guess your motives. Are you trying to replace the baby who died by requesting the same sex? Is it fair or even desirable to have a choice, when if you were pregnant, you wouldn't? Even if you decide to state "no preference," it's normal to harbor a wish for one or the other. Neither preference is wrong. It just is what it is.

Regarding the sex of the child, I still feel that the match is more important as to whether it is a boy or girl. However, I do deliberate this in my mind at times. Would a girl be more "fitting"? Then at the same time, I do like boys . . . but maybe we should have been specific about gender and decided on a girl purely as a contrast. Then I think rationally: if I were able to have a child naturally, I wouldn't be able to choose and whatever the sex—we will love that child as we do Tom and Alex. I will let fate decide, after all isn't this what it is all about?

—Victoria

Whether you're pregnant or adopting, strong desires for a certain sex are legitimate. Whenever you find out, it's helpful to be aware of your feelings so that you can face them, rather than having them go underground and affect your growing relationship with your little one. If you are disappointed, it is important that you acknowledge this loss and go with the flow of your emotions. Saying "This is not what I wanted" can help you mindfully observe and accept these feelings, and also accept your little boy or girl. And it can also help soften your disappointment to remember the bottom line—as Anne says, "Honestly, it really does not matter. Boy or girl. I just pray for a healthy baby."

THE BIRTH

Our obstetrician agreed to induce me at thirty-eight weeks for my mental health. The day I was to be induced I remember walking through the door of the hospital thinking, "Is this baby going to die in childbirth? We seem to have lost them at every other stage. No reason why it couldn't be us."

—*Melanie*

The final weeks of your pregnancy may be an anxious time as the "moment of truth" approaches. Like many bereaved mothers, you may be especially aware of your baby's movements or visit your doctor daily. As the due date draws near you may find yourself hoping, even as your worry mounts. When you're getting ready for the birth, you may feel an odd mixture of impatience and dread, elation and anxiety, optimism and pessimism. It is normal to feel this way. It is normal to have flashbacks. It is normal to feel bereft. It is normal to feel relieved, excited, or overwhelmed with trepidation.

During the last weeks I felt increasing terror, especially since it was only a year before that I delivered another baby. It was such a blend: it was hard to figure out the grieving, the hormones are going crazy and just being pregnant you're a mess anyway. I can't even compare pregnancies. You go into one pregnancy excited to see your baby and you go into the next one being sure the baby is going to be dead.

—*Sara*

I felt anxiety and fear, but also a little bit of investment, looking forward to it. I actually went out a few days before she was born and bought a dress for her to wear home from the hospital.

—*Holly*

I couldn't wait to have him. I was so anxious for him to be born. I wasn't worried so much about the birth part of it, but just to have him here with everything going right. . . . I wanted to have this baby. The doctor took my cerclage out when I was thirty-seven weeks and nothing happened. After months of stopping premature labor, we thought, "When we take this out there's nothing that's going to hold this baby back," but nothing happened. I kept waiting and waiting and waiting and finally, a week later, I went into labor.

—*Peg*

I'm in a bit of a weird place. I'd like to just stop the clock and be pregnant for a while longer. I'm desperately trying to hold on to every moment I have. I feel very overwhelmed at the thought of giving birth and having a baby and the risk of losing this baby too.

—*Karen*

Particularly if you experienced a traumatic labor or birth with your baby who died, you may feel transported back to that harrowing time. Emotionally triggered, you may revisit distressing feelings like sadness, anger, or anxiety. This alone would be a reason to proactively seek a brain-based treatment for trauma. There is no reason to add unnecessary suffering to this birth experience. (See also "Trauma and Suffering" in chapter 3; "Counseling" in chapter 13.)

If you are worried about yourself (or your laboring partner) or your baby's health status, ask for the monitoring and reassurance you need. Discuss with your doctor or midwife whether having a fetal monitor during labor is a good idea. The sound of the baby's heartbeat can be distracting or anxiety provoking, and it also restricts your movement, which can be uncomfortable. Or it might be reassuring. You could choose to have it silenced and just let your health practitioners keep track of it so you can focus on giving birth. If you deliver by Cesarean, you may want to be awake to feel more in control, or you may wish you could have a general anesthetic to spare yourself the anxiety. As Martina recalls, "I didn't want to be awake in case something was wrong."

This is where a birth plan can come in handy. (See "Taking Action" in chapter 15.) After discussing your wishes and your overall vision with your doctor or midwife, you'll be able to relax a little more. You'll also benefit from special care if you request that everyone who takes care of you be informed that you had a baby who died.

During the prep and the surgery I kept asking if my blood pressure was okay and telling the anesthesiologist that I still had feeling in my belly and legs. Ever since I lost Judah, I had been preoccupied with the baby and/or myself dying during labor. Luckily, the anesthesiologist was like having a sweet grandfather with me—he even held my hand the whole time, reassuring me that I was doing great and everything was going as planned and that my blood pressure was fine.

—*Jolie*

Many mothers are afraid of losing control during labor or being consumed with grief and thoughts of the baby who died. Bryn recalls, "When she was born, everything I was going back to was my first experience—all the rooms, the doctors, the procedures . . . I was terrified when my water broke because that's when it all started before." Sophie remembers, "I was afraid I would get real crazy in terms of thinking about Stephanie and crying and sobbing uncontrollably, and that wouldn't help labor at all." But Sophie, like most, found she was able to focus on the present birth. As mentioned earlier, focusing on the differences between this experience and the other can help you cope and feel more optimistic.

> When Nicole was stillborn it was so quiet. It seemed like the whole hospital got quiet, and you could hear a pin drop, it was so quiet and peaceful. When Emily was born, it was so loud. Everybody was talking and laughing and crying, and so it was a really big difference. I loved the noise.
>
> —Cindy

> Once I went into labor it was a matter of existing in the "here and now." My midwife was fantastic and made sure I felt safe and let me dictate when and how things went. My waters were broken at midnight and Nico was delivered fourteen minutes later. I had skin-to-skin straightaway and we delayed cord clamping, my husband got to hold Nico while I got a few stitches and cleaned up. It was as perfect and uncomplicated as it could be.
>
> —Karen

COPING AFTER THE BIRTH

> The first thing I said was, "Is he breathing?" I wanted to make sure he was alive. I think I was so enthralled that this baby came out alive.
>
> —Erin

> I finally DID get to hear that cry, and I remember Charlie and I looking at each other. We were both laughing and crying.
>
> —Jolie

> We were so happy that everything went well. But I must say Cheeni brought out a lot of emotions and longing for Dayani.
>
> —Destrida

> When Francesco was finally born, I think I went through some kind of postpartum depression. I had "won at the video game" but I still kept thinking of my first child, "fagiolino" (little bean in Italian).
>
> —Annalaura

> Mixed emotions—intense love for this new baby and total sadness, as I should have had **two** boys . . . . No one can prepare you for how you will feel.
>
> —Lorna

Just when you expected to be fulfilled with maternal joy, you may be also drowning in sorrow. It may help to remember that feelings of sadness are normal for all new mothers. There are physical reasons, such as hormones fluctuating, sleep deprivation, and the around-the-clock demands of nursing and caring for an infant. Giving birth is also a "letting go" and this in itself can feel like a loss. Feelings of emptiness can be literal, since you no longer have a baby inside you. You also may have some grief over the birth—perhaps unplanned interventions were necessary or you were separated from your baby for a while. Or you may be sad because this is (or might be) your last pregnancy. All of these sources of sadness are part of normal postpartum recovery.

As a bereaved mother, you are likely dealing with other issues that can dampen your joy. Perhaps this birth was eerily similar to the one that didn't turn out so well. Particularly if your new baby strongly resembles the baby who died, you may be experiencing distressing or frightening flashbacks. Or you may feel anxious until your baby gets a thorough checkup.

At birth, Owain looked so much like his big brother Ronin, which was scary. It was like I was holding Ronin, but he was alive. To be faced with a live baby who looked like a child I had loved greatly, but I would never get to hear him cry, hold him ever again, or watch him grow—it was scary.

—*Lorna*

I was obviously happy but still concerned for her well-being. She seemed okay, but I was holding my breath in case something went wrong or was found to be wrong. It wasn't until our pediatrician saw her the next day and told us everything was fine that I began to breathe easier.

—*Destrida*

I was highly monitored and felt like I was in the best hands at our hospital. But let's be honest: I didn't take a huge breath of relief until he was in my arms crying! It was scary. He came out blue and we were told he'd need to go to the NICU, but then they took him over to the little table and he passed his Apgar scores with flying colors. So before I knew it he was on my chest. The best . . .

—*Abby*

Furthermore, your adjustment to parenting this baby is complicated. Even when you finally bring home this healthy baby, it may feel unreal to you. Your dream has come true, but after months of being afraid it would never happen, it can be quite a shock. And even when cradling your little one safely in your arms, you may wonder what tragedy lies around the corner. After all, you know for a fact that mothers don't get to keep every baby they bring into the world. Postpartum depression may also descend.

I found the first few weeks pretty tough. It is hard with the exhaustion of sleep deprivation and all the hormones, but I also felt I was constantly on edge. We finally had her but what was going to happen to take her away?

—*Melanie*

I struggled with postpartum depression after having Aviana, and that was a real struggle indeed. However, I have since gotten on medication and I feel a million times better. I wish I'd done it sooner so I could have enjoyed those first eight weeks, but it is better late than never.

—Jolie

Most significantly, whether you waited two months or two years before getting pregnant, feelings of grief can intensify after your new baby's birth. Even if you feel as though you have put your grief behind you, having this baby in your arms can trigger emotions you've yet to express. You may come to another level of realization that the baby you lost will never be recovered, even by having this baby. As Lauren points out, "You always hope deep down that maybe another child could fill the void in your heart." The pain may surprise you. As Melanie says, "In Zara's first year, Kate's and Zac's birthdays were pretty tough. It was hard to reconcile that grief, now that we had a wee baby." You may also feel torn between two worlds, two kinds of devotion—to the dead and to the living.

Once you have a real living baby and you see that you're actually dealing with a baby, then it really made me start to think about the other babies quite a bit. I went through a period where it was bothering me more than it had before. . . . My grief was something I felt I had pretty much gotten over, and then when I had Justin it brought it back to me and I realized, "It still bothers me."

—Peg

The thing that has taken me by surprise is how much I miss having the middle of the night to myself with Elizabetta. It was when I could just be still and "be" with her, and now that time has to be shared. There have been tears and the unwelcome return of that gnawing longing for Elizabetta. The why and unfairness, the missing and guilt have come back, but at the same time I have this beautiful little boy who I've fallen in love with, and finding a balance is difficult.

—Karen

Some mothers try to suppress their grief so it won't dampen their joy. Unfortunately, by stifling emotions, you won't feel sad, but you won't feel happy either. Bryn recalls, "I was so happy and yet I could still not enjoy it. I was not ready to really enjoy anything. I couldn't savor things." If you permit yourself to feel sad emotions, you also open yourself up to feel the happy ones. Finding a balance rather than trying to repress feelings will benefit you and your baby.

Within a couple of days I was really starting to grieve again. I think a lot of it was probably relief, and maybe I had suspended some of the grief during the pregnancy. I remember while I was in the hospital, just crying a lot, carrying her around, just being so happy with her. At the same time, it seems like I really got a lot of that grief out the first month.

—Liza

I thought having another baby would make me feel better, and during the pregnancy I had something to look forward to, but after Alysia's birth, something was gnawing at me. I've been feeling angry and feeling strongly that I should have another baby. Then last week it dawned on me that I want another baby because it feels like a baby is missing—Steven is missing. I wish I didn't miss him so much, and I thought I'd feel better and go forward instead of backward.

—Alison

It's important to remember that sometimes, going backward is actually a part of your adjustment going forward. And, instead of trying to leave behind the baby you miss, do keep your bond and take your memories of that precious baby with you, forward into the future. Keeping your bond and your memories can help you feel connected and less discouraged when you find yourself continuing to grieve. Then over time, and as you settle in with your new baby, you will feel less bereft and soon you'll notice that your baby who died isn't center stage anymore, and that's okay because he or she remains an integral part of you. You can also see that your lovely new baby requires you to adjust your focus, and you feel gratitude for how this child graces your life. And your healing continues.

Losing Judah shook me to my core and changed me as a person, and in that way he is always, always a part of me. I thought of him at Christmastime and how he would've been old enough to "help" me make cookies now. Sometimes Aviana stares at his pictures on the wall. I think about him in moments that are as fleeting as those, and I can acknowledge the thought and emotion and then let it pass. I feel more at peace.

—Jolie

Having that new baby in our arms was actually very healing. Not the same as having Ashley back, but healing nonetheless.

—Shellie

Bonding with Your Newborn

I held her so tight that my midwife had to say, "You need to loosen your hold on her so she can breathe!" And it took ten minutes before I was even interested in whether she was a girl or a boy, I was just so thankful she was here and she was okay.

—Melanie

Meeting Owain and seeing him for the first time was amazing. I also felt I could breathe normally again as I finally had this perfect human in my arms and he was alive. The love I felt was instant. I don't think Owain will ever realize that he was my sunshine after the storm I had lived through.

—Lorna

I just remember being in awe—that's the only way I can describe it.
All I could say was "I love you."

—Jolie

Some parents fall instantly in love with their newborns. But many other parents need time. Their love blooms as they hold, care for, and get acquainted with their little one. Lorna recalls, "After getting the all clear, and once I got to properly look at and hold him, I was able to relax and bring down those barriers, allow myself to love him, and enjoy my baby." Other parents are hesitant, as they feel anxious that this baby isn't theirs to keep. Kitty remembers, "I didn't fall instantly in love with her because I felt like someone was going to snatch her away, just like with Melanie." Martina agrees: "Up until she was about a year old, I went through times of feeling like I was taking care of a baby that wasn't mine, that she wasn't really ours and someone was going to come and take her and I wouldn't see her again."

At first I was afraid to love Nicholas, a child full of life, for fear of losing him. For so long, I felt as though I only knew how to love dead children and I was frightened that Nicholas, too, would die.

—Sheila

Whether you're struggling or not, you can cultivate your bond by holding your baby skin-to-skin (also called "kangaroo care"). Putting your naked baby (maybe with a diaper) on your bare chest is an extremely effective way to feel close to your baby. Skin-to-skin contact has powerful effects on the mother's brain and body that can ward off postpartum depression, reduce anxiety, promote feelings of devotion and confidence, and increase the production of breast milk. Fathers and coparents can reap some of these benefits as well. Equally important, kangaroo care is beneficial to your baby's well-being, with powerful positive effects on physical, emotional, and intellectual development. It's also soothing to your baby's brain, helping your baby feel calm and sleep better. Starting at birth, precious little should come between you and your newborn.

Once I saw Brenna I knew I loved her, but the feeling was much more intense once I held her skin-to-skin and I got to see my little girl and bond with her. I got to listen to her cry and the sounds she makes when she sleeps, and just hold her. Brenna still loves being next to me. She sleeps longer next to me than she does in her cot. It is so special and doesn't last long so I am enjoying it while it lasts.

—Lorna

If you're adopting, you may have additional concerns about bonding. Can you feel connected to a child you didn't carry in your body? What if you missed early infancy? Adoption certainly does require a leap of faith. But bonding experiences like skin-to-skin contact will have the same benefits and endear you to each other. And like a birth parent, as you spend time holding, taking care of, and getting acquainted, you'll discover that your heart expands to love this child who's been entrusted to you.

> *I can't believe Charlie has been with us for over ten weeks now! It really seems as though he has always been with us. And the bond? Somehow, it is happening. On meeting him for the very first time at the carer's home, I remember the look on his face—that's when it started. And so for nine days we kept visiting, and our time spent with Charlie grew longer and so the bond deepened further. In the meantime, Charlie is doing wonderfully. We have been truly blessed.*
>
> —Victoria

Five months later, Victoria describes how the bond has grown and strengthened over time. "I've allowed nature to take its course; the love appears like a shot from nowhere and the nurturing just happens. It's been the same for Tom and his bond with his brother. At first, I was trying to put A and B together, but things in life happen in their own time, as we now know very well."

Whatever route you've taken, when you welcome your new child into your family, the bond does grow, even if the path is quite bumpy or complicated. In fact, you may be surprised by how messy and demanding the newborn period can be. Even experienced mothers like Karen are not immune to postpartum struggles. She says, "I am in the process of getting some supports put in place and will be put under the care of the Postnatal Adjustment Team which I'm hoping will be enough to keep me afloat." Thankfully, many societies recognize the value of postpartum support for mothers and families.

> *Nico is a truly delightful wee boy who recognizes his mummy and wants her when he is unhappy. His older siblings are besotted with him and his daddy seems to be getting a lot of joy from him. But the journey that is unfolding is starting to look a little like it's unraveling. The lack of sleep and a highly demanding baby are taking their toll and I'm starting to struggle with my mood. I'm at a point where I just want to sit and cry when he is upset and inconsolable. I know there is a light at the end of the tunnel and I know I can do this, but it's going to be a long, hard journey until we get to the other side.*
>
> —Karen

> *It was really hard for me being home alone with Aviana at first. Charlie works ten-hour days and we don't have any family nearby, so I was on my own getting used to an entirely different schedule and lifestyle. That, together with postpartum depression, made it feel almost unbearable most days and I couldn't imagine how (or why) stay-at-home moms did it. It was awful. Postpartum depression is seriously just so awful! After getting help from antidepressants and counseling though, I felt like I could finally bond with Aviana and enjoy her. I am a totally different person than I was a few weeks ago and I have a totally different relationship with Aviana.*
>
> —Jolie

If kangaroo care doesn't seem to be the whole solution and you have nagging concerns about your maternal feelings, ask your doctor or midwife for an evaluation for postpartum depression. Either parent could benefit from extra support and perhaps a brain-based treatment for trauma. Do whatever frees you to enjoy your baby and form a sturdy bond. Parenting an infant is such a precious and fleeting time. You deserve to enjoy it. (See also "Postpartum Depression" in chapter 5; "Counseling" in chapter 13; chapter 4, "Mindfulness-Based Coping Strategies.")

PARENTING SUBSEQUENT CHILDREN

I am so eternally grateful to have Zara. She is such a dear wee thing. I don't take her for granted. Not that I took my other daughters for granted, but our experiences have solidified how fragile life can be.

—*Melanie*

Most parents find that the death of a baby profoundly affects their relationship with the children born afterward. Parents often mention a heightened appreciation for these precious children, protective feelings, and a desire to be the best parent possible. Many also have a strong desire to make sure their subsequent children know about the baby who died. In the past, some of these reactions were considered unhealthy, but in reality, they are usually harmless, often beneficial, and a natural consequence of bereavement. Moreover, these feelings are common and normal.

If you have older children or a surviving baby or babies from a multiple pregnancy, you may notice similar effects on your relationships with them.

Losing Willow had a profound impact on my life, including my experience of fathering Noa, Blossom, and River. I'm not sure how exactly. I guess that ever since losing Willow I have had a clearer understanding of the fragility and the dignity of life.

—*Nathan*

TALKING ABOUT THE BABY WHO DIED

You may wonder when your subsequent children are able to understand or appreciate the significance of a baby sibling who isn't around. Liza notes, "I've shown Michelle [age three] his picture, but she just seems to think it's a little baby." You may decide to wait until your children are older or start asking questions.

I want to wait until the kids are eight or nine. I guess I want them to understand. I think they'll be sad and I think they'll want to go see the grave, but I don't want Meg going to kindergarten and bragging, "I had a brother" and showing off about it and chatting about it like it meant nothing. So I thought if she was a little older she might understand it. I just don't want it to become trite.

—*Bess*

I know a lot of people who say, "Well, my mom had a stillborn," like that didn't really matter, it wasn't important. But that was your sister or brother! I want Emily to feel, "Yeah, I had a sister that was older than me, but she died and her name was Nicole."

—Cindy

If you don't want to wait, you can start by pointing to pictures and other mementos and gradually explaining in simple terms what happened to this brother or sister of theirs. Many parents just matter-of-factly talk about the baby whose photograph is prominently displayed and let their children's responses be their guide. Shellie says, "We are open about Ashley's life and death, and death in general. We talk about her. We keep photos in our house and celebrate her birthday. We go to the cemetery together. I don't want them to be scared of death but rather to know that it's a natural part of the cycle for all living things."

Just know that because death is abstract, no matter how carefully you explain, most young children will harbor strange ideas. But this is rarely a cause for concern. If you remain available for questions, your children can engage your help if they do have worries. Having an ongoing conversation is both a way to integrate your baby into the family and a way to accommodate your children's curiosity and growing knowledge. (See also "Integrating Your Baby into the Family" in chapter 17.)

James is almost four now. He learned about death initially by seeing dead animals, so we were able to talk about what happens when bodies die: how they go back into the earth, but how the people (or animals) who loved them might miss them and be very sad. And when you live close to a cemetery, as we do, you learn what they're all about, even if you don't have a dead sibling. On one of our recent walks to Thor's grave, he asked me what was written on the gravestone—he's at an age where he's interested in letters and how words are put together. So I showed him the letters in Thor's name and explained who he was. He processed this news in a very kid-logical kind of way. He understood that Thor had grown in my tummy but then had died, so he concluded that he, James, must have grown in Glenn's tummy. Then I had to double back and give a refresher on the subject of adoption. No, not my tummy, but not Daddy's tummy either.

—Elizabeth

At one time Gary [age three] wanted to know if he could dig Jamie up and play with him. I thought I did a really great job of explaining death to him, and then he asks, "Can we go dig him up and play with him?" Then I showed him a picture of Jamie, and you think you're so smart with your kids and you're just not. I thought I did this great discussion, "This is your brother, he died, etc.," and like a week later there's a picture of him at my mother's house—of him [Jamie] when he was a baby—and he said, "Oh look, there's me when I was dead." So I don't know what he understands.

—Sara

Even though it may be a while before they can grasp the concept of death or of a sibling who isn't visible, your children will simply fit the information into their own intellectual framework. As they get older and more sophisticated, your ongoing conversations can help them reorganize their ideas. (Also see "Children's Understanding of Death" in chapter 12.)

HEIGHTENED APPRECIATION

Parents typically feel an enhanced appreciation for all their surviving children. You don't take for granted their health and survival. You may also reorder your priorities and strive to be closer to them. Kara notes, "You realize things aren't forever and you appreciate everything they do and what they are." Destrida agrees, "One thing for sure, I am enjoying more of the little things and every moment I get to spend with my children now than before." Embry adds, "I'm just really reminding myself to enjoy them, to make them a priority, to count them as very special gifts that I've been entrusted with." Jane elaborates: "I view Jenny as a child that wouldn't have been if I hadn't lost the other one."

> *My husband in the last year has become a stay-at-home dad as we felt that we needed one of us to be home, to be there to look after our children. It has also given us a lot more opportunity for family time, which our kids love. . . . And Dave and I do not sweat the small stuff, such as sleepless nights. I believe we are much more relaxed in some areas, as we appreciate having our children with us.*
>
> *—Lorna*

You may particularly acknowledge how much having a subsequent child has added to your emotional healing and feel profound gratitude, and even redemption. Victoria notes, "I now walk with my head in the air, though soon after Alex's death, I didn't have this attitude or body language. This changed when Charlie joined the family." Like most parents, you may consider this deeper appreciation to be one of the positive lessons acquired from dealing with the death of your baby.

The downside to heightened appreciation is that it may spark feelings of vulnerability. When you think about how special your children are, it seems you would have that much more to lose should tragedy strike. Abby notices, "Emma has made my life deeper and more meaningful, so without a doubt I am a better parent because of that. In the same breath I have moments where I feel terrified for Conner to hurt himself and I always go to the worst-case scenario." Karen vows, "I will move heaven and earth to make sure all my children are protected—physically, emotionally, and spiritually."

PROTECTIVENESS

> *All parents worry about their children, but I think there's a certain amount of denial that exists that allows you to really believe in your*

heart that something is not going to happen to them. And then when something does happen to one of your children, you know it can happen, you know it's for real.

—Anya

It stands to reason that protective feelings would arise from firsthand experience with the death of a baby. You may feel that life is very tenuous, that you can't count on everything turning out all right. It is normal to be vigilant.

I think about the fact that she could die, probably more than most parents, and that scares me. I don't think most parents think about that or want to, but it's reality. It could happen.

—Cindy

I'm a lot more protective and smothering. I worry every night whether he will wake up in the morning and I check on him so many times in the night. I worry about the little things. Some days I feel as if I have him wrapped up in cotton wool a bit too tightly.

—Fleur

When he was jaundiced at birth I was sure that he had liver problems; the first cold, I was sure it was pneumonia. Everything that kid did I was sure was going to end his life. I didn't leave that baby with a sitter for over a year. I did not let that child nap without my interrupting the nap for a year. I was terrified he was going to die and I was gonna be sure that I was going to be there when he did. I didn't even want to leave him with my husband because I just knew that if something happened to him and I wasn't there, that would be it for me, if that happened with two kids. I remember thinking, "I will just definitely kill myself then, definitely."

—Sara

Parents vary on how vulnerable they feel, but many have these and other fears to some extent. For some, anxiety may subside quite a bit after the baby is born and safely in arms. Others find it gradually easier to relax as the child survives infancy. But it's common to always feel susceptible to the fact that this child could die too, especially when injuries and illnesses come along, or as the child starts going out into the world. Rose sums up her fears: "With Lori, I just never knew. I thought if she didn't have some kind of problem internally, that she would die of SIDS [sudden infant death syndrome]. If she didn't die of SIDS she'd die of something else, get hit by a car, whatever."

I worried that there could be something wrong with Francesco. I was obsessed with this idea. Francesco was a colicky baby; he kept crying and I had no way of soothing him. I was in this spell for a few months, and only when we got out of the colic did I start to feel reassured that there was nothing wrong with him.

—Annalaura

We are very protective of them. Especially my husband, for example, with sickness it's "straight to A&E" [Accident and Emergency] when I know it's nothing more than just sickness. Mathew likes to be sure and panics a little. He Googles info and is very attentive. I'm more laid back.

—*Victoria*

The babysitter texted me that Aviana wouldn't stop screaming. So, we decided to go to the doctor right away to see what was up. On the way there my mind started going. What if it's something more serious that we can't see? I was paranoid, and I thought to myself, "Is this grief-induced?" Well, the obvious answer was "yes." I know first-time moms can be overprotective and concerned, but I'm assuming most don't go from thinking "ear infection" to "death."

—*Jolie*

Even if your baby is strong and healthy, you may worry about exposure to contagious diseases or a mild illness turning into a life-threatening situation. You may be on guard against accidents such as choking, falling, or car wrecks. If your child does have health problems, or becomes seriously ill, your overprotective feelings can be intensified. On the flip side, be careful that you don't overcompensate for your protective urges by ignoring signs of illness or neglecting hazardous situations. This could actually endanger your child's health and safety.

I always worried about him choking on something and I always thought I was going to feed him Cream of Wheat until he was five so I would never have to worry about him choking. I have had a first-aid class so I know what to do, but that doesn't mean I could do it if I had to. I think of all these off-the-wall things that could happen to him.

—*Peg*

*I can handle a little sickness, but if they get really sick, I become very uptight and supersensitive to them. Like the time Kim had pneumonia when she was sixteen months old and I immediately escalated that into something really life-threatening. Unfortunately, when Jared was eight days old we discovered he had meningitis, which **is** life-threatening. It was real scary because I thought, "This baby is going to be taken away from me too."*

—*Anya*

*He got a rash and I didn't want to rush him to the doctor. I didn't want to be one of **those** mothers because I had been to the doctor so much, and I thought, "We're not going to start this." Then it turned out to be a serious staph infection!*

—*Desi*

To ease feelings of vulnerability and anxiety, try the mindfulness practices and brain-calming strategies in chapter 4. Other skills that come in handy are being attuned to your children and discerning between your imaginary fears and what you're actually observing in the present moment (see "Acknowledging Your Imagination" and "Tuning into Your Intuition" in chapter 15.) You may also benefit from supportive counseling or a brain-based therapy to release you from the trauma of your baby's death. (See "Counseling" in chapter 13.)

Like many parents, you may notice that as your tiny newborn grows into a robust baby and child, your confidence grows too. Melanie admits, "I was always checking on her in the night expecting to find her dead. And that continued until she was probably one. She is now fifteen months and that feeling has definitely eased." Cindy notes her progress, observing, "In her first bath she screamed and I cried, so my mom bathed her. Now I dunk her in there and say, 'You're okay.' I feel more comfortable now since we lived through the newborn period."

Also continue to go with the flow of your grief and engage in your tasks of mourning. As your grief softens, you'll likely feel less reactive and vulnerable. Your budding sense of peace and healing can also be accompanied by a budding sense of trust in a benevolent universe. And if you have more subsequent children, you may notice that you can be more relaxed.

The other day we went to a park with one of my girlfriends, and she has a girl who's three days older than Emily. Her little girl went over to the slides and just started playing. And I thought, "I can't let Emily go down the slide by herself; I can't sit back and let her do it alone! I have to be there and stand there!" But I can't go in the sand since I have a cast on my foot, so I had to decide—let her go or she won't be able to play. And I let her go and it was really hard. She got up those slides and did like every other kid, and it was a good feeling to me. I said, "Wow, I let her go and she did it!" I didn't even realize I could do that.

—Cindy

I had a successful baby. Lori was alive and well, and I knew I could do it. A baby of mine could live past five days. So with Anna, I'm probably raising her a little bit more normally. I've gotten in the routine of having healthy kids and I know that they'll probably be fine. I'm over those paranoid feelings, other than little surges of panic. I don't think Anna is going to die every time I leave her in the bedroom.

—Rose

BEING THE BEST PARENT YOU CAN BE

As part of the transformative experience of mourning the death of your baby, you may also be keen on transforming your approach to parenting. Indeed, raising your children can be a transformative journey into the kind of parent you want to be.

A loss like this changes us in so many ways, so I'd be naive to think it hasn't affected my parenting. If anything I think I take time to enjoy

my son more than I would have when I was busy, busy, busy, and
stressed with work and life. I have slowed down a lot more.

—*Abby*

Indeed, bereaved mothers and fathers tend to come into parenthood with a special eagerness to be the best parents possible. You may feel extra devoted and take your parenting very seriously, with an added sense of responsibility to do the right thing with your precious children.

I think you better appreciate something that's harder to get. I think
he's more special. I would hope that I would treat any baby that I
had well and do my best, but I think it just makes me more aware of
how much I did want him and how special babies really are and that
you're really responsible once you have them for how they grow up.

—*Peg*

I'm home with them most of the days, so I spend a significant amount
of time with them. Bodhi has been a reminder to me to focus on
mentally being there for my kids, while allowing them to be kids—to
play, learn on their own, fall on their own, succeed on their own.
Bodhi never got those opportunities and I owe it to him to let Claeson
and Paige experience them.

—*Ben*

I think I'm more patient or more tolerant of some things than I would
have been if I hadn't lost a baby. Not to the extent of not feeling
comfortable stopping certain things, but it just makes you stop and
think, "Is this really important?" You know, he might not even be here.
I'm concerned about doing the right thing, the right parenting things.
I want to do things that are basically good for him. I want to provide
him with good experiences. I don't believe in Super Baby, but I want
to give him the best, be a good parent.

—*Hannah*

Wanting to do your best is a positive goal. Unfortunately, there is a lot of conflicting parenting advice out there. Indeed, there is no formula or one "right way" to raise a child. Parenting is an art that must make room for the uniqueness of each child and parent, and any philosophy must accommodate all the different pathways to success. So as you sift through social trends, the latest tricks of the trade, and the stream of parenting advice that's readily available, focus on learning "how to think," not just "what to think."

Thanks to Bodhi, I am more aware of how I react and feel, and I pay
attention to how Claeson and Paige react and feel about things too.
The entire experience with Bodhi has led to me analyzing myself and
life in a way that helps and will likely help me with those two, in ways
that I don't think many parents ever get to experience.

—*Ben*

What Ben describes could be considered "mindful parenting." Mindful parenting is the practice of being self-aware and reflective so you can consciously strive for communicating effectively, guiding appropriately, and setting wise priorities. Mindful parents are intent on nurturing their children, respecting them as individuals, supporting healthy and whole development, and giving them what they need to thrive.

> *My emphasis is on my new family, to focus on Tom and Charlie. To provide them with what they deserve in life and hopefully reap some of the benefits. Yes I am tired, but it's so worth it. I will do my darnedest to teach Charlie what love is, what kindness is, how to respect an honor oneself and others, to have faith and hope and generally, try to be a good person.*
>
> —Victoria

> *I think just being there for him and loving him and giving him security so he can grow, to me is the most important thing that I can do for him.*
>
> —Sara

Mindful parenting can include approaches like *attachment parenting, developmentally supportive parenting, conscious parenting,* and *brain-based parenting.* These are philosophies and strategies of parenting rather than sets of instructions. They can be practiced concurrently, as there is much overlap and consistency. All of them accommodate the need for individually tailored parenting. And all of them recognize that parenting is a journey, not of perfection, but of continuous learning and constant adjusting, because the landscape is always changing. Your child continues to grow and develop, as do you. Inevitably, just as you've figured out a solution to a challenge, your child moves on to the next challenge—and now you're in new territory and it's back to the drawing board. And that's why most parents can attest to the fact that there's never a dull moment.

> *I had some idea that there was some kind of perfect parent and I was going to do that, that I would never scold her, and I just let my imagination go wild with me. I felt like I could just be Super Mom because of what had happened. It's been kind of a shock to find out that I'm pretty ordinary. . . . I somehow thought I could read all the books and be a perfect mother, and it's been difficult to realize that no one has all the answers and that I really have to go from day to day.*
>
> —Liza

> *It's hard learning the balance between knowing when to raise my voice and when to just stop and hug and when to just leave them alone, but that's probably a lifetime of learning what they need, when. The experience with Bodhi is a constant reminder to do what I can with them.*
>
> —Ben

WHEN ANOTHER BABY DIES

After Laura died, I had a miscarriage and that was real hard. It was depressing. It made me think, "Maybe I really am not going to be a mother." I felt like a victim, like maybe there was something out there that was going to get me, and that was a bad feeling.

—*Hannah*

The miscarriage hurt too. It was like, add another one to the list. When I think about getting pregnant—I had a miscarriage, I had a stillbirth, I had an almost-premature baby—I mean, what's going to happen next?

—*Cindy*

To have these miscarriages that once again you had no answers for and you couldn't control . . . the miscarriages really compounded my grief and just made it more difficult to keep going, to function, to want to continue. I just would have rather been dead. The pain was unbearable sometimes.

—*Holly*

After your first experience with a baby dying, your greatest fear is that it will happen again. If it does, it can be devastating. You may wonder if it's a sign of deeper problems, a prelude to chronic infertility, or a definite inability to bear a healthy baby. You may feel like even more of a failure. You may lose faith in optimism, good intentions, and the universe. You may feel shocked, like you just don't *understand*. And you may feel even more angry than ever. It's *so* unfair.

I fell pregnant nine months later but went on to have a miscarriage, which felt like a punch when I was already knocked down.

—*Embry*

With Michael, most people around me could not understand my anxiety being pregnant, including my husband. Just when I was starting to feel hopeful around fourteen to fifteen weeks, I was told that our baby died inside of me, again. After his birth, it was hard. I did not understand it. I was sad, and mad. Confused.

—*Anne*

At twenty-seven weeks, we went up to the labor ward and they hooked me up to the machine and they found a heartbeat, which was a huge relief. I told the midwife our story of our loss of Kate and how anxious we were. My stomach was still rock hard. Then she couldn't find the heartbeat. She called another midwife in to try, and she couldn't so they went and got another machine, and she still couldn't find it. So they called the on-call registrar to come and do a scan. But by now I am losing it. That this cannot be happening again to us. We cannot be losing another baby. My husband is down the end of the bed where the doctor and ultrasound are and I can see it in his face, there is no heartbeat. I just cannot believe that this has happened again.

—Melanie

I got my hopes up though I knew I shouldn't. I thought that the beautiful coincidences were "signs" that this time we would make it. That this was the one. But that rainbow in the sky at fourteen weeks was not for me. Perhaps somewhere some other mother was getting her miracle. I was not getting mine.

—Tanya

After a number of losses, you may feel more anxious than ever at the prospect of being pregnant. You may fear that you could never survive another baby's death. But you are probably more resilient than you think, and like many of the mothers above, you might gather up the courage to try yet again. And if you decide you're done trying, your resilience will help you discover another fulfilling path.

Points to Remember

- During subsequent pregnancies, it is normal for bereaved parents to feel hesitant about investing in the baby or a positive outcome.
- If investing in the new baby makes you feel guilty or disloyal to your baby who died, this only reflects your ongoing grief and a desire to protect your baby's memory.
- Although it is challenging, it is possible to manage competing feelings—to express hope for the future *and* grief for the past. Continuing to mourn enhances your adjustment to your baby's death *and* prepares a healthy foundation for your relationship with the subsequent baby.
- Over the course of the pregnancy, you will likely make more and more small gestures that reveal the growing bond you have to your baby. There are many simple activities and thoughts that count as bonding.
- Like subsequent pregnancy, adoption can also be an arduous process that includes happy anticipation, anxiety, fear, and guarded optimism.
- It is normal to have strong preferences about your new baby's sex. If you are disappointed, saying, "This is not what I wanted" can help you mindfully observe and accept these feelings, and also accept your little boy or girl.
- During the birth, it is normal to think about your previous experiences. If you experienced a traumatic labor or birth with your baby who died, to avoid being transported back to that harrowing time, proactively seek a brain-based treatment for trauma. There is no reason to add unnecessary suffering to this birth experience.
- After the birth, it is normal for you to grieve deeply, as having another baby can act as a catalyst for your grief about the baby who died.
- Make room for your grief and your joy. Finding a balance rather than trying to suppress emotions will benefit you and your baby.
- Mothering an infant is a precious and fleeting time. You deserve to enjoy it. Seek postpartum support and if necessary, treatment for postpartum depression.
- Most parents find that the death of a baby profoundly affects their relationships with the children born afterward. Parents often mention a heightened appreciation for these precious children, protective feelings, and a desire to be the best parent possible.
- If you experience the death of another baby, you can use what you have learned about grief and gathering memories. You will survive this too.

17

LIVING IN REMEMBRANCE

And so life goes on, but we're not the same. We look at life through different eyes and with a different heart.
                                                            —Victoria

These tiny souls should never be underestimated. Their lives are undeniably short but the profound lessons they bring us will last a lifetime.
                                                            —Emmerson

You will always remember your baby. As you grieve and come to terms with your baby's death, you find that life goes on. Your sadness never completely disappears, but it does soften and your baby's life acquires new meaning. Instead of creating endless suffering, grief settles into the background, and you integrate this entire journey into the larger tapestry of your life. All you've learned, how you've grown, and what you'll do going forward is a result of you prevailing in the face of tragedy and living in honor of your baby. You can acquire a new or renewed sense of purpose and meaning in your life, and with that, you become a part of your baby's legacy.

Prior to the past month or so I had accepted that my purpose in life was simply to be a wandering soul. I always knew there was something that I was born to do, that I was going to excel at, and that God had given me the gifts to spend my life doing, but I just could never find what it was. It was such an unbelievably frustrating feeling—having the motivation and the yearning to do something but not know what it was! I have spent so many days daydreaming, praying, and brainstorming about this. It has always made me so depressed thinking that I may not find my purpose in life, or maybe that my purpose in life doesn't have as much meaning as I had hoped. The current training I am in and my most recent decision to go on to obtain my master's in clinical counseling . . . it holds the meaning to my life. In no way does the idea of getting the opportunity to help other bereaved families make my losses seem "worth it," but it sure does restore some of the purpose and meaning that my life lacked and lost.
                                                            —Jolie

My world is completely changed from that experience. In my daughter's honor I worked on so many things that were holding me back. I wanted that experience and her life (death) to have had a purpose and meaning. For me, it was a very strong impetus to work on myself and our marriage.
                                                            —Julie

I have found great meaning in this experience. There were many gifts that came out of Ashley's brief life. I have a closer relationship with a few people who weren't as important to me before. I was able to help other parents—by listening, by sharing our story, and by lovingly making the hospital care packages. I know that our story has touched and inspired other people, and that is a beautiful legacy for Ashley. My career change after ten years of teaching was greatly inspired by our experiences with Ashley. I am just about to start my first job in my new field [genetic counseling]. I'm excited and feel it will be a way to honor our daughter.

—Shellie

I knew from the very beginning that Pearl's life was not going to be for nothing. I knew something good had to come out of this . . . something to help others not to feel so alone. I longed to create a legacy for my baby . . . my other children were creating their legacy each day and Pearl would be no different.

—Laura

She has made me a better person and I try on a daily basis to honor her. I am really looking forward to my next journey, which is leading a Share bereavement group. It's an amazing organization and I am honored to have gone through their training and to be bringing a chapter to our city. I feel blessed that I will be helping other families heal and work through their grief.

—Abby

I was determined for Willow's sake to live beyond her death in a way that would serve tribute to her. Both my wife and I very early on decided that the most beautiful way that we could honor Willow's life was to grieve her well, and to eventually live beyond that grief in graceful and meaningful ways. That was incredibly important to us.

—Nathan

It doesn't matter whether you reach outward to make a difference in the lives of others, or you reach inward to make a difference in your own life and how you live it. Either way, you can emanate mindfulness as you make your way in the world. Through you, your baby's legacy can have an impact that is more far-reaching than you'll ever know.

YOUR HEALING TRANSFORMATION

For a long time after we lost Kate I spent a lot of time wishing I could get back to being the happy carefree person I was. I was so lost and overwhelmed and so consumed by my grief, I felt I was never going to be happy again. Why can't I be like I was? But we are all shaped by our experiences. And I feel like I am a different person now than before I lost Kate and Zac. I would describe my life in two versions: the "before-baby-loss" and the "after-baby-loss."

—Melanie

*I've changed completely. I'm more aware, understanding, at times
a little selfish (as advised by our counselor), caring, interested in
others, not afraid to talk to people who are bereaved. And I'm more
confident, not only completing the marathon and adopting a little boy,
but I'm now two months away from completing a degree, with honors,
all because of Alex.*

—Victoria

As grief softens, most parents notice that they've changed. Not only do
they see the world differently, they see themselves differently. And after
wishing they could return to "normal," they discover that they can adjust
to a "new normal" and even embrace how they've changed and grown.
Here are nine "ways of being" that are described by many parents as key
parts of their healing transformations.

NEW STRENGTHS REVEALED

For many parents, grieving and surviving the death of a baby teaches
them about life and reveals new strengths. You may surprise yourself with
the courage, stamina, and resilience you have displayed. Liza reports, "I
must be a lot stronger than I thought I was. I'm amazed that a person can
reinvest in life after going through this." Lena observes, "I've acquired the
courage to face things I wouldn't have been able to face before as easily."

*My life was mostly charmed before this happened. Going through
this helped me to grow as a person. I realized I am stronger than I
thought and that I can get through difficult times.*

—Shellie

*Although at times I feel incredibly weak on this journey of ups and
downs, I now know and acknowledge how truly strong I am.*

—Emmerson

*I must say that I can't believe that I am still here, that I can lose a
child and still live! This was unfathomable to me before. So in a way,
life today is easier than I thought it would be.*

—Destrida

NEW EMOTIONAL SKILLS

You may acquire skills that serve your emotional regulation and your relationships, new and old. You may feel more in touch with your feelings and
understand the value of mindfully observing them, acknowledging them, and
letting them flow through you. As a result of your own emotional wholeness,
you may find that you are better able to accept a wide range of emotions
in your partner, your children, and others close to you. Your relationships
may feel more satisfying and your life may feel more aligned with your true
self. Abby notes, "This has taken awhile to see but I know now I am more

connected to life than I was before. She has empowered me in so many ways from friendships to my marriage to figuring out my next career."

I'm grateful for how much we grew from this experience and how much better our marriage is. I also feel gratitude for our friends, family, and therapist who ushered us through that horrible year after. Once you go through that with somebody, they are with you for life.

—Julie

We definitely took a big step in our marriage in terms of knowing that we were there for each other. Bodhi's death, it's just sort of a binder—it feels like a rope that circles our family and it's there for us to grab on when we're distracted, busy, or things are just hectic. Not essential to keep us together, but just another connection.

—Ben

After something like a stillbirth, there are all sorts of microadjustments. Some of my friendships have changed, but they've all survived. And those friendships have been affected by other things as well: other tragedies, other insults, other gestures of generosity or moments of joy. The stillbirth is now part of a very complex tapestry in my friendships.

—Elizabeth

I always thought life was precious, and this experience has reinforced for me the importance of allowing people to be how they need to be, to respect our differences, to love openly and honestly, and how critical communication is.

—Emmerson

New Sense of Self

You may become more assertive. You stand up for yourself instead of trusting your fate to others. You also take care of yourself first, instead of always sacrificing for others. Winnie explains, "I've learned to say 'No.' Now I ask myself whether I'm doing this or that because I want to, or because I *should*. I'm tossing out the *shoulds*." Lena agrees: "I have come to value more what I do and realizing I have to do things for me too. I can't be all things to all other people."

I'm my own person now and I don't know if I'd have become that way if I hadn't lost Jessica. I think that forces you to get in touch with yourself, what you need.

—Rose

Now I look out for me first and then I do for others, because when Scott died I discovered nobody watches out for me, but me! Since I made this decision, I feel much better about myself and I have more self-respect.

—Kelly

I am learning to speak my truth, take care of myself, and to let go of friendships and relationships that no longer serve me.

—Tanya

Practicing self-compassion can seem mandatory now. Julie says, "When I think of her and that time in our lives, there is a strong feeling of tenderness, both for her and for us, and what we went through." As you develop a more nurturing, compassionate relationship with yourself, you can feel more compassion for others. In particular, you may be more sensitive to other bereaved people and better able to offer kindness and support. Karen says, "I'm blessed that I have walked this path and that I can hopefully help others. I have learned a lot about forgiveness and healing."

I think I found a lot more compassion for myself and for others—consideration, understanding, accepting other people and myself.

—Meryl

I have been humbled. Greatly. I think losing them, experiencing death, has enabled me to slow down, and really listen to people's struggles in life. I do not judge as quickly as I had in the past. You rarely know the full story. I am able to give sincere, honest empathy and sympathy in a variety of circumstances.

—Anne

Jedidiah's legacy has seriously given me a whole new set of lenses for people and I am forever grateful to him for that. It opened my eyes to take life more seriously, be more selfless, and treat people differently, to have grace on others, knowing we all have our stories, usually involving some level of pain or trauma.

—Embry

Losing my daughter has sent me on a path to raise awareness, to speak my truth, to help others in the same situation, to pay it forward, and do "random acts of kindness" so my baby's name is spoken in the world.

—Emmerson

NEW PRIORITIES

You may feel a heightened appreciation for what you have. You may have clarified your values and straightened out your priorities. Holly remarks, "I value life more and my child more. I try not to take things for granted or dwell on picky little things that don't matter." Peg agrees: "It makes me aware of what's really important. I worry about the big things, try and deal with those, and I'm much calmer about the little things." Lena adds, "I treasure life more than I ever did—my own, my children's, even the ants on the driveway." Many parents sense a spiritual component to this.

I am not interested in being caught up in people's petty dramas and I think that comes from really not sweating the small stuff anymore.
—Melanie

I used to worry about small stupid insignificant stuff, now I just go, "Oh well, I can deal with that and it will be okay."
—Lorna

I am a more appreciative and thankful person now. Even in the darkest of times, I couldn't swear off life, God, or the universe. I have been so blessed for having had my daughter.
—Destrida

NEW MINDFULNESS

You may have learned to become more mindful about life in general. Perhaps you slow down your pace, appreciate the simple things, stay connected to your body, and live in the present moment. Instead of rushing around *doing*, you savor *being*. And life seems richer.

Though at times life can be hard, it's just about putting on the brakes and being grateful and happy for what we have in front us.
—Victoria

I live a lot more for the moment. I think before I was so busy rushing that I was missing out on enjoying the moment. I spend a lot of time at the beach with the girls and it's been so nice to take in a deep breath, feel the warmth of the sun on my face, watch the girls digging holes in the sand and playing in the driftwood, and be able to smile.
—Melanie

I am much more accepting of my spiritual side since I had Finley. I integrate every aspect of myself in my work and daily life now, and it is a very pleasant way to be.
—Mel

I don't take things for granted anymore, and because of this I live an enriched life compared to before she died.
—Abby

I have changed in my outlook on life. I have to chosen to be happy, finding the small joys in things, laughing when I can. Knowing its okay to be sad and its okay to ring friends and ask for a cuppa. They always have time.
—Sarah

NEW AWARENESS

You're also more jaded. Now you *know* how vulnerable you are to tragedy. And you realize the extent to which certain aspects of your life are beyond your control. Anya admits, "This experience was good for me in the sense that it taught me that you can't think that things go a certain way just necessarily because you do all the right things." At first this is frightening, but as you discern what's out of your hands, there is freedom in just doing what you can and letting the rest fall into place, as it will. This attitude lets you put your energy where it matters—toward trying to control only what is actually controllable. This includes controlling *yourself* and making conscious choices. You can even choose how to perceive the world around you and choose how to make your way through it.

> *My whole life changed that day. At first it changed for the worse. Everything I had ever believed, I suddenly questioned. Everything suddenly became scary and unknown and I felt like anything could happen at any time . . . until not too far down the road I realized I didn't want to live that way. And I didn't want my baby's death to "be for nothing" so I let it change me for the good, for the better.*
>
> —Embry

> *My outlook on life has changed a little, in that it really is too short and to make the most of what you can. And treasure the moments you have with your loved ones, as you don't know what is around the corner.*
>
> —Kylie

New Courage

You may focus on what you really want out of life. When you realize that life is too short to waste a minute of it, you may take leaps you'd never had the courage to make. Or perhaps you take those leaps far sooner than you'd planned. You start living fully now, instead of waiting for who-knows-what, and you take advantage of the time you have.

> *I know more than ever that life is fleeting. The strength I found to get through losing her might have helped me find the courage to change careers. You definitely see the old adage "Life is too short" in a whole new way when you lose a child.*
>
> —Shellie

> *I might not have taken the leap of quitting a regular job as soon as I did. That's another "doing" thing that's all led to a whole different world.*
>
> —Ben

New Perspective

More assertive, brave, and focused on controlling what you can, you may also feel more self-reliant, that in a crisis you can count on yourself—but not necessarily others. You may feel wiser and older for your age, less naive, and more serious. This, along with awareness of your vulnerability to life's twists and turns, adds up to having a more realistic perspective that allows you to proceed with greater maturity, self-respect, and forgiveness.

> *What I have learned from this tragedy is not to trust others but to trust in oneself. To be listened to, heard and responded to, as well as respected. This is something I will take with me forever.*
>
> —*Victoria*

> *I am a bit more discerning about people, and sadly, less trusting. My eyes have been opened. I have been forced to see things that I didn't want to before.*
>
> —*Emmerson*

> *I am more somber. I take less for granted than I used to. I find it easier to accept disappointment and I have fewer expectations. I do not hold grudges. I find forgiveness to be easier.*
>
> —*Lavender*

NEW CONFIDENCE

With all these lessons learned, skills acquired, and relationships made stronger, you likely feel better equipped to face whatever life throws your way. Feelings of vulnerability become less frightening when coupled with feelings of confidence in your ability to prevail. Most parents eventually feel that through adversity, they have grown in ways that prepare them to cope with whatever the future holds.

> *I am acutely aware of death and how everything can change in an instant. I don't take anything for granted. I anticipate having more of those moments in my life and I'll be much better prepared emotionally the next time.*
>
> —*Julie*

> *Death doesn't affect or scare me like it used to. No matter what life has to throw at me, I can deal with it.*
>
> —*Fleur*

> *I have learned that if I can get through the death of my child—which has been the hardest thing I have had to live through—I can deal with anything.*
>
> —*Lorna*

And sometimes, what the future holds can be quite lovely, as Lorna can attest.

> *We went to decorate the Sands Christmas tree today and put all the decorations on from all the families who have lost a baby over the years. Interesting, as the last time I went to see the tree and hang our decoration for Ronin, I had no children and I couldn't imagine a*

future at that point. Now six Christmases on, I was there with three beautiful children.

—Lorna

ACCEPTANCE, PEACE, AND GRATITUDE

With a restored sense of control and a newfound confidence in your ability to prevail, you can accept your sense of vulnerability without undue fear. Vulnerability can even inspire you to live fully and appreciate what you have, knowing that nothing is guaranteed. But instead of being fearful, you see the value of accepting how your life unfolds. You can accept *what is*. You take things in stride. As Meryl says, "It made me more accepting to life and that these things happen. Sometimes we have all the control in the world and other times, there isn't any control at all." Abby agrees, "Accepting that this happened has been huge for my grief journey. It sucks but it's our reality. We cannot escape life's misfortunes."

I am coming to a different place in my grieving with Emily and Michael. I am coming to more of the "Acceptance" of it all. Not that I wouldn't change it, if I could. But I can't. I am feeling more at peace with embracing all that I do have, and am blessed with.

—Anne

I am not afraid of death. I'm accepting that no matter how we plan or try to direct, I understand that it is totally in God's hands and he knows exactly what's going on. My faith continues to develop and helps me in my everyday life, and I thank Alex for giving me this.

—Victoria

This newfound attitude of acceptance grants you the ability to go with the flow instead of fighting it. Accepting *what is* also enables you to let go of worries and any lingering guilt or regrets.

I am a lot more accepting that I cannot control everything. We have no control over a lot of what happens in life and there is no point expending energy worrying about what might happen.

—Melanie

To make peace with regrets, I acknowledge them, and understand decisions were made at that time and carried out to the best of the health care professionals' abilities. And I accept "it happened" and this certainly has made me the person I am today.

—Victoria

I have made peace knowing, with Michael especially, that I tried asking all of the right questions, and having tests done to see what I could do differently. I have learned that sometimes things are just out of our control. We like to think that we can control outcomes, but that is not always the case.

—Anne

Acceptance also includes being thankful for what you have instead of wishing for what you haven't. From this comes a sense of peace and gratitude. As Daniela says simply, "I love you baby Laure and I am so happy you came." In fact, for many parents, gratitude centers on their babies. A testament to the power of healing, raw grief turns into gratitude for the time they had with their babies. These are cherished memories, held close.

The time we had with Jamie was so brief, but now I can look back on that and smile. And I didn't think I'd ever smile about that. Every time I thought about that, it would make me cry. But now I'm grateful that I had that time, that I had him for three days, instead of none.

—*Sara*

My bond with Melina started before I saw her—when I felt her kick, when I sang to her, talked to her, imagined our future together. But seeing her and holding her and being with her was an experience that I truly cherish. So I am grateful to Melina for giving me the opportunity to love her and to mother her in our short thirty-six weeks together.

—*Helen*

I feel grateful that Oren was alive long enough (thirty-eight weeks in the womb) for him to react to the world outside the womb, rolling around while listening to my son Derek drumming, kicking me through the layers of flesh and muscle that held him tight. I am grateful that the little dude did not feel anything in his life but the warm embrace of his mom.

—*Lavender*

*I'm grateful that I had the opportunity to hold both of them. That I have that memory of **me with my children**.*

—*Sonya*

I'm grateful for Jed. I'm grateful for the fact that he was mine and I got to carry him and feel him alive in me for almost ten months. I'm grateful for all that I've learned because of him.

—*Embry*

I'm grateful for the opportunity to be Miriam's mother even for such a short time. For our bodies and souls intertwined.

—*Tanya*

Adisyn will always be my brightest shining light; I feel honored she chose us to be her parents.

—*Emmerson*

Gratitude can also be felt for the subsequent children who might not have been born if it weren't for the baby(s) who died.

I think another part of being grateful—I'm not sure Paige would be here if we hadn't lost Bodhi. If we'd had him with us, we may have considered being done with Clae. That's a tough thing to think of, but it's true. I'm not sure what I'd do without her busting through everything and making her opinion known. Death really changes life, that's for sure.

—Ben

INTEGRATING YOUR BABY INTO YOUR LIFE

Instead of being on your mind all the time, it becomes part of your history. You know, you don't meet new people and discuss your dead baby anymore. I actually know people that don't know that I've lost a baby, and it isn't because I'm hiding it, it's just because it isn't part of my conversation. It just happened to me and I'll always be sad and I'll always have one less child.

—Sara

A hallmark of healing is integrating your baby's life and death into the larger tapestry of your life. At first, grieving your baby's death is front and center, but as you mourn, you adjust and adapt to a different future, and your relationship with your baby changes from a relationship of presence to a relationship of memory. In other words, instead of raising this child into adulthood, you remember this child for the rest of your life. Remembering entails finding a comfortable place for this baby in your family, in your life, and in your heart.

It's very different nine years later. We are in a really good place and have been for quite some time. I think about Ashley most days, but now it's more with fondness or with "what if?" and wondering what she would be like, rather than with great sadness. I don't really cry, only rarely if a certain memory or song comes up, or if I hear about another family losing a child. I do wish she was here with us, but at the same time I'm grateful for the many blessings in our lives.

—Shellie

Now that we have Charlie, I bought a picture frame to include three heart-shaped photos. Well, you can guess what I intend to do with that. Alex fits in so well between my older son Tom and baby Charlie . . .like a sweet sandwich or a custard cream biscuit. It now makes sense, and Charlie has finally completed my family.

—Victoria

INTEGRATING YOUR BABY INTO YOUR FAMILY

Now I think of her more as a sister to my other children than I do the baby that I didn't have. We think of her as a part of our family, and Paul [age six] talks about her. When Julie [age one] is old enough to understand, she's going to understand that she did have a sister.

—Kitty

Tom asked me during the early weeks after Charlie arrived whether Alex was still his baby brother. I answered very clearly that "of course" he was, but just couldn't be his brother here on earth. Tom came up with the title that Alex is to be his "heavenly brother," which I absolutely love and he sometimes talks about how "if Alex were here, I'd have two brothers!"

—Victoria

For many parents, a meaningful way to integrate the baby into the family is by talking to their children about the baby sibling who died. Particularly for your subsequent children, you may want them to know there was a brother or sister before them. To talk about the baby is another way to acknowledge his or her existence and to validate your love. Jessie comments, "I hold a place for her. She's still our first child and Lynn's older sister." Lorna agrees, "Owain is four and starting to understand who Ronin is in photos. I want my children to know that they have an older brother and that he was loved and part of our family."

When People Ask, "How Many Kids Do You Have?"

I always say we are a family of five; we just don't physically look like one.

—Abby

Another way parents integrate the baby who died into the family is to talk about all their children. You may decide to do this with everyone or just certain people. Holly explains, "It depends on who it is and how much of an explanation you want to get into and whether you want to see their jaws fall open and have them feel like they stuck their foot in their mouth." Hannah adds, "I sort of play it by ear. If I don't say that I had her, I feel bad about it. But then I think, 'Well, I didn't want to get into a lengthy discussion, so it's okay.'" Maiya feels comfortable with this simple statement: "I have three children; two are with me, and one died." Here's an even simpler version that speaks volumes: "I have two living children."

Even if you tell people, they may not recognize your baby as a member of your family. Jessie points out, "It upsets me sometimes when they see my one-year-old and they say, 'Oh, this is your first child' or 'This is your first Mother's Day.' I feel bad that Meghan is being deprived of those things that were rightfully hers." Lorna agrees, "I think I make some people uncomfortable as I still talk about Ronin openly and count him as part of my family. But I feel bad when I have said that I only have three children and have not acknowledged Ronin."

Your Identity as a Parent

I'm not sure what I want to become just yet but I know I will always be Adisyn's mummy and she will always be our first child.

—Emmerson

If you have older children, or if you decide to have another baby or to adopt a child, being an active parent can help you overcome feelings of failure, restore a sense of purpose, and satisfy that part of your identity. Parenthood can also add a sense of fullness to your life. Lena notices, "I feel like a much more caring, loving, nurturing person since having Ryan." Peg adds, "It kind of makes up for what I've been through. I don't feel like I'm waiting for something anymore." For many parents, having a child to raise helps them to move forward in remembrance, because this child is another link, a sibling to the baby who died.

> With Leslie being born, it really helped me because here was somebody who needed me. I wasn't going to be able to sit around and be depressed because I needed to be there for her. She helped me. She filled my life, she filled my hours. When she was two years old, somehow I could tell I was better.
>
> —Bryn

Whether you have a child to raise or not, it helps to remember that you will always be your baby's mother, father, or coparent. As Ben recalls, "Bodhi taught us what it meant to be not only expectant parents, but parents, real parents!"

> Instead of wiping her nose or making sure she brushes her teeth, I have to decide which memories to share. How much of her story is told. Those sorts of things are still ways of parenting my child.
>
> —Sarah

REMEMBERING, IN CELEBRATION OF LIFE

Your baby's life made an impact. First on you, and then through you—either by you inviting others to share in your baby's life and death, or by you being inspired to become a better person and pay it forward. You may want to honor your baby's life, however brief, by remembering and celebrating it, and dedicating your good works to it.

> As the time goes by (I am two and a half years After Finley), the emotion is not so raw and I get a simple kind of pleasure and pride about hearing people say how Finley has stayed in their hearts, how their lives have changed, how when they heard the news they held their child, imagining what it would be like to lose that. If one person appreciates their life more because of Finley, then his life has not been wasted. He lives on through their smiles.
>
> —Mel

> I'm glad that we were open to including others in our story. We openly shared what was going on with the pregnancy, inviting family to be with us during the birth, and included many friends and coworkers in the service to celebrate her brief life. It was very

meaningful for us. Many other people said it was meaningful for them, too. It was a way to mark her brief life—she was here, she did make an impact on the world. When you don't have the next forty years with your child, that legacy is extremely important.

—Shellie

And though you wouldn't wish this bereavement on anyone, healing makes it possible for you to ultimately feel grateful that this child came into your life. With healing, you can also accept *what is*, embrace your personal growth, and make peace with your regrets. *Because you prevailed*, your grief and heartache over your baby's death transform into a healing celebration of your baby's life. And your baby will be loved and remembered, always.

I have found all the gifts Emma has given me—making me a mother, empowering me, and enriching my life. She has made my life more meaningful and deeper and I thank her every day for that. She also gives me daily gifts that I cherish and those help me feel connected to her, from the color yellow to hummingbirds to the song from her blessing, "Tupelo Honey."

—Abby

If anything, perhaps Willow's greatest gift for me has been a profound confirmation that our lives are so deeply precious and fragile and sacred, and that love itself somehow irrefutably and mysteriously and fundamentally transcends death.

—Nathan

YOUR CONTINUING BOND

I strongly feel that we can truly experience much healing by deciding to remember and include our babies in our lives going forward . . . and not in trying to move on and put it behind us, to forget them, like that is even possible.

—Lori

We love all four of our children very, very much. We talk about Willow all of the time. It is a privilege to love and nurture such precious young human beings.

—Nathan

Some parents worry that "healing" means "forgetting." In fact, you may have read this somewhere or someone might have insisted it was true. But as you know by now, forgetting is not an option. Your bond with your baby remains ever-present. You move along your life's path *with* your memories, the gifts of your transformation, and your baby tucked away in your heart, and perhaps often on your mind.

I really feel it's important you just don't forget about them. Christopher is a real part of our lives. And I'll never forget him. I don't want to.

—Rayleen

I feel grateful for our babies, Emily and Michael. It is bittersweet. Bitter, because we had two babies die in the second trimester. But sweet, because they are still our babies. I will meet them again someday.

—Anne

And when you let your mind rest on your baby, or when you take the time to look at photographs or handle keepsakes, you may still be transported back to that indelible time.

I almost think a new word should be created that describes this state of making a new life, with the loved one in it, in a different form. A balanced life with hope and sadness, and the ability to live between the two. I can see I have moved forward, but a part of me continues to be in August 2nd, 2009, with Finley. Sometimes that part is bigger or smaller, but always a part of me is back at that time.

—Mel

After three years I finally could be who I am without being "a person who had a dead baby." I finally separated myself from that . . . but I can still picture him when I was holding him. Now I can't remember what his face looked like, but I can remember feeling the weight on my arm.

—Bryn

I came to realize how precious "remembering" really was in the early days of grief. Sleepless nights spent imitating Lindsay's little sighs as she was dying in my arms. . . . Such painful memories and yet so tender! Even the smallest incident had monumental importance: words said, glances and nuances, her hand clutching mine, her breath in my ear, her silky hair caressing my cheek. I pored over the few photographs we had, enlarging this one, cropping that one just so, to bring her face a little closer. And then while I was remembering one day, I smiled. I almost felt guilty, but, oh, she was just so very precious! The same memories that once brought me such heartache and pain were the very same ones I have come to cherish and cling to with such tenacity. In the beginning, I could not imagine "going on" without her, until I realized she could "go on" with me.

—Dana

SONG FOR AN EMPTY CRADLE
For Andrea

Out my bedroom window rests my gaze
Through the mist of emptiness and pain's grey haze
I watch the patterns softly formed and changed,
The hillsides' grasses gently rearranged
By the winds' caressing touch.

From my womb she fell; my breath was stilled
By fear and pain and yet my heart was filled
By the overwhelming wonder of what was Andrea
That now lay white and quiet in my hand.
My baby, my prayers, the life that I had planned

Were gone. And in their place was left
A desert. Hot and empty so bereft
of hope, save for the splintered dreams I'd planned
That shined like broken bottles in the sand.

And soon the minutes into long months turn,
And even with time's comfort still I yearn
To hold her once in warm embrace
And say goodbye, and yet, there is a place
I carry her still, within my heart, steadfast;
For even the briefest of memories last.

Out my bedroom window rests my gaze
Through the mist of emptiness and pain's grey haze
I watch the patterns softly rearranged
And know my life, my dreams have all been changed.
My daughter's life was brief yet such
That in my emptiness I have so much.

—Clara Wilbrandt-Koenig

INDEX

Praise for the previous edition of
Empty Cradle, Broken Heart

"*Empty Cradle, Broken Heart* is written with great awareness and sensitivity. Deborah Davis gets it just right."

—Sheila Kitzinger, author of
The Complete Book of Pregnancy and Childbirth

"There is comfort in these pages."

—*Mothering* magazine

"This gentle book fills a void often overlooked how it feels to lose a baby during or shortly after pregnancy."

—*Booklist*

"Davis speaks directly to the emotional and physical needs of bereaved parents."

—Judith Lasker, author of *When Pregnancy Fails*

"This book is a comprehensive resource for bereaved parents and the practitioners who help them."

—*Thanatos, A Realistic Journal Concerning Dying, Death and Bereavement*